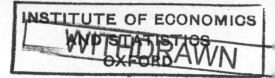
Equilibrium analysis
Essays in honor of Kenneth J. Arrow, Volume II

Equilibrium analysis

Essays in honor of Kenneth J. Arrow, Volume II

Edited by

WALTER P. HELLER
University of California, San Diego

ROSS M. STARR
University of California, San Diego

DAVID A. STARRETT
Stanford University

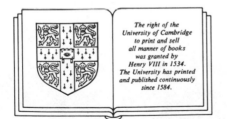

The right of the
University of Cambridge
to print and sell
all manner of books
was granted by
Henry VIII in 1534.
The University has printed
and published continuously
since 1584.

CAMBRIDGE UNIVERSITY PRESS

Cambridge
London   New York   New Rochelle
Melbourne   Sydney

Published by the Press Syndicate of the University of Cambridge
The Pitt Building, Trumpington Street, Cambridge CB2 1RP
32 East 57th Street, New York, NY 10022, USA
10 Stamford Road, Oakleigh, Melbourne 3166, Australia

First published 1986

Printed in the United States of America

Library of Congress Cataloging in Publication Data
Equilibrium analysis.
(Essays in honor of Kenneth J. Arrow; v. 2)
Includes index.
1. Equilibrium (Economics)   I. Heller, Walter P.
II. Starr, Ross M.   III. Starrett, David A.   IV. Arrow,
Kenneth Joseph, 1921- .   V. Series.
HB145.E674 1986   339.5   86-11693

British Library Cataloguing in Publication Data
Equilibrium analysis : essays in honor of
Kenneth J. Arrow, volume II.
1. Economic development   2. Equilibrium
(Economics)
I. Heller, Walter P.   II. Starr, Ross M.
III. Starrett, David A.   IV. Arrow, Kenneth J.
339.5   HD75

ISBN 0 521 30455 5

Contents

Essays in honor of Kenneth J. Arrow, Volumes I, II, III

Contributors

Yves Balasko*
Université de Genève

Theodore Bergstrom*
University of Michigan

David F. Bradford
Woodrow Wilson School of Public
  and International Affairs
Princeton University

Graciela Chichilnisky*
Columbia University

John D. Geanakoplos
Yale University

Louis Gevers
Faculté Notre Dame de la Paix
Namur, Belgium

W. M. Gorman
Nuffield College
Oxford

Jerry R. Green
Harvard University

Frank Hahn*
Churchill College
Cambridge

Peter J. Hammond
Stanford University

John C. Harsanyi
University of California, Berkeley

Walter P. Heller*
University of California, San Diego

Leonid Hurwicz
University of Minnesota

Michael D. Intriligator
University of California, Los Angeles

Takatoshi Ito*
University of Minnesota

Heinz Koenig*
University of Mannheim

Mordecai Kurz*
Stanford University

Jean-Jacques Laffont
Université des Sciences Sociales
Toulouse

Robert C. Lind
Cornell University

Thomas Marschak
University of California, Berkeley

Eric S. Maskin
Harvard University

Roger B. Myerson
Northwestern University

Marc Nerlove*
University of Pennsylvania

Hajime Oniki
Osaka University

Heraklis M. Polemarchakis
Columbia University

Roy Radner
AT&T Bell Laboratories

Michael Rothschild
University of California, San Diego

Herbert E. Scarf
Yale University

Amartya Sen
All Souls College
Oxford

*Contributors to Volume II.

Karl Shell*
University of Pennsylvania

Eytan Sheshinski
Hebrew University
Jerusalem

Robert M. Solow*
Massachusetts Institute of Technology

Ross M. Starr*
University of California, San Diego

David A. Starrett
Stanford University

Nancy L. Stokey*
Northwestern University

Laurence Weiss*
University of California, San Diego

Menahem E. Yaari
Hebrew University
Jerusalem

Editors' preface

This three-volume work is composed of essays written by many of Kenneth Arrow's students and collaborators. Although it is impossible to cover the entire range of his contributions to economics, we have organized the presentation around the major topics of his research career: Volume I treats "Social Choice and Public Decision Making," Volume II covers "Equilibrium Analysis," and Volume III deals with "Uncertainty, Information, and Communication."

We would like to thank all contributors to these volumes not only for their cooperation in helping expedite on-time production but also for voluntary efforts contributed in reading and commenting on each other's essays. In addition, we acknowledge with thanks the help of the following outside referees: Chuck Blackorby, Mark Johnson, Mark Machina, John McMillan, and Joel Sobel.

Special thanks go to Deborah Bailey who coordinated our (sometimes chaotic) correspondence among authors, editors, and publisher; she cheerfully dealt with potential disasters and enabled us to deliver the completed manuscript as scheduled. Also, we would like to thank Colin Day and his staff at Cambridge University Press for a highly professional effort at their end.

Finally, and most importantly, we speak for all contributors in thanking Kenneth Arrow for being an inspirational teacher and colleague over the years. The intellectual standards he set and the enthusiasm with which he approaches our subject are surely part of all of us. We can only hope that these essays convey some sense of our appreciation and esteem.

Kenneth J. Arrow

The impact of Kenneth Arrow's work on twentieth century economics has been to change fundamentally economists' understanding of their discipline and their view of several major classes of problems.[1] Arrow was a leader in the post–World War II push to bring the full power of mathematics and statistics to bear on economic analysis. The fields of general equilibrium, social choice and welfare economics, mathematical programming, and economics of uncertainty have been fundamentally altered by his contributions. In addition, Arrow is a man of wide learning, refreshing spontaneity, personal warmth, and remarkable absence of pretension.

Born in 1921 to Harry and Lillian Arrow of New York City, Kenneth Arrow was raised in and around New York. He pursued his undergraduate studies at City College of New York. On graduation from CCNY in 1940, he was awarded the Gold Pell Medal for highest grades in the graduating class. He studied then at Columbia, in particular with Harold Hotelling, and received an M.A. in mathematics in 1941.

Arrow's studies were interrupted by World War II. He served with the Weather Division of the Army Air Force and there wrote his first scientific paper ("On the use of winds in flight planning"). However, his other professional activities in the division almost prevented this line of research. The new young group of statisticians in the Weather Division subjected the prevailing prediction techniques to statistical test against a simple null hypothesis based on historical averages for the date in question. Finding that prevailing techniques were not significantly more reliable, several junior officers sent a memo to the general in charge suggesting that the unit be disbanded and the manpower reallocated. After a succession of such memos, the general's secretary is reported to have replied brusquely on his behalf, "The general is well aware that your division's forecasts are worthless. However, they are required for planning purposes." The division remained intact.

---

[1] Arrow has a rich personal intellectual history. This is best summarized in the headnotes to his research papers in the *Collected papers of Kenneth J. Arrow*. We have borrowed freely from this material. A discussion of Arrow's contributions to each of the topics treated in this collection appears in the introductions to the individual sections.

In 1946, Arrow returned to Columbia for doctoral study with Hotelling. In 1947, he joined the Cowles Commission at the University of Chicago, then under the direction of Jacob Marschak. Cowles was then virtually synonymous with mathematical economics and econometrics in
North America. With Hurwicz, Klein, Koopmans, and Marschak there,
it formed an active research environment. Arrow was unsure then of his
vocation. He considered the possibility of pursuing a nonacademic career
as an actuary. Tjalling Koopmans advised him that actuarial statistics
would prove unrewarding, saying, with characteristic reticence, "There is
no music in it." Fortunately for economic science, Arrow followed this
advice and decided to continue a research career.

In 1947, Arrow married Selma Schweitzer, then a graduate student in
economics at the University of Chicago. Jacob Marschak, in his capacity
as Cowles Commission Research Director, had arranged for the Commission to administer the Sarah Frances Hutchinson Fellowship. This
fellowship was held by Sonia Adelson (subsequently married to Lawrence
Klein) and then by Selma Schweitzer. The succession of fellows generated some administrative scrutiny. Upon review, it was determined that
the terms of the bequest establishing the fellowship required the fellows
to be women of the Episcopal Church of Seneca Falls, New York, and
the fellowship was withdrawn from Cowles' administration. Nevertheless,
the fellowship was clearly a great social success while at Cowles.

In 1948, Arrow joined the recently formed RAND Corporation in Santa
Monica, California. RAND was then an active center for fundamental
research, particularly in the fast-developing area of mathematical game
theory. He returned to RAND during several subsequent summers. There,
in the summers of 1950 and 1951, the collaboration with Leonid Hurwicz
was initiated.

In 1949, Arrow accepted an assistant professorial appointment in economics and statistics at Stanford University. The research work and pub-
lications of the next decade represent an extraordinary burst of creativity
and scientific progress. In the space of four years, 1951–4, three of Arrow's
most important works of economic theory appeared: *Social choice and
individual values* (1951), "An extension of the basic theorems of classical
welfare economics" (1951), and "Existence of equilibrium for a competitive economy" (with G. Debreu, 1954). Work on the theory of social
choice, started at RAND, was a particularly distinctive act of creation,
since the theory was developed with very few antecedents. Arrow describes
it as "a concept that took possession of [him]...development of the theorems and their proofs...required only about three weeks, although writing
them as a monograph...took many months" (Arrow, *Collected papers*).

The Ph.D. from Columbia was awarded in 1950; and the dissertation, *Social choice and individual values,* was published in 1951. "Extension of the basic theorems of classical welfare economics" was developed for the Second Berkeley Symposium on Mathematical Statistics and Probability to which Arrow was invited in his capacity as a statistician.

In the early 1950s, Arrow pursued – largely by correspondence – joint work on general equilibrium theory with Gerard Debreu, who was then at the Cowles Commission in Chicago. Abraham Wald, with whom Arrow had studied at Columbia, had written several papers in the field but had run up against fundamental mathematical difficulties. It was the recognition by Arrow and Debreu of the importance of use of a fixed point theorem that led to major progress in this area.[2] Publication of Arrow and Debreu's "Existence of equilibrium for a competitive economy" represented a fundamental step in the revision of economic analysis and modeling, demonstrating the power of a formal axiomatic approach with relatively advanced mathematical techniques.

During the mid-1950s, Leonid Hurwicz was a frequent academic visitor to Stanford. In 1955–6 Hurwicz was at the Center for Advanced Study in the Behavioral Sciences at Stanford, and in 1957–8 he was a visiting faculty member in the economics department. Collaboration with Hurwicz led to papers in mathematical programming, decentralization, and classic work on the stability of competitive equilibrium. The research faculty in mathematical economics was housed in a converted residence, Serra House. Colleagues there included Herbert Scarf and Hirofumi Uzawa. The informal, quiet, and somewhat isolated setting resulted in a particularly friendly atmosphere and esprit de corps.

Arrow was rapidly promoted at Stanford: to associate professor in 1950 and to full professor in 1953. The full professorship included appointment to the new Department of Operations Research, in addition to economics and statistics. Mathematical programming is a recurrent area of Arrow's research interest, and the new department was founded with Arrow's vigorous support. Although the profession is used to it now, the mathematical complexity of the body of work was then regarded as a bit forbidding. This reputation was a source of some humor when Arrow received the 1957 John Bates Clark Award of the American Economic Association. At the presentation ceremony, introductory remarks were made by George Stigler, who reportedly advised Arrow, in a loud stage-whisper, "You should probably say, 'Symbols fail me.'"

---

[2] Credit for independent discovery of the importance of fixed point theorems in this context is due to Lionel McKenzie ["On equilibrium in Graham's model of world trade and other competitive systems," *Econometrica,* 22: 147–61 (1954)].

In 1962, Arrow served on the research staff of the Council of Economic Advisers. In 1963–4, he was visiting fellow at Churchill College, Cambridge. The collaboration with Frank Hahn on *General competitive analysis* was pursued there and continued at Stanford in 1967. During the late 1960s, Arrow took up a research program in continuous-time optimal control (a topic touched on twenty years earlier in his Army Air Force service). In collaboration with Mordecai Kurz of Stanford, the result was *Public investment, the rate of return, and optimal fiscal policy*.

In 1968, Arrow accepted a professorship at Harvard and moved to Cambridge, Massachusetts. For the next decade, Harvard was the center of his activity, though he returned to Stanford annually for summer-long seminar series.

When the Nobel Prize in Economics was created in the mid-1960s, a common parlor game among professional economists was to forecast the next recipient. Arrow was on virtually everyone's short list. It was hence no surprise when the 1972 Nobel Prize in Economic Sciences was announced. Arrow was the laureate, jointly with the distinguished British economic theorist, John Hicks of Oxford. Age 51 at the time of the award, he is (at this writing) by far the youngest recipient of the Nobel Prize in Economics.

In 1979, Arrow returned to Stanford; he has been on the faculty there continually since then. Arrow lives on the Stanford campus with his wife, Selma. They have two sons, David and Andrew.

At both Stanford and Harvard, Arrow has been active in the affairs of the faculty and institution. Indeed, he has sometimes advised students, "true academic freedom is freedom from committee assignments." At both institutions and within the profession at large, he has been a source of intellectual excitement and ferment. He holds honorary doctorates from a variety of universities around the globe, including his alma mater, CCNY. He is a fellow of the Econometric Society, Institute of Mathematical Statistics, and American Statistical Association and a distinguished fellow of the American Economic Association. He is past president of the Econometric Society, American Economic Association, Institute of Management Sciences, and Western Economic Association. He holds the distinction, particularly rare among non-Japanese, of membership in the Second Class Order of the Rising Sun, an award presented by the Emperor of Japan.

Arrow is personally accessible and unpretentious, addressed as Ken by students, colleagues, and staff. The student, however junior, who steels his nerve to talk with the distinguished professor discovers that he has Arrow's undivided attention. To devoted students and colleagues, Arrow is a legendary figure, larger than life. Stories abound, highlighting his abilities:

- Arrow thinks faster than he – or anyone else – can talk. Hence conversation tends to take place at an extremely rapid pace; no sentence is ever actually completed.

- The breadth of Arrow's knowledge is repeatedly a surprise, even to his friends. By the end of an evening's dinner party whose guests included a professor of art specializing in the art of China, it seemed clear to the host that Arrow was as well versed as the specialist in this subject.

- Arrow can quote passages of Shakespeare and facts of English history accurately and at length.

- Arrow's presence in seminars is legendary. He may open his (abundant) mail, juggle a pencil, or give every evidence of inattention. He will then make a comment demonstrating that he is several steps ahead of the speaker.

Those of us who have had the chance to know him well are particularly fortunate. We are far richer for the experience.

Contents

PART I

General equilibrium

Arrow, along with Debreu, initiated modern general equilibrium theory in their landmark 1954 paper. The importance of rigorous analysis to economics is nowhere so highlighted as in this subject. On the one hand, economists had long been used to haphazard reasoning ranging from a naive belief that any economic system of importance had to have a solution to the slightly more methodical approach of the counting of equations and unknowns. On the other hand, a major benefit of Arrow and Debreu's work was the realization that the conditions for existence were strikingly restrictive. In particular, the importance of convexity to the existence of equilibrium was first recognized by them. For example, convexity is rarely true of the individual firm's technology set, and so the importance of large numbers of agents as a precondition for the workability of competition is now better understood.

A third major use of the Arrow–Debreu model is in applications. Once the way was paved in the abstract setting, countless papers utilized the basic framework and methods to extend the analysis to a variety of more concrete settings. Chichilnisky's contribution is a good example. She examines a general equilibrium model of international trade intended to represent an advanced industrial nation trading with a less developed country rich in resources. Under more general assumptions than heretofore considered, she shows that it is possible that trade will lower the real wages and the welfare of workers in the labor-abundant country.

Bergstrom studies a general equilibrium model of indivisible occupational choice. He examines conditions under which simple lotteries with purely monetary prizes can improve welfare. In addition, he shows that a simple lottery equilibrium exists where an Arrow–Debreu equilibrium might not.

Stokey considers a model of industry structure in which there is "industrywide learning by doing," namely, average cost declines as a function of industry output. She shows that price always falls over time, as it should, and that a unique symmetric Nash equilibrium exists. She also shows that increasing the number of firms can lower welfare, because free-rider incentives grow larger with the number of firms and can over-whelm the loss of monopoly power.

Starr examines the problem of how transactions are accomplished in general equilibrium in the absence of a central clearing mechanism that accepts all goods in trade. Even if prices are set at equilibrium levels, without the double coincidence of wants, traders must exchange money or IOUs. If there is a lack of trust and of money, Starr shows that a simple bank credit arrangement will suffice. Moreover, other arrangements, such as commodity money or multiple credit instruments are shown to create coordination problems.

Shell, in collaboration with Balasko, extends their earlier joint work on the overlapping-generations model. They show that, in the infinite-horizon case, a perfect foresight competitive equilibrium with a positive price of money exists if the public debt is forever zero after some date. Counterexamples are given to show that asymptotically zero public indebtedness will not suffice for existence of such equilibria, nor will the requirement that public debt be zero infinitely often.

Heller considers a simple general equilibrium oligopoly model with a full set of markets. Consumers earn income in industries that produce output they do not desire. Conditions are given under which there are multiple Pareto-ranked equilibria. The situation is akin to pecuniary externalities. It is also similar to effective demand failures, but with perfectly flexible prices and perfect foresight. Policy remedies are examined.

CHAPTER 1

A general equilibrium theory of
North–South trade

Graciela Chichilnisky

This chapter presents an application of competitive general equilibrium theory of markets in the spirit of Walras, formalized in the 1950s by K Arrow and by G. Debreu. In using general equilibrium theory to generate insights into current policy issues, it follows a tradition established by Arrow in his work on welfare economics of medical care (1963), on the organization of economic activity (1969), on the evaluation of public investment (Arrow and Lind, 1970), and in urban economic development (1970).

The intention is to use formalized general equilibrium theory to derive general statements about the economic behavior and interrelations between two groups of countries: industrial and developing countries. The first group is represented by a cluster of competitive market economies called the *North,* and the second by a similar cluster of competitive economies called the *South:* thus the name North–South trade. The goal is to obtain simple and general results, and for this purpose we consider a stylized model with the minimum of characteristics needed for the task: two regions, two produced goods, and two factors of production. Within this simple model, we explore issues of current import, such as export-led policies and the transmission of economic activity between regions. The underlying theme is that general equilibrium analysis is indeed useful for disclosing patterns of economic behavior and for suggesting policies, a point of view that guided classical international economics.

Research support was provided by the Institute for Mathematics and its Applications, University of Minnesota, and NSF Grant SES–84–09857. Comments from M. Aoki, R. Aumann, K. Arrow, J. Benhabib, P. Dasgupta, A. Fishlow, F. Hahn, G. Heal, R. Jones, M. Kurz, D. McLeod, A. Mas-Colell, R. Riezman, L. Taylor, A. Sen, J. Stiglitz, E. Sheshinski, and N. Wallace are acknowledged. The computer programs and simulations were produced by Eduardo Jose Chichilnisky, Princeton University. This essay was presented at the I.M.S.S.S. at Stanford University, July 1984.

1   Policy issues and main results

The classical trade models developed by Heckscher, Ohlin, Lerner, and Samuelson were concerned with gains from trade between countries having similar preferences and technologies, but with different endowments of factors of production. These models explained why trade takes place between similar countries. In the earliest part of this century, trade among similar countries, indeed industrial countries, was the most important segment of international trade. However, North–South trade, which now accounts for 40 percent by value of OECD trade, takes place between countries of very different characteristics. They differ not only in factor endowments but also in preferences and technologies. To understand this important and growing component of world trade, we need a framework that can incorporate explicitly the diversity of technologies and demand patterns as well as the more traditional differences in factor endowments and that can relate this diversity to the welfare effects of trade.

This chapter develops a rigorous general equilibrium analysis of trade between two competitive market economies with significant differences both in technologies and in endowments. Within this framework, we use general equilibrium comparative statics analysis to study the welfare effects of changes in the volume of trade across free trade equilibria. We study changes in the market equilibrium in response to changes in parameters that are exogenous to the model. We also examine the comparative statics effects that an expansion in the North has on the South. These are two current topics: Export policies of the developing countries are at the forefront of discussions on the international debt, and the issue of whether or not an economic expansion in the industrial countries is transmitted to the developing countries underlies many policy prescriptions. Many oil-exporting countries and exporters of other raw materials show disappointing records after a decade of concentration on production for exports.

The aim of this essay is to explain why, in the words of Arthur Lewis, the international market works at times to concentrate rather than to diffuse the gains from trade (Lewis 1983). I hope to explore in some detail how the international market transmits economic activity from one region to the other. The explanations that I seek are in terms of the primitive structural characteristics of the domestic economies of the trading regions, such as technologies factor supplies and demand structures, and not in terms of the derived parameters of international markets, such as elasticities of international demand at a market equilibrium.

For many developing countries, the degree of involvement in the international economy is a major policy decision, with export-oriented domestic production having been strongly recommended by international agencies for many years. However, as Samuelson has noted, even under the assumptions of classical trade theory we cannot, in general, claim that a country will benefit from orienting its production toward international trade.[1] The policy issue facing most countries is not one of choosing between free trade and autarky. It is one of choosing between policies that would result in more or less emphasis on an international sector of the economy. The classical theorems on the welfare effects of trade provide little information about such choices. This is the issue we study here.

Initial results on these problems were obtained in Chichilnisky (1981), who dealt with trade between an industrial country and a labor-abundant developing country and showed how the structural differences between the countries (and also between sectors within a country) play an important role in determining the welfare impact of changes in the volume of trade and in the transmission of economic activity through international markets.

A feature of the 1981 results that seemed counterintuitive and attracted attention is that an increase in the exports of a labor-intensive product could lower real wages and terms of trade in the labor-abundant South. Labor abundance was described by the responsiveness of labor supply to real wages, and it was proved that even in cases where the labor supply is abundant, an expansion of labor-intensive exports could have these negative effects. Of course, these same effects occur when labor is *not* abundant, and in this chapter we give necessary and sufficient conditions for such results. We consider here cases where the South's demand for basics derives both from capital and from wage income.

Another feature of the results that attracted attention was that an expansion in the North parameterized by an increase in its demand for industrial goods could lead to an expansion in the South's exports and simultaneously could lower terms of trade and real wages in the South. This result led to several comments that centered on the question: How is it possible that in a stable market economy such as that of the North–South model, one can have simultaneously an increase in the volume of exports from the South demanded by the North and a drop in their market prices? This chapter deals with this question. It shows how under conditions similar to those discussed above, a move toward an equilibrium with a higher industrial demand in the North leads indeed to a higher volume of exports of labor-intensive goods from the South but to lower terms of trade and lower real wages in the South, within a stable market economy. The results are traced to simultaneous supply and demand responses, which are not readily perceived within a partial equilibrium framework but appear quite naturally in general equilibrium models. Further results are obtained here showing that in such cases the North may actually consume more of both goods and the South less, following the industrial expansion in the North and the increase in exports from the South.

Of course, precisely the opposite effects can also happen. This essay also examines sufficient conditions for *positive* outcomes of an export expansion: As exports increase, terms of trade and real wages improve. It also examines conditions for a positive transmission of an expansion in the North to the South: As the North increases its industrial demand, its imports increase, leading to better terms of trade and real wages in the South. The purpose of our general equilibrium analysis is to provide a rigorous framework to analyze which case is likely to occur and under which specifications of the economies. We also discuss some empirical aspects on the basis of recent econometric implementations of the model for the case of trade between Sri Lanka and the United Kingdom in Chichilnisky, Heal, and Podivinsky (1983) and for the case of Argentina and the United States in Chichilnisky and McLeod (1984).

2   The North–South model and its solutions

This section summarizes the general equilibrium model in Chichilnisky (1981, 1984a, b). A version of this model is a special case of an Arrow–Debreu general equilibrium model: This is shown in Section f of the appendix.

There are two regions, North and South. The North represents the industrial countries, the South the developing countries. Each region produces and consumes two goods: basics (B) and industrial goods (I). There are two inputs to production: capital (K) and labor (L). The two regions trade with each other.

Consider first the economy of the South. It produces basics and industrial goods using labor and capital, as described by the Leontief production functions

$$B^S = \min(L^B/a_1, K^B/c_1),$$

$$I^S = \min(L^I/a_2, K^I/c_2),$$

where the superscripts B and I denote the sector in which inputs are used, and the superscript S denotes supply. Basics are labor-intensive and in-

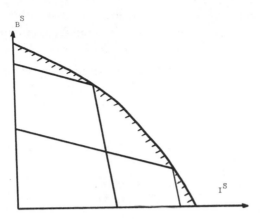

Figure 1. The overall production possibility frontier across equilibria when $D \neq 0$. For each set of prices, the production possibility frontier is piecewise linear; as prices change, endowments of factors vary and a new piecewise linear production set arises. The overall frontier is smooth.

dustrial goods capital-intensive, that is, $D = a_1 c_2 - a_2 c_1 > 0$. These production functions were chosen for the sake of analytic tractability. More general production functions can be utilized with no significant changes in the results (see, e.g., Benhabib and Chichilnisky 1984). In any case, across equilibria, this economy exhibits substitution between the total amount of labor and capital employed; this is discussed below.

We can now write the equations that specify equilibrium of the model. Competitive behavior on the part of the firms ensures zero profits, so that

$$p_B = a_1 w + c_1 r, \tag{2.1}$$

$$p_I = a_2 w + c_2 r, \tag{2.2}$$

where p_B and p_I are the prices of B and I; w and r are the wages and the rate of return on capital.[2]

Labor and capital supplied are increasing functions of their rewards:

$$L^S = \alpha(w/p_B) + \bar{L} \quad (\alpha > 0), \tag{2.3}$$

$$K^S = \beta r + \bar{K} \quad (\beta > 0). \tag{2.4}$$

Since factor supplies vary with factor prices by equations (2.3) and (2.4), the model exhibits substitution in the total use of capital and labor across equilibria when $D = a_1 c_2 - a_2 c_1 \neq 0$. Figure 1 illustrates the production possibility frontier: Across equilibria, commodity prices change and factor prices change so that factor endowments change too, by (2.3) and (2.4).

The diagram exhibits a piecewise linear production possibility frontier for each price vector of prices and indicates the overall frontier as the envelope of the piecewise linear frontier across different prices. The market clearing conditions (superscript S denotes supply and D denotes demand) are

$$L^S = L^D, \tag{2.5}$$

$$K^S = K^D, \tag{2.6}$$

$$L^D = L^B + L^I = B^S a_1 + I^S a_2, \tag{2.7}$$

$$K^D = K^B + K^I = B^S c_1 + I^S c_2, \tag{2.8}$$

$$B^S = B^D + X_B^S, \tag{2.9}$$

where X_B^S denotes exports of B,

$$I^D = X_I^D + I^S, \tag{2.10}$$

where X_I^D denotes imports of I, and

$$p_B X_B^S = p_I X_I^D, \tag{2.11}$$

that is, the value of exports equals the value of imports.[3]

The North is specified by a set of equations similar to (2.1)–(2.11), with possibly different technology and factor supply parameters. In a world equilibrium, the prices of traded goods are equal across regions (factors K and L are not traded) and exports match imports:

$$p_I(S) = p_I(N), \tag{2.12}$$

$$p_B(S) = p_B(N), \tag{2.13}$$

$$X_B^S(S) = X_B^D(N), \tag{2.14}$$

$$X_I^S(N) = X_I^D(S), \tag{2.15}$$

where (S) and (N) denote South and North, respectively.

In each region, there are eight exogenous parameters: $a_1, a_2, c_1, c_2, \alpha, \bar{L}$, β, and $\bar{K}$, making a total of *sixteen exogenous parameters* for the North–South model. When we add the price-normalizing condition,[4]

$$p_I = 1, \tag{2.16}$$

we have a *total of twenty-six independent equations:* (2.1)–(2.11) for North; (2.1)–(2.11) for South, (2.12)–(2.14), and (2.16).[5] There are in total twenty-eight *endogenous variables,* fourteen for each region: p_B, p_I, w, r, L^S, L^D, K^S, K^D, B^S, B^D, X_B^S, I^S, I^D, and X_I^D. Therefore, the system is undetermined so far up to two variables.[6] Thus, we now specify two more variables exogenously, industrial demand in the South, $I^D(S)$, and in the North, $I^D(N)$, adding two more equations:

$$I^D(N) = \bar{I}^D(N), \tag{2.17}$$

$$I^D(S) = \bar{I}^D(S). \tag{2.18}$$

Obviously, we could have solved the model by specifying exogenously other variables or else by postulating demand equations; this will be done in the following sections. The demand specifications of the model are chosen to meet two criteria: analytical tractability and empirical plausibility.

The North–South model is, therefore, a system of twenty-eight equations in twenty-eight variables, depending on eighteen exogenous parameters: a_1, a_2, c_1, c_2, α, $\bar{L}$, β, $\bar{K}$, and $\bar{I}$ for each region.

The economies of the North and of the South are identical except possibly for the values of their exogenous parameters. Differences in the structural characteristics of the two regions are described by differences in their exogenous parameters. For instance, in the North the two sectors (B and I) use approximately the same technology, that is, the economy is technologically homogeneous. This means that $a_1/c_1 \sim a_2/c_2$ so that the determinant $D(N)$ of the matrix of technical coefficients

$$\begin{pmatrix} a_1 & c_1 \\ a_2 & c_2 \end{pmatrix}$$

is close to zero in the North. In the South, instead, technologies are dualistic: The two sectors use factors very differently, and $D(S)$ is therefore large. In both regions, $D(N)$ and $D(S)$ are positive, which indicates that the B sector uses labor more intensively than the I sector. Another difference arises in factor markets. In the North, labor is relatively more scarce, that is, less responsive to increases in the real wage w/p_B. This means $\alpha(N)$ is small. In the South the opposite is true, $\alpha(S)$ is large. The reciprocal relations hold in capital markets: $\beta(N)$ is large and $\beta(S)$ is small. These parameter specifications can be presented so as to be independent of the units of measurements.

It is worth noting that whereas most equations are linear in the variables, some are not [e.g., (2.3) is nonlinear]. The solutions also display nonlinearities, as we shall see in the following.

Proposition 1. The North–South model has at most one equilibrium.[7] This equilibrium can be computed explicitly by solving one equation that depends on all exogenous parameters of the model.

Proof: From

$$X_I^D(S) = X_I^S(N),$$

we have

$$\bar{I}^D(S) - I^S(S) = I^S(N) - \bar{I}^D(N). \tag{2.19}$$

Inverting (2.7) and (2.8), we obtain

$$B^S = \frac{c_2 L - a_2 K}{D}, \qquad I^S = \frac{a_1 K - c_1 L}{D}, \tag{2.20}$$

and inverting (2.1) and (2.2),

$$w = \frac{p_B c_2 - c_1}{D}, \qquad r = \frac{a_1 - p_B a_2}{D}. \tag{2.21}$$

Using (2.3), (2.4), (2.20), and (2.21), we can rewrite equation (2.19) as a function of one variable only, p_B (which is the *terms of trade* of the South, since $p_I = 1$) and obtain

$$p_B^2(A + A(N)) + p_B[C + C(N) + \bar{I}^D(S) + \bar{I}^D(N)] - (V + V(N)) = 0, \tag{2.22}$$

where

$$A = \frac{\beta a_1 a_2}{D^2}, \qquad V = \frac{\alpha c_1^2}{D^2},$$

and

$$C = \frac{1}{D}\left(c_1 \bar{L} - a_1 \bar{K} + \frac{\alpha c_1 c_2 - \beta a_1 a_2}{D}\right),$$

and where expressions A, V, and C contain parameter values for the South, and $A(N)$, $V(N)$, and $C(N)$ for the North. Solving equation (2.22) yields an equilibrium level of terms of trade p_B^* as a function of all eighteen exogenous parameters of the system.

It is easy to check that equation (2.22) has at most one positive root p_B^* because the constant term is negative and the quadratic term is positive. From this and (2.21), one obtains the equilibrium values of w^* and r^* for each region; from (2.3) and (2.4), L^* and K^* for each region; from (2.20), $(B^S)^*$ and $(I^S)^*$ for each region. From (2.9), (2.10), and (2.11) we then obtain $(B^D)^*$, $(X_B^S)^*$, and $(X_I^D)^*$ for each region. All endogenous variables have been computed, and the solution is complete. ∎

In the following, we shall consider different specifications of demand. Equation (2.18) in the South is substituted by one of three different specifications of equilibrium levels of demand:

$$X_B^S(S) = \bar{X}_B^S, \tag{2.18a}$$

$$B^D(S) = \frac{wL}{p_B}, \tag{2.18b}$$

and finally,

$$B^D(S) = \gamma \frac{wL}{p_B} + \lambda rK, \tag{2.18c}$$

for $\gamma, \lambda < 1$ and at least one positive.

A different specification of the North's demand will also be considered. Equation (2.17) is substituted by

$$B^D(N) = \bar{B}^D, \tag{2.17a}$$

that is, an exogenous specification of the North's demand for basics at the equilibrium.

In the following section, we show that all these different specifications of demand lead to similar results. The specification with equation (2.18a) is useful to parameterize the solutions of the model by one real variable denoting the volume of exports $X_B^S(S)$: As $\bar{X}_B^S$ varies [and $I^D(N) = \bar{I}^D(N)$ remains fixed], we obtain a one-dimensional path of equilibria across which we may carry out comparative statics exercises about the effects of changes in the volume of exports of the South on the equilibrium levels of endogenous variables. This was done in Chichilnisky (1981) and is also done in the following section. Equation (2.18b) is useful to derive necessary and sufficient conditions for increases or decreases in terms of trade as exports change in cases where labor is not necessarily abundant. Equation (2.18c) shows that the results obtain even when the demand for basics comes also from capital income. Equation (2.17a) is used to show that an increase in the North's demand for basics may lead to increased exports of basics from the South and simultaneously to a lower price of basics. This is also done in the following section.

The model's specification with equations (2.17) and (2.18) was used in Chichilnisky (1981) to study the impact of an industrial expansion in the North (an increase in the exogenous value of $\bar{I}^D(N)$) [Proposition 2, Chichilnisky (1981)].

In all cases, an exogenous change in $\bar{I}^D$, or $\bar{X}_B^S$, is simply a change in a number that is exogenously given to the model. Such an exogenous change can be interpreted in many different fashions, thus making the results rather general. For instance, an increase in $\bar{I}^D(N)$ could be a result of a shift in underlying preferences in the North leading to a new equilibrium level of demand for industrial goods; see Section f of the appendix. We have therefore indexed the utility function in the North by $\bar{I}$ and considered a change in this utility index. Other different possibilities are that industrial demand $\bar{I}^D(N)$ is fixed by a quota, or that it is random. Whatever the reason, any model in which all equations but (2.17) are satisfied, and in which a change in $I^D(N)$ has taken place, will have the same properties predicted in our theorems. The theorems are therefore rather general: They apply to a large class of models all of which share the equilibrium equations (2.1)–(2.11) in each region, and (2.12)–(2.14), (2.16), and (2.18). Similarly, an exogenous change in X_B^S could be regarded as a change in preferences in the North that led to a change in the equilibrium volume of exports of the South; or as a similar change in the South leading to a change in its exports; or finally, as a change in an import quota of the North. In all these cases, the comparative statics results of all exogenous change in X_B^S remain unchanged.

Note, finally, that no information has been given so far about (disequilibrium) excess demand or supply functions: Outside of the equilibrium, demands are not defined so far. Supply functions are not defined outside of an equilibrium either, because we have constant returns to scale. Therefore, the above information does not suffice to discuss stability: This task is taken up in a subsequent section.

3   Further results on export-led strategies

This section concentrates on the comparative statics results. The appendix provides a program for the model, as well as numerical simulations that reproduce the propositions.

The first two propositions deal with the 1981 version of the model, which we call the North–South model. The model consists of twenty-eight equations, or equations (2.1)–(2.11) in each region; (2.12)–(2.14); and (2.16), (2.17), and (2.18). There are twenty-eight variables: In each region, these are p_B, p_I, r, w, B^S, B^D, I^S, I^D, X_I^S, X_I^D, K^S, K^D, L^S, L^D. We now parameterize the solutions of the North–South model by varying the equilibrium level of industrial demand in the North, $I^D(N)$, in equation (2.17). For each value of $\bar{I}^D(N)$, there is (at most) a unique solution to the model, by Proposition 1. Therefore, as $\bar{I}^D(N)$ varies, we obtain a one-dimensional set of equilibria (under regularity conditions, a one-dimensional manifold) contained in the space of all endogenous variables, R^{28}. Comparative statics results arise from studying the relationships between two or more endogenous variables along this set of equilibria. The following propositions study the relationship between the export level X_B^S, the terms of trade p_B, and the real wages w/p_B of the South across different equilibria of the North–South model.

Proposition 2. Consider the North–South economy, where the South exports basic goods, has abundant labor, α large, and dual technologies, that is, $c_2/D < 2w/p_B$. Then a move to an equilibrium with a higher level of exports of basics leads to lower terms of trade and to lower real wages in the South. [Proposition 1 in Chichilnisky (1981).]

When labor is abundant and real wages are low, or else technologies are homogeneous, that is, $c_2/D > 2w/p_B$, then a move to an equilibrium with a higher level of exports X_B^S leads to better terms of trade and higher real wages in the South. [Proposition 2 in Chichilnisky (1981).]

Proof:

$$X_B^S(S) = B^S - B^D;$$

by equation (2.20),

$$B^S = \frac{c_2 L - a_2 K}{D};$$

and by Walras' law and equation (2.17),

$$B^D = \frac{wL + rK - \bar{I}^D(S)}{p_B}.$$

Therefore,

$$X_B^S = \frac{c_2 L - a_2 K}{D} - \frac{wL + rK - \bar{I}^D(S)}{p_B}$$

$$= \frac{\alpha c_1}{D^2 p_B}\left(c_2 - \frac{c_1}{p_B}\right) + \frac{\beta a_1}{D^2}\left(a_2 - \frac{a_1}{p_B}\right) + \frac{c_1\bar{L} - a_1\bar{K}}{Dp_B} + \frac{\bar{I}^D(S)}{p_B}, \qquad (3.1)$$

and the derivative of X_B^S with respect to p_B across equilibria is

$$\frac{dX_B^S}{dp_B} = \frac{\alpha c_1}{D^2 p_B^2}\left(\frac{2c_1}{p_B} - c_2\right) + \frac{\beta a_1^2}{D^2 p_B^2} + \frac{a_1\bar{K} - c_1\bar{L}}{p_B^2} - \frac{\bar{I}^D(S)}{p_B^2}. \qquad (3.2)$$

Therefore, when $\alpha(S)$ is large, dX_B^S/dp_B has the sign of $(2c_1/p_B) - c_2$, which equals that of $c_2/D - 2w/p_B$ by equation (2.21). Finally note that by (2.21), across equilibria, $d(w/p_B)/dp_B > 0$. ∎

An intuitive explanation of this result is in Arrow (1981):

> Very loosely the argument is the following. Suppose the rise in export demand for the B commodity were followed by an increase in its price. Since its production is highly labor intensive, there would be a rise in real wages and since labor supply is higher responsive to the real wage,

a considerable increase in labor supply. The rise in both real wage and labor supply increases even more rapidly the domestic demand for the B commodity, since it is all directed to the B commodity. Hence supply available for export would *decrease* and therefore would not match the increased demand for exports. It follows that the only way the (rise in) export demand could be met, under these conditions, would be a decrease in the price of commodity B and of real wages.

In this light, it seems useful to explain the role of the assumption $c_2/D < 2w/p_B$. The term c_2/D represents a supply response and the term $2w/p_B$ a demand response across equilibrium. The inequality $<$ indicates that the demand response exceeds the supply response, as discussed in Arrow (1981).

Remarks: The expression $c_2/D - 2w/p_B$ is simple and has a ready economic interpretation: It describes a relationship between real wages and technological parameters. Intuitively speaking, when technologies are "dual," D is large and c_2/D is small; thus, we call the condition $c_2/D < 2w/p_B$ *technological duality*. This condition has also the advantage of being relatively easy to test econometrically since real wages and input–output coefficients are relatively accessible data (see Chichilnisky et al. 1983).

However, from a theoretical viewpoint, this condition is not presented in a standard fashion because it mixes parameters (c_2/D) with endogenous variables $(2w/p_B)$. It seems therefore useful to express $c_2/D - 2w/p_B$ as a function of exogenous parameters only. We can then check *inter alia* its consistency with the other condition in Proposition 2, that is, $\alpha(S)$ large. From equation (2.21), $c_2/D < 2w/p_B$ is equivalent to $p_B > 2(c_1/c_2)$. Since p_B is a function of exogenous parameters only, by equation (2.22), we obtain that $c_2/D < 2w/p_B$ is equivalent to an expression that depends solely on exogenous parameters:

$$\frac{\gamma + (\gamma - 4(V + V(N))(A + A(N))^{1/2}}{2(A + A(N))} > 2\frac{c_1}{c_2} \tag{3.3}$$

where A and V were defined in Proposition 1, and

$$\gamma = C + C(N) + \bar{I}^D(S) + \bar{I}^D(N).$$

It is easy to check that inequality (3.3) is indeed a plausible combination of parameters, when $\alpha(S)$ is large. For example, the simulations in Section a of the appendix have numerical values of the exogenous parameter values where both $\alpha(S)$ large and (3.3) are satisfied simultaneously.

Sufficient conditions can also be given for (3.3) to be satisfied along with $\alpha(S)$ large in terms of an interval of values of $D(S)$ (note that $\bar{L}$ is generally negative; otherwise there would be positive labor supply at zero real wages): One proves this by showing that when α and D are rather large in the South, by (2.22), p_B is approximated by

$$\frac{c_1^2}{(D/\alpha)(c_1\bar{L}-a_1\bar{K})+c_1c_2},$$

where all parameters are for the South. This expression exceeds $2c_1/c_2$ when the denominator is positive and small. This will occur within an interval for the exogenous parameter D.

Proposition 3 [Proposition 3 in Chichilnisky (1981)]. Assume the South has abundant labor and dual technologies: α large and $c_2/D < 2w/p_B$. Then a move to a new equilibrium with a higher level of industrial demand in the North leads to a higher level of exports of basics from the South, but to lower terms of trade, real wages, and domestic consumption in the South. This occurs in Walrasian stable markets.

Proof: From equation (2.22) and the implicit function theorem,

$$\frac{dp_B}{dI^D(N)} = \frac{p_B}{2p_B(A+A(N))+C+C(N)+\bar{I}^D(S)+\bar{I}^D(N)}, \tag{3.4}$$

where A and C are defined in (2.22).

When α is large in the South, the sign of the term in α determines the sign of $C+C(N)$. Since the term in α within $C+C(N)$ is $\alpha c_1 c_2/D^2$, a positive number, $C+C(N)$ is positive in this case. Furthermore, A and $A(N)$ are always positive. It follows that

$$dp_B/d\bar{I}^D(N) < 0 \tag{3.5}$$

when α in the South is large. Therefore when α is large, an increase in the equilibrium level of industrial demand in the North leads to a drop in the equilibrium price of basics.

Now, consider the equation relating exports of basics with their price across equilibria:

$$X_B^S = \frac{\alpha c_1}{D^2 p_B}\left(c_2 - \frac{c_1}{p_B}\right) + \frac{\beta a_1}{D^2}\left(a_2 - \frac{a_1}{p_B}\right) + \frac{c_1\bar{L}-a_1\bar{K}}{Dp_B} + \frac{\bar{I}^D(S)}{p_B}.$$

As seen in Proposition 2, $dX_B^S/dp_B < 0$ when $c_2/D < 2w/p_B$. Added to inequality (3.5), this implies $dX_B^S/d\bar{I}^D(N) > 0$.

To summarize: A move to an equilibrium with a higher level of industrial demand in the North [i.e., an increase in the parameter $\bar{I}^D(\text{N})$] leads both to a larger volume of imports of basic goods by the North (higher X_B^S) and to lower terms of trade for the South (lower p_B).

To complete the proof, it suffices now to point out that real wages w/p_B are always positively associated with the price of basics [by (2.21)] and that in equilibrium the consumption of basics is also positively associated with their price in the South when α is large. This is because $B^D = [wL + rK - \bar{I}^D(\text{S})]/p_B$, and this expression is dominated by the term in α, that is, by $\alpha(w/p_B)^2$, which is an increasing function of p_B. Stability was established in the appendix of Chichilnisky (1981) and is discussed further in the following section. ∎

Our next step is to extend the 1981 results. The next proposition sharpens Proposition 1 of Chichilnisky (1981): It obtains results not only on terms of trade but also on *total export revenues* following an export expansion. These results are obtained without any assumptions on the international elasticities of demand.

Proposition 4. In the North–South economy, assume that the South has abundant labor, α large, and dual technologies, $c_2/D < 2w/p_B$. Then a move to a new equilibrium with a higher volume of exports leads not only to lower terms of trade but also to lower export revenues in the South. However, when $c_2/D > 2w/p_B$, terms of trade and export revenues increase following the expansion in exports.

Proof: When $c_2/D < 2w/p_B$ and α is large, by Proposition 2, as the level of exports X_B^S increases, the South's terms of trade p_B drop at the new equilibrium. By (2.21), wages decrease and the rate of profit increases. This implies from (2.3) and (2.4) that total capital available increases, and total labor employed decreases. Therefore, the domestic supply of industrial goods I^S increases, since $I^S = (a_1 K - c_1 L)/D$. Since the industrial demand in the South is constant by (2.18), and the supply I^S has increased, the volume of imports of industrial goods $X_I^D(\text{S}) = I^D(\text{S}) - I^S(\text{S})$ must therefore decrease when the price of basics drops. By the balance-of-payments condition $p_B X_B^S = X_I^D$, the total revenue from exports, $p_B X_B^S$, decreases when $c_2/D > 2w/p_B$ by Proposition 2. When $c_2/D > 2w/p_B$, a rise in exports leads to better terms of trade so that export revenues increase as well. ∎

The next proposition studies changes in *both* regions, following either an increase of exports X_B^S or an industrial expansion in the North, that is, an increase in $\bar{I}^D(N)$; or an increase in demand for basics $\bar{B}^D(N)$. These are exogenous changes in either of three numbers: $I^D(N)$, $X_B^S(S)$, or $B^D(N)$. Cases with exogenous changes in X_B^S refer to the version of the model where equation (2.18) of the North–South model is replaced by (2.18a); all other equations remain unchanged. Cases where $B^D(N)$ increases exogenously refer to the North–South model where equation (2.17) is replaced by equation (2.17a): All others remain unchanged.

Proposition 5. Assume that technologies are dual, $c_2/D < 2w/p_B$, and α is large in the South. Furthermore, assume that labor supply in the North is unresponsive to the real wage [$\alpha(N)$ small] and that industrial goods in the North use little labor (a_2 small). Then:

i. A move to a new equilibrium with a higher level of industrial demand in the North, $\bar{I}^D(N)$, leads to higher levels of imports of basics and of consumption of basic goods in the North. The North consumes simultaneously more of both goods and is in this sense strictly better off. The South exports more basics, at lower prices, and receives lower export revenues. In the South, real wages and consumption decrease. The South consumes fewer basics and the same amount of industrial goods: It is therefore strictly worse off at the new equilibrium.

ii. Identical results obtain when the exogenous parameter is $\bar{X}_B^S(S)$. A move to a new equilibrium with an increased level of exports of the South, $X_B^S(S)$, or of import quotas in the North, $X_B^D(N)$ (allowing now either $I^D(N)$ or $I^D(S)$ to adjust), leads to lower terms of trade, export revenues, wages, and consumption in the South.

iii. Finally, identical results occur when the initial exogenous change is in the equilibrium level of demand for basics in the North, $\bar{B}^D(N)$. At the new equilibrium, the North's demand for basics and its imports of basics increase, but the price of basics goes down. The North consumes more of both goods; the South consumes the same amount of industrial goods and less basics. The North is therefore strictly better off, and the South is worse off.

All these results occur in Walrasian stable markets.

Proof: Consider first the case where in the North $\alpha(N) = 0$ and $a_2(N) = 0$. The supply of basics in the North is then a constant, since

$$B^S = (c_2 L - a_2 K)/D = c_2 \bar{L}/D \quad \text{when} \quad \alpha = a_2 = 0.$$

(Note that $\bar{L}$ must be positive in this case.) Since the consumption of basics of the North is the sum of domestic supply plus imports, $B^D(N) = B^S(N) + X_B^D(N)$, and $B^S(N)$ is a constant, when imports of basics $X_B^D(N)$ increase, consumption of basics in the North, $B^D(N)$, must increase as well.

Proposition 3 shows that, under the conditions, a move to an equilibrium with a higher level of industrial demand in the North, $I^D(N)$, leads to more exports of basics, $X_B^S(S) = X_B^D(N)$. Therefore, in our case, this leads to increased consumption of basics in the North. The equilibrium levels of demand for industrial goods $I^D(N)$ and for basics $B^D(N)$ have therefore increased simultaneously in the North. For any reasonable welfare measure, the North is strictly better off. By continuity, the same results obtain when $a_2(N)$ and $\alpha(N)$ are close to zero, proving the first part of the theorem.

In the South, export revenues decrease as shown in Proposition 4 above. As the terms of trade p_B decrease, real wages and the consumption of basics decrease in the South, as shown in Proposition 3. Since industrial demand remains constant in the South, the South is strictly worse off.

The statement in ii follows from the fact that parameterizing the solutions by the level of exports X_B^S or by the level of industrial demand in the North, $I^D(N)$, leads to the same comparative statics results. Finally, we prove part iii.

Assume $\bar{B}^D(N)$ is exogenously increased, $\alpha(N) = 0$, and $a_2(N) = 0$. Then, as shown above, B^S remains constant, $B^S = c_2 \bar{L}/D$. The increase of demand must be met by a higher level of imports of basics, $X_B^D(N) = X_B^S(S)$. But $c_2/D < 2w/p_B$ and $\alpha(S)$ large imply that at the new equilibrium with a higher level of $X_B^S(S)$, both p_B and $p_B X_B^S$ are lower, as shown in Proposition 4. This means that exports of industrial goods $X_I^S(N)$ are lower ($p_B X_B^S = X_I^S$). As p_B is lower, r and K are higher, that is, supply of I increases in the North. Therefore $I^D = I^S - X_I^S$ increases too: The North now consumes more basics *and* more industrial goods. The rest of the theorem is an application of Propositions 1–4. Stability is established in Section 4.   ∎

Having extended the comparative statics results of the 1981 model in Propositions 4 and 5, we now turn to an extension of the model itself. This allows us to obtain sharper and more general results. The new results are applicable to economies that may or may not have abundant labor.

The extension of the model proposed here was formulated in Chichilnisky (1981, p. 179).

An extension of the North–South model

The North–South model presented in Section 2 is altered now in a rather simple fashion already discussed in Section 2. The change is in the specification of demand in the South. Rather than assuming that the equilibrium level of industrial demand in the South is a given constant, we assume instead that, in equilibrium, wage income in the South is spent on the basic good. This entails replacing equation (2.18), that is, $I^D(S) = \bar{I}^D(S)$, by

$$p_B B^D = wL. \tag{2.18b}$$

This version of the North–South model (denoted II) consists therefore of the same equations as in the North–South model but for equation (2.18), which is replaced by (2.18b). As before, the model has a unique solution. Note that in the following results no assumption is made about labor abundance in the South. Comparative statics is performed by varying exogenously either X_B^S or $I^D(N)$: The comparative statics results obtained under these two exogenous changes are the same.

Proposition 6. Consider a North–South economy II where capital stocks in the South are fixed ($K = \bar{K}$), *and* $L = \alpha w/p_B$ ($\bar{L} = 0$). Then a necessary and sufficient condition for an increase in exports to lower the South's terms of trade, real wages, and consumption is technological duality: $c_2/D < 2w/p_B$. In particular, when the economy is homogeneous, $c_2/D > 2w/p_B$, the South's terms of trade always improve as the South increases its exports, and its real wages and consumption of basics increase as well.

When $\bar{L} \neq 0$, the necessary and sufficient condition is, instead, $c_2/D < 2w/p_B + \bar{L}$.

Proof: Consider the equation for the equilibrium volume of exports, $X_B^S(S) = B^S(S) - B^D(S)$. From $B^S = (c_2 L - a_2 K)/D$ and $B^D = wL/p_B$ and substituting for L and K from equations (2.3) and (2.4), we obtain

$$\frac{dX_B^S}{dw/p_B} = \alpha\left(\frac{c_2}{D} - \frac{2w}{p_B}\right) - \bar{L}. \tag{3.6}$$

When $\bar{L} = 0$, the necessary and sufficient condition for $dX_B^S/d(w/p_B)$ to be negative is $c_2/D < 2w/p_B$. When $\bar{L} \neq 0$, we obtain, instead, $c_2/D < 2w/p_B + \bar{L}$.

To complete the proof, note that the real wage is an increasing function of the price of basics across equilibria [from equation (2.21)].

Finally, the consumption of basics is an increasing function of the real wage across equilibria, since $B^D = w/p_B L = \alpha(w/p_B)^2 + w/p_B \bar{L}$ by (2.3) and (2.18b).   ∎

The following proposition obtains results analogous to those of Proposition 3 but for the North–South model II.

Proposition 7. Consider a North–South economy II where the capital stock in the South is fixed ($K = \bar{K}$) and $L = \alpha w/p_B$ ($\bar{L} = 0$). Labor in the South need not be abundant. Then an increase in the North's industrial demand leads to an increase in exports and to lower terms of trade, real wages, and consumption of basics in the South if and only if the duality condition holds in the South, $c_2/D < 2w/p_B$. When $\bar{L} \neq 0$, the condition is $c_2/D < 2w/p_B + \bar{L}$. Furthermore, if the rate of profit in the South is sufficiently low that $r < a_1/D$, an increase in exports lowers also total export revenues of the South.

The consumption of basics and of industrial goods increases simultaneously in the North provided industrial goods use little labor [$a_2(N)$ small] and labor is rather unresponsive to the real wage [$\alpha(N)$ small].

When $c_2/D > 2w/p_B$, the results are positive: An increase in the North's industrial demand leads to an increase in exports and to higher terms of trade, real wages, and consumption of basics in the South. The sign of $c_2/D - 2w/p_B$ determines therefore whether the international market transmits or hinders economic expansion across the two regions under the conditions.

Proof: First, we study the relationship between the equilibrium price of basics and the level of industrial demand of the North. Since Walras' law is always satisfied in an equilibrium, $p_B B^D + I^D = wL + rK$, and by assumption (2.18b), $p_B B^D = wL$, it follows that

$$I^D = rK = \beta r^2 + r\bar{K}.$$

Across equilibria, therefore,

$$\frac{dr}{dI^D} = \frac{1}{2r\beta + \bar{K}} > 0. \tag{3.7}$$

Furthermore, from equation (2.3), across equilibria,

$$\frac{dr}{dp_B} = \frac{-a_2}{D} < 0. \tag{3.8}$$

Therefore, from equations (3.7) and (3.8), it follows that

$$\frac{dp_B}{dI^D(\text{N})} < 0,$$

that is, an increase in the industrial demand in the North leads to a lower price of basics at the new equilibrium.

We have already proved in Proposition 6 that (under the conditions) a necessary and sufficient condition for a negative association of export levels and the price of basics is duality in the South: $c_2/D < 2w/p_B$ when $\bar{L} = 0$, or $c_2/D < 2w/p_B + \bar{L}$ when $\bar{L} \neq 0$. Therefore, since p_B is negatively associated with $I^D(\text{N})$, these two conditions are also necessary and sufficient for an *increase* in exports and for a simultaneous *decrease* in the terms of trade of the South, as the industrial demand in the North, $I^D(\text{N})$, increases. Since Proposition 6 showed that real wages and consumption of basics in the South all decrease with the price of basics, this completes the first part of the proof.

Next consider the condition on profits $r < a_1/D$. By (2.18b) and Walras' law, imports of the South equal

$$X_I^D(\text{S}) = I^D(\text{S}) - I^S(\text{S}) = rK - \frac{a_1 K - c_1 L}{D} = \left(r - \frac{a_1}{D}\right)K + \frac{c_1}{D}L.$$

It follows that, across equilibria,

$$\frac{dX_I^D(\text{S})}{dp_B} = \left(r - \frac{a_1}{D}\right)\frac{dK}{dp_B} + \frac{c_1}{D}\frac{dL}{dp_B}.$$

By assumption, $r < a_1/D$; since $dK/dp_B < 0$ and $dL/dp_B > 0$, it follows that $dX_I^D(\text{S})/dp_B > 0$. The imports of the South decrease as the price of basics drops, across equilibria.

By the balance-of-payments condition, total export revenues $p_B X_B^S(\text{S})$ equal the value of imports $X_I^D(\text{S})$. Therefore, we have proved that when $c_2/D < 2w/p_B$, export revenues fall with a decrease in the price of basics, across equilibria. The opposite happens when $c_2/D > 2w/p_B$: p_B and export revenues increase.

Finally, under the conditions, the consumption of basics will increase in the North following an expansion in industrial demand whenever $a_2(\text{N})$ is small and $\alpha(\text{N})$ is small, as proved in Proposition 5. ∎

The North–South model with fixed factor endowments

The last two propositions in this section consider economies with fixed factor endowments, that is, $K = \bar{K}$ and $L = \bar{L}$ ($\alpha = \beta = 0$). The first proposition refers to the North–South model, and the last two to its versions II and III.

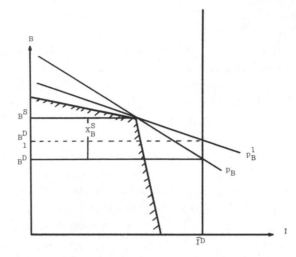

Figure 2. The North–South model with fixed factor endowments: The production possibility frontier has a shaded piecewise linear boundary. Across equilibria, the demand for industrial goods $\bar{I}^D$ is constant and an *increase* in the price of basics from p_B to p_B^1 leads always to a *drop* in the volume of exports X_B^S. Note that domestic supply B^S remains constant, but domestic demand for basics B^D increases to B_1^D when the price of basics increases from p_B to p_B^1.

Proposition 8. Consider a North–South model with fixed factor endowments. In this case, a move to a new equilibrium with higher levels of exports always lowers the terms of trade and export revenues of the South and leads also to lower real wages and consumption of basics in the South. Figure 2 illustrates this result.[8]

Proof: When $\alpha = 0$ and $\beta = 0$, the cross-equilibria relation between exports and their price p_B is

$$X_B^S = \frac{c_2 \bar{L} - a_2 \bar{K}}{D} - \frac{w\bar{L} + r\bar{K} - \bar{I}^D(S)}{p_B}$$

$$= \left(\frac{c_2}{D} - \frac{w}{p_B}\right)\bar{L} - \left(\frac{a_2}{D} + \frac{r}{p_B}\right)\bar{K} + \frac{\bar{I}^D}{p_B}.$$

Substituting w and r, one obtains

$$X_B^S = \frac{c_1 \bar{L} - u_1 \bar{K}}{D p_B} + \frac{\bar{I}^D(S)}{p_B},$$

so that

$$\frac{dX_B^S}{dp_B} = \frac{a_1 \bar{K} - c_1 \bar{L}}{D p_B^2} - \frac{\bar{I}^D(S)}{p_B^2},$$

which is always negative since $a_1 \bar{K} > c_1 \bar{L}$ [see, e.g., equation (2.20)]. As the price of basics drops, the real wage drops as well. Also, the consumption of basic goods, $B^D = (w\bar{L} + r\bar{K} - \bar{I}^D(S))/p_B$, decreases when $\bar{L}$ is large since dB^D/dp_B is dominated by the expression $\bar{L}(d(w/p_B)/dp_B)$, which is positive. ∎

Proposition 9. Consider a North–South model II with fixed factor endowments in the South. Then a move to an equilibrium with increased exports of the wage good leads always to a drop in the South's terms of trade. It also leads to a drop in real wages and in the consumption of the wage good in the South. However, in the new equilibrium, the South imports more industrial goods.

Proof: In the North–South model II, we have $X_B^S = (c_2 \bar{L} - a_2 \bar{K})/D - w/p_B \bar{L}$, that is,

$$X_B^S = \left(\frac{c_2}{D} - \frac{w}{p_B}\right)\bar{L} - \frac{a_2 \bar{K}}{D}.$$

By substitution from equation (2.21), this equals $X_B^S = (c_1/p_B D)\bar{L} - a_2 \bar{K}/D$, so that $dX_B^S/dp_B = -c_1 \bar{L}/p_B^2 D$, which is always negative. Therefore, a move to an equilibrium with increased exports of the wage good leads always to a decrease in their price, p_B. Since $w/p_B = c_2/D - c_1/p_B D$, the real wage decreases, and domestic demand for wages goods, being $B^D = w\bar{L}/p_B = (c_2/D - c_1/p_B D)\bar{L}$, also decreases as $dB^D/dp_B = c_1 \bar{L}/p_B^2 D > 0$. Finally, we show that imports of industrial goods increase. Consider the domestic demand for industrial goods in the South: In this case, this is $I^D = r\bar{K}$. Since p_B decreases following the export expansion, the new equilibrium profits r are higher, by equation (2.4). Therefore, industrial demand $I^D(S)$ increases in the South. However, since factor endowments are constant, industrial supply I^S has not changed. Therefore, the higher level demand of industrial goods at the new equilibrium must be due to increased imports of industrial goods. ∎

The last proposition in this section substitutes the demand specification (2.18) by (2.18c), that is, demand from basics derives both from wages and from capital income:

$$B^D = \gamma \frac{w}{p_B} L + \lambda rk, \quad \gamma, \lambda < 1,$$

and at least one positive in the South. All other equations remain unchanged. We call this the North–South model III.

Proposition 10. Consider the North–South model III where the demand for basics derives both from labor and capital income and from fixed factor endowments ($L = \bar{L}$, $K = \bar{K}$). If all capital income is spent on the basic good B, increasing the volume of exports leads always to better terms of trade but to lower domestic consumption of basics. If demand for basics comes both from labor and capital income, the terms of trade may increase or decrease as exports expand. Their response depends on the sign of the expression

$$\lambda a_2 \bar{K} - \gamma \frac{c_1}{p_B^2} \bar{L}.$$

Proof: In the South, across equilibria,

$$X_B^S = B^S - B^D = \frac{c_2}{D} \bar{L} - \frac{a_2}{D} \bar{K} - \left(\gamma \frac{w}{p_B} \bar{L} + \lambda r \bar{K} \right)$$

$$= \bar{L} \left(\frac{c_2}{D} - \frac{\gamma w}{p_B} \right) - \bar{K} \left(\frac{a_2}{D} + \lambda r \right)$$

$$= \bar{L} \left(\frac{c_2}{D} (1 - \gamma) + \frac{\gamma c_1}{D p_B} \right) - \bar{K} \left(\frac{a_2}{D} (1 - p_B \lambda) + \lambda \frac{a_1}{D} \right),$$

and

$$\frac{dX_B^S}{dp_B} = -\bar{L} \frac{\gamma c_1}{D p_B^2} + \frac{a_2}{D} \lambda \bar{K}.$$

When $\gamma = 0$, $dX_B^S / Dp_B > 0$. When $\lambda = 0$, $dX_B^S / dp_B < 0$, as in Proposition 9. The sign of dX_B^S / dp_B is that of $a_2 \lambda \bar{K} - (\gamma c_1 / p_B^2) \bar{L}$. Finally, note that $(dB^D / dp_B) < 0$ when $B^D = rK$. ∎

4   Stability

This section studies the stability of the North–South model and discusses several comments that address this issue.

It was shown in Chichilnisky (1981) that the North–South model is stable under the conditions of Propositions 2 and 3. Arrow (1981) pointed out that individual equilibria are stable in the usual sense of general equilibrium theory.[9] Heal and McLeod extended and generalized the 1981 stability results to a wide family of adjustment processes that contain, as a special case, the process in Chichilnisky (1981). Other commentators (e.g., Gunning, Findlay, Bhagwati, Srinivasan, Ranney, and Saavedra) proposed an adjustment process quite different from that in Chichilnisky (1981), but these authors nevertheless all agree on the stability of the model.[9]

For a discussion of stability, we must now define our disequilibrium adjustment process. This is necessary because the previous sections studied only moves from one equilibrium to another, and no information has been given so far that could be used to decide whether shocking the system away from one equilibrium would make it return to the equilibrium or not. All equations given so far are equilibrium relations. For instance, each proposition of Sections 2 and 3 assumes that profits are zero, namely, that commodity prices are linear combinations of factor prices, given by the commodity–factor price equations:

$$p_B = a_1 w + c_1 r, \qquad p_I = a_2 w + c_2 r, \tag{4.1}$$

or the equivalent inverse equations, the factor–commodity price relations:

$$w = (p_B c_2 - c_1)/D, \qquad r = (a_1 - p_B a_2)/D.$$

Profits must be zero in equilibrium because the North–South model has constant returns to scale, and the producers are competitive. But profits are typically *not* zero during an adjustment process that leads from a disequilibrium position to an equilibrium. Classical studies of stability in constant returns-to-scale economies such as Samuelson (1949) and Arrow and Hurwicz (1963) use profits as a driving force in the adjustment processes: In disequilibrium, producers increase output when profits are positive, and they decrease it when profits are negative. More recently, Mas-Colell (1974) has studied Walrasian stability in a constant returns-to-scale economy that is very similar, indeed an enlarged version of the model presented here. He too uses profits as a driving force in the adjustment process, a process he attributes to Walras: Profits in his model are only zero at equilibrium. Similarly, the adjustment process of Chichilnisky (1981, 1984) and the more general processes in Heal and McLeod (1984) all have nonzero profits in disequilibrium and, indeed, these profits play an important role in the adjustment process. In all of these adjustment processes, therefore, the commodity–factor price equations (4.1) do *not* hold outside of an equilibrium.

This point is worth noting because some commentators, that is, Findlay, Bhagwati, Srinivasan, and Ranney, use a different process, one in which profits are assumed to be identically zero at every disequilibrium point even while commodity markets adjust. They assume that the *zero profit* commodity–factor price relations (4.1) hold at every disequilibrium position of the commodity markets. Formally, the process used by these commentators cannot be Walrasian because the price equations (4.1) imply that factor prices are continuously varying as functions of good prices, even though their factor markets are continuously at an equilibrium, and excess demand in these markets is always zero: In a Walrasian process, there can be no price changes in markets that remain with zero excess demand. The process used by these commentators, which assumes zero profits at every disequilibrium point, rules out those processes of Samuelson, Arrow and Hurwicz, Mas-Colell, and Heal and McLeod, all of which assume nonzero profits outside of equilibrium. It also rules out the process of Chichilnisky (1981), so that these authors are working on a different model altogether.

We now define the process given in the appendix of Chichilnisky (1981). First, we study one region, and then we study both North and South. The North–South model has four markets in each region, for capital, labor, basics, and industrial goods. A typical Walrasian adjustment requires that market prices be positively associated with the excess demand in that market. Therefore, for each (disequilibrium) price vector $p = (p_B, p_I, w, r)$, we assume

$$\dot{p}_b = DB(p) - SB(p), \qquad \dot{p}_I = DI(p) - SI(p),$$
$$\dot{w} = DL(p) - SL(p), \qquad \dot{r} = DK(p) - SK(p), \tag{4.2}$$

where the letters D and S preceding a variable indicate (disequilibrium) demand and supply, respectively. This notation is deliberately different from that for equilibrium supply and demand and also different from the notation in the appendix of Chichilnisky (1981) so as to avoid confusion between, for example, the *equilibrium level of demand* B^D and the *demand function* for basics $DB(p)$.

To avoid the technicalities of a four-dimensional dynamical system, we assume, in a fashion analogous to Arrow and Hahn (1971, Chapter 12) and to much of the trade literature, that some of the markets are always at an equilibrium and that the burden of adjustment lies on the other markets. Factor markets are assumed always to clear DL = SL and DK = SK; by (4.2), this implies $\dot{w} = \dot{r} = 0$. Also, since industrial goods are the *numéraire, p_I* is identically equal to 1, so that $\dot{p}_I = 0$. The market for basics is therefore the only one in which price and quantity adjustments take place along the adjustment process, following the differential equation $\dot{p}_B = DB(p) - SB(p)$.

The next step is to define the supply and demand functions $SB(p)$ and $DB(p)$ for all disequilibrium prices. This includes, in particular, price vectors $p = (p_B, 1, w, r)$ where profits are not zero, that is, where the commodity–factor price equations (4.1) do not necessarily hold. Such a supply function has not been defined previously in this chapter, and we do so now. Note that as the North–South model has constant returns to scale, profit maximization conditions do not determine standard supply functions independently from demand considerations: Disequilibrium supply functions are not well defined with constant returns to scale [see, e.g., Arrow and Hahn (1971), Chapter 12, Section 10]. Several alternatives are possible, and we follow one that appears reasonable. For any given price vector $p = (p_B, 1, w, r)$, we use the factor supply equations

$$SL(p) = \alpha w/p_B + \bar{L} \quad \text{and} \quad SK(p) = \beta r + \bar{K}$$

to determine the level of factors supplied at p. Since factor markets always clear, supplies of labor and capital must match demand,

$$SL(p) = DL(p) = L(p) \quad \text{and} \quad SK(p) = DK(p) = K(p),$$

and thus we obtain the level of capital and labor employed at price p. If firms use their factors efficiently, this means that at the (disequilibrium) price vector p, supply of B is

$$SB(p) = \frac{c_2 L(p) - a_2 K(p)}{D} = \frac{c_2}{D}\left(\alpha \frac{w}{p_B} + \bar{L}\right) - \frac{a_2}{D}(\beta r + \bar{K}). \tag{4.3}$$

This defines the *supply function for basics* at any (disequilibrium) price vector p.

We now define the demand function for basics $DB(p)$ and for industrial goods $DI(p)$ for any price vector p. These definitions must be consistent with *Walras' law,* which states that at any (disequilibrium) price p, the value of expenditures equals the value of income:

$$p_B DB(p) + DI(p) = wL(p) + rK(p) + \Pi(p), \tag{4.4}$$

where $\Pi(p)$ denotes profits at p. Recall that unit profits at the price vector p are given by $p_B - a_1 w - c_1 r$ in the B sector and $1 - a_2 w - c_2 r$ in the I sector. Total profits $\Pi(p)$ are therefore equal to

$$\Pi(p) = SB(p_B - a_1 w - c_1 r) + SI(1 - a_2 w - c_2 r) \tag{4.5}$$

and are generally not zero outside an equilibrium.

The disequilibrium *demand function for basics* $DB(p)$ was defined on page 190 of Chichilnisky (1981) [denoted $B^D(p)$] as

$$p_B DB(p) = wL(p) + rK(p) - \bar{I}^D(p), \tag{4.6}$$

that is,

$$DB(p) = \alpha \left(\frac{w}{p_B} \right)^2 + \frac{w\bar{L} + r\bar{K}}{p_B} + \frac{\beta r^2}{p_B} - \frac{\bar{I}^D}{p_B},$$

where w and r are the equilibrium values and $\bar{I}^D$ is the constant defined in equation (2.17).

By Walras' law, this definition of $DB(p)$ is *equivalent* to defining the (disequilibrium) *demand function for industrial goods* $DI(p)$ as

$$DI(p) = \bar{I}^D + \Pi(p). \tag{4.7}$$

Therefore, the definition of DB in the appendix of Chichilnisky (1981) implies that profits $\Pi(p)$ are always spent in the industrial sector. In particular, since profits are nonzero and an increasing function of p_B in disequilibrium, $DI(p)$ is *not* a constant out of equilibrium; rather it is an increasing function of p_B, or equivalently $DI(p)$ is downward sloping in the relative price of p_I, as stated in Chichilnisky (1981, p. 168). This is worth noting because some of the commentators (e.g., Findlay, 1984a, b; Srinivasan and Bhagwati, 1984) drew a *vertical* disequilibrium demand function for industrial goods; that is, they postulated that in disequilibrium, industrial demand is always a constant $\bar{I}^D$. This is not correct since, as seen above, a constant demand function for I would contradict Walras' law and the definition of the demand for B in Chichilnisky (1981, p. 190).

We define now the disequilibrium *supply function for industrial goods* in analogy with the supply of basics [equation (4.3)]. At a disequilibrium price $p = (p_B, 1, w, r)$, let

$$SI(p) = \frac{a_1 K(p) - c_1 L(p)}{D} = \frac{a_1}{D}(\beta r + \bar{K}) - \frac{c_1}{D}\left(\alpha \frac{w}{p_B} + \bar{L} \right). \tag{4.8}$$

By construction, Walras' law is satisfied, that is, the value of excess demand is equal to zero.

Having defined the supply and demand functions for basics and industrial goods, we may now compute whether the system is stable in a neighborhood of one equilibrium. To study stability in the neighborhood of one equilibrium, $p^* = (p_B^*, 1, w^*, r^*)$ under the adjustment process defined above, one considers a shock to p^*. From equation (4.2), the factor prices w and r must remain at the equilibrium values during a Walrasian adjustment process ($\dot{w} = \dot{r} = 0$) because factor markets have been assumed to clear at all times.[10] From here on, I shall therefore assume that $w = w^*$ and $r = r^*$. Stability in a neighborhood of one equilibrium requires that all the eigenvalues of the Jacobian of the system (4.2) have negative real parts. This Jacobian is the 4×4 matrix of the partial derivatives of the four functions $DB(p) - SB(p)$, $DI(p) - SI(p)$, $DL(p) - SL(p)$, and $DK(p) - SK(p)$ with respect to the four variables p_B, p_I, w, and r. However, since $\dot{p}_I = \dot{w} = \dot{r} = 0$, the matrix has only one nonzero term, which is the partial derivative of the excess demand for basics with respect to the price of basics, that is, $\partial/\partial p_B[DB(p) - SB(p)]$. For stability, this partial derivative must be negative.

From the above definitions of supply and demand [equations (4.3) and (4.6)], we have, for any (disequilibrium) price p, the expression for *excess demand for basics:*

$$DB(p) - SB(p) = \frac{wL(p) + rK(p) - \bar{I}^D}{p_B} - \frac{c_2}{D}L(p) + \frac{a_2}{D}K(p), \qquad (4.9)$$

which by the definition of supply of labor and capital in disequilibrium is equal to $\alpha(w/p_B)^2 + \beta(r^2/p_B) + w/p_B(\bar{L} - \alpha c_2/D) + r(\beta a_2/D + \bar{K}/p_B) + (\bar{K}a_2 - \bar{L}c_2)/D - \bar{I}^D/p_B$. For stability, the partial derivative of the excess demand function $DB(p) - SB(p)$ with respect to p_B must be negative, that is,

$$\frac{\partial}{\partial p_B}(DB(p) - SB(p)) = \frac{\alpha w}{p_B^2}(c_2/D - 2w/p_B) - \frac{w\bar{L}}{p_B^2} - \frac{\beta r^2}{p_B^2} - \frac{\bar{K}r}{p_B^2} + \frac{\bar{I}^D}{p_B^2}$$

$$< 0. \qquad (4.10)$$

When α is sufficiently large, the term $\alpha w/p_B^2(c_2/D - 2w/p_B)$ dominates the expression (4.10). Therefore, *the B market is stable when the duality condition $c_2/D < 2w/p_B$ is satisfied.* This is, of course, the stability condition on pages 190–191 of Chichilnisky (1981) and is also the condition obtained by Heal and McLeod (1984) in their adjustment process of Section 4.1.

It is now immediate to show stability in the industrial goods market, for which it is required that the *partial derivative $\partial/\partial p_B(DI(p) - SI(p))$* be positive. This is a direct application of Walras' law. Since the value of excess demand is zero, that is, $p_B(DB(p) - SB(p)) + DI(p) - SI(p) = 0$, it follows that

$$\frac{\partial}{\partial p_B}(\mathrm{DI}(p)-\mathrm{SI}(p)) = \frac{\mathrm{DI}(p)-\mathrm{SI}(p)}{p_B^2} - \frac{\partial}{\partial p_B}(\mathrm{DB}(p)-\mathrm{SB}(p)).$$

Near an equilibrium, $\mathrm{DI}(p)-\mathrm{SI}(p)$ is close to zero, and therefore $(\partial/\partial p_B)(\mathrm{DI}(p)-\mathrm{SI}(p))$ is indeed positive when $\partial/\partial p_B(\mathrm{DB}(p)-\mathrm{SB}(p))<$ 0. Thus *the market for industrial goods is also stable when α is large and $c_2/D < 2w/p_B$*. Figures 3 and 4 reproduce numerically the disequilibrium supply and demand equations for B and for I for a simulation of the model with initial parameter values satisfying the above conditions. These figures illustrate stability of both markets.

We have therefore proved the stability results in Chichilnisky (1981):

Proposition 11. [Appendix 2, Chichilnisky (1981)]. Under the Walrasian adjustment process $\dot{p} = \mathrm{DB}(p)-\mathrm{SB}(p)$ of Chichilnisky (1981), the economy of the South is stable when α is large and $c_2/D < 2w/p_B$.

Proof: See the preceding text starting from equation (4.6) to the statement of this proposition. ∎

As mentioned above, the process in Chichilnisky (1981) assumes that $I^D = \bar{I}^D + \Pi(p)$: Profits are spent in the I sector. Heal and McLeod (1984) have studied more general adjustment processes for the North–South model, in particular, one where a proportion λ of profits is spent on basics and the rest on industrial goods. For each (disequilibrium) price vector $p = (p_B, 1, w, r)$, this changes the demand equation (4.6) for basics into

$$\mathrm{DB}(p) = \frac{wL(p)+rK(p)-\bar{I}^D}{p_B} + \frac{\lambda\Pi(p)}{p_B}$$

$$= \frac{wL(p)+rK(p)-\bar{I}^D}{p_B} + \frac{\mathrm{SB}(p)(p_B-a_1 w-c_1 r)\lambda}{p_B}.$$

Since $\mathrm{SB}(p) = (c_2 L(p)-a_2 K(p))/D$, we obtain

$$\mathrm{DB}(p) = L(p)\left[\frac{w}{p_B} + \frac{\lambda}{D}\left(c_2 - \frac{c_2 a_1 w}{p_B} - \frac{c_2 c_1 r}{p_B}\right)\right]$$

$$+ K(p)\left[\frac{r}{p_B} - \frac{\lambda}{D}\left(a_2 - \frac{a_2 a_1 w}{p_B} - \frac{a_2 c_1 r}{p_B}\right)\right] - \frac{\bar{I}^D}{p_B}.$$

Therefore, the new *excess demand function for basics* $\mathrm{DB}(p)-\mathrm{SB}(p)$ is

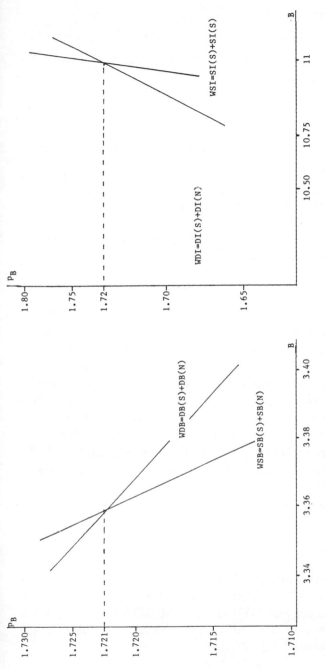

Figure 3. [Left] Simulation of the world's disequilibrium supply and demand curves: world market for basics. Curves were simulated from the given data set at the equilibrium corresponding to $I^D(N) = 7.0$. WSB = world disequilibrium supply of basics; WDB = world disequilibrium demand for basics. The world market for basics is stable when $\alpha(S)$ is large, and $c_2/D < 2w/p_B$ in the South, Proposition 12, Section 4. WSB = SB(N) + SB(S); WDB = DB(N) + DB(S); slope of WSB = -0.38, slope of WDB = -0.22.

Figure 4. [Right] Simulation of the world's disequilibrium supply and demand curves: world market for industrial goods. Curves were simulated from the given data set at the equilibrium corresponding to $I^D(N) = 7.0$. WSI = world disequilibrium supply of industrial goods; WDI = world disequilibrium demand for industrial goods. The world market for industrial goods is also stable, under the conditions of Proposition 12, Section 4. WSI = SI(N) + SI(S), WDI = DI(N) + DI(S); slope of WSI = 2.27, slope of WDI = 0.29.

$$DB(p) - SB(p) = L(p)\left[\frac{w}{p_B} + \frac{(\lambda-1)c_2}{D} - \frac{\lambda}{D}\left(\frac{c_2 a_1 w}{p_B} + \frac{c_2 c_1 r}{p_B}\right)\right]$$
$$+ K(p)\left[\frac{r}{p_B} - \frac{(\lambda-1)a_2}{D} - \frac{\lambda}{D}\left(\frac{a_2 a_1 w}{p_B} + \frac{a_1 c_1 r}{p_B}\right)\right]$$
$$- \frac{\bar{I}^D}{p_B}. \tag{4.11}$$

Therefore, when α is sufficiently large, this excess demand function is dominated by the terms in α, that is, by

$$\alpha\left[\left(\frac{w}{p_B}\right)^2 + \frac{w(\lambda-1)c_2}{p_B D} - \frac{\lambda w}{p_B^2 D}(c_2 a_1 w + c_2 c_1 r)\right],$$

and thus the sign of the *partial derivative* of the excess demand function for basics with respect to their price is that of

$$\alpha\left[-\frac{2w^2}{p_B^3} + \frac{(1-\lambda)c_2 w}{p_B^2 D} + \frac{2\lambda w}{p_B^3 D}(c_2 a_1 w + c_2 c_1 r)\right].$$

Since all the terms in λ are positive, it follows that the larger is λ, that is, the higher the proportion of profits spent on basics, the more positive is the expression above, and the less likely is stability. When $\lambda = 0$, all profits are spent on the industrial good, and we recover the results of Chichilnisky (1981): The above expression reduces then to $\alpha w/p_B^2(c_2/D - 2w/p_B)$, which is negative when the duality condition $c_2/D < 2w/p_B$ is satisfied. Therefore, the most favorable case for stability is when profits are allocated to the industrial sector, and the adjustment process in Chichilnisky (1981) summarized in Proposition 11 above is the one most favorable to stable markets.

It was also stated in Chichilnisky (1981, p. 191) that the *world market* for basics was stable under the same conditions, but this was not proved there. We provide a proof now:

Proposition 12. Consider the Walrasian adjustment process for the world economy described above, where the price of basics rises with the world excess demand for basics: $\dot{p}_B = \text{WDB}(p) - \text{WSB}(p)$. Then the world economy is stable when the economy of the South has abundant labor [$\alpha(S)$ large] and dual technologies ($c_2/D < \alpha w/p_B$).

Proof: Consider a trade equilibrium in the North–South model where the equilibrium exports of the South, $X_B^S(S)$, are matched by equilibrium imports of the North, $X_B^D(N)$, and the equilibrium exports of the North, $S_I^S(N)$, are matched by equilibrium imports of the South, $S_I^D(S)$.

There are now six markets: Two markets for commodities, basics and industrial goods, and four markets for factors, capital and labor in each region. Note that since factors are not traded internationally, they constitute different markets in each region: A price vector is now $p = (p_B, p_I, w(S), w(N), r(S), r(N))$. A Walrasian adjustment process is now described by prices increasing with the *world excess demand:*

$$\dot{p}_B = DB(S)(p) - SB(S)(p) + DB(N)(p) - SB(N)(p) = WEDB(p),$$

$$\dot{p}_I = DI(S)(p) - SI(S)(p) + DI(N)(p) - SI(N)(p) = WEDB(p),$$

$$\dot{w}(S) = DL(S)(p) - SL(S)(p), \qquad \dot{r}(S) = DK(S)(p) - SK(S)(p),$$

$$\dot{w}(N) = DL(N)(p) - SL(N)(p), \qquad \dot{r}(N) = DK(N)(p) - SK(N)(p).$$

As before, we assume that all factors markets clear and that industrial goods are the *numéraire,* so that $\dot{p}_I = \dot{w}(S) = \dot{r}(S) = \dot{r}(N) = 0$. Therefore, wages and profits always remain at their equilibrium levels, and we only need to prove that the first differential equation in $\dot{p}_B$ leads to stability. Supply of basics is defined in the same way as before. For any disequilibrium price vector, we obtain one supply function for each region:

$$DB(S)(p) = (c_2(S)L(S)(p) - a_2(S)K(S)(p))/D(S)$$

and

$$SB(N)(p) = (c_2(N)L(N)(p) - a_2(N)K(N)(p))/D(N),$$

where in each region

$$K(p) = SK(p) = \beta r + \bar{K} \quad \text{and} \quad L(p) = SL(p) = \alpha w/p_B + \bar{L}$$

for each (disequilibrium) price vector $p = (p_B, 1, w(S), w(N), r(S), r(N))$.

Next we define the world demand for basics at any (disequilibrium) price p. In each region Walras' law is now

$$p_B DB(p) + DI(p) = wL(p) + rK(p) + \Pi(p) + NX,$$

where NX denotes net export revenues at price p. This implies that at any price vector p, the demand function for basics in each region is now

$$DB(p) = [wL(p) + rK(p) - \bar{I}^D(p)]/p_B + \mu(NX/p_B),$$

where μ is the proportion of net export revenues allocated to the B sector. Here we have assumed as before that $DI(p) = \bar{I}^D + \Pi(p)$, so that profits are spent in the industrial goods.

At an equilibrium, net export revenues NX are, of course, zero: This is the balance-of-payments condition. Outside of an equilibrium, however, NX need not be zero. However, the world's net export revenues, which are the sum of the North's and the South's, $NX(N)+NX(S)$, must be zero. In particular, when $\mu(S)=\mu(N)$, that is, when the same proportion of export revenues goes to basics in both regions,

$$\mu(NX(N)/p_B)+\mu(NX(S)/p_B)=0.$$

Therefore, the world excess demand for basics (WEDB), which is the sum of the North's and the South's, does not contain any term in NX. We obtain

$$WEDB(p)=(DB(N)(p)+DB(S)(p))-(SB(N)(p)+SB(S)(p))$$

$$=\alpha\left(\frac{w}{p_B}\right)^2+\frac{\beta r^2}{p_B}+\frac{w}{p_B}\left(\frac{\bar{L}-\alpha c_2}{D}\right)+r\left(\frac{\beta a_2}{D}+\frac{\bar{K}}{p_B}\right)$$

$$+\frac{\bar{K}a_2-\bar{L}c_2}{D^2}-\frac{I^D}{p_B}+\alpha(N)\left(\frac{w(N)}{p_B}\right)^2+\frac{\beta(N)r(N)^2}{p_B}$$

$$+\frac{w(N)}{p_B}\left(\bar{L}(N)-\frac{\alpha(N)c_2(N)}{D(N)}\right)+r(N)\left(\frac{\beta(N)a_2(N)}{D(N)}+\frac{\bar{K}(N)}{p_B}\right)$$

$$+\frac{\bar{K}(N)a_2(N)-\bar{L}(N)c_2(N)}{D(N)^2}-\frac{I^D(N)}{p_B}, \tag{4.12}$$

where all the parameters are for the South unless otherwise indicated.

We may now study the stability of the world market for basics, that is, the sign of the partial derivative of $WEDB(p)$ with respect to the price p_B:

$$\frac{\partial}{\partial p_B}(WEDB(p))=\alpha\frac{w}{p_B^2}\left(\frac{c_2}{D}-\frac{2w}{p_B}\right)-\frac{\beta r^2}{p_B^2}-\left(\frac{\bar{L}w+r\bar{K}}{p_B^2}\right)+\frac{I}{p_B^2}$$

$$+\alpha(N)\frac{w(N)}{p_B^2}\frac{c_2(N)}{D(N)}-\frac{2w(N)}{p_B}-\frac{\beta(N)(r(N))^2}{p_B^2}$$

$$-\frac{\bar{L}(N)w(N)+r(N)\bar{K}(N)}{p_B^2}+\frac{\bar{I}(N)}{p_B^2}, \tag{4.13}$$

where all parameters, unless otherwise indicated, are for the South. Equation (4.13) shows that when $\alpha(S)$ is sufficiently large in the South, so that the terms in $\alpha(S)$ dominate, $(\partial/\partial p_B)WEDB(p)$ has the sign of the expression $\alpha w/p_B(c_2/D-2w/p_B)$ in the South. Therefore, when $c_2/D<2w/p_B$ in the South, the world market for basics is stable. As in the one-region case, the world market for industrial goods is also stable from Walras' law. We have thus proved Proposition 12. ■

To summarize: the adjustment process defined in Chichilnisky (1981) was analyzed in detail and extended to the two-region economy. It was shown to yield Walrasian stability under the conditions postulated in Chichilnisky (1981). This process has an element in common with the process defined in Arrow and Hahn (1971) for constant returns-to-scale economies: Some of the markets (in our case, factor markets) are always in equilibrium. It also has an element in common with the processes defined in Samuelson (1949), Arrow and Hurwicz (1963), Mas-Colell (1974), and Heal and McLeod (1984): There are nonzero profits outside of an equilibrium, and these have indeed a nontrivial role in determining the stability of the model.

A final task is to compare the stability process in Chichilnisky (1981) with the comments of Findlay, Bhagwati, Srinivasan, Ranney, and Saavedra. All these comments are based on a particular adjustment process initially proposed by Findlay, as pointed out by Srinivasan and Bhagwati (1984), a process that is quite different from that in Chichilnisky (1981). Yet, with this different process, these authors still obtain stability of the model (for details, see note 9).

Figures 2 and 3 of Bhagwati and Srinivasan [first proposed by Findlay (1984)] are useful for this task. They state that (disequilibrium) demand for industrial goods is constant, that is, $DI(p) = \bar{I}^D$, and therefore that the (disequilibrium) demand function for industrial goods is a vertical line. Yet we know from equation (4.7) that the disequilibrium demand for industrial goods must necessarily be $DI = \bar{I}^D + \Pi(p)$ (otherwise Walras' law is violated) and therefore $DI(p)$ is definitely not a constant function because profits $\Pi(p)$ are not zero outside an equilibrium and indeed vary with p. The conclusions drawn by these authors, derived from their assumption that DI is a constant, are therefore inapplicable to the North–South model because they violate Walras' law. Their assumptions require that profits be always zero outside an equilibrium, that is, equations (4.1).

The same problem appears in Findlay and Srinivasan and Bhagwati's analysis of the market for basics. The downward-sloping cross-equilibria curve X_B^S is confused there with a disequilibrium excess supply curve in the usual sense, that is, with the curve $SB(S) - DB(S)$, defined in (4.9) and in page 190 of Chichilnisky (1981). Yet the curves X_B^S and $SB(S) - DB(S)$ are very different indeed: In fact, one is downward sloping precisely when the other is upward sloping: When $c_2/D < 2w/p_B$, as shown in Proposition 2, dX_B^S/dp_B is *negative*, while $\partial/\partial p_B(SB(S) - DB(S))$ is *positive*, as shown in Proposition 11. Obviously X_B^S is *not* an excess supply curve in the usual sense: This was pointed out in Arrow (1981) as well.[11] The correct disequilibrium excess demand for basics in (4.9) has nonzero profits outside an equilibrium. However, since in equilibrium profits are necessarily zero and the two approaches differ only in the value of profits, the two approaches give exactly the same set of equilibria. This explains why all these comments agree on the whole with the comparative statics results of Chichilnisky (1981), which study properties of the set of equilibria. That is, there is agreement on the facts that the export volumes of the South are negatively associated to their price and that higher values of industrial demand in the North lead to lower prices and higher volumes of exports of basic goods from the South (when α is large and $c_2/D < 2w/p_B$ in the South). There is also agreement on the fact that the model is stable, even though stability is defined differently by some of the commentators (see note 9).

The differences that arise are therefore rather minor. Neither the stability nor the comparative statics results are questioned. The only point at stake is the interpretation of how the comparative statics results arise, which is only natural since the adjustment process has been changed.

The difference of interpretation is most acute when some of these authors state that a drop in the South's terms of trade following an expansion of the industrial demand in the North, "must follow from a decrease in the North's demand for basics."[12] This is incorrect. Both Propositions 3 and 5 of Section 3 and Theorem 1 in Heal and McLeod (1984) show that the terms of trade of the South drop even with an increase in (domestic or international) demand for basics in the North. This point has also been substantiated by the simulation reported in Heal and McLeod, Section 3, Table 2, where the demand for basics in the North rises and the equilibrium price of basics drops. Furthermore, the appendix to this essay also shows numerically that an increase in the demand for basics in the North, DB(N), accompanied by a positive shift in the excess demand for basics of the North, WD (which intersects X_B^S from above), lead to a *drop* in the price of basics, p_B, and in the purchasing power of the South. This is due to the fact that there is also a positive shift in the excess supply curve of the South when $\bar{I}^D$ increases in the North. The point is simple: In a general equilibrium context, a change in an exogenous parameter leads typically to simultaneous changes in excess supply and excess demand curves, so that even in stable markets, an outward shift in excess demand may be accompanied by a lower new equilibrium price.

It is easy to trace the source of the erroneous conclusion that a drop in the price of basics must be due to a drop in the North's demands for basics. It derives from the confusion of the cross-equilibrium curve X_B^S defined in Proposition 2 with the actual excess supply curve of basics of the

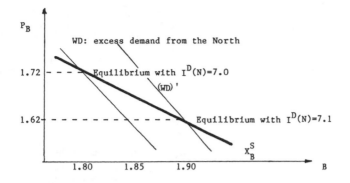

Figure 5. International market for basic goods. This figure reproduces Figure 2(b) in Chichilnisky (1981), where the curves have been computed numerically from the basic data set. For $I^D(N) = 7.0$, we obtain WD, and for $I^D(N) = 7.1$, we obtain (WD)'. Slope of $X_B^S = -0.9$, slope of WD $= -1.1$, slope of (WD)' $= -1.1$.

South, defined in the appendix of Chichilnisky (1981) and in equation (4.9). The erroneous conclusion that a drop in the price of basics must be due to a drop in the North's demand for basics derives from a partial equilibrium view in which only one curve shifts at a time (e.g., excess demand for the North) *and* in which the zero-profit cross-equilibrium relation X_B^S is confused with an (unmovable) excess supply curve. Walrasian stability of the model, in which we all agree, would in this erroneous partial equilibrium view lead to an excess demand curve that meets X_B^S from above and must shift downward to reach a lower new equilibrium price. However, when the curve X_B^S is seen properly as an equilibrium locus, and it is understood that the excess supply and demand curves both shift with $\bar{I}^D(N)$, this partial equilibrium interpretation collapses.

Propositions 3 and 5 and the numerical simulations in the appendix show clearly that the terms of trade of the South drop after an increase $I^D(N)$ even when the North's demand for basics is higher (i.e., shifts outward) at the new equilibrium. This occurs within a Walrasian stable market because both demand and supply curves vary simultaneously when $\bar{I}^D(N)$ increases. Figure 2b in Chichilnisky (1981) illustrates this fact. This figure is reproduced from a numerical simulation of the model in the appendix (Figs. 5 and 6). In a Walrasian stable market, a drop in the price of basics will clearly follow an upward shift in demand for basics when the supply curve for basics shifts sufficiently. This is precisely what was shown in Chichilnisky (1981). When the equilibrium value of industrial

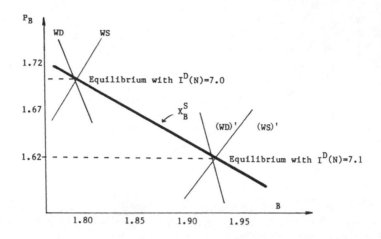

Figure 6. Simulation of X_B^S as a locus of equilibria in the international market for basic goods. $WD = DB(N) - SB(N)$, $WS = SB(S) - DB(S)$, WD and WS correspond to $I^D(N) = 7.0$. $(WD)'$ and $(WS)'$ correspond to $I^D(N) = 7.1$. The curve X_B^S is computed from a range of different values of $I^D(N)$, which are of course associated to different equilibrium prices p_B. Slope of $WD = -1.1$, slope of $WS = 1$, slope of $(WD)' = -1.1$, slope of $(WS)' = 1.6$, slope of $X_B^S = -0.9$.

demand in the North $\bar{I}^D(N)$ increases, both supply and demand curves for basics shift. This is because at the new $\bar{I}^D(N)$, a new equilibrium set of prices emerges $(p_B^*, 1, w^*, r^*)$, the only set of prices compatible with the new $\bar{I}^D(N)$. From the definitions of the supply and demand functions for basics [equations (4.3) and (4.6)], it is clear that both of these functions shift at the new equilibrium. Obviously, when both demand and supply shift simultaneously, an increase in demand may be accompanied by lower prices, within a Walrasian stable market. This is what was shown to happen in Chichilnisky (1981, Propositions 3 and 5) and in the appendix to this chapter.

In sum: the curve X_B^S is a cross-equilibrium locus of export volumes and export prices and not a disequilibrium excess supply curve valid for testing Walrasian stability. This was pointed out clearly in Chichilnisky (1981) and in Arrow (1981) (see note 11). The use of X_B^S as an excess supply curve is not appropriate for testing Walrasian stability because it requires profits to be zero outside of an equilibrium, that is, the use of price equations (4.1) outside an equilibrium. In addition, when price equations are assumed to be satisfied at all times, factor prices are continuously varying as functions of goods prices, even though the factor markets are continuously at an equilibrium and the excess demand in these markets is always zero, whereas in a Walrasian adjustment process, there can be no price changes in a market that remains with zero excess demand. The disequilibrium excess supply of the South, $SB(S) - DB(S)$, was defined in Appendix 2 of Chichilnisky (1981) and in equation (4.9) above and is clearly very different from X_B^S.

A numerical simulation of the model produces Figure 2(b) of Chichilnisky (1981) with the proper excess supply function of the South, $S = SB(S) - DB(S)$ (see Figs. 5 and 6). These figures show X_B^S as the locus of the intersections of two curves: the (disequilibrium) excess demand curve of the north, WD, and the (disequilibrium) excess supply curve of the South, WS, at different equilibria. Stability is therefore perfectly consistent with a downward-sloping cross-equilibrium relation X_B^S met from above by the North's excess demand curve, WD, that is, with Figure 2(b) in Chichilnisky (1981). How the North's excess demand curve WD meets X_B^S is totally irrelevant for stability; what matters for stability is only how each excess demand of the North, WD, crosses the corresponding excess supply of the South, WS. Since each excess demand WD is downward sloping and the corresponding excess supply WS is upward sloping, an equilibrium is obviously stable (see Figs. 5 and 6).

5   Conclusions and empirical studies

This chapter summarizes and extends the model and results of Chichilnisky (1981, 1984).

Section 2 establishes uniqueness of the solutions and computes an equilibrium explicitly.

Section 3 gives straightforward proofs of Propositions 1, 2, and 3 in Chichilnisky (1981). It also obtains new, more general propositions about the effects of an export expansion. Necessary and sufficient conditions are given for positive and negative outcomes of an export expansion for the South. These conditions are on the internal structures of the economies, technologies, factor endowments, and initial levels of trade and do not depend on international elasticities of demand. Outcomes are in general negative when

  (a) labor is abundant and there is "duality," that is, $c_2/D < 2w/p_B$;
  (b) the country exports a wage good and there is duality; or
  (c) factor endowments are fixed and the country exports a wage good.

We also considered cases where demand for the export good comes from capital income or from a combination of capital and wage incomes. Similar results obtain.

Under certain conditions, following an export expansion of the South, the North consumes simultaneously more of both goods. In contrast, the South's terms of trade, export revenues, and consumption all decrease. There is therefore a transfer of welfare from the South to the North, working its way through the operation of competitive international markets.

The effects of an export expansion typically become positive when the South is more "homogeneous," $c_2/D > 2w/p_B$. The conditions for positive outcomes depend on the initial volume of exports because the sign of the expression $c_2/D - 2w/p_B$ changes as real wages adjust to the new export levels. Therefore, the results address the problem of whether to increase or decrease exports rather than a choice between trade and autarchy. Domestic policies may be used to alter the sign of this expression, $c_2/D - 2w/p_B$, or the responsiveness of labor to real wage, leading to a more positive environment for export-led strategies.

Section 4 discussed stability. It summarized the adjustment process in Chichilnisky (1981) and generalized it to a two-region economy. This section shows the role of profits in the stability of the model and discusses in this context several comments on the 1981 results.

The model introduced in 1981 and developed further above shows that under certain conditions an expansion of labor-intensive exports leads to disadvantageous outcomes for the South, even when this is associated to an expansion of the North's demand for basics. The critical conditions concern the domestic structure of the South's economy as reflected by the inequality $c_2/D \lesssim 2w/p_B$, and the responsiveness of labor supplies to real wages. To evaluate the basic structure of the model and to test its implications for particular cases, a sequence of econometric case studies has been undertaken. The first of these is reported in Chichilnisky, Heal, and Podivinsky (1983). This deals with trade between Sri Lanka and the United Kingdom, which is characterized by the exchange of primary products (mainly tea) for industrial goods.

For this empirical implementation, the equilibrium equations of the North–South model in Section 2 were treated (in reduced form) as describing the long-run steady state of a dynamic system. The system was then assumed to adjust toward this steady-state configuration by a partial adjustment process, in which it adjusts in each period to remove a fraction of the deviations of its variables from their equilibrium values. This is a standard time series implementation of an equilibrium or steady-state model.

The resulting system of nonlinear simultaneous equations was estimated using a twenty-five-year data series by both nonlinear FIML and three-stage least squares. Full details of the results are contained in Chichilnisky et al. (1983): These results confirmed that a dynamic adaptation of the model defined by the equations in Section 2 can provide a good statistical explanation of patterns of trade between Sri Lanka and the United Kingdom and their relationship to technologies and factor prices. The case study also established that in Sri Lanka, where labor is certainly abundant, the inequality $c_2/D < 2w/p_B$ held for every year but one in the sample period 1952–80. In view of Propositions 2 and 3 above, this implies that during the sample period a change in demand in the United Kingdom that led to an expansion of Sri Lanka's exports would lead in statistical terms to a reduction in Sri Lanka's real wages and terms of trade. Statistical analysis of the data confirms this result. The case study thus confirms both the appropriateness of the general structure of the model and the potential importance of the domestic structural issues that it highlights.

A second empirical study was undertaken in Chichilnisky and McLeod (1984) for the case of Argentina and the United States. Here the econometric analysis was restricted to the estimation of the exogenous parameters of the model, in particular the factor supply equations. The model was then simulated on the basis of the estimations of these parameters. An empirical study of export levels and of terms of trade and real wages was undertaken simultaneously. The results showed that when the inequality $c_2/D < 2w/p_B$ was satisfied (plus or minus a standard deviation), terms of trade were negatively associated with export volumes; otherwise, the association was statistically positive. Similar results were obtained with respect to changes in the real wages. The model used for Argentina and the United States was North–South II since Argentina exports a wage good, which is labor intensive (agricultural products).

Appendix

The first few sections of this appendix contain a program in BASIC for solving the model, and the results of several computer runs that reproduce numerically the comparative statics propositions in Section 3 and the stability results in Section 4. These were produced by Eduardo-José Chichilnisky.

a   *Computer code names for the variables and parameters*

Variables and parameters (North and South)	Computer code	
	South	North
α	MS	MN
β	NS	NN
a_1	A1	A3
a_2	A2	A4
c_1	C1	C3
c_2	C2	C4
$\bar{L}$	LS	L (*not* LN)
$\bar{K}$	KS	KN
D	DS	DN
A	AS	AN
V	VS	VN
C	CS	CN
W	WS	WN
r	RS	RN
L	L1	L2
K^S	K1	K2
B^D	B3	B4
B^S	B1	B2
I^D	I3	I4
I^S	I1	I2
X_B^S	X1	$-$X1
X_I^D	X2	$-$X2

b   *Program for the North–South model*

```
1000:  INPUT "SOUTH:ALPHA,BETA,A1,A2?";MS,NS,A1,A2
1010:  INPUT "SOUTH:C1,C2,L*,K*?";C1,C2,LS,KS
1020:  INPUT "NORTH:ALPHA,BETA,A1,A2?";MN,NN,A3,A4
1030:  INPUT "NORTH:C1,C2,L*,K*?";C3,C4,L,KN
1040:  LF 2:TEXT :CSIZE 1:LPRINT "PARAMETERS":LF 1
1050:  LPRINT "SOUTH:";MS;",";NS;",";A1;".";A2
1060:  LPRINT TAB 6;C1;",";C2;",",LS;",";KS;LF 1
1070.  LPRINT "NORTH:";MN,",";NN;",",A3:",";A4
1080.  LPRINT TAB 6;C3;",";C4;",";L;",";KN:LF 1
1090.  INPUT "ID(S)?";I1
1100.  INPUT "ID(N)?";I2.LF 2
1110:  DS=A1*C2-A2*C1:DN=A3*C4-A4*C3
1115:  IF DS=0THEN1500: 1F DN=0THEN 1500
1120:  AS=NS*A1*A2/(DS*DS):AN=NN*A3*A4/(DN*DN)
1130:  VS=MS*C1*C1/(DS*DS):VN=MN*C3*C3/(DN*DN)
1140:  CS=(1/ (DS/*DS))*(DS*(C1*LS-A1*KS)+MS*C1*C2-NS*A1*A1)
1150:  CN=(1/DN*DN))*(DN*(C3*L-A3*KN)+MN*C3*C4-NN*A3*A3)
1160:  J=CS+CN+I1+I2:K=J*J+4*(VS+VN)*(AS+AN)
1170:  IF K<0THENGOTO 1500
1180:  PB=(-J+ K)/(2*(AS+AN))
1190:  WS=(PB*C2-C1)/DS:WN=(PB*C4-C3)/DN
1200:  RS=(A1-PB*A2)/DS:RN=(A3-PB*A4)/DN
1210:  L1=MS*WS/PB+LS:L2=MN*WN/PB+L
1220:  KI=NS*RS+KS:K2=NN*RN+KN
1230:  I3=(A1*K1-C1*L1)/DS:I4=(A3*K2-C3*L2)/DN
1240:  B1=(WS*L1+RS*K1-I1)/PB:B2=(WN*L2+RN*K2-I2)/PB
1250:  B3=(C2*L1-A2*K1)/DS:B4=(C4*L2-A4*K2)/DN
1260:  X1=B3-B1:X2=PB*X1
1265:  LPRINT TAB 6;"PB  =";PB:LF 2
1270:  LPRINT "SOUTH:";TAB 18;"NORTH:":LF 1
1272:  LPRINT TAB 16;"W":LF 1
1274:  LPRINT WS;TAB 18;WN:LF1
1280:  LPRINT TAB 15;"W/PB";:LF1
1290:  LPRINT WS/PB;TAB 18;WN/PB:LF 1
1300:  LPRINT TAB 16;"R":LF 1
1310:  LPRINT TAB RS;TAB 18;RN:LF1
1320:  LPRINT TAB 16;"L":LF 1
1330:  LPRINT L1;TAB 18,L2:LF1
1340:  LPRINT TAB 16;"K":LF 1
1350:  LPRINT K1; TAB 18;K2:LF1
1360:  LPRINT TAB 16;"BS":LF 1
1370:  LPRINT B3;TAB 18;B4:LF1
1380:  LPRINT TAB 16;"BS":LF 1
1390:  LPRINT B1;TAB 18;B2:LF1
1400:  LPRINT TAB 16;"IS":LF 1
1410:  LPRINT I3;TAB 18;I4:LF
1420:  LPRINT TAB 16;"ID":LF 1
1430:  LPRINT I1;TAB 18;I2:LF2
1440:  LPRINT "XSB(S) =";X1:LF1
1450:  LPRINT "XDI(S) =";X2
1460:  GOTO 1100
1500:  LPRINT :THIS IS NO CUP OF TEA":GOTO1999
1999:  END
```

c   *Computer runs*

Data set: initial parameters

	α	β	a_1	a_2	c_1	c_2	$\bar{L}$	$\bar{K}$	D
South:	75	0.025	4.5	0.02	0.01	3	-2	2.7	13.5
North:	6	9.7	2	0.15	1.8	1.7	0.5	12	3.13

$I^D(\text{S}) = 4.00$

Run 1, $I^D(\text{N}) = 6.00$ Run 2, $I^D(\text{N}) = 7.00$

Solutions: endogenous variables

	South		North	
	Run 1	Run 2	Run 1	Run 2
p_B	3.252	1.721	3.252	1.721
w	0.7232	0.3818	1.194	0.3598
w/p_B	0.2220	0.2218	0.3666	0.2090
r	0.3285	0.3308	0.4829	0.5565
L	14.65	14.63	2.7000	1.754
K	2.70822	2.70826	16.683	17.398
B^S	3.352	3.248	0.6667	0.1190
B^D	2.297	1.443	1.621	1.925
X_B^S	0.9541	1.806	-0.9541	-1.806
I^S	0.89189	0.8913	9.108	10.108
I^D	4.00	4.00	6.00	7.00
X_I^D	3.10810	3.10807	-3.1081	-3.10807
$c_2/D - 2w/p_B$	-0.2218	-0.2214	-0.1901	0.1251

d   *Simulation of comparative statics results*

Runs 1 and 2 reproduce numerically the results of Propositions 2–5 in Section 3, and Propositions 1 and 3 in Chichilnisky (1981).

The initial data show that labor is abundant in the South [$\alpha(\text{S}) = 75$] and much less abundant in the North [$\alpha(\text{N}) = 6$]. The duality condition

$c_2/D < 2w/p_B$ is satisfied in both runs of the South. The North has more abundant capital than the South [$\beta(N) = 9.7$ whereas $\beta(S) = 0.025$, and $\bar{K}(N) = 12$ whereas $\bar{K}(S) = 2.7$]. The level of duality is much higher in the South, $D(S) = 13.5$, whereas in the North, $D(N) = 3.13$.

In both runs, the industrial demand in the South, $I^D(S)$, is equal to 4.00. In the first run, the industrial demand in the North is 6.00 and is increased to 7.00 in the second run.

As proved in Proposition 3 of Chichilnisky (1981) and Proposition 3 of Section 3, this increase in the value of $I^D(N)$ has the following general equilibrium effects: Exports of basic goods in the South, X_B^S, increase from 0.9541 to 1.806; the price of basics p_B decreases from 3.252 to 1.721; wages in the South decrease from 0.7232 to 0.3818; and consumption of basics in the South decreases from 2.297 to 1.443. As proved in Proposition 4 of Section 3, total export revenues of the South decrease also (even though export volume has increased), from 3.10810 to 3.10807.

Finally, these runs illustrate the results of Proposition 4 in Section 3: Following an exogenous increase in industrial demand $I^D(N)$, the North's demand for basics increases as well, from 1.621 to 1.925. Thus, an industrial expansion in the North [a higher $I^D(N)$] leads it to consume more of both goods simultaneously, so that the North's welfare strictly increases. The South, instead, exports more basics at lower prices and consumes fewer basics at home. Real wages decrease in the South. Since $I^D(S)$ remains constant, the welfare of the South strictly decreases.

e   *Stability*

The world's market for basics. Using always the same exogenous data, we compute now numerically the world's (disequilibrium) supply and demand curves for basics, corresponding to a neighborhood of the equilibrium given by $I^D(N) = 7.00$, where the equilibrium price is $p_B^* = 1.721$. From equation (4.6), the world demand function for basics is $\text{WDB}(p) = \text{DB(N)}(p) + \text{DB(S)}(p)$, which equals

$$\alpha(N)\left(\frac{w(N)}{p_B}\right)^2 + \frac{w(N)\bar{L}(N) + r(N)\bar{K}(N)}{p_B} + \frac{\beta(N)(r(N))^2}{p_B} - \frac{\bar{I}^D(N)}{p_B}$$

$$+ \alpha\left(\frac{w}{p_B}\right)^2 + \frac{w\bar{L} + r\bar{K}}{p_B} + \frac{\beta r^2}{p_B} - \frac{I^D(S)}{p_B},$$

where as usual all parameters and variables are from the South unless

Table 1. *Numerical values for Figure 3, simulated at the equilibrium with $I^D(N) = 7.0$.*

p_B	World supply function for basics, WSB[a]	World demand function for basics, WDB[b]
1.60	3.6982	3.9433
1.61	3.6690	3.8906
1.62	3.6401	3.8388
1.63	3.6115	3.7881
1.64	3.5833	3.7383
1.65	3.5555	3.6894
1.66	3.5280	3.6415
1.67	3.5008	3.5944
1.68	3.4740	3.5482
1.69	3.4474	3.5028
1.70	3.4215	3.4582
1.71	3.3953	3.4144
1.721	3.367	3.367
1.73	3.3444	3.3292
1.74	3.3193	3.2877
1.75	3.2946	3.2470
1.76	3.2701	3.2070
1.77	3.2459	3.1676
1.78	3.2220	3.1289
1.79	3.1984	3.0909
1.80	3.1750	3.0536

[a] Slope of WSB $= -0.38$.   [b] Slope of WDB $= -0.22$.

otherwise indicated. The world supply function for basics is

$$WSB(p) = SB(N)(p) + SB(S)(p)$$

$$= \frac{c_2(N)}{D(N)} \left(\frac{\alpha(N)w(N)}{p_B} + \bar{L}(N) \right) + \frac{a_2(N)}{D(N)} (\beta(N)r(N) + \bar{K}(N))$$

$$+ \frac{c_2}{D} \left(\frac{\alpha w}{p_B} + \bar{L} \right) - \frac{a_2}{D} (\beta r + \bar{K}).$$

Figure 3 shows that the world's market for basics is stable when $\alpha(S)$ is large and $c_2/D < 2w/p_B$ in the South, as proved in Proposition 12 of Section 4 and noted on page 191 of the Appendix of Chichilnisky (1981). Table 1 gives the numerical values from the computer runs of WSB and WDB, depicted in Figure 3.

The world's market for industrial goods. We study next, for the same data, the stability of the industrial market at the same equilibrium, where $I^D(N) = 7.0$ and $p_B^* = 1.721$. We compute numerically the world's (disequilibrium) supply and demand functions for industrial goods, WSI and WDI, respectively. From equations (4.7) and (4.8),

$$
\begin{aligned}
\text{WSI}(p) &= \text{SI}(S)(p) + \text{SI}(N)(p) \\
&= (a_1/D)(\beta r + \bar{K}) - (c_1/D)(\alpha w/p_B + \bar{L}) \\
&\quad + (a_1(N)/D(N))(\beta(N)r(N) + \bar{K}(N)) \\
&\quad - (c_1(N)/D(N))(\alpha(N)w(N)/p_B + \bar{L}(N))
\end{aligned}
$$

and

$$
\begin{aligned}
\text{WDI}(p) &= \text{DI}(S)(p) + \text{DI}(N)(p) \\
&= \bar{I}^D(S) + \bar{I}^D(N) + \Pi(S)(p) + \Pi(N)(p) \\
&= \bar{I}^D(S) + (p_B - a_1 w - c_1 r)[(c_2/D)(\alpha w/p_B + \bar{L}) \\
&\qquad\qquad\qquad\qquad - (a_2/D)(\beta r + \bar{K})] \\
&\quad + \bar{I}^D(N) + (p_B - a_1(N)w(N) - c_1(N)r(N)) \\
&\quad \times [(c_2(N)/D(N))(\alpha(N)w(N)/p_B) + \bar{L}(N) \\
&\qquad\qquad - (a_2(N)/D(N))(\beta(N)r(N) + \bar{K}(N))].
\end{aligned}
$$

Table 2 gives the numerical values of simulating WDI and WSI in a neighborhood of the equilibrium with $I^D(N) = 7.0$ and $p_B^* = 1.721$.

Figure 2b from Chichilnisky (1981). Next we reproduce, for the same data base, Figure 2b of Chichilnisky (1981). As discussed in Section 4, this figure depicts two curves: The cross-equilibria relation X_B^S relating the exports of the South and their price:

$$
X_B^S = \frac{\alpha c_1}{D^2 p_B}\left(c_2 - \frac{c_1}{p_B}\right) + \frac{\beta a_1}{D^2}\left(a_2 - \frac{a_1}{p_B}\right) + \frac{c_1 \bar{L} - a_1 \bar{K}}{D p_B} + \frac{\bar{I}^D(S)}{p_B},
$$

where all parameters are for the South; and the North's disequilibrium excess demand for basics, denoted WD in Chichilnisky (1981), which from equation (4.9), is

$$
\begin{aligned}
\text{WD} &= \text{DB}(N)(p) - \text{SB}(N)(p) \\
&= \alpha\left(\frac{w}{p_B}\right)^2 + \frac{\beta r^2}{p_B} + \frac{w}{p_B}\left(\bar{L} - \frac{\alpha c_2}{D}\right) + r\left(\frac{\beta a_2}{D} + \frac{\bar{K}}{p_B}\right) + \frac{\bar{K}a_2 - \bar{L}c_2}{D} - \frac{\bar{I}^D}{p_B},
\end{aligned}
$$

48   **Graciela Chichilnisky**

Table 2. *Numerical values for Figure 4, simulated at the equilibrium with $I^D(N) = 7.0$.*

p_B	World supply of industrial goods, WSI[a]	World demand for industrial goods, WDI[b]
1.60	10.944	10.553
1.61	10.949	10.593
1.62	10.954	10.632
1.63	10.959	10.671
1.64	10.964	10.710
1.65	10.968	10.748
1.66	10.973	10.785
1.67	10.978	10.822
1.68	10.982	10.858
1.69	10.987	10.893
1.70	10.991	10.928
1.71	10.995	10.963
1.721	10.999	10.999
1.73	11.004	11.030
1.74	11.008	11.063
1.75	11.012	11.096
1.76	11.016	11.128
1.77	11.020	11.159
1.78	11.024	11.190
1.79	11.028	11.221
1.80	11.032	11.250

[a] Slope of WSI = 2.27.   [b] Slope of WDI = 0.29.

where all parameters and variables are for the North. Table 3 gives the numerical values of X_B^S at different world equilibria corresponding to different values of $I^D(N)$ (and thus to different prices p_B) and of two disequilibrium excess demand curves of the North, WD and (WD)'. WD is computed in a neighborhood of the equilibrium given by $I^D(N) = 7.0$ and (WD)' is computed at the equilibrium given by $I^D(N) = 7.1$.

Finally, we consider a full version of Figure 2b in Chichilnisky (1981), where X_B^S is plotted together with two other curves at two nearby equilibria. These curves are excess demand of the North, WD = DB(N) − SB(N), and excess supply of the South, WS = SB(S) − DB(S), both of which are disequilibrium curves. Both WD and WS are computed from the same basic data set; WD and WS are computed in a neighborhood of the equi-

Table 3. *Numerical values for Figure 5.*[a]

p_B	X_B^S	WD = DB(N) − SB(N) at $I^D(N) = 7.0$	(WD)′ = DB(N) − SB(N) at $I^D(N) = 7.1$
1.56	1.992	1.963	1.978
1.58	1.967	1.941	1.957
1.60	1.943	1.920	1.937
1.62	1.915	1.900	1.915
1.64	1.895	1.880	1.898
1.66	1.872	1.860	1.880
1.68	1.850	1.842	1.862
1.70	1.828	1.823	1.844
1.721	1.807	1.807	1.827
1.74	1.786	1.788	1.810
1.76	1.766	1.772	1.794
1.78	1.746	1.755	1.778
1.80	1.727	1.739	1.763

[a] Slope of $X_B^S = -0.9$; slope of WD = −1.1; slope of (WD)′ = −1.1.

librium determined by $I^D(N) = 7.0$, and (WD)′ and (WS)′ are computed for the equilibrium corresponding to $I^D(N) = 7.1$. The equations for WD and WS were given in Chichilnisky (1981) and in Table 3 of this appendix. Table 4 gives the values of the simulations of WS and WD depicted in Figure 6.

f   *The North–South model and the Arrow–Debreu model*

We now exhibit a version of the North–South model as a particular case of the Arrow–Debreu model. This version of the model appears in Propositions 8 and 9.

Consider an Arrow–Debreu economy with six commodities, two agents, and four firms. The commodities are B, I, $K(N)$, $L(N)$, $K(S)$, and $L(S)$. Firms 1 and 2 produce B and I using $L(N)$ and $K(N)$ according to the production functions

$$B^S = \min(L(N)^B/a_1, K(N)^B/c_1), \qquad I^S = \min(L(N)^I/a_2, K(N)^I/c_2),$$

where the superscripts B and I indicate the sector in which $L(N)$ and $K(N)$ are used. Firms 3 and 4 produce B and I using similar production functions, but with $L(S)$ and $K(S)$ as inputs. All four firms are perfectly competitive.

Table 4. *Numerical values for Figure 6.*[a]

p_B	WD[b]	WS	X_B^S	(WD)′ [c]	(WS)′
1.56	1.963	1.619	1.992	1.978	1.858
1.58	1.941	1.649	1.967	1.957	1.879
1.60	1.920	1.677	1.943	1.937	1.897
1.62	1.900	1.702	1.915	1.915	1.915
1.64	1.880	1.726	1.895	1.898	1.930
1.66	1.860	1.748	1.872	1.880	1.944
1.68	1.842	1.769	1.850	1.862	1.958
1.70	1.823	1.788	1.828	1.844	1.969
1.721	1.806	1.806	1.806	1.827	1.980
1.74	1.788	1.821	1.786	1.810	1.989
1.76	1.772	1.836	1.766	1.794	1.997
1.78	1.755	1.850	1.746	1.778	2.005
1.80	1.739	1.862	1.727	1.763	2.011

[a] Slope of $X_B^S = -0.91$; slope of WD $= -1.1$; slope of WS $= 1$; slope of (WD)′ $= -1.1$; slope of (WS)′ $= 1.6$.
[b] WD is the North's excess demand for basics, computed near the equilibrium determined by $I^D(N) = 7.0$ and $p_B^* = 1.721$. WS is the excess supply curve of the South computed near the same world equilibrium. Note that X_B^S, WD, and WS all meet at $p_B = 1.721$.
[c] (WD)′ is the North's excess demand for basics computed near the equilibrium determined by $I^D(N) = 7.1$, and (WS)′ is the excess supply of the South computed near the same equilibrium. X_B^S, (WD)′, and (WS)′ all meet at $p_B = 1.62$.

Agent 1 has the initial endowment vector (in terms of the commodities defined above)

$$(0, 0, 0, 0, \bar{K}(S), \bar{L}(S)),$$

and *agent 2* has the endowment vector

$$(0, 0, \bar{K}(N), \bar{L}(N), 0, 0).$$

For any values of $\bar{K}(S)$, $\bar{L}(S)$, $\bar{K}(N)$, and $\bar{L}(N)$, agent 1's preferences are of the form indicated in Figure 7. This implies that there exists an $\epsilon > 0$ such that for any price $p_B > \epsilon$ this agent consumes the fixed amount $\bar{I}^D(S)$ of good I, and the rest of his or her income is used to consume good B. This agent will consume zero amounts of all other commodities. Agent 2 has similar preferences, but the "kink" occurs at $I = \bar{I}^D(N)$.

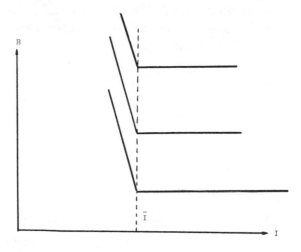

Figure 7. An agent's preference curves.

We thus have all the components of an Arrow–Debreu model: six commodities, two agents with their endowments and preferences, and four firms and their technologies. The next step is to show how the equilibrium equations of our North–South model emerge from the equilibrium equations of the Arrow–Debreu model. The North–South model is defined by the twenty-eight equations (2.1)–(2.11) for each country and (2.12)–(2.18); recall that one of these latter seven equations is always satisfied where all others are.

Equations (2.1) and (2.2) for the North, that is,

$$p_B = a_1 w(N) + c_1 r(N), \qquad p_I = a_2 w(N) + c_2 r(N),$$

are the zero-profit conditions for firms 1 and 2, where $w(N)$ is the equilibrium price of commodity $L(N)$ and $r(N)$ that of $K(N)$. These zero-profit conditions are satisfied at an equilibrium in our Arrow–Debreu model because it has constant returns to scale.

Similarly, we obtain equations (2.1) and (2.2) for the South; they are the zero-profit conditions of firms 3 and 4 in the South. Each region uses specific inputs for production.

Equations (2.3) and (2.4) in each region are given by the initial endowments of our Arrow–Debreu model. Equations (2.5) and (2.6) are the equilibrium conditions in the markets for $L(N)$ and $K(N)$ and for $L(S)$ and $K(S)$, respectively. Equations (2.7) and (2.8) for each region simply state that all firms use their inputs efficiently: They minimize costs. Equations (2.9) and (2.10) are obtained in each region from the market-clearing condition in markets for B and I of our Arrow–Debreu model.

Equation (2.11) in each region derives from Walras' law, as we shall show in the following. The two agents maximize utility subject to their budget constraints. Consider, for example, agent 1 (the South). Then at the price vector

$$(p_B, p_I, w(N), r(N), w(S), r(S)),$$

this agent consumes I^D and B^D satisfying

$$p_B B^D + p_I I_D = w(S)L(S) + r(S)K(S).$$

In view of equations (2.7) and (2.8) (efficient use of inputs), we have

$$w(S)L(S) + r(S)K(S) = (a_1 w(S) + c_1 r(S))B^S + (a_2 w(S) + c_2 r(S))I^S.$$

By the zero-profit conditions (2.1) and (2.2), this implies

$$w(S)L(S) + r(S)K(S) = p_B B^S + p_I I^S.$$

Therefore,

$$p_B B^D + p_I I^D = p_B B^S + p_I I^S.$$

Since

$$B^D = B^S - X_B^S \quad \text{and} \quad I^D = I^S + X_I^D,$$

it follows that

$$p_B(B^S - X_B^S) + p_I(I^S + X_I^D) = p_B B^S + p_I I^S,$$

so that

$$p_B X_B^S = p_I X_I^D,$$

which is equation (2.11). Thus, equation (2.11) follows in our Arrow–Debreu model from utility maximization under a budget constraint, zero profits, and cost-minimizing use of inputs. Equations (2.12)–(2.15) are the standard equilibrium conditions in the Arrow–Debreu model, and equations (2.17) and (2.18) follow from utility maximization, with the agents' preferences defined in Figure 7 provided the equilibrium price p_B exceeds some $\epsilon > 0$. Therefore, for any (nonzero) equilibrium price p_B^* of the North–South model, we can find a set of preferences (and thus an $\epsilon > 0$) for which equations (2.17) and (2.18) emerge as the usual utility maximization conditions under a budget constraint of the Arrow–Debreu model. This shows that all the equations of the North–South model are equilibrium equations of the Arrow–Debreu model.

The North–South model utilized so far has fixed factor endowments $[L(S) = \bar{L}(S), K(S) = \bar{K}(S), L(N) = \bar{L}(N),$ and $K(N) = \bar{K}(N)]$. We have shown that this model is a special case of the Arrow–Debreu model.

It is also possible to consider the North–South model with "variable endowments" (a notation used in the literature on international trade), where, for example, in one region

$$L^S = \alpha w/p_B + \bar{L}.$$

In this case, the result is as follows: At each equilibrium, the equilibrium equations of this North–South model will be those of an Arrow–Debreu model where in addition to the preferences and technologies defined above, the supply of commodity L is provided by utility-maximizing behavior under budget constraints. The supply equation for L defined above may not emerge as a supply function of the Arrow–Debreu model. However, at each equilibrium, the supply L^S is fixed, and it can be described as the equilibrium level L^S that emerges from utility-maximizing behavior in a standard Arrow–Debreu model.

An equilibrium of the North–South model is thus also an equilibrium of a standard Arrow–Debreu model.

NOTES

1 "Practical men and economic theorists have always known that trade may help some people and hurt others." "What in the way of policy can we conclude from the fact that trade is a potential boon? ... Very little" (Samuelson 1962).

2 Equations (2.1) and (2.2) are equivalent to the production functions when firms are competitive. In equilibrium, profits are zero so that revenues equal costs, i.e., $p_B B^S = wL^B + rK^B$. Now from the production functions $B^S = L^B/a_1 = K^B/c_1$, so that $p_B B^S = a_1 wB^S + c_1 rB^S$, or $p_B = a_1 w + c_1 r$, equation (2.1). Similarly, one derives equation (2.2).

3 Note that when all markets clear, the value of domestic demand $p_B B^D + p_I I^D$ equals the value of domestic income $wL + rK$. This is Walras' law or the national income identity at the equilibrium. From equations (2.1)–(2.11), one obtains

$$p_B B^D + p_I I^D = p_B (B^S - X_B^S) + p_I (I^S + X_I^P) = p_B B^S + p_I I^S$$
$$= (a_1 w + c_1 r) B^S + (a_2 w + c_2 r) I^S = wL + rK.$$

Section f in the appendix exhibits preferences, endowments, and technologies that turn this model into a standard Arrow–Debreu model. The results are unchanged.

4   All relations in this model are homogeneous of degree 0 in prices, i.e., only relative prices matter. Therefore, one may normalize the model by fixing the price of one good (the *numéraire*) equal to 1.

5   Equation (2.15) is not independent: It is always satisfied when (2.11) is satisfied in each region and (2.12)–(2.14) hold.

6   This is not surprising, since demand behavior, or preferences, have not been specified so far.

7   Existence requires standard restrictions on the exogenous parameters to ensure that the equilibrium prices are all positive, e.g., $a_1/a_2 > p_B > c_1/c_2$, where p_B satisfies equation (2.22).

8   This observation and Figure 2, which illustrates it, were suggested by Ron Jones.

9   Arrow (1981, p. 2) states: "Individual equilibria are stable in the usual sense of general equilibrium theory." Gunning (1984) states, in the paragraph after equation (14): "Hence equilibrium is stable in the Walrasian sense." Heal and McLeod (1984, Section 4) state: "It will be shown that under either of these approaches Chichilnisky's model is stable under the conditions assumed in her paper." Findlay's (1982) last section states: "Examination of the structure of the model shows that it possesses a unique equilibrium that is Walras stable." Ranney (1984), in the paragraph after equation (6), states: "Thus an increase in p_B results in a decline in the production of I goods in both countries, and the model is Walrasian stable." Saavedra (1984) states in Section 2: "We know from the preceding section that Walrasian stability of equilibrium always holds in this model." Finally, Srinivasan and Bhagwati (1984) state: "One could not therefore get a stronger result; the equilibrium is unique and evidently Walras-stable."

10 Arrow and Hahn (1971, Chapter 12, p. 317) define an adjustment process where the price equations (4.1) hold, but this is because their commodity markets are assumed to remain at an equilibrium throughout, and their factor markets adjust (see their p. 317, lines 21–3). Since commodity prices are in equilibrium, profits are zero. In our case, instead, factor markets remain in equilibrium and commodity markets adjust; profits are not zero.

11 The difference between X_B^S and an excess supply curve valid for stability analysis was clearly pointed out in Chichilnisky (1981, footnote 10, p. 175, and p. 189, lines 15–31). A similar point is made by Arrow (1981, pp. 1, 2): "Methodologically, the papers are exemplary applications of general equilibrium analysis. *A clear distinction is made between the downward sloping response of the economy as a whole and supply curves in the strict sense. The reaction curve* (X_B^S) *links alternative equilibria of the economy and is not a curve relevant to any one equilibrium.* It is shown, in fact, that the individual equilibria are stable in the usual sense of the general equilibrium theory." (italics added)

12 A clear version of this error appears in Findlay (1984), who states: "A shift in the demand of the North towards the South's exports in her model actually can only produce the completely standard result that it would improve the terms of trade of the latter." This comment, as already noted, is incorrect.

REFERENCES

Arrow, K. J. (1963), "Uncertainty and the welfare economics of medical care," *American Economic Review,* 53: 941–73.

Arrow, K. J. (1969), "Issues pertinent to the choice of market vs. non-market allocation," in U.S. Congress, Joint Economic Committee, *The analysis and evaluation of public expenditures: the PPB system,* Vol. I, pp. 47–66.

Arrow, K. J. (1970), "The effects of the price system and market on urban economic development," in K. J. Arrow et al., *Urban processes as viewed by the social sciences,* Washington, D.C.: the Urban Institute, pp. 11–20.

Arrow, K. (August, 1981), "Evaluation of the UNITAR project, technology, domestic distribution and North–South relations," UNITAR, New York.

Arrow, K., and F. Hahn (1971), *General competitive analysis,* San Francisco: Holden-Day.

Arrow, K. and L. Hurwicz (1963), "Decentralization and computation in resource allocation," in R. Pfouts (Ed.), *Essays in economics and econometrics in honor of Harold Hotelling,* Chapel Hill: University of North Carolina Press.

Arrow, K. J. and R. C. Lind (1970), "Uncertainty and the evaluation of public investment decisions," *American Economic Review,* 60: 364–78.

Benhabib, J. and G. Chichilnisky (1984), "North–South trade and export-led policies: A generalization," working paper, New York.

Chichilnisky, G. (1978), "Terms of trade and domestic distribution: Export-led growth with abundant labor," Discussion Paper No. 41, Harvard Institute for International Development.

Chichilnisky, G. (1981), "Terms of trade and domestic distribution: Export-led growth with abundant labor," *Journal of Development Economics,* 8, April, 163–92.

Chichilnisky, G. (1984a), "North–South trade and export-led policies," *Journal of Development Economics,* 15, 131–60.

Chichilnisky, G. (1984b), "North–South trade: A rejoinder to rejoinders," *Journal of Development Economics,* 15, 177–84.

Chichilnisky, G. and D. McLeod (1984), "Agricultural productivity and trade: The case of Argentina," Working Paper, The World Bank.

Chichilnisky, G., G. Heal, and J. Podivinsky (1983), "Trade between Sri Lanka and the U.K.: A case study in North–South trade," Working Paper, Columbia University, Graduate School of Business.

Findlay, R. (1984a), "Growth and development in trade models," Chapter 4 in *Handbook of International Economics,* P. Kenen and R. Jones (Eds.), Amsterdam: North-Holland.

Findlay, R. (1984b), "A comment on North–South trade and export led policies," *Journal of Development Economics,* 15, 161–7.

Gunning, J. W. (1984), "Export-led growth with abundant labor: A defense of orthodoxy," *Journal of Development Economics,* 15, 97–103.

Heal, G. and D. McLeod (1984), "Gains from trade, stability and profits: A comment on Chichilnisky's 'Terms of trade and domestic distribution: Export-led growth with abundant labor'," Working Paper, Woodrow Wilson School of

International Affairs, Princeton University, *Journal of Development Economics,* 15, 117–30.

Lewis, W. A. (1983), "Development economics in the Eighties," Working Paper, Princeton University.

Mas-Colell, A. (January 1974), "Algunas observaciones sobre la teoria del tâtonnement de Walras en economias productivas," *Anales de Economia,* 21: pp. 191–224.

Ranney, S. (1984), "Terms of trade and domestic distribution: A comment," *Journal of Development Economics,* 15, 89–96.

Saavedra, N. (1984), "Terms of trade and domestic distribution: A comment," *Journal of Development Economics,* 15, 105–10.

Samuelson, P. (1949), "Market mechanisms and optimization," in J. Stiglitz (Ed.), *Collected papers of Paul Samuelson,* Cambridge, Mass.: MIT Press, pp. 425–92.

Samuelson, P. (1962), "The gains from trade once again," *Economic Journal,* December, pp. 820–29.

Sen, A. (August 1981), "Evaluation of work carried out under the UNITAR project on technology, domestic distribution and North–South relations, co-directed by Graciela Chichilnisky and Sam Cole," UNITAR, New York.

Srinivasan, T. N. and J. Bhagwati (1984a), "On transfers paradoxes and immiserizing growth, Part II," *Journal of Development Economics,* 15, 111–15.

Srinivasan, T. N. and J. Bhagwati (1984b), "A rejoinder," *Journal of Development Economics,* 15, 173–5.

CHAPTER 2

Soldiers of fortune?

Theodore Bergstrom

1 Recruiting an army for a homogeneous country

A *The fortunes of soldiers in the absence of private lotteries or insurance*

Imagine a country where all N citizens have the same tastes and abilities. There is just one consumption good, bread. To defend itself, this country must raise an army of A soldiers. The other $N-A$ citizens are farmers who produce a total of W units of bread. Farmers are taxed to pay the soldiers. Let w_A be the wage rate paid to soldiers and w_F be the amount of bread left to each farmer after taxes. The net wages, w_A and w_F, must satisfy the social feasibility constraint

$$Aw_A + (N-A)w_F = W. \tag{1.1}$$

Equivalently, if we define $\bar{\pi} = A/N$ and $\bar{w} = W/N$,

$$\bar{\pi}w_A + (1-\bar{\pi})w_F = \bar{w}. \tag{1.2}$$

We will call (w_A, w_F) a *feasible wage structure* if (1.2) is satisfied.

Being a soldier is unpleasant and dangerous. If soldiers and farmers were paid the same wage, everyone would want to be a farmer. The country could offer high enough wages to soldiers to attract a volunteer army or it could select its army by lottery. A *fair draft lottery* would give everyone the same probability $\bar{\pi} = A/N$ of being drafted. For an arbitrarily chosen

I am grateful for helpful comments and encouragement from Sherwin Rosen of the University of Chicago, P. Srinagesh of the University of Illinois, Chicago Circle, Dan Usher of Queens University, and my colleagues Paul Courant, John Cross, George Johnson, Richard Porter, and Hal Varian at Michigan. I am especially grateful to Oliver Hart of the London School of Economics, whose insightful criticism of an earlier (1982) version of this essay has led me to new and, I think, more interesting results. Of course, none of these scholars should be implicated in any unpopular views or false statements found herein.

feasible wage structure, citizens will not be indifferent about whether or not they are selected for the army. But since everyone faces the same probability of being drafted, they will all have the same ex ante expected utility.

Let us assume that each citizen is an expected utility maximizer with a utility function

$$U(\pi, c_A, c_F) = \pi u_A(c_A) + (1 - \pi) u_F(c_F), \tag{1.3}$$

where π is the probability that he will be in the army, c_A and c_F are the amounts of bread that he would consume in the army and on the farm, and $u_A(c_A)$ and $u_F(c_F)$ are smooth, increasing, strictly concave functions. In the absence of private lottery arrangements and insurance markets, it would have to be that $c_A = w_A$ and $c_F = w_F$. In this case, if there is a fair draft lottery with wage structure (w_A, w_F), then the utility of a representative citizen will be

$$U(\bar{\pi}, w_A, w_F) = \bar{\pi} u_A(w_A) + (1 - \bar{\pi}) u_F(w_F). \tag{1.4}$$

We define the *optimal wage structure* to be the feasible wage structure that maximizes the expected utility of a representative citizen if the army is chosen by a fair lottery. The optimal wage structure (w_A^*, w_F^*) therefore maximizes equation (1.4) subject to the constraint (1.2). Simple calculus informs us that there is a unique solution for (w_A^*, w_F^*) and that, at this solution,

$$u_A'(w_A^*) = u_F'(w_F^*). \tag{1.5}$$

For any wage w paid to farmers, let us define $c(w)$ to be the *compensating wage differential* that would have to be paid to induce people to be soldiers when farmers are paid w. Since preferences are continuous and monotonic, $c(w)$ is a well-defined function. In general, $c(w)$ could be either positive or negative, depending on which occupation is more attractive, or even positive for some values of w and negative for others. It is also logically possible that for some wage rates of farmers no premium would be large enough to induce a person to voluntarily choose the army, in which case we define $c(w) = \infty$. Where it is finite valued, the compensating differential function $c(w)$ is defined implicitly by the equation

$$u_A(w + c(w)) = u_F(w). \tag{1.6}$$

If there is to be a volunteer army, then the prospect of being a soldier must be just as attractive as that of being a farmer. Let us assume that if soldiers got all the bread and farmers got none, then everyone would want to be a soldier, and that if farmers got all the bread and soldiers got none, then everyone would want to be a farmer. It then follows from continuity and monotonicity of preferences that there will be a unique feasible wage structure $(\hat{w}_A, \hat{w}_F)$ that is consistent with a volunteer army. The wage structure $(\hat{w}_A, \hat{w}_F)$ satisfies equation (1.2) and

$$\hat{w}_A = \hat{w}_F + c(\hat{w}_F) \tag{1.7}$$

so that

$$u_A(\hat{w}_A) = u_F(\hat{w}_F). \tag{1.8}$$

The utility level achieved by all citizens if there is a volunteer army would also be attained with a fair draft lottery in which the wage structure is $(\hat{w}_A, \hat{w}_F)$. This allows us to make the following simple, but useful, observation.

Proposition 1.1. If all citizens have identical preferences and if there are no private lotteries or insurance markets, then the expected utility of the representative citizen will be at least as high with a fair lottery, given the optimal wage structure, as it would be with a volunteer army.

In fact, except for a very special class of preferences, it will be the case that a fair lottery with an optimal wage structure dominates the volunteer army. The volunteer army wage structure equalizes *total* utilities $u_A(\hat{w}_A)$ and $u_F(\hat{w}_F)$, whereas, as we have shown, the optimal equalitarian wage structure equalizes *marginal* utilities $u'_A(w_A^*)$ and $u'_F(w_F^*)$. Only in the special case that the former condition implies the latter will the volunteer army be as good as a fair lottery with the optimal wage structure.

Two easy examples

Example 1.1. Consider a country where all citizens have identical von Neumann–Morgenstern utility functions such that for all w, $u_A(w) = u_F(w) - \alpha$, where $\alpha > 0$, $u'_F(w) > 0$, and $u''_F(w) < 0$. The optimal wage structure must satisfy $u'(w_A^*) = u'(w_F^*)$, which in this instance implies that $w_A^* = w_F^*$. Then $u_A(w^*) = u_F(w^*) - \alpha < u_F(w^*)$. Therefore, the optimal wage structure pays soldiers and farmers the same wage rate and leaves those who are chosen for the army worse off than those who are not.

Example 1.2. Suppose that all citizens have von Neumann–Morgenstern utility functions such that for all w, $u_A(w) = u_F(w - \alpha)$, where, as before

$\alpha > 0$, $u'_F(w) > 0$, and $u''_F(w) < 0$. Then $u'_A(w^*_A) = u'_F(w^*_F)$ implies that $w^*_A - \alpha = w^*_F$ and therefore $u_A(w^*_A) = u_F(w^*_F)$. In this case, the optimal wage structure makes farmers and soldiers equally well off. Therefore, the optimal wage structure is the same as the wage structure for the volunteer army.

There is a very simple condition that determines whether in a fair draft lottery with the optimal wage structure farmers will be better off than soldiers or vice versa. If the compensating differential function $c(w)$ is increasing in w, then the wage premium for the amenity of being a farmer rather than a soldier is an increasing function of wealth. It therefore is natural to make the following definition.

Definition. Farming is a *normal good at w* if $c'(w) > 0$ and an *inferior good at w* if $c'(w) < 0$.

Proposition 1.2. Let (w^*_A, w^*_F) be the optimal wage structure. With this wage structure, everyone will prefer being a farmer to being a soldier if and only if farming is a normal good at w^*_F. With the optimal wage structure, everyone will prefer being a soldier to being a farmer if and only if farming is an inferior good at w^*_F.

Proof: Differentiating both sides of the identity (1.6), one has

$$u'_A(w + c(w))(1 + c'(w)) = u'_F(w). \tag{1.9}$$

Therefore $u'_A(w^*_F + c(w^*_F)) < u'_F(w^*_F)$ if and only if $c'(w^*_F) > 0$. Since $u'_A(w^*_A) = u'_F(w^*_F)$ and since by assumption $u'_A(\cdot)$ is monotone decreasing, it must be that $w^*_A < w^*_F + c(w^*_F)$ if and only if $c'(w^*_F) > 0$. But

$$u_A(w^*_F + c(w^*_F)) = u_F(w^*_F)$$

and $u_A(\cdot)$ is monotone increasing in w. Therefore, $u_A(w^*_A) < u_F(w^*_F)$ if and only if $c'(w^*_F) > 0$. This proves the first assertion of Proposition 1.1. The second assertion is established by a similar argument. ∎

Notice that, by our definition, the condition that determines whether farming is a normal good is a condition on the sign of the *derivative* of $c(w)$ and not on the sign of $c(w)$ itself. For example, if $c(w)$ were always negative and $c'(w)$ always positive, then it would be the case that at equal wages the army would be preferred to the farm, but with the optimal wage structure, farming would be preferred to the army.

B   *A draft lottery with private draft insurance*

Suppose that the country selects its army by a fair draft lottery but chooses a feasible wage structure (w_A, w_F) different from (w_A^*, w_F^*). Then there is a reason for private markets in "draft insurance" to develop. A citizen who can buy actuarially fair insurance can afford to consume contingent consumptions c_A if drafted and c_F if not so long as

$$\bar{\pi} c_A + (1 - \bar{\pi}) c_F = \bar{\pi} w_A + (1 - \bar{\pi}) w_F = \bar{w}. \tag{1.10}$$

Since each citizen will choose (c_A, c_F) to maximize expected utility subject to equation (1.10), the problem solved is precisely the same as the problem we solved to find the optimal wage structure (w_A^*, w_F^*). Therefore we can assert the following.

Proposition 1.3. If the army is selected by a fair draft lottery with any feasible wage structure and if there are actuarially fair draft insurance markets, citizens will buy insurance so that their contingent consumptions are $c_A = w_A^*$ and $c_F = w_F^*$ where (w_A^*, w_F^*) is the wage structure of the best fair lottery.

From Proposition 1.3 we see that if the army is chosen by a fair lottery, then even if the government sets the "wrong" wage structure, private insurance contracts can "correct the mistake" so that after insurance contracts are settled, the contingent consumptions of farmers and soldiers are the same as the wages corresponding to the best fair draft lottery.

C   *Is a draft lottery needed when fair financial lotteries are available?*

In an earlier draft of this chapter, it was argued that if all citizens had the same tastes and abilities, Propositions 1.1–1.3 would constitute a strong case for selecting an army by a draft lottery rather than having a volunteer army. Of course, in a world where preferences and abilities differ, there will be more reasons to use markets that sort people according to taste and comparative advantage.

Professor Oliver Hart suggested in private correspondence that this view is misleading because even with a volunteer army, it would be possible for private lotteries to achieve a Pareto-optimal allocation. It should be no surprise that efficiency could be achieved if there were private lotteries for ordinary goods as well as lotteries in which the "prizes" were obligations to join the army. But Professor Hart's claim is stronger. He argued that if the government offers the utility-equalizing wages $(\hat{w}_A, \hat{w}_F)$, then the availability of actuarially fair lotteries with prizes of ordinary goods is all that is necessary to enable individuals to achieve the utility level of a fair lottery with the optimum wage structure. [A recent article by Marshall (1984) advances a similar idea.] This turns out to be essentially correct and, at least to me, quite surprising.

Suppose that there is a volunteer army with the wage structure $(\hat{w}_A, \hat{w}_F)$ and let (w_A^*, w_F^*) be the optimal wage structure defined in the previous section. Consider a lottery in which with probability $\bar{\pi}$ the prize is $w_A^* - \hat{w}_A$ and with probability $1 - \bar{\pi}$ the prize is $w_F^* - \hat{w}_F$. (From Proposition 1.2, it follows that if farming is a normal good, then the former prize will be positive and the latter negative.) Since the volunteer army wage structure and the optimal wage structure are both feasible, it must be that

$$\bar{\pi}(w_A^* - \hat{w}_A) + (1 - \bar{\pi})(w_F^* - \hat{w}_F) = 0. \tag{1.11}$$

Therefore, this lottery is actuarially fair.

Now suppose the citizen participates in this lottery and adopts the following strategy: If the prize is $w_A^* - \hat{w}_A$, then he joins the army, and if the prize is $w_F^* - \hat{w}_F$ then he farms. With this strategy, the citizen will have a probability $\bar{\pi}$ of being in the army and consuming $\hat{w}_A + (w_A^* - \hat{w}_A) = w_A^*$ and a probability of $1 - \bar{\pi}$ of being on the farm and consuming $\hat{w}_F + (w_F^* - \hat{w}_F) = w_F^*$. But this is precisely what the prospects would be if there were a fair draft lottery with the optimal wage structure. Furthermore, if all citizens choose this strategy, then the fraction $\bar{\pi}$ of the population will receive prizes that induce them to choose the army. This observation can be phrased as follows:

Proposition 1.4. If consumers have access to actuarially fair lotteries and if the wage structure fully compensates for the utility difference between being a farmer and being a soldier, then it is possible for consumers to replicate the prospects they would have with a fair draft lottery and the optimal wage structure by the device of making purely financial bets and conditioning their occupational choice on the outcome of the financial bets.

A skeptical reader may wonder whether the strategy that we have proposed for replicating the optimal wage structure by private lotteries is *self-enforcing* in the sense that those who "lose" the lottery (i.e., win the negative prize $w_A^* - \hat{w}_A$) will want to choose the army rather than the farm in the event that they lose the lottery. Similarly one may ask whether "winners" will choose the farm after they have learned the outcome of the lottery. To show that those who lose in the lottery will choose the army, we need to show that

$$u_A(\hat{w}_A + (w_A^* - \hat{w}_A)) \geq u_F(\hat{w}_F + (w_A^* - \hat{w}_A)). \tag{1.12}$$

From convexity of the function $u_F(\cdot)$ and equation (1.11), it follows that

$$\bar{\pi} u_F(\hat{w}_F + (w_A^* - \hat{w}_A)) + (1 - \bar{\pi}) u_F(\hat{w}_F + (\hat{w}_F - \hat{w}_F)) \leq u_F(\hat{w}_F). \tag{1.13}$$

But, according to Proposition 1.1,

$$\bar{\pi} u_A(w_A^*) + (1 - \bar{\pi}) u_F(w_F^*) \geq u_F(\hat{w}_F). \tag{1.14}$$

Subtracting inequality (1.13) from (1.14) and simplifying terms, we have inequality (1.12). An exactly parallel proof establishes that

$$u_F(\hat{w}_F + (w_F^* - \hat{w}_F)) \geq u_A(\hat{w}_A + (w_F^* - \hat{w}_F)) \tag{1.15}$$

so that winners will always choose to farm.

The fact that the proposed strategy is self-enforcing is important because if this were not the case, then in order to achieve the utility level associated with this strategy, citizens would have to *precommit* themselves by means of some contract that forced them to join the army if they lost in the lottery. This would be contrary to the spirit of our discussion, since we sought a solution in which the only bets that citizens made were bets with financial prizes. As it turns out, although losers in the lottery may complain about their "bad luck" and may wish they had not bet, there is no better option for them, given that they have lost, than to "make up some of their losses" by joining the army.

But this is not quite the end of the story. We have shown that given the wage structure $(\hat{w}_A, \hat{w}_F)$, there is a strategy whereby citizens *can* achieve the expected utility generated by an optimal wage structure. We have *not* shown that this is the *expected utility-maximizing* strategy for citizens who have access to actuarially fair financial lotteries. In fact, this is in general not the case. With the wage structure $(\hat{w}_A, \hat{w}_F)$, citizens who are able to make any actuarially fair financial bets and to condition their choice of occupation on the outcome of the financial bet will not choose strategies that send them to the army with probability $\bar{\pi}$. Therefore, if citizens have access to all such bets, the wage structure $(\hat{w}_A, \hat{w}_F)$ will not be an "equilibrium" because it will *not* attract an army of expected size $\bar{\pi}$. Generally, however, there will exist *some* wage structure such that citizens using optimal strategies will join the army with probability $\bar{\pi}$. We pursue this matter in the next section.

D   *Probabilistic recruitment equilibrium with private lotteries*

Suppose that the wage structure is (w_A, w_F) and that citizens can participate in any actuarially fair financial lottery. A citizen is able to choose an occupation after having determined the outcome of the financial bet. Since we assume that the functions $u_A(\cdot)$ and $u_F(\cdot)$ are concave, a citizen will not be interested in "pure gambles" where his occupational choice is independent of the outcome of the lottery. Therefore, the only lotteries of interest are those in which his winnings take on two possible values, where one outcome induces the citizen to join the army and the other induces him to stay on the farm. He can choose any lottery with probability π of winning the prize x_A and probability $1 - \pi$ of winning prize x_F so long as $\pi x_A + (1 - \pi)x_F = 0$. If he chooses to join the army whenever the prize is x_A and to farm whenever the prize is x_F, then with probability π the citizen will be in the army and have consumption $c_A = w_A + x_A$ and with probability $1 - \pi$ he will be on the farm with consumption $c_F = w_F + x_F$. An equivalent way to say this is that he can choose any probability π and consumptions c_A and c_F such that

$$\pi c_A + (1 - \pi)c_F = \pi w_A + (1 - \pi)w_F. \tag{1.16}$$

We can now define an equilibrium wage structure for the model of this section.

Definition: Where citizens have identical preferences, a wage structure $(\tilde{w}_A, \tilde{w}_F)$ is a probabilistic recruitment equilibrium if all citizens choose $\pi = \bar{\pi}$ when they are allowed to choose π, c_A, and c_F to maximize expected utility subject to

$$\pi c_A + (1 - \pi)c_F = \pi \tilde{w}_A + (1 - \pi)\tilde{w}_F.$$

Let us define $V(\pi, w_A, w_F)$ to be the maximum expected utility that a citizen can obtain when the wage structure is (w_A, w_F) if he makes actuarially fair financial bets and joins the army with probability π. Thus $V(\pi, w_A, w_F)$ is the maximum of expected utility function (1.3) subject to the constraint that c_A and c_F satisfy the budget equation (1.16). If the wage structure is (w_A, w_F) and actuarially fair lotteries are available, expected utility is maximized by the following strategy. Choose π to maximize $V(\pi, w_A, w_F)$. For this value of π, choose c_A and c_F to maximize the expected utility subject to (1.16). Make a bet that with probability π pays $c_A - w_A$ and with probability $1 - \pi$ pays $c_F - w_F$. In case of the first outcome, join the army. In case of the second outcome, stay on the farm.

We are able to prove the following result.

Proposition 1.5. Let consumers have identical, continuous von Neumann–Morgenstern utility functions such that $u_A(\cdot)$ and $u_F(\cdot)$ are strictly concave and let there be some feasible wage structure such that everyone prefers being a farmer to being a soldier and another feasible wage structure such that everyone prefers being a soldier to being a farmer. Then there exists a unique wage structure $(\tilde{w}_A, \tilde{w}_F)$ that is a recruitment equilibrium with fair lotteries in consumption goods. In general, this wage structure is not the same as the volunteer army wage structure in the absence of lotteries.

The existence result asserted in Proposition 1.5 is a special case of a result proved in the next section. Here we show by an example that the recruitment equilibrium with fair lotteries may, depending on the variables of the problem, pay soldiers either more or less than the volunteer army wage in the absence of lotteries.

Example 1.3. An equilibrium with financial lotteries. Let all citizens' von Neumann–Morgenstern utility functions take the special form $u_F(c_F) = f(c_F)$ and $u_A(c_A) = f(c_A) - \alpha$ where $f'(\cdot) > 0$ and $f''(\cdot) < 0$. Then the expected utility function expressed in general form by (1.3) becomes

$$U(\pi, c_A, c_F) = \pi(f(c_A) - \alpha) + (1 - \pi)f(c_F). \tag{1.17}$$

The special expected utility function (1.17) is maximized subject to (1.16) when

$$c_A = c_F = \pi w_A + (1 - \pi)w_F. \tag{1.18}$$

Therefore

$$V(\pi, w_A, w_F) = U(\pi, c_A, c_F) = f(\pi w_A + (1 - \pi)w_F) - \pi\alpha. \tag{1.19}$$

Then $V(\pi, w_A, w_F)$ is maximized over π when

$$f'(\pi w_A + (1 - \pi)w_F)(w_A - w_F) = \alpha. \tag{1.20}$$

To secure a volunteer army of the right size, the government must offer a feasible wage structure $(\tilde{w}_A, \tilde{w}_F)$ such that (1.20) is satisfied for $\bar{\pi} = \bar{\pi}$. The fact that $(\tilde{w}_A, \tilde{w}_F)$ must be a feasible wage structure implies that

$$\bar{\pi}\tilde{w}_A + (1 - \bar{\pi})\tilde{w}_F = \bar{w}. \tag{1.21}$$

It follows from equations (1.20) and (1.21) that in the presence of actu-arially fair lotteries, the wage structure $(\tilde{w}_A, \tilde{w}_F)$ will secure a volunteer army of size $\bar{\pi}$ when

$$f'(\bar{w})(\tilde{w}_A - \tilde{w}_F) = \alpha. \tag{1.22}$$

To get an explicit solution for $\tilde{w}_A$ and $\tilde{w}_F$, we specialize the example further by assuming that $f(c) = \ln c$ for all $c > 0$. Then equation (1.22) implies that

$$\tilde{w}_A - \tilde{w}_F = \bar{w}\alpha, \tag{1.23}$$

and from (1.21) and (1.23) it follows that

$$\tilde{w}_F = (1 - \alpha\bar{\pi})\bar{w} \quad \text{and} \quad \tilde{w}_A = (1 + \alpha - \alpha\bar{\pi})\bar{w}. \tag{1.24}$$

In this example it is straightforward to compare the two wage structures $(\hat{w}_A, \hat{w}_F)$ and $(\tilde{w}_A, \tilde{w}_F)$. With a bit of calculation we can show that when $f(c) = \ln c$,

$$\hat{w}_F = \frac{1}{1 + \bar{\pi}(e^\alpha - 1)}\bar{w} \quad \text{and} \quad \hat{w}_A = \frac{1}{1 + \bar{\pi}(e^\alpha - 1)}\bar{w}e^\alpha. \tag{1.25}$$

Direct computation shows that $\hat{w}_A > \tilde{w}_A$ if $\alpha = 5$ and $\bar{\pi} = 0.1$ whereas $\hat{w}_A < \tilde{w}_A$ if $\alpha = 1$ and $\bar{\pi} = 0.5$. Therefore, we see that, depending on the size of the parameters α and $\bar{\pi}$, $\tilde{w}_A$ can be either larger or smaller than $\hat{w}_A$.

2   Marching to different drums

When people's tastes and abilities differ, it is important that an alloca-tion mechanism selects people for occupations according to principles of comparative advantage. A volunteer army is better able to do this than a draft lottery. But if private lotteries in consumption goods are available, it is typically the case in equilibrium that some citizens will choose to make a gamble in consumption goods and determine their occupation by the outcome of the gamble. In this section, we extend the definition of a probabilistic recruitment equilibrium to the case of a heterogeneous pop-ulation and we show that this equilibrium is Pareto optimal. To simplify exposition, we will confine our attention here to differences in prefer-ences while assuming that there are no differences in productivity between people and that all income comes from wages.

If there are heterogeneous citizens and no private lotteries, then a vol-unteer army wage structure $(\hat{w}_A, \hat{w}_F)$ would have the property that there are A citizens i for whom $u_i(\hat{w}_A) \geq u_i(\hat{w}_F)$ and $N - A$ for whom $u_i(\hat{w}_F) \geq u_i(\hat{w}_A)$. Since preferences differ, it will be true that in equilibrium some of the citizens who choose the army will strictly prefer the army at equilibrium wages and some of the citizens who choose to farm will strictly prefer the farm.

Suppose now that actuarially fair lotteries in private goods are available to all consumers. Much as we did in the case of identical consumers, let us define for each i an indirect utility function:

$$V_i(\pi^i, w_A, w_F) = \max_{\pi^i, c_A^i, c_F^i} \pi^i u_A(c_A^i) + (1 - \pi^i) u_F(c_F^i) \tag{2.1}$$
$$\text{subject to } \pi^i c_A^i + (1 - \pi^i) c_F^i \leq \pi^i w_A + (1 - \pi^i) w_F.$$

If the wage structure is (w_A, w_F), then $V_i(\pi^i, w_A, w_F)$ is the highest utility level that i can attain by the following type of strategy: Make an actuarially fair bet where with probability π^i the prize is $c_F^i - w_A$ and with probability $1 - \pi^i$ the prize is $c_F^i - w_F$, and then choose to join the army if you get the former prize and to farm if you get the latter.

A consumer with access to actuarially fair lotteries when the wage structure is (w_A, w_F) will maximize his expected utility by choosing π^i between 0 and 1 so as to maximize $V_i(\pi^i, w_A, w_F)$. It turns out that under reasonable assumptions, this maximum is unique.

Proposition 2.1. If the functions $u_A^i(\cdot)$ and $u_F^i(\cdot)$ are twice differentiable and strictly concave and if farming is a normal good, then for any wage structure (w_A, w_F) there is one and only one value of π^i that maximizes $V_i(\pi^i, w_A, w_F)$.

Proof: The existence of at least one maximizing π^i is immediate from standard arguments of continuity and boundedness. Taking derivatives and applying the envelope theorem, we find that $\partial^2 V_i(\pi^i, w_A, w_F)/\partial \pi^{i2} < 0$ whenever $\partial V_i(\pi^i, w_A, w_F)/\partial \pi^i = 0$. It is then straightforward from the Kuhn–Tucker conditions that there can be only one value of π^i in the interval $[0, 1]$ that maximizes $V_i(\pi^i, w_A, w_F)$. ∎

We are therefore entitled to define a *probabilistic supply function* as follows.

Definition. Consumer i's probabilistic supply function for serving in the army is $\pi^i(w_A, w_F)$ where $\pi^i(w_A, w_F)$ is the value of π^i that maximizes $V_i(\pi^i, w_A, w_F)$ on the interval from 0 to 1.

An *allocation* will be fully described by a specification of the probability π^i that each i will be in the army and the contingent consumptions

c_A^i and c_F^i that he will consume if he is in the army and if he farms. We define a *probabilistic recruitment equilibrium wage structure* as one that attracts an army of the right expected size and that makes expected total wages equal to total wealth and a *probabilistic recruitment equilibrium allocation* as an allocation induced by such a wage structure.

Definition. A wage structure $(\tilde{w}_A, \tilde{w}_F)$ is a probabilistic recruitment equilibrium wage structure if $\bar{\pi}\tilde{w}_A + (1-\bar{\pi})\tilde{w}_F = \bar{w}$ and if $1/N \sum_{i=1}^{N} \pi^i(\tilde{w}_A, \tilde{w}_F) = \bar{\pi}$. An allocation $(\bar{\pi}^i, \tilde{c}_A^i, \tilde{c}_F^i)$, $i=1,\ldots,N$, is a probabilistic recruitment equilibrium allocation if $\bar{\pi}^i = \pi^i(\tilde{w}_A, \tilde{w}_F)$ and if $\tilde{c}_A^i$ and $\tilde{c}_F^i$ maximize $\bar{\pi}^i u_A^i(c_A^i) + (1-\bar{\pi}^i)u_F^i(c_F^i)$ subject to $\bar{\pi}^i c_A^i + (1-\bar{\pi}^i)c_F^i \leq \bar{\pi}^i \tilde{w}_A + (1-\bar{\pi}^i)\tilde{w}_F$.

Proposition 2.2. If all consumers have twice differentiable concave expected utility functions, if farming is a normal good, and if no one would choose an occupation with zero wages if all the bread were paid to the other occupation, then there exists a probabilistic recruitment equilibrium.

Proof: Define the function $\Phi(w_A)$ for $w_A \in [0, \bar{w}/\bar{\pi}]$ so that

$$\Phi(w_A) = \frac{1}{N} \sum_{i=1}^{N} \pi^i\left(w_A, \frac{\bar{w} - \bar{\pi}w_A}{1-\bar{\pi}}\right). \tag{2.2}$$

Our assumptions imply that $\Phi(w_A)$ is a continuous function and that $\Phi(0) = 0$ and $\Phi(\bar{w}/\bar{\pi}) = 1$. From the intermediate value theorem, it follows that as w_A is varied continuously from 0 to $\bar{w}/\bar{\pi}$, $\Phi(w_A)$ takes on all intermediate values between 0 and 1 and in particular for some $\tilde{w}_A \in [0, \bar{w}/\bar{\pi}]$, $\Phi(\tilde{w}_A) = \bar{\pi}$. It is straightforward to verify that $(\tilde{w}_A, \tilde{w}_F)$ is a probabilistic recruitment equilibrium wage where $\tilde{w}_F = (\bar{w} - \bar{\pi}\tilde{w}_A)/(1-\bar{\pi})$. ∎

If each individual i joins the army with probability $\pi^i(w_A, w_F)$, then the expected proportion of the population to join the army will be $1/N \sum_{i=1}^{N} \pi^i(w_A, w_F)$. If the country is large and the lotteries are independent, then with very high probability, the proportion of the population joining the army will be very close to the expected proportion. Likewise, the expected consumption per capita will be very close to $1/N \sum_{i=1}^{n} [\pi c_A^i + (1-\pi)c_F^i]$. It is therefore reasonable to define a feasible allocation in the following way. [*Remark:* Although the independent lotteries would not take on exactly their expected values, since they will with very high probability come very close in per capita terms, the cost per citizen of insuring this residual risk would be very small and can safely be ignored.]

Definition. An allocation (π^i, c_A^i, c_F^i), $i = 1, \ldots, N$, is feasible for a country that requires the fraction $\bar{\pi}$ of its population to be in the army and that has a per capita endowment of bread equal to $\bar{w}$ if $\sum_{i=1}^N \pi^i = N\bar{\pi}$ and $1/N \sum_{i=1}^n [\pi c_A^i + (1-\pi)c_F^i] \le \bar{w}$.

Definition. An allocation is Pareto optimal if it is feasible and if there is no other feasible allocation that gives all citizens at least as high an expected utility and at least one citizen a higher expected utility.

Proposition 2.3. A probabilistic recruitment equilibrium allocation is Pareto optimal.

Proof: Let $(\tilde{w}_A, \tilde{w}_F)$ be a probabilistic recruitment equilibrium wage structure and let the corresponding equilibrium allocation be $(\tilde{\pi}^i, \tilde{c}_A^i, \tilde{c}_F^i)$, $i = 1, \ldots, N$. Then $\sum_{i=1}^N \tilde{\pi}^i = N\bar{\pi}$, and for each i,

$$\pi^i \tilde{c}_A^i + (1-\pi^i)\tilde{c}_F^i \le \pi^i \tilde{w}_A + (1-\pi^i)\tilde{w}_F.$$

Summing these inequalities and dividing by N, we have

$$1/N \sum [\pi^i \tilde{c}_A^i + (1-\pi^i)\tilde{c}_F^i] \le \bar{\pi}\tilde{w}_A + (1-\bar{\pi})\tilde{w}_F \le \bar{w}. \tag{2.3}$$

Therefore the allocation $(\tilde{\pi}^i, \tilde{c}_A^i, \tilde{c}_F^i)$, $i = 1, \ldots, N$, is feasible.

Suppose that some allocation (π^i, c_A^i, c_F^i), $i = 1, \ldots, N$, is Pareto superior to $(\tilde{\pi}^i, \tilde{c}_A^i, \tilde{c}_F^i)$, $i = 1, \ldots, N$. Since by construction $V_i(\tilde{\pi}^i, \tilde{w}_A, \tilde{w}_F) \ge V_i(\pi^i, \tilde{w}_A, \tilde{w}_F)$, it must be that $\pi^i c_A^i + (1-\pi^i)c_F^i \ge \pi^i \tilde{w}_A + (1-\pi^i)\tilde{w}_F$ for all i with strict inequality for some i. Therefore $1/N \sum_{i=1}^N [\pi^i c_A^i + (1-\pi^i)c_F^i] > \pi^i \tilde{w}_A + (1-\pi^i)\tilde{w}_F$. But this means that the allocation (π^i, c_A^i, c_F^i), $i = 1, \ldots, N$, is not feasible. This proves the theorem. ∎

Two examples of probabilistic recruitment equilibrium with heterogeneous tastes

Example 2.1. Here we let utility take the same special functional form as in Example 1.3, but we allow for differences in tastes. In particular, we assume that for each i, $u_F^i(c_F) = \ln c_F$ and $u_A^i(c_A) = \ln c_A - 1/T_i$. The parameter T_i can be interpreted as citizen i's tolerance for the army. Just as in Example 1.3, a consumer with this utility function who can make actuarially fair bets will choose $c_A = c_F$. Then

$$V_i(\pi^i, \tilde{w}_A, \tilde{w}_F) = \ln[\pi^i \tilde{w}_A + (1-\pi^i)\tilde{w}_F] - \frac{\pi^i}{T_i}. \tag{2.4}$$

Let us assume, provisionally, that the value of π that maximizes $V_i(\pi^i, \tilde{w}_A, \tilde{w}_F)$ is an interior solution in the open interval $(0, 1)$. Differentiating with respect to π^i and rearranging terms, we find that the first-order condition for this maximization is equivalent to

$$\pi^i = T_i - \frac{\tilde{w}_F}{\tilde{w}_A - \tilde{w}_F} \tag{2.5}$$

for all i. From (2.5) it follows that

$$\bar{\pi} = \bar{T} - \frac{\tilde{w}_F}{\tilde{w}_A - \tilde{w}_F}, \tag{2.6}$$

where $\bar{T} = 1/N \sum_{i=1}^{N} T_i$. From (2.6) and the feasibility constraint

$$\bar{\pi}\tilde{w}_A + (1 - \bar{\pi})\tilde{w}_F = \bar{w},$$

we deduce that

$$\tilde{w}_F = \frac{\bar{T}\bar{w}}{\bar{T} + \bar{\pi}} \quad \text{and} \quad \tilde{w}_A = \frac{(\bar{T} + 1)\bar{w}}{\bar{T} + \bar{\pi}}. \tag{2.7}$$

From (2.5) and (2.6), it follows that, for each i,

$$\pi^i = \bar{\pi} + T_i - \bar{T}. \tag{2.8}$$

Therefore, our provisional assumption that π^i is an internal solution for every i is justified if and only if $0 \leq \bar{\pi} + T_i - \bar{T} \leq 1$ for all i.

The equilibrium contingent consumptions for each i will satisfy

$$\tilde{c}_A^i = \tilde{c}_F^i = \pi^i \tilde{w}_A + (1 - \pi^i)\tilde{w}_F = \tilde{w}_F + \pi^i(\tilde{w}_A - \tilde{w}_F). \tag{2.9}$$

From equations (2.5) and (2.9), it follows that

$$\tilde{c}_A^i = \tilde{c}_F^i = T_i(\tilde{w}_A - \tilde{w}_F). \tag{2.10}$$

For this example, let us choose parameter values so that in equilibrium everyone is at an "interior" solution. Specifically, let $\bar{\pi} = 0.25$ and let the individual T_i's be uniformly distributed on the interval $[1, 1.5]$. Then $\bar{T} = 1.25$ and $0 \leq \bar{\pi} + T_i - \bar{T} \leq 1$ for all i. From equation (2.7), we calculate that

$$\tilde{w}_A = 1.5\bar{w} \quad \text{and} \quad \tilde{w}_F = 0.833\bar{w}. \tag{2.11}$$

Although the equilibrium wages of soldiers are higher than the wages of farmers, each individual will plan contingent consumptions $\tilde{c}_A^i = \tilde{c}_F^i$. But the bigger the risk one takes of losing the preliminary bet and joining the army, the higher will be both of these contingent consumptions. In equilibrium, people with higher tolerance will accept a greater probability of being in the army. In this example, a citizen with tolerance T_i will enter a lottery in which with probability $T_i - 1$ he loses the amount $\tilde{w}_A - \tilde{c}_A^i$ and joins the army and with probability $2 - T_i$ he wins $\tilde{c}_F^i - \tilde{w}_F$ and stays on the farm. In this instance, we find from equation (2.10) that

$$\tilde{c}_A^i = \tilde{c}_F^i = 0.666 T_i. \tag{2.12}$$

If there were no private lotteries, then the wage structure would have to be such that the one-fourth of the population with the highest tolerance for the army would choose the army. The marginal individual would be a citizen with tolerance $T_i = \frac{11}{8}$. The voluntary equilibrium wage structure $(\hat{w}_A, \hat{w}_F)$ in the absence of private lotteries would be a feasible wage structure that makes such an individual indifferent between the two occupations. It turns out that

$$\hat{w}_A = 1.63\bar{w} \quad \text{and} \quad \hat{w}_F = 0.789\bar{w}. \tag{2.13}$$

Example 2.2. In this example, preferences will be as in Example 2.1, but we will allow wider variation of the parameter T_i so that in equilibrium some citizens will choose the army with certainty, some will choose to farm with certainty, and some will enter a lottery and make their occupations conditional on the outcome of the lottery. We assume that $\bar{\pi} = 0.25$ and that the T_i's are uniformly distributed over the interval $[1, 4]$.

As in Example 2.1, those citizens who choose π^i in the interior of the interval $[0, 1]$ must satisfy the first-order conditions [eq. (2.5)]

$$\pi^i = T_i - \frac{\tilde{w}_F}{\tilde{w}_A - \tilde{w}_F}.$$

There will be critical tolerance levels T^* and T_* such that in equilibrium all consumers with $T_i \geq T^*$ will choose the army with certainty and all consumers with $T_i \leq T_*$ will farm with certainty. Then T^* and T_* are the upper and lower boundaries of the range of T_i's for which the right side of equation (2.5) takes values between 0 and 1. From equation (2.5), we see that

$$1 = T^* - \frac{\tilde{w}_F}{\tilde{w}_A - \tilde{w}_F} \quad \text{and} \quad T_* = T^* - 1. \tag{2.14}$$

The fraction $\frac{1}{3}(4 - T^*)$ of the population that has $T_i \geq T^*$ will join the army with certainty. The remaining recruits for the army will come from citizens that have $T_* < T_i < T^*$ and whose gambling outcomes result in their joining the army. From equation (2.5), it follows that the expected fraction of the total population that comes from this group to join the army will be

$$\frac{1}{3}\int_{T^*-1}^{T^*}\left(T-\frac{\tilde{w}_F}{\tilde{w}_A-\tilde{w}_F}\right)dT=\frac{1}{3}\left(T^*-0.5-\frac{\tilde{w}_F}{\tilde{w}_A-\tilde{w}_F}\right) \qquad (2.15)$$

In equilibrium, the expected fraction of the total population to join the army must be $\bar{\pi}$. Adding the fraction $\frac{1}{3}(4-T^*)$ of the population that will join the army with certainty to the expression (2.15), we find that in equilibrium

$$\bar{\pi}=\frac{1}{3}\left(T^*-0.5-\frac{\tilde{w}_F}{\tilde{w}_A-\tilde{w}_F}+4-T^*\right). \qquad (2.16)$$

Using equations (2.14) and (2.16) and substituting in $\bar{\pi}=0.25$, one can show that

$$T^*=3.75 \quad \text{and} \quad \frac{\tilde{w}_F}{\tilde{w}_A-\tilde{w}_F}=2.75. \qquad (2.17)$$

Finally, from (2.17) and the constraint $\bar{\pi}\tilde{w}_A+(1-\bar{\pi})\tilde{w}_F=\bar{w}$, it follows that

$$\tilde{w}_A=1.25\bar{w} \quad \text{and} \quad \tilde{w}_F=0.9175\bar{w}. \qquad (2.18)$$

In this example, all citizens with $T_i\geq 3.75$ will join the army with certainty and consume $\tilde{w}_A=1.25\bar{w}$. Citizens with $T_i\leq 2.75$ will be certain to stay out of the army and will consume $\tilde{w}_F=0.9175\bar{w}$. A citizen with tolerance level T_i in the interval $[2.75,3.75]$ will enter a lottery in which with probability $T_i-2.75$ he loses $\tilde{w}_A-\tilde{c}_A^i$ and with probability $3.75-T_i$ he wins $\tilde{c}_F^i-\tilde{w}_F$. If he loses the lottery, he joins the army; if he wins, he farms. In either case, his consumption will be equal to $\frac{1}{3}T_i\bar{w}$.

3   Toward a general theory of occupational choice

Much of what we have said about soldiers and farmers applies as well to garbagemen and bank clerks or to certified public accountants and college professors. The theory generalizes cleanly to the case of many occupational alternatives and to a technology where total output depends in a neoclassical way on the numbers of persons engaged in each occupation. Although the model can be extended without much complication to the level of generality of the Arrow–Debreu model of general equilibrium, to simplify exposition and to emphasize the novel features of our treatment, we will draw our model more starkly.

Let there be N laborers and M occupations where N is "large" relative to M. Each laborer must select exactly one of these occupations. A single consumption good is produced. Total output is determined by a differentiable, concave, linear homogeneous production function, $F(N_1, \dots, N_M)$, where N_i is the number of laborers who select occupation i. Each individual i is assumed to have a (state-dependent) von Neumann–Morgenstern utility function of the form

$$U(\pi^i, c^i) = \sum_{j=1}^{M} \pi_j^i u_j^i(c_j^i),$$ (3.1)

where π_j^i is the probability that his occupation will be j and c_j^i is his consumption contingent on the occupation being j.

Let the consumption good be the *numéraire* and let w_j denote the wage rate of occupation j. If laborers have access to all actuarially fair lotteries in consumption goods, then laborer i could obtain any vector of contingent commodities $c^i = (c_1^i, \dots, c_M^i)$ and probability distribution of occupations $\pi^i = (\pi_1^i, \dots, \pi_M^i)$ that satisfies the condition

$$\sum_{j=1}^{M} \pi_j^i c_j^i = \sum_{j=1}^{M} \pi_j^i w_j.$$ (3.2)

The way that a laborer can obtain this combination is to participate in a lottery in which for each j there is a probability π_j^i of winning $c_j^i - w_j$. From equation (3.2), we see that this lottery is actuarially fair. If the prize turns out to be $c_j^i - w_j$, then he selects occupation j. The net result of this strategy is that for each j the laborer has the probability π_j^i of selecting occupation j, and his consumption when he collects the wage for that occupation and adds it to his net winnings or losses in the lottery is $w_j + (c_j^i - w_j) = c_j^i$.

With the wage structure $w = (w_1, \dots, w_M)$, the highest expected utility that laborer i can achieve by a strategy of this type with probability distribution π^i is

$$V_i(\pi^i, w) = \max_{c^i} U(\pi^i, c^i) \quad \text{subject to} \quad \sum_{j=1}^{M} \pi_j^i c_j^i \leq \sum_{j=1}^{M} \pi_j^i w_j.$$ (3.3)

At wage structure w, the laborer will choose π^i to maximize $V_i(\cdot, w)$. If π^i maximizes $V_i(\cdot, w)$ and $V_i(\pi^i, w) = \sum_{j=1}^{M} \pi_j^i u(c_j^i)$, then the strategy in which he enters a lottery that gives him for each occupation j a probability π_j^i of winning $c_j^i - w_j$ is self-enforcing in the sense that if the prize turns out to be $c_j - w_j$ he can do no better than to select occupation j. Suppose he could do better, either by choosing an alternative occupation with certainty or by entering a second actuarially fair lottery and then choosing an occupation. Then the probability distribution π'^i of occupational outcomes and the vector of contingent consumptions c'^i that would obtain after the second stage in the lottery would still satisfy the inequality $\sum_{j=1}^{M} \pi_j'^i c_j'^i \leq \sum_{j=1}^{M} \pi_j'^i w_j$. Therefore, since π^i maximizes $V(\cdot, w)$, it follows that $U(\pi^i, c^i) \geq U(\pi'^i, c'^i)$.

In general, there might be more than one choice of π^i that solves the maximization problem (3.3). For each i, let us define the correspondence $\Pi^i(w)$ from the nonnegative orthant of R^M to the subsets of the M-simplex S^M such that

$$\Pi^i(w) = \{\pi^i \in S^M \mid \pi^i \text{ maximizes } V_i(\pi^i, w)\}.$$

We define the correspondence $\Psi(w) = \sum_{i=1}^{N} \Pi^i(w)$. A point $(N_1, ..., N_M)$ in $\Psi(w)$ is a distribution of expected numbers of laborers supplied to each occupation at the wage structure w.

Definition. An equilibrium wage structure with lotteries is a vector of wages $\tilde{w}^* = (w_1^*, ..., w_M^*)$ such that for some $N^* = (N_1^*, ..., N_M^*) \in \Psi(w^*)$ and for all $j = 1, ..., M$,

$$w_j^* = \partial F(N^*)/\partial N_j. \tag{3.4}$$

An equilibrium allocation with lotteries is an allocation (c^{*i}, π^{*i}), $i = 1, ..., N$, such that π^{*i} maximizes $V_i(\pi^i, w^*)$ on S^M and such that

$$V_i(\pi^{*i}, w^*) = U_i(\pi^{*i}, c^{*i}).$$

To prove the existence of an equilibrium wage structure, we will define a correspondence that satisfies the conditions of the Kakutani fixed point theorem and show that a fixed point for this correspondence is an equilibrium. Let the set $A = \{(N_1, ..., N_M) \geq 0 \mid \sum_{i=1}^{M} N_i = N\}$ and let $B = \{(w_1, ..., w_M) \geq 0 \mid w_i \leq \max_{N \in A} F(N)\}$. Define the correspondence $\Phi(\cdot, \cdot)$ from the convex set $A \times B$ into its subsets so that $\Phi(N, w) = \Psi(w) \times \nabla F(N)$ is the gradient function of $F(N)$. To apply the Kakutani theorem, we must establish that the image sets $\Phi(N, w)$ are convex sets for all (N, w) in $A \times B$. The following result is needed to prove that this is the case.

Proposition 3.1. If the expected utility function $U_i(\pi^i, c^i)$ is concave in c^i for fixed π^i, then the function $V_i(\pi^i, w)$ is a concave function of π^i.

Proof: Consider the probability distributions π and π' in the simplex S^M and let

$$V_i(\pi, w) = \sum_{j=1}^{M} \pi_j u_j^i(c_j^i), \tag{3.5}$$

and

$$V_i(\pi', w) = \sum_{j=1}^{M} \pi'_j u^i_j(c'^i_j), \tag{3.6}$$

where

$$\sum_{j=1}^{M} \pi_j c^i_j = \sum_{j=1}^{M} \pi_j w_j, \tag{3.7}$$

and

$$\sum_{j=1}^{M} \pi'_j c'^i_j = \sum_{j=1}^{M} \pi'_j w_j. \tag{3.8}$$

For λ between 0 and 1, the probability vector

$$\pi(\lambda) = (\pi_1(\lambda), \ldots, \pi_M(\lambda)) = \lambda \pi + (1-\lambda)\pi' \tag{3.9}$$

is also in the simplex S^M. To prove that $V_i(\pi, w)$ is a concave function of π, it suffices to show that $V_i(\pi(\lambda), w) \geq \lambda V_i(\pi, w) + (1-\lambda) V_i(\pi', w)$ for all $\lambda \in [0, 1]$.

Multiplying equations (3.7) and (3.8) by λ and $1-\lambda$, respectively, and adding, we obtain

$$\sum_{j=1}^{M} [\lambda \pi_j c^i_j + (1-\lambda)\pi'_j c'^i_j] = \sum_{j=1}^{M} \pi_j(\lambda) w_j. \tag{3.10}$$

For each occupation, $j = 1, \ldots, M$, and for $\lambda \in [0, 1]$, let us define

$$\theta_j = \lambda \pi_j / \pi_j(\lambda). \tag{3.11}$$

Then

$$1 - \theta_j = (1-\lambda)\pi'_j / \pi_j(\lambda). \tag{3.12}$$

Equation (3.10) can be rewritten as

$$\sum_{j=1}^{M} \pi_j(\lambda)[\theta_j c^i_j + (1-\theta_j)c'^i_j] = \sum_{j=1}^{M} \pi_j(\lambda) w_j. \tag{3.13}$$

It follows from the definition of $V_i(\pi, w)$ that

$$V_i(\pi(\lambda), w) \geq \sum_{j=1}^{M} \pi_j(\lambda) u^i_j(\theta_j c^i_j + (1-\theta_j)c'^i_j). \tag{3.14}$$

But, by assumption, the functions $u^i_j(\cdot)$ are concave functions. Therefore, equation (3.14) implies

$$V_i(\pi(\lambda), w) \geq \sum_{j=1}^{M} \pi_j(\lambda)[\theta_j u^i_j(c^i_j) + (1-\theta_j)u^i_j(c'^i_j)]. \tag{3.15}$$

Using equations (3.11) and (3.12), we see that (3.15) is equivalent to

$$V_i(\pi(\lambda), w) \geq \lambda \sum_{j=1}^{M} \pi_j u_j^i(c_j^i) + (1-\lambda) \sum_{j=1}^{M} \pi_j' u_j^i(c_j'^i). \tag{3.16}$$

Recalling equations (3.1) and (3.2), we see that (3.16) is equivalent to

$$V_i(\pi(\lambda), w) \geq \lambda V_i(\pi, w) + (1-\lambda) V_i(\pi', w). \tag{3.17}$$

Therefore, $V_i(\pi, w)$ is concave in π. ∎

With the help of Proposition 3.1, we can prove that Φ has all of the properties needed to apply the Kakutani theorem.

Lemma 3.1. If the expected utility function $U(\pi^i, c^i)$ is continuous and concave in c^i for fixed π, then for each i, the correspondence $\Phi(N, w)$ is an upper semicontinuous correspondence from the closed bounded convex set $A \times B$, and the image sets $\Phi(N, w)$ are convex subsets of $A \times B$ for all (N, w) in $A \times B$.

Proof: It is easily verified that Φ maps the convex set $A \times B$ into its subsets. According to well-known arguments, continuity of preferences and production functions imply that this correspondence is upper semicontinuous. From Proposition 3.1, it follows directly that the image sets of $\Pi^i(w)$ are convex sets for all $w \in A$. Therefore, $\Psi(w) = \sum_{i=1}^{N} \Pi^i(w)$ has convex image sets. The function $\nabla F(N)$ is single valued and hence (trivially) has convex image sets. Therefore, $\Phi(N, w) = (\Psi(w), \nabla F(N))$ must have convex image sets for all $(N, w) \in A \times B$. ∎

Now we can prove the existence of equilibrium.

Proposition 3.2. For the model of this section, there exists an equilibrium wage structure with lotteries.

Proof: According to Lemma 3.1, the correspondence Φ satisfies the conditions of the Kakutani fixed point theorem. Therefore, there must exist $N^* \in A$ and $w^* \in B$ such that $N^* \in \Psi(w^*)$ and $w^* = \nabla F(N)$. ∎

If equilibrium occurs with large numbers of laborers in each occupation and if the lotteries in which individuals participate are independent, then the proportion of the labor force that selects each occupation will be very close to its expected value. Since the production function has constant returns to scale, per capita output and the marginal products of all factors will be very close to their expected values. It is therefore reasonable to approximate this stochastic economy by a certainty equivalent economy in which feasibility means equality of expected total consumption and aggregate output. (See Remark following Proposition 2.2.)

Definition. A feasible allocation consists of contingent consumptions c_j^i and probabilities π_j^i for all laborers $i = 1, \dots, N$ and occupations $j = 1, \dots, M$ such that

$$\sum_{i=1}^{N} \sum_{j=1}^{M} \pi_j^i c_j^i = F(N_1, \dots, N_M), \tag{3.18}$$

where $N_j = \sum_{i=1}^{N} \pi_j^i$.

When feasibility is defined in this way, an equilibrium wage structure generates a Pareto-optimal allocation.

Proposition 3.3. An equilibrium allocation with lotteries is Pareto optimal.

Proof: We first observe that an equilibrium allocation is feasible. Let (π^{*i}, c^{*i}), $i = 1, \dots, N$, be an equilibrium allocation. Then for each laborer i,

$$\sum_{j=1}^{M} \pi_j^{*i} c_j^{*i} \leq \sum_{j=1}^{M} \pi_j^{*i} w_j^*. \tag{3.19}$$

Summing equation (3.19) over all i, one has

$$\sum_{i=1}^{N} \sum_{j=1}^{M} \pi_j^i c_j^i \leq \sum_{j=1}^{M} N_j w_j^*, \tag{3.20}$$

where $N_j = \sum_{i=1}^{N} \pi_j^i$. But $w^* = \nabla F(N^*)$. Since $F(N)$ is assumed to be homogeneous of degree 1, it follows from Euler's theorem on homogeneous functions that

$$\sum_{j=1}^{M} N_j w_j^* = F(N^*). \tag{3.21}$$

Therefore,

$$\sum_{i=1}^{N} \sum_{j=1}^{M} \pi_j^i c_j^i \leq F(N^*), \tag{3.22}$$

which establishes that the equilibrium allocation (π^{*i}, c^{*i}), $i = 1, \dots, N$, is feasible.

Let (π^i, c^i), $i = 1, \ldots, N$, be an allocation that is Pareto superior to (π^{*i}, c^{*i}), $i = 1, \ldots, N$. Since $V_i(\pi^{*i}, w^*) \geq V_i(\pi_i, w^*)$, it must be that if $U_i(\pi^i, c^i) > U_i(\pi^{*i}, c^{*i})$, then

$$\sum_{j=1}^{M} \pi_j^i c_j^i > \sum \pi_j^i w_j^*. \tag{3.23}$$

Since preferences are assumed to be strictly monotonic in consumption, it also follows from a familiar argument that if $U_i(\pi^i, c^i) \geq U_i(\pi^{*i}, c^{*i})$, then

$$\sum_{j=1}^{M} \pi_j^i c_j^i > \sum \pi_j^i w_j^*. \tag{3.24}$$

Summing the inequalities (3.23) and (3.24) over all i, we find that

$$\sum_{i=1}^{N} \sum_{j=1}^{M} \pi_j^i c_j^i > \sum_{j=1}^{M} N_j w_j^* = F(N). \tag{3.25}$$

Therefore, the allocation (π^i, c^i), $i = 1, \ldots, N$, is not feasible. It follows that (π^{*i}, c^{*i}), $i = 1, \ldots, N$, is Pareto optimal. ∎

4   Comments on related literature

Debreu's (1959) discussion of consumers in general equilibrium suggests a way in which occupational choice can be incorporated into a general equilibrium model. He treats a *consumption plan* as a vector the components of which are consumer inputs (with positive signs) and outputs (with negative signs) where "Typically, the inputs of a consumption are various goods and services (related to food, clothing, housing...dated and located); its only outputs are the various kinds of labor performed (dated and located)" (p. 59).

Similarly, Arrow and Hahn (1971) treat labor offered by an individual in different occupations as different commodities. To preserve monotonicity of preferences, they use the convention of treating "time spent not doing work of type x" rather than "time spent doing work of type x" as the commodities, but this is a difference of notation and not of substance.

"Thus, if the individual is capable of teaching for 12 hours a day and also capable of driving a bus for 12 hours a day and if, in fact, he teaches for eight hours a day and does not drive a bus at all, then his demand for 'teaching leisure' is four hours and that for 'bus-driving leisure' is 12 hours" (p. 75).

This modeling strategy is powerful and allows for a natural way of treating most of the issues likely to arise in matters of occupational choice and the allocation of time. But it does introduce a difficulty, both in the interpretation of the major theorems of general equilibrium analysis and in standard applications of comparative statics. The difficulty is that in the model so constructed, it does not seem very reasonable to assume convex preferences. Convexity would demand that a consumer who is indifferent between a certain income with 4 hours of teaching leisure and 12 hours of bus-driving leisure and another income with 12 hours of teaching leisure and 4 hours of bus-driving leisure would be at least as well off with an income halfway between the two incomes and with 8 hours of each kind of leisure. Not only does this assumption seem unappealing on casual grounds but it also seems contrary to the evidence offered by the fact that most people specialize in a single occupation.

Our general model can be thought of as a polar case within the Arrow–Debreu general structure, where instead of assuming that preferences and consumption possibility sets are convex in time spent in each occupation, we assume that each individual must specialize completely. Of course, a more realistic model could be constructed in which there was some convexity and some nonconvexity so that some individuals might in equilibrium choose to allocate their time among several occupations.

The idea of allocating by lottery in the presence of indivisibilities or other nonconvexities is familiar in game theory where equilibrium in mixed strategies plays an essential role (von Neumann and Morgenstern 1944). This idea has also received attention in the literature on the economics of location (see, for example, Mirrlees 1972), the theory of clubs (Hillman and Swan 1983), and the theory of taxation (Stiglitz 1982). Starr (1969) and Arrow and Hahn (1971) demonstrate that in appropriately large economies approximate competitive equilibria will exist even if there are nonconvexities in individual preferences. A careful survey of the recent literature and development of the theme that aggregation smooths can be found in Trockel (1984). The general development of our model of occupational choice is similar in spirit to this work. The extra ingredient of our discussion is that we are able to develop an explicit description of the way in which simple lotteries, with financial prizes only, can be used to achieve the requisite smoothing of aggregate behavior when individuals must make discrete choices.

REFERENCES

Arrow, K. and F. Hahn (1971), *General competitive analysis,* San Francisco: Holden-Day.
Debreu, G. (1959), *The theory of value,* New York: Wiley.

Hillman, A. and P. Swan (1983), "Participation rules for Pareto optimal clubs," *Journal of Public Economics*, February: 55–76.

Marshall, J. (1984), "Gambles and the shadow price of death," *American Economic Review*, March: 73–86.

Mirrlees, J. (1972), "The optimal town," *Swedish Journal of Economics*, March: 115–35.

Starr, R. (1969), "Quasi-equilibrium in markets with non-convex preferences," *Econometrica*, 37(1): 25–38.

Stiglitz, J. (1982), "Utilitarianism and horizontal equity: The case for random taxation," *Journal of Public Economics*, June: 1–34.

Trockel, W. (1984), *Market demand – An analysis of large economies with nonconvex preferences*, New York: Springer-Verlag.

von Neumann, J. and O. Morgenstern, *The theory of games and economic behavior*, Princeton: Princeton University Press.

CHAPTER 3

The dynamics of industrywide learning

Nancy L. Stokey

1   Introduction

In "The Economic Implications of Learning by Doing," Professor Arrow (1962) emphasizes that inefficiencies arise if *doing* generates external effects on the *learning* of others. That such externalities are pervasive seems obvious. Communication between individuals takes place through the usual channels, and communication between firms occurs when individuals move from one firm to another, or when learning by one firm is transferred to the supplier of a capital good and then embodied in the equipment purchased by another.

In the presence of externalities in learning, inefficiencies arise because for each firm the private benefits of experience are less than the social benefits, leading to underproduction even with perfectly competitive markets. This is why subsidies to "infant" industries may be called for. In fact, the free-rider problem is more severe the greater the number of firms, so there is no presumption that entry is socially beneficial – even with constant returns to scale in production and no cost of entry. Thus, second-best policies may include those – like patents – that restrict entry.

The analysis of any such policies requires an understanding of how firms compete in industries where learning occurs. A model of such competition, based on the framework of differential games, is studied below.

The dynamics of a single industry are examined under the assumption that spillovers in learning are complete, that is, that learning is industrywide. Specifically, it will be assumed that unit cost for any firm in the industry depends only on cumulative industry production to date.[1] This

I am grateful to Robert E. Lucas, Jr. and Sherwin Rosen for helpful discussions. This research was supported by National Science Foundation Grant No. SES–8411361 and by the Center for Advanced Studies in Managerial Economics and Decision Sciences, Northwestern University.

assumption, while extreme, captures an important aspect of many infant industries. Indeed, many of the arguments in favor of public policies to promote new industries rest exactly on this externality.

In Section 2, the model is described, and in Section 3, the efficient (surplus-maximizing) and monopoly (profit-maximizing) solutions are characterized. In Section 4, industry behavior under oligopoly is analyzed. The firms in the industry are viewed as players in a (noncooperative) infinite-horizon differential game. Theorems 1 and 2 establish the existence and uniqueness of a symmetric Nash equilibrium in decision rules, and Theorems 3 and 4 provide a qualitative characterization of the equilibrium output path. In Section 5, computational results are presented for a series of examples. These illustrate how industry structure interacts with other features of the model. In the presence of externalities in learning, increasing the number of firms in an industry has two opposing effects: Aggregate output tends to increase for the same reason it does in a static model but tends to decrease because the free-rider problem becomes more severe. In the examples in Section 5, the first effect dominates when demand is inelastic and the interest rate high, and the second dominates when demand is elastic and the interest rate low. Conclusions are drawn in Section 6. Proofs of the more difficult results are gathered in the appendix.

2   The environment

The model is formulated in continuous time with an infinite horizon, $t \in [0, \infty)$. At date $t = 0$, $n \geq 1$ identical firms enter the industry. At each date, all firms operate with the same constant returns-to-scale technology. That is, unit cost of production is constant for each firm at each date and is identical across firms at each date. The industrywide learning curve is captured in the fact that unit cost declines as cumulative industrywide production, call it x, increases. Let $c(x)$ denote unit cost when cumulative production is x.

Assumption 1. $c: \mathbb{R}_+ \to \mathbb{R}_+$ is once continuously differentiable. For some $X_1 \geq 0$, it is strictly decreasing and strictly convex on $[0, X_1)$ and constant on $[X_1, \infty)$.

Thus, unit cost decreases smoothly as experience increases from 0 to X_1 and is constant thereafter.

Demand is described by a stationary inverse demand curve.

Assumption 2

(i) $p: \mathbb{R}_+ \to \mathbb{R}_+$ is twice continuously differentiable on $\mathbb{R}_{++}$;

(ii) $p'(y) \leq 0$, with equality only if $p(y) = 0$;

(iii) $2p'(y) + yp''(y) \leq 0$, with equality only if $p(y) = 0$;

(iv) $\lim_{y \to 0}[p(y) + yp'(y)] > c(0)$;

(v) for some $Y > 0$, $p(Y) = c(X_1)$.

Assumption 2 says that the demand and marginal revenue curves are both downward sloping; that it is possible for profits to be positive at every date (although in equilibrium they may or may not be); and that demand is bounded when price is equal to the minimum attained by unit cost.

Under Assumption 2, for any number of firms $n \geq 1$ and constant unit cost $c \in [c(X_1), c(0)]$, there exists a unique Cournot–Nash equilibrium in the static quantity game, and this equilibrium is symmetric. Define $q_n(c)$ to be the Nash equilibrium quantity produced by each firm when there are n firms and unit cost is c,

$$p(nq_n(c)) + q_n(c)p'(nq_n(c)) - c \equiv 0, \qquad c \in [c(X_1), c(0)]. \qquad (1)$$

It is straightforward to show that $q_n(c)$ is decreasing in n and c and that $nq_n(c)$ is increasing in n and decreasing in c.

3   Industry behavior under monopoly and surplus maximization

A baseline for efficiency comparisons is the output path that maximizes the present discounted value of total surplus, where surplus at each date is measured by the area under the demand curve minus current costs of production. Since learning effects are industrywide and the technology displays constant returns to scale at each date, costs of production depend only on the path for aggregate production and not on how it is disaggregated among producers. Thus, the efficient path for aggregate production is simply the solution to the variational problem

$$\max_{[x(t)]} \int_0^\infty e^{-rt} \left[\int_0^{x'(t)} p(u)\, du - x'(t)c(x(t)) \right] dt, \quad \text{s.t. } x(0) = 0.$$

The Euler equation for this problem, in integral form, is

$$p(x'(t)) = c(x(t)) + \int_t^\infty e^{-r(s-t)} x'(s) c'(x(s))\, ds. \qquad (2)$$

Price equals marginal cost along the efficient path, where the latter is defined to include the indirect effect of current production on future costs. Integrating the right side of (2) by parts, one finds that the Euler equation can also be written as

$$p(x'(t)) = r \int_t^\infty e^{-r(s-t)} c(x(s)) \, ds. \tag{2'}$$

Characterizing the efficient path is straightforward. Consider the situation while learning is still going on (before cumulative experience reaches X_1). Since c is decreasing in x, the right side of (2') is decreasing over time. Thus price is falling over time and the rate of production rising. Upper and lower bounds on the price path can also be derived. Since $c(x) > c(X_1)$, (2') implies that price exceeds minimum unit cost, and since $c'(x(t)) < 0$, (2) implies that price is less than current unit cost. Thus price lies in the interval $(c(X_1), c(x))$, and profits are negative. After experience reaches X_1 and learning stops, price is constant at unit cost $c(X_1)$, and profits are zero.

The production path for a profit-maximizing monopolist[2] can be found as the solution to a similar variational problem, with revenue replacing the area under the demand curve in the objective function. Thus, the production path for a monopolist solves

$$\max_{[x(t)]} \int_0^\infty e^{-rt} x'(t)[p(x'(t)) - c(x(t))] \, dt, \quad \text{s.t.} \quad x(0) = 0.$$

The Euler equation for this problem is

$$p(x'(t)) + x'(t) p'(x'(t)) = c(x(t)) + \int_t^\infty e^{-r(s-t)} x'(s) c'(x(s)) \, ds \tag{3}$$

$$= r \int_t^\infty e^{-r(s-t)} c(x(s)) \, ds. \tag{3'}$$

Equation (3) says that at each date the monopolist produces where marginal revenue equals marginal cost, where the latter is defined as before.

Consider the case while learning is still going on. Equation (3') implies that unit cost and hence marginal revenue are decreasing over time, the rate of production thus increasing. Bounds on the monopolist's strategy can also be derived from (3) and (3'). From (3') it follows that marginal revenue exceeds minimum unit cost, and from (3) that it is less than current unit cost. Thus, marginal revenue lies in the interval $(c(X_1), c(x))$, and profits may be either positive or negative. After experience reaches X_1, unit cost is constant at $c(X_1)$, and production is constant at $q_1(c(X_1))$.

Comparing (2) and (3), one finds the usual inefficiency from monopoly: for any given marginal cost, the monopolist underproduces since marginal revenue rather than price is set equal to marginal cost. However, the situation is even worse than that. Because the monopolist produces less at each date, costs fall more slowly. Thus, at any date t when learning is still going on, the integral in (3′) exceeds the one in (2′). Hence, at any date when learning is still going on, the relevant marginal cost for the monopolist exceeds marginal cost for the efficient producer.

4   Industry behavior under oligopoly

In this section, equilibrium will be studied for oligopolistic market structures. Thus, at date $t = 0$, $n \geq 2$ firms enter the industry. Each firm seeks to maximize the present discounted value of its profit stream over the horizon $[0, \infty)$, and each discounts future profits at the constant rate of interest $r > 0$.

The firms will be viewed as players in a noncooperative dynamic game in which the state variable is cumulative industry production, the strategies are decision rules describing production decisions, and the payoffs are discounted profits. The equilibrium concept employed will be subgame perfect Nash equilibrium. Thus, a strategy for any player $i = 1, \ldots, n$, is a piecewise continuous function $g_i : \mathbb{R}_+ \to \mathbb{R}_+$, where $g_i(x)$ is firm i's production rate when cumulative industry production to date is x. History-dependent strategies are ruled out. The payoff to any player i if the vector of strategies $(g_1, \ldots, g_n)$ is adopted and the initial state is $\hat{x}$, is

$$\pi_i(g_1, \ldots, g_n, \hat{x}) = \int_0^\infty e^{-rt} g_i(x(t))[p(\Sigma_j g_j(x(t))) - c(x(t))]\, dt$$

where

$$x'(t) = \Sigma_j g_j(x(t)), \qquad x(0) = \hat{x}.$$

A subgame perfect Nash equilibrium is a vector of strategies $(g_1, \ldots, g_n)$ such that

$$\pi_i(g_1, \ldots, g_n, \hat{x}) \geq \pi_i(g_1, \ldots, g_{i-1}, g_i', g_{i+1}, \ldots, g_n, \hat{x}), \quad \text{for all } g_i', i, \hat{x}.$$

The approach here will be to construct a symmetric equilibrium. By standard arguments (see, e.g., Starr and Ho 1969), such an equilibrium is completely characterized by a value function $v : \mathbb{R}_+ \to \mathbb{R}_+$ and a strategy $g : \mathbb{R}_+ \to \mathbb{R}_+$ satisfying

$$rv(x) = g(x)[p(ng(x)) - c(x)] + ng(x)v'(x) \tag{4}$$

$$= \max_y y[p(y + (n-1)g(x)) - c(x)] + [y + (n-1)g(x)]v'(x), \tag{5}$$

for all x. The interpretation is that for each firm $v(x)$ is the present discounted value of future profits and $g(x)$ the rate of production when the current state is x.

The existence and uniqueness of a symmetric Nash equilibrium will be established by using (4) and (5) to develop a single functional equation in the unknown function g. Briefly, the first-order condition arising from (5) gives an equation for $v'(x)$ in terms of $g(x)$, and modifying (4) slightly and integrating gives an equation for $v(x)$. Using these to eliminate v and v' from (4) then gives the functional equation in g. First, though, we must consider v and g at the boundary point $x = X_1$.

If $x \geq X_1$, then no further learning occurs, and from that point on, the firms behave like ordinary Cournot competitors. Thus, any equilibrium strategy must satisfy

$$g(x) = q_n(c(X_1)), \qquad x \geq X_1, \tag{6}$$

where q_n is defined in (1). It then follows from (4) that the value function satisfies

$$v(x) = q_n(c(X_1))[p(nq_n(c(X_1))) - c(X_1)]/r$$
$$= -g^2(x)p'(ng(x))/r, \qquad x \geq X_1. \tag{7}$$

where the second line uses (1) and (6).

Next, note that under Assumption 2, the right side of (5) is strictly concave in y, so that the first-order condition describes an interior maximum. Therefore, at a symmetric equilibrium with positive production, (v, g) must satisfy

$$p(ng(x)) + g(x)p'(ng(x)) - c(x) + v'(x) = 0. \tag{8}$$

Using (8) to eliminate $p - c$ from (4) and multiplying by $n/(n-1)$, we find that

$$ng(x)v'(x) - \rho v(x) = (n/(n-1))g^2(x)p'(ng(x)),$$

where $\rho = rn/(n-1)$. Then integrating and using the boundary condition (7), we find that, for all $0 \leq t \leq T$,

$$e^{-\rho t}v(x(t)) = \frac{-n}{n-1}\int_t^T e^{-\rho s}g^2(x(s))p'(ng(x(s)))\,ds + e^{-\rho T}v(X_1), \tag{9}$$

where

$$x(0) = 0, \qquad x(T) = X_1,$$
$$x'(s) = ng(x(s)), \qquad 0 \leq s \leq T.$$

Finally, substituting from (8) and (9) into (4) to eliminate v' and v, we find that for all $X_0 \in [0, X_1]$, g must satisfy

$$-\rho \int_0^T e^{-\rho s} g^2(x(s)) p'(ng(x(s))) \, ds + e^{-\rho T} r v(X_1)$$

$$= -[(n-1)g(X_0)[p(ng(X_0)) - c(X_0)] + ng^2(X_0) p'(ng(X_0))] \quad \text{(10a)}$$

where

$$x(0) = X_0, \qquad x(T) = X_1,$$
$$x'(s) = ng(x(s)), \qquad 0 \le s \le T.$$
$$\text{(10b)}$$

The following theorem will be used to establish the existence and uniqueness of a function g satisfying (6) and (10).

Theorem 1. Consider the following functional equation in the unknown function g:

$$\rho \int_0^T e^{-\rho s} \gamma(g(x(s))) \, ds + e^{-\rho T} V = \phi(g(X_0), X_0), \quad \text{(11)}$$

where $x(s)$ is given by (10b), and where $\rho > 0$, $n \ge 1$, $X_1 \ge 0$, and $V \ge 0$ are known as are $\gamma : \mathbb{R}_+ \to \mathbb{R}$ and $\phi : \mathbb{R}_+ \times [0, X_1] \to \mathbb{R}$. Suppose there exists a continuous increasing function $a(x)$ on $[0, X_1]$, and $A \ge a(X_1)$, such that

(a) γ is continuous and strictly increasing on $[a(0), A]$.
(b)   There exists $w > 0$ such that

$$|\gamma(y) - \gamma(y')| \le w|y - y'|, \qquad y, y' \in [a(0), A]. \quad \text{(12)}$$

(c) $\phi(y, x)$ is continuous, strictly increasing in y, and strictly decreasing in x on $S = \{(y, x) \mid y \in [a(x), A], x \in [0, X_1]\}$.
(d)   For some $k_1 > 0$ and $k_2 \ge 0$,

$$k_1|y - y'| \le |\phi(y, x) - \phi(y', x)|, \qquad (y, x), (y', x) \in S,$$
$$|\phi(y, x) - \phi(y, x')| \le k_2|x - x'|, \qquad (y, x), (y, x') \in S.$$
$$\text{(13)}$$

(e)   For each $X_0 \in [0, X_1]$, the range of $\phi(\cdot, X_0)$ on $[a(X_0), A]$ contains $[\gamma(a(X_0)), \gamma(A)]$.
(f) $V \in [\gamma(a(X_1)), \gamma(A)]$.

Then there exists a function g satisfying (11) for all $X_0 \in [0, X_1]$, and the solution is unique in the space of continuous functions f on $[0, X_1]$ satisfying the bounds

$$a(x) \le f(x) \le A, \qquad x \in [0, X_1]. \tag{14}$$

If ϕ is once continuously differentiable, then so is g.

The proof is in the appendix. To apply this theorem to the problem at hand, define

$$\gamma(y) = -y^2 p'(ny), \tag{15a}$$

$$\phi(y, x) = -(n-1)y[p(ny) - c(x)] - ny^2 p'(ny), \tag{15b}$$

$$V = rv(X_1). \tag{15c}$$

Then (10a) has the form of (11), and it only remains to show that the hypotheses of Theorem 1 are satisfied.

Theorem 2. Let c and p satisfy Assumptions 1 and 2, and fix $n > 1$. Then there exists a function g satisfying (6) and (10). This solution is once differentiable and is unique in the space of continuous functions on $[0, X_1]$ satisfying

$$q_1(c(x))/n \le f(x) \le Y/n, \qquad 0 \le x \le X_1. \tag{16}$$

Proof: It is sufficient to show that Theorem 1 applies, where γ, ϕ, and V are given by (15), ρ is as above, and

$$a(x) = q_1(c(x))/n, \qquad 0 \le x \le X_1, \tag{17a}$$

$$A = Y/n. \tag{17b}$$

It follows immediately from part (i) of Assumption 2 that γ is continuous and differentiable and that γ' is bounded on $[q_1(c(0))/n, Y/n]$. It follows from part (iii) that $\gamma' \ge 0$, with equality only if $y = Y/n$. Hence γ satisfies (a) and (b).

It follows immediately from Assumptions 1 and 2 that ϕ is once continuously differentiable, with

$$\phi_1(y, x) = -(n-1)[p(ny) + nyp'(ny) - c(x)] + n\gamma'(y).$$

The term in square brackets is negative on the relevant range, approaching zero only as $y \to q_1(c(x))/n$, and γ' is positive, approaching zero only as $y \to Y/n$. Hence ϕ is strictly increasing in y on $[q_1(c(x))/n, Y/n]$, and for some $0 < k_1$, the first bound in (d) holds. Next, note that $\phi_2(y, x) = (n-1)yc'(x)$. By Assumption 1, c is strictly decreasing and strictly convex on $[0, X_1]$. Hence $\phi(y, x))$ is strictly decreasing in x on the relevant range, and the second bound in (d) holds for $k_2 = (n-1)(Y/n)|c'(0)|$. Hence ϕ satisfies (c) and (d).

To show that (e) holds, note that for each $x \in [0, X_1]$,

$$\phi(a(x), x) = \phi\left(\frac{q_1(c(x))}{n}, x\right)$$

$$= -(n-1)\frac{q_1(c(x))}{n}[p(q_1(c(x))) - c(x)] + n\gamma\left(\frac{q_1(c(x))}{n}\right)$$

$$= (n-1)\frac{q_1^2(c(x))}{n}p'(q_1(c(x))) + n\gamma\left(\frac{q_1(c(x))}{n}\right)$$

$$= (n(1-n)+n)\gamma\left(\frac{q_1(c(x))}{n}\right)$$

$$\leq 0 \leq \gamma\left(\frac{q_1(c(x))}{n}\right) = \gamma(a(x)),$$

where the third line uses (1) and the last uses the fact that $\gamma > 0$ and $n \geq 2$. Also,

$$\phi(A, x) = \phi(Y/n, x)$$

$$= -(n-1)(Y/n)[p(Y) - c(x)] + n\gamma(Y/n)$$

$$= (n-1)(Y/n)[c(x) - c(X_1)] + n\gamma(Y/n)$$

$$> \gamma(Y/n) = \gamma(A),$$

where the third line uses the definition of Y and the last uses the fact that $n \geq 2$ and $c(x) \geq c(X_1)$. This establishes that (e) holds.

Finally, note that, from (6) and (7),

$$V = rv(X_1) = \gamma(g(X_1)) = \gamma(q_n(c(X_1))).$$

Since $q_n(c(X_1)) \in [q_1(c(X_1))/n, Y/n] = [a(X_1), A]$, and γ is monotone, it follows that (f) holds.   ∎

Theorem 2 establishes that there is a unique symmetric Nash equilibrium in the space of production strategies for which aggregate industry production $nf(x)$ is at least as great as the quantity $q_1(c(x))$ that a monopolist in a static environment with unit cost $c(x)$ would produce, but no more than the quantity Y at which price equals minimum unit cost $c(X_1)$.

The equilibrium point g of Theorem 2 can be characterized more sharply by showing that Theorem 1 still holds when the bounds in (16) are narrowed and by applying the following result.

Theorem 3. If the hypotheses of Theorem 1 hold and if in addition $V = \gamma(A)$, then the solution g is strictly increasing.

The proof is in the Appendix.

Theorem 4. The unique function g of Theorem 2 is strictly increasing and satisfies

$$q_n(c(x)) \le g(x) \le q_n(c(X_1)). \tag{18}$$

Proof: It is sufficient to show that Theorems 1 and 3 apply when we choose

$$a(x) = q_n(c(x)), \qquad A = q_n(c(X_1)).$$

Conditions (a)–(d) are as before, and $V = \gamma(A)$, so (f) holds. To see that (e) holds, fix $x \in [0, X_1]$. From (15b) and (1), it follows that

$$
\begin{aligned}
\phi(a(x), x) &= \phi(q_n(c(x)), x) \\
&= -(n-1)q_n(c(x))[p(nq_n(c(x))) - c(x)] \\
&\quad - nq_n^2(c(x))p'(nq_n(c(x))) \\
&= -q_n^2(c(x))p'(nq_n(c(x))) \\
&= \gamma(q_n(c(x))) = \gamma(a(x)).
\end{aligned}
$$

Also, since ϕ is decreasing in x,

$$
\begin{aligned}
\phi(A, x) &= \phi(q_n(c(X_1)), x) > \phi(q_n(c(X_1)), X_1) \\
&= \gamma(q_n(c(X_1))) = \gamma(A).
\end{aligned}
$$

Hence the range of $\phi(\cdot, x)$ on $[a(x), A]$ includes the interval $[\gamma(a(x)), \gamma(A)]$, and (e) holds. ■

The functions satisfying (18) represent strategies with the following property: For any level of cumulative production x, each firm's current production rate $f(x)$ lies between the static Cournot–Nash equilibrium rates $q_n(c(x))$ and $q_n(c(X_1))$ corresponding to unit costs $c(x)$ and $c(X_1)$, respectively. In other words, if all firms adopt strategies satisfying (18), then as under monopoly, when current unit cost is $c(x)$, marginal revenue lies in the interval $[c(X_1), c(x)]$.

Theorem 4 shows that for any demand and cost functions and any number of firms $n \ge 2$, the unique symmetric Nash equilibrium has the qualitative characteristics one would expect: The rate of production increases monotonically as learning proceeds and costs fall, and at any date, marginal revenue lies between minimum unit cost and current unit cost.

Next consider the value function v given by (9), which can be interpreted as the market value of the firm. Note that $x(t)$ is strictly increasing, g is strictly increasing on $[0, X_1]$, $\gamma(y)$ is positive and strictly increasing, and $v(X_1) = \gamma(g(X_1))/r$. Hence it follows from (9) that v is positive and strictly increasing on $[0, X_1]$. That is, the market value of each firm increases as learning occurs.

Although entry is not incorporated in the analysis above, the model does suggest a line of attack using backward induction. Let $v_n(x)$ denote the present discounted value of the profits of each of n firms at the symmetric equilibrium beginning at x. Since $v_n(X_1)$ is proportional to profits in an n-firm (static) Cournot equilibrium [with unit cost $c(X_1)$], it is decreasing in n. Suppose there is a fixed cost Γ of entry. Then the number of firms in the "mature" industry will be given by N satisfying

$$v_N(X_1) \leq \Gamma < v_{N+1}(X_1).$$

The profits of the Nth firm cover its cost of entry, but those of the $(N+1)$th firm would not. Moreover, since $v_N(x)$ is continuous and strictly increasing in x, the Nth firm enters when industry experience is X_N satisfying $v_N(X_N) = \Gamma$.

Extending the argument further back is difficult, however, since there is no obvious way to guarantee that the value Γ is attained in the $(N-1)$-firm game terminating at X_N; that is, there seems to be no way of ensuring that the $(N-1)$th firm ever has an incentive to enter.

5 The effect of industry structure: some examples

Given demand and cost functions, it is straightforward to compute the equilibrium strategies for different numbers of firms: Equation (10) can be solved stepwise from right to left, starting at X_1 and working back to the origin. In this section, results are presented for several such examples.[3] These are designed to illustrate the possible effects of industry structure on equilibrium behavior. As might be expected, varying the number of firms has quite different effects depending on the price elasticity of demand and the interest rate. This is because increasing the number of firms has two opposing effects: The aggregate rate of production tends to rise for the reason it does in a static Cournot model but tends to fall because the free-rider problem associated with learning becomes more severe.

For a given cost function, the first effect predominates when demand is relatively inelastic and the interest rate is high, and the second when demand is elastic and the interest rate low.

In the examples below, the inverse demand function is assumed to have the constant-elasticity form

$$p(y) = Ay^{-1/B},$$

so that $B > 1$ is the price elasticity of demand. The cost function is also of the constant-elasticity form,

$$c(x) = \begin{cases} C(x+1)^{-D} & \text{if } C(x+1)^{-D} > 1, \\ 1 & \text{otherwise}, \end{cases}$$

so that $D > 0$ is the elasticity of cost with respect to cumulative output. Thus, the industry is assumed to start with one unit of experience, so that initial unit cost is C, and thereafter doublings of cumulative experience cause unit cost to fall by a factor of 2^{-D} until the minimum cost of unity is reached. In each example, solutions were computed for $n = 1, 2, 3, 4$, and 8 firms, for a competitive industry, and for an efficient (total surplus-maximizing) producer.

In the first set of examples, the parameter values are $A = 10$, $B = 1.5$, $C = 10$, and $D = 0.32$, and the interest rate is $r = 0.1$. Thus, demand is moderately elastic, and output doublings cause unit cost to decline by 20 percent, starting at a unit cost of 10 and falling to a minimum of 1. Figure 1(a) shows price as a function of cost for several industry structures and Figure 1(b) shows price as a function of time. Note that as unit cost reaches its minimum in Figure 1(a), or equivalently, as time passes in Figure 1(b), the price level for any industry structure reaches what it would be in a static model with constant unit cost equal to 1. Note, too, that at any cost level or any date, an efficient producer charges a lower price than is found under any other industry structure. These two features are, of course, independent of the specific cost and demand curves chosen.

Next, note that for these parameter values, the price curves are ordered: At every cost level in Figure 1(a) and at every date in Figure 1(b), the highest price is found under monopoly, the next highest under duopoly, and so on (this also holds for $n = 3, 4, 8$, not displayed in the figures). As will be seen below, this feature is *not* general. This ordering of the cost curves implies that only the efficient producer ever prices below unit cost. This can be seen from Figure 1, where the competitive industry is, of course, represented by the 45° line. The price curve for the efficient

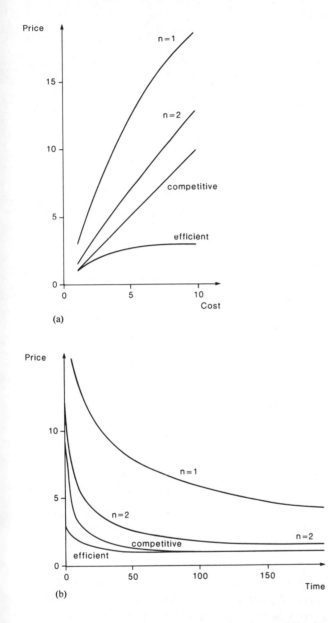

Figure 1. Price as a function of (a) cost and (b) time for various industry structures. The price elasticity of demand is 1.5, the interest rate is 0.1, and the elasticity of cost with respect to cumulative output is 0.32.

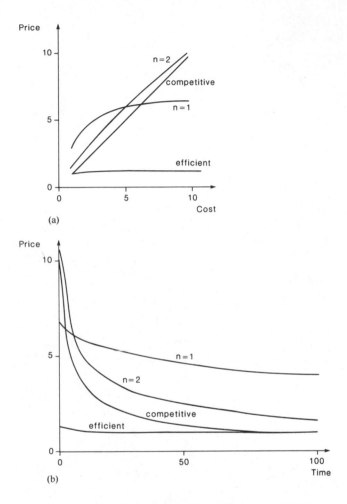

Figure 2. Price as a function of (a) cost and (b) time for various industry structures. The price elasticity of demand is 1.5, the interest rate is 0.01, and the elasticity of cost with respect to cumulative output is 0.32.

producer lies below this curve, just touching it when cost is at its minimum, whereas the curves for all other industry structures lie above it.

Figures 2(a) and 2(b) show the effect of lowering the interest rate; the other parameter values are as before, but the interest rate is $r = 0.01$. This leads to a major change in the behavior of a monopolist producer. A lower interest rate increases the importance of learning, and a monopolist responds to this by initially pricing below unit cost. Under duopoly, however, the free-rider problem still predominates, so that price is always above unit cost. (In this case, initial prices are *not* ordered for $n = 3, 4, 8$ firms. When unit cost is 10, price is 10.9 in an industry with three firms, 11.0 with four firms, and 10.7 in an industry with eight firms.) Note, too, that with this low interest rate, the efficient price is almost constant over time. But the monopolist, even though he internalizes all of the externalities in learning, charges a higher price initially, and allows price to fall gradually as costs fall.

In the next example, the elasticity of demand is increased to $B = 2.3$, the interest rate is kept at $r = 0.01$, and the other parameters are as before. Recall that with a higher elasticity of demand, increasing the number of firms has a relatively smaller effect in a static Cournot model. Here, with a low interest rate and a high elasticity of demand, the free-rider problem clearly dominates until unit cost is quite low. When unit cost is high, the curves in Figures 3(a) and 3(b) lie in just the reverse of their usual Cournot order: As shown, price is lower with one firm than with two and is highest of all under perfect competition. Over an intermediate cost range, the curves cross and resume their usual ordering as cost reaches its minimum. [The curves for $n = 3, 4, 8$ (not shown) are ordered and lie between those for $n = 2$ and perfect competition for $c = 1$ and $c = 10$ and they cross at intermediate values.] Note that both the efficient producer and the monopolist now charge a virtually constant price.

These examples illustrate that changes in industry structure have a wide range of possible effects depending on other parameters of the model and that changes in the elasticity of demand or the interest rate can interact in rather complicated ways.

6   Conclusions

In this chapter, the dynamics of industry behavior have been studied under the assumption of industrywide learning.[4] The existence and uniqueness of a symmetric equilibrium for any industry structure was established, and qualitative properties of the equilibria were developed. In particular, it was shown that price falls over time and that marginal revenue at any date lies between current unit cost and minimum unit cost. As shown by example, price may lie below current unit cost during the early phases of the industry. That is, firms may earn initial losses. Examples were also provided to illustrate some of the possible effects of industry structure on the equilibrium price path.

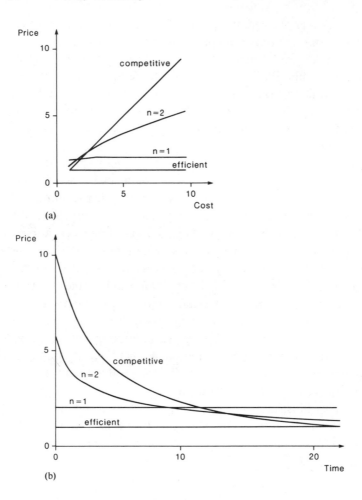

Figure 3. Price as a function of (a) cost and (b) time for various industry structures. The price elasticity of demand is 2.3, the interest rate
is 0.01, and the elasticity of cost with respect to cumulative output is
0.32.

Perhaps the most dramatic feature of the examples is the wide diver-
gence, in the early stages of an industry, between efficient prices and
equilibrium prices for *any* industry structure. This suggests that under-
investment in learning is not a minor source of inefficiency. The efficacy
of policies designed to compensate for externalities in learning is a subject for further research.

Appendix

Overview of the proof of Theorem 1

The proof will draw on a series of lemmas. Let $\mathcal{F}$ be the space of continuous functions satisfying the bounds in (14), with the sup norm. Lemmas 1 and 2 show that (11) can be used to define an operator on $\mathcal{F}$. Lemma 3 shows that this operator maps $\mathcal{F}$ into the subspace of itself, $\mathcal{F}_k$, consisting of functions that satisfy a Lipschitz condition. Lemmas 4 and 5 show that this operator is a contraction on each of a sequence of spaces $\mathcal{F}_k[X_i, X_1]$ of functions with restricted domain. The proof of the theorem then rests on an induction argument that involves the contraction property at each stage. It is assumed throughout the appendix that the hypotheses of Theorem 1 hold.

Define $H: \mathcal{F} \times [0, X_1] \to \mathbb{R}$ by

$$H(f, X_0) = \rho \int_0^T e^{-\rho t} \gamma(f(x(t)))\, dt + e^{-\rho T} V \qquad (19)$$

where

$$x(0) = X_0, \qquad x(T) = X_1, \qquad x'(t) = nf(x(t)).$$

Also define $b(x) \equiv \gamma(a(x))$, $x \in [0, X_1]$, and $B \equiv \gamma(A)$. The relevant properties of H are given in Lemma 1.

Lemma 1. H as given by equation (19) is well defined, with

$$b(X_0) \le H(f, X_0) \le B, \qquad f \in \mathcal{F},\ X_0 \in [0, X_1]. \qquad (20)$$

Moreover, H is once continuously differentiable with respect to X_0, with

$$|\partial H(f, X_0)/\partial X_0| \le \rho[B - b(0)]/na(0) = k_0, \qquad f \in \mathcal{F},\ X_0 \in [0, X_1]. \qquad (21)$$

Proof: Since $a(x)$ is increasing, $a(x) \le A$, and f satisfies (14), it follows that the integrand in (19) lies in the interval $[\gamma(a(X_0)), \gamma(A)] = [b(X_0), B]$, for all $t \in [0, T]$. Then (f) implies (20).

For any $f \in \mathcal{F}$, $X_0 \in [0, X_1]$, and $\delta > 0$, define

$$\hat{H}(f, X_0, \delta) = e^{\rho \delta}\left[\rho \int_\delta^T e^{-\rho t} \gamma(f(x(t)))\, dt + e^{-\rho T} V\right],$$

where $x(t)$ and T are as in (19). Note that for any $\epsilon > 0$, if $\delta > 0$ is chosen so that $x(\delta) = X_0 + \epsilon$, then by definition $\hat{H}(f, X_0, \delta) = H(f, X_0 + \epsilon)$. Moreover, for $\epsilon > 0$ sufficiently small, $\epsilon \approx \delta nf(X_0)$. Therefore,

$$\left|\frac{\partial H(F, X_0 + \epsilon)}{\partial \epsilon}\right|_{\epsilon=0} = \left|\frac{\partial \hat{H}(f, X_0, \delta)}{\partial \delta}\right|_{\delta=0} \left|\frac{d\delta}{d\epsilon}\right|_{\epsilon=0}$$

$$= |\rho \hat{H}(f, X_0, 0) - \rho\gamma(f(X_0))|/nf(X_0)$$

$$= \rho|H(f, X_0) - \gamma(f(X_0))|/nf(X_0)$$

$$\leq \rho[B - b(X_0)]/na(X_0)$$

$$\leq \rho[B - b(0)]/na(0),$$

where the last line uses the fact that $a(x)$ and $b(x)$ are both increasing. ∎

Next, note that (c)–(e) imply that ϕ has an inverse with respect to its first argument. For each $X_0 \in [0, X_1]$, define ψ by

$$\phi(\psi(z, X_0), X_0) = z, \qquad z \in [b(X_0), B]. \tag{22}$$

Lemma 2. ψ as given by (22) is well defined, and for each $X_0 \in [0, X_1]$, the range of $\psi(\cdot, X_0)$ on $[b(X_0), B]$ is contained in $[a(X_0), A]$. Moreover, $\psi(z, X_0)$ is continuous and satisfies the Lipschitz conditions

$$0 < |\psi(z, x) - \psi(z', x)| \leq |z - z'|/k_1, \qquad z, z' \in [b(x), B], \; x \in [0, X_1],$$
$$\tag{23}$$
$$0 \leq |\psi(z, x) - \psi(z, x')| \leq k_2|x - x'|/k_1, \qquad z \in [b(x), B], \; x, x' \in [0, X_1],$$

and if ϕ is once differentiable, then so is ψ.

Proof: The claims follow directly from (c)–(e), the inverse function theorem, and the chain rule. ∎

From Lemmas 1 and 2, it follows that (11) can be written as

$$\psi(H(g, X_0), X_0) = g(X_0), \qquad X_0 \in [0, X_1]. \tag{24}$$

The next step is to use (24) to define an operator T on $\mathcal{F}$. For $f \in \mathcal{F}$, let

$$Tf(X_0) = \psi(H(f, X_0), X_0), \qquad X_0 \in [0, X_1]. \tag{25}$$

Lemma 3. The operator T on $\mathcal{F}$ given by (25) is well defined, and $T: \mathcal{F} \to \mathcal{F}$. Moreover, Tf satisfies the Lipschitz condition

$$|Tf(X_0) - Tf(X_0')| \leq [k_0/k_1 + k_2/k_1]|X_0 - X_0'| = k|X_0 - X_0'|. \tag{26}$$

If ϕ is once differentiable, then so is Tf.

Proof: It follows from (20) and (22) of Lemmas 1 and 2 that Tf is well defined, continuous, and satisfies the bounds in (14). Hence, $T: \mathfrak{F} \to \mathfrak{F}$. It follows directly from (25), (23), and (21) that

$$|Tf(X_0) - Tf(X_0')| = |\psi(H(f, X_0), X_0) - \psi(H(f, X_0'), X_0')|$$

$$\leq |H(f, X_0) - H(f, X_0')|/k_1 + |X_0 - X_0'|k_2/k_1$$

$$\leq |X_0 - X_0'|[k_0/k_1 + k_2/k_1].$$

The differentiability of Tf follows directly from the differentiability of ψ and H.   ■

The proof that (24) has a unique solution will be by induction. Each stage in the induction will use a contraction argument, which in turn requires defining an appropriate sequence of function spaces.

For any $X_i \in [0, X_1]$, suppose that there exists a continuous function g_i on $[X_i, X_1]$ satisfying (14) and (24). Then for any X_{i+1}, with $0 \leq X_{i+1} \leq X_i \leq X_1$, define $\mathfrak{F}[X_{i+1}, X_1]$ to be the space of continuous functions on $[X_{i+1}, X_1]$ that satisfy (14), and coincide with g_i on $[X_i, X_1]$. Let $\mathfrak{F}_k[X_{i+1}, X_1]$ be the space of functions that in addition satisfy the Lipschitz condition

$$|f(x) - f(x')| \leq k|x - x'|, \tag{27}$$

where k is given by (26). Note that $F_k[X_{i+1}, X_1]$ is a complete metric space.

The main step in the proof is to show that for an appropriate choice of X_i's, T is a contraction on each of the sequence of spaces defined above. A preliminary result is proved in Lemma 4.

Lemma 4. Let X_i, g_i, X_{i+1}, and $\mathfrak{F}_k[X_{i+1}, X_1]$ be as above, let $f_1, f_2 \in \mathfrak{F}_k[X_{i+1}, X_1]$, with $\|f_1 - f_2\| = \delta$, and let $\tau = (X_i - X_{i+1})/na(0)$. Choose $X_0 \in [X_{i+1}, X_i]$. Then

$$|x_1(t) - x_2(t)| \leq \frac{\delta}{k}(e^{nkt} - 1), \qquad t \geq 0, \tag{28}$$

and

$$|T_1 - T_2| \leq \frac{\delta}{kna(0)}(e^{nk\tau} - 1), \tag{29}$$

where $x_1(t)$, $x_2(t)$, T_1, and T_2 are given by

$$x_j(0) = X_0, \qquad x_j(T_j) = X_i, \tag{30}$$

$$x_j'(t) = nf_j(x_j(t)), \qquad 0 \le t, \ j = 1, 2.$$

Proof: First consider (28). Let $\Delta(t) = x_1(t) - x_2(t)$. Then

$$|\Delta'(t)| \le n[|f_1(x_1(t)) - f_1(x_2(t))| + |f_1(x_2(t)) - f_2(x_2(t))|]$$

$$\le n[k|\Delta(t)| + \delta],$$

and (28) follows directly.

Next consider (29). Note that

$$\int_0^{T_1} nf_1(x_1(t)) \, dt = (X_i - X_0) = \int_0^{T_2} nf_2(x_2(t)) \, dt.$$

Without loss of generality, suppose $T_2 \ge T_1$. Then

$$|T_2 - T_1| na(0) \le |T_2 - T_1| na(X_0)$$

$$\le \left| \int_{T_1}^{T_2} nf_2(x_2(t)) \, dt \right|$$

$$= \left| \int_0^{T_1} n[f_1(x_1) - f_1(x_2) + f_1(x_2) - f_2(x_2)] \, dt \right|$$

$$\le \int_0^{T_1} n[k|x_1 - x_2| + \delta] \, dt$$

$$\le \int_0^{T_1} n\delta(e^{nkt} - 1 + 1) \, dt$$

$$\le \frac{\delta}{k} [e^{nk\tau} - 1],$$

where the last line uses the fact that since f_1 satisfies (14), $T_1 \le \tau$. ∎

The next lemma uses these bounds to show that given $X_i \le X_1$ and a solution g_i on $[X_i, X_1]$ for a suitable choice of $X_{i+1} < X_i$, the operator T is a contraction on the space of functions $\mathcal{F}_k[X_{i+1}, X_1]$ defined above.

Lemma 5. Suppose that for $0 < X_i \le X_1$, there exists a continuous function g_i on $[X_i, X_1]$ satisfying (14) and (24). Choose $0 < \beta < 1$, and choose $0 \le X_{i+1} < X_i$, such that

$$\frac{\rho}{k_1}\left[\frac{w}{nk-\rho}(e^{(nk-\rho)\tau}-1)+\frac{B-b(0)}{kna(0)}e^{-\rho\theta}(e^{nk\tau}-1)\right]<\beta, \qquad (31)$$

where $\tau=(X_i-X_{i+1})/na(0)$ and $\theta=(X_i-X_{i+1})/nA$, and such that

$$X_i-X_{i+1}<na(0)A/\rho(A-a(0)). \qquad (32)$$

There exists a unique continuous function g_{i+1} on $[X_{i+1},X_1]$ that satisfies (14) and (24) and coincides with g_i on $[X_i,X_1]$. Moreover, g_{i+1} is once continuously differentiable.

Proof: Let X_i, g_i, and X_{i+1} satisfy the hypotheses of the lemma, and let the space $\mathcal{F}[X_{i+1},X_1]$ be defined as above. Any continuous function g_{i+1} satisfying (14) and (24) and coinciding with g_i on $[X_i,X_1]$ is a fixed point of the operator T defined in (25) applied to $\mathcal{F}[X_{i+1},X_1]$. By Lemma 3, any such function is once continuously differentiable on $[X_{i+1},X_1]$. Hence it is sufficient to show that T has a unique fixed point on $\mathcal{F}_k[X_{i+1},X_1]$. Since $\mathcal{F}_k[X_{i+1},X_1]$ is a complete metric space, it is sufficient to show that T is a contraction on it.

Define

$$v_i=\rho\int_0^T e^{-\rho t}\gamma(g_i(x(t)))\,dt+e^{-\rho T}V,$$

where

$$x(0)=X_i, \qquad x(T)=X_1, \qquad x'(t)=ng_i(x(t)).$$

Since f satisfies the bounds in (14), it follows that $b(x(t))\le\gamma(g_i(x(t))\le B$ for $t\in[0,T]$. Since $a(x)$ is increasing, (f) implies that $v_i\in[b(X_i),B]$.

For any $X_0\in[X_{i+1},X_i]$, it follows from the definitions of T and H and from Lemma 2 that, for $f_1,f_2\in\mathcal{F}_k[X_{i+1},X_1]$,

$$|Tf_1(X_0)-Tf_2(X_0)|=|\psi(H(f_1,X_0),X_0)-\psi(H(f_2,X_0),X_0)|$$

$$\le\frac{1}{k_1}|H(f_1,X_0)-H(f_2,X_0)|$$

$$=\frac{1}{k_1}\left|\int_0^{T_1}e^{-\rho t}\rho\gamma(f_1(x_1(t)))\,dt+\int_0^{T_2}e^{-\rho t}\rho\gamma(f_2(x_2(t)))\right.$$

$$\left.+(e^{-\rho T_1}-e^{-\rho T_2})v_i\right|,$$

where $x_1(t)$, $x_2(t)$, T_1, and T_2 are given by (30).

Let $\delta=\|f_1-f_2\|$. Without loss of generality, suppose that $T_2\le T_1$. Note, too, that since f_1,f_2 satisfy (14), $\theta\le T_1,T_2\le\tau$. Hence it follows from (b), the bounds on v_i, and Lemma 4 that the expression above is

$$\leq \frac{1}{k_1} \left[\int_0^{T_2} e^{-\rho t} \rho [|\gamma(f_1(x_1)) - \gamma(f_1(x_2))| \right.$$

$$+ |\gamma(f_1(x_2)) - \gamma(f_2(x_2))|] \, dt$$

$$\left. + \left| \int_{T_2}^{T_1} e^{-\rho t} \rho \gamma(f_1(x_1)) \, dt + (e^{-\rho T_1} - e^{-\rho T_2}) v_i \right| \right]$$

$$\leq \frac{1}{k_1} \left[\int_0^{T_2} e^{-\rho t} \rho w [k |x_1 - x_2| + \delta] \, dt \right.$$

$$\left. + \left| \int_{T_2}^{T_1} e^{-\rho t} \rho [\gamma(f_1(x_1)) - v_i] \, dt \right| \right]$$

$$\leq \frac{1}{k_1} \left[\int_0^{T} e^{-\rho t} \rho w \delta e^{nkt} \, dt \right.$$

$$\left. + (B - b(X_0)) e^{-\rho T_2} [1 - e^{\rho(T_2 - T_1)}] \right].$$

Since $X_{i+1} - X_i$ satisfies (32), and f_1, f_2 satisfy (14), it follows that $0 \leq \rho |T_1 - T_2| \leq \rho(\tau - \theta) < 1$. Now for any $z > -1$, $\ln(1+z) \leq z$, so that $-z \geq 1 - e^z$. Hence it follows from Lemma 4 that the expression above is

$$\leq \frac{1}{k_1} \left[\frac{\delta w \rho}{nk - \rho} [e^{(nk - \rho)\tau} - 1] + (B - b(0)) e^{-\rho \theta} \rho(T_1 - T_2) \right]$$

$$\leq \frac{\delta \rho}{k_1} \left[\frac{w}{nk - \rho} [e^{(nk - \rho)\tau} - 1] + \frac{B - b(0)}{kna(0)} e^{-\rho \theta} (e^{nk\tau} - 1) \right]$$

$$\leq \beta \delta.$$

Since all functions in $\mathfrak{F}_k[X_{i+1}, X_1]$ coincide on $[X_i, X_1]$, it follows that for $X_0 \in [X_i, X_1]$, $|Tf_1(X_0) - Tf_2(X_0)| = 0$. Hence

$$\|Tf_1 - Tf_2\| \leq \beta \|f_1 - f_2\|, \qquad \text{for all } f_1, f_2,$$

and T is a contraction on $\mathfrak{F}_k[X_{i+1}, X_i]$.   ■

Proof of Theorem 1: Since $V \in [b(X_1), B]$, by Lemma 2, there exists a unique value g_1 satisfying

$$g_1 = \psi(V, X_1).$$

Moreover, $g_1 \in [a(X_1), A]$. Clearly, any solution of (11) must satisfy $g(X_1) = g_1$.

Then by repeated application of Lemma 5, this solution has a unique extension to the interval $[0, X_1]$. If ϕ is differentiable, then by Lemma 3, so is Tf, for all $f \in \mathcal{F}$. Hence the solution g is continuously differentiable. ∎

Proof of Theorem 3: If $V = B$ and f is nondecreasing, then it follows from (19) and the hypotheses of Theorem 1 that $H(f, X_0)$ is nondecreasing in X_0. Hence by (25) and Lemmas 2 and 3, Tf is strictly increasing. Hence the arguments above apply when attention is restricted to the space $\mathcal{F}' = (f \in \mathcal{F} \mid f$ is nondecreasing$)$. Hence $g \in \mathcal{F}'$, and since $g = Tg$, g is strictly increasing. ∎

NOTES

1 In this respect the model is quite different from those of Rosen (1972), Spence (1981), and Fudenberg and Tirole (1983), in which firm-specific learning is considered. Rosen considers the decision problem facing a single firm, Spence analyzes industry equilibria in path strategies (i.e., with precommitment), and Fudenberg and Tirole compare equilibria in path and decision rule strategies (i.e., with and without precommitment) for a two-period version of Spence's model, showing that they may be qualitatively very different. See Reinganum and Stokey (1985) for a discussion of equilibria with and without precommitment and an example where the difference is crucial.

2 An analysis of the monopoly problem, including more general specifications of the cost and demand functions, may be found in Clarke, Darrough, and Heineke (1982).

3 The solutions were computed using a BASIC program, available on request from the author.

4 The analysis in this essay also applies, with one sign change, to an industry extracting a common property resource, where unit cost increases with cumulative extraction to date.

REFERENCES

Amit, R. (1985), "Cost leadership strategy and experience curves," mimeo, Northwestern University.

Arrow, K. J. (1962), "The economic implications of learning by doing," *Review of Economic Studies,* 29: 153–73.

Bass, F. M. (1980), "The relationship between diffusion rates, experience curves, and demand elasticities for consumer durable technological innovations," *Journal of Business,* 53: 51–67.

Clarke, F. H., M. N. Darrough, and J. Heineke (1982), "Optimal pricing policy in the presence of experience effects," *Journal of Business,* 55: 517–30.

Fudenberg, D. and J. Tirole (1983), "Learning-by-doing and market performance," *Bell Journal of Economics,* 14: 522–30.

Ghemawat, P. and M. Spence (1983), "Learning curve spillovers, shared experience and market performance," Harvard Institute of Economic Research Discussion Paper No. 968, Harvard University.

Hall, W. P. (1983), "The learning curve, industry equilibrium, and economic performance," Economic Policy Office Discussion Paper No. 83-15, Antitrust Division, U.S. Department of Justice.

Lieberman, M. B. (1984), "The learning curve and pricing in the chemical processing industry," *The Rand Journal of Economics,* 15: 213–28.

Rapping, L. (1965), "Learning and World War II production functions," *Review of Economics and Statistics,* 48: 81–6.

Reinganum, J. and N. L. Stokey (1985), "Oligopoly extraction of a common property natural resource," *International Economic Review,* 26: 161–73.

Rosen, S. (1972), "Learning by experience as joint production," *The Quarterly Journal of Economics,* 86: 366–82.

Ross, D. R. (1984), "The significance of learning in reducing costs," Mimeo, Department of Economics, Williams College.

Sheshinski, E. (1967), "Tests of the learning-by-doing hypothesis," *Review of Economics and Statistics,* 49: 568–78.

Spence, A. M. (1981), "The learning curve and competition," *Bell Journal of Economics,* 8: 49–70.

Starr, A. W. and Y. C. Ho (1969), "Nonzero-sum differential games," *Journal of Optimization Theory and Applications,* 3: 184–206.

CHAPTER 4

Decentralized trade in a credit economy

Ross M. Starr

The enemy was repelled. But victory was not won. The war
dragged on for a year and there was no decision. Gold grew
scarce, and again the Government was in despair.

I easily relieved them. "Write," I said, "promises on paper
to be repaid in gold." They did as I advised – paying me (at
my request) a trifle of half a million for the advice. I handled
the affair – on a merely nominal profit. I punctually met for
another year every note that was paid in. But too many were
presented, for the war seemed unending and entered a third
year.

Then did I conceive yet another stupendous thing. "Bid them,"
said I to the Sultan, "take the notes as money. Cease to repay.
Write, not 'I will on delivery of this paper pay a piece of gold,'
but, 'this is a piece of gold.'"

He did as I told him. The next day the Vizier came to me
with the story of an insolent fellow to whom fifty such notes
had been offered as payment for a camel for the war and who
had sent back, not a camel, but another piece of paper on which
was written "This is a camel."

"Cut off his head!" said I.

It was done, and the warning sufficed. The paper was taken
and the war proceeded.

Hilaire Belloc, The mercy of Allah, 1922

1 Bilateral trade

It is shown by Ostroy and Starr (1974) that the use of money (a single
good entering asymmetrically in the trading process) allows a decentralized trading procedure to achieve a market equilibrium allocation in a

Financial support of NSF Grant SOC–78–15429 is gratefully acknowledged. I became interested in this problem through conversations with Neil Wallace at the Cornell Conference on Economic Theory, August 1981. Conversations with Peter Kim, comments of
W. P. Heller, and the UCSD Advanced Economic Theory class have been most helpful.
Oversights are my own.

fixed, relatively short trading time. The allocation could otherwise be achieved equally rapidly using more elaborate organization. Alternatively, nonmonetary decentralized trade can approach the equilibrium allocation as the limit of a slower process (Starr 1976). A maintained assumption throughout the above studies is nonnegativity of commodity holdings. This represents a restriction on the issue of IOUs. The result of this restriction is that sufficient conditions for successful execution of monetary trade are relatively strong. All agents require sufficiently large money endowment to support monetary trade. The theorems in this chapter investigate a relaxation of the nonnegativity restriction to allow the use of credit. This allows the extension of effective decentralized trade to economies without sufficient initial money stocks to support effective monetary trade.

There is a trivial and unsatisfactory sense in which relaxation of the nonnegativity requirement on goods holdings can allow effective decentralized trade. If we delete the nonnegativity restriction (A.1), rule μ of Ostroy and Starr (1974) will always lead to full execution (E) in one round. Taking advantage of the relaxed condition would amount to some agents delivering goods (particularly good m) that they do not own. They would hold negative stocks of the goods to be replenished on subsequent trades. They are assured that they will have the opportunity to do so since prices and demands are market clearing. The difficulty here is not for those whose stocks would occasionally become negative but rather for the recipients in trade of these goods. They would be required to accept and use an IOU for good m as though it were good m. Obviously, this is impractical. A serious investigation of the role of credit arrangements must distinguish as separate commodities goods and IOUs for those goods. This is the approach taken in this essay.

Three credit structures are considered: bank credit, trade credit, and commodity credit. Under the bank credit regime, agents borrow bank notes or bank deposits at the outset of trade that they repay at trade's end. The bank notes or deposits are traded as money. Trade moves to the equilibrium allocation almost as expeditiously as in a fully monetary economy; extra time is required at the start and end of trade only to arrange loans and their repayment. The simplicity of monetary trade is preserved under the bank credit regime.

Commodity credit is characterized by promissory notes for specific goods. Trade in nonmonetary goods here requires twice the time of the preceding models since essentially all goods – or promises to deliver them –

are acting as money. A typical commodity promised in exchange will not go directly from supplier to demander. Rather, those goods needed to fulfill promissory notes go from suppliers to those who have incurred debts denominated in them to the creditors who are final demanders.

Trade credit consists of promises to pay money – when available – in exchange for the current receipt of goods. The delivery of nonmonetary goods is expeditiously arranged, with promissory notes accepted in payment, but repayment of the notes may take a long time as the limited supply of the monetary commodity is used to retire the debt. The efficacy and decentralization of this process with respect to delivery of goods is demonstrated, but repayment of debt may be complex. Indeed, I conjecture that it is not generally decentralizable; hence it will not generally terminate in finite time without the use of a centralized clearing mechanism – a bank. There is a family resemblance of the difficulties here with those of Townsend and Wallace (1984). Effective solutions are possible in principle, but achieving them expeditiously requires coordination, which may not be possible in a decentralized fashion.

Alternative credit arrangements are capable of overcoming a shortage of the monetary commodity as an impediment to trade. Bank credit allows the convenience of monetary trade but requires an additional institution and the time and resources required to arrange financing. Repayment of commodity credit is completed in a relatively short time, but the frequency and complexity of trade is greater than for the alternate arrangements. Trade credit does not require an additional financial institution but may require long waits for repayment of monetary debt and may not be fully decentralizable.

It is unsurprising – to the point of triviality – that sufficient credit arrangements should overcome a shortage of medium of exchange to allow full execution of a trading plan. Hence the bank credit results are useful but not deep. The curious and somewhat unsettling result of this study is in the nature of a partial converse to the efficacy of bank credit. The simplification provided by the single bank (or banking system) and by the uniqueness of its credit instruments appears to be essential to the efficacy of a credit trading process. Among the credit arrangements considered, it is unique in combining simplicity with decentralization. Commodity credit is decentralizable but complicated by the variety of goods acting as media of exchange. Trade credit does not seem to be decentralizable for convergence in finite trading time.

Bilateral trade: the setting

Let there be N commodities indexed by $n = 1, \ldots, N$ and a set of J traders, I, indexed by $i = 1, \ldots, J$. Let each trader have an *endowment bundle* b_i. Prices are assumed strictly positive. Trader i's desired net trade vector at price vector p is z_i; the matrix of b_i is denoted B, and the matrix of z_i is denoted Z, where $p, b_i, z_i \in \mathbb{R}^N$.

The vector p is said to be an equilibrium price vector if

(U.1) $p \cdot z_i = 0$,   each $i \in I$,

(U.2) $\sum_i z_i = 0$,   and

(U.3) $z_i \geq -b_i$ componentwise.

Trade is supposed to take place between one trader and another, in pairs. A trader can be a member of only one pair at a time; it requires τ periods for each trader to form a pair with every other trader precisely once, where

$$\tau = \begin{cases} J-1 & \text{if } J \text{ is even,} \\ J & \text{if } J \text{ is odd.} \end{cases}$$

A sequence of meetings in τ periods in which each trader meets each other trader precisely once is called a round.

At the start of the tth period, trader i's holdings will be represented by w_i^t with $w_i^1 = b_i$. The change in i's holdings between t and $t+1$, $a_i^t = w_i^{t+1} - w_i^t$, is the trade i performs in period t. Trader i's hitherto unsatisfied excess demands on entering period t are

$$v_i^t = v_i^1 - \sum_{T=1}^{T=t-1} a_i^T, \quad \text{with } v_i^1 = z_i.$$

Consider the meeting and trade between i and j. $\pi^t(i) = j$ means that i meets j at time t. Positive entries in a_i^t indicate goods going from j to i, and negative entries indicate goods going from i to j. We consider the following three restrictions on a_i^t and a_j^t:

(A.1)   Nonnegativity of holdings, no IOUs,

$$w_i^t + a_i^t \geq 0, \qquad w_j^t + a_j^t \geq 0.$$

(A.2)   Conservation of commodities,

$$a_i^t = -a_j^t.$$

(A.3)   Quid pro quo,

$$p \cdot a_i^t = 0 = p \cdot a_j^t.$$

At the end of one round, the outcome is $w_i^{\tau+1} = b_i + \Sigma_{t=1}^\tau a_i^t$. If

(E) $\displaystyle\sum_{t=1}^{t=\tau} a_i^t = z_i,$ for all $i \in I,$

we will say that *full execution* of the competitive equilibrium has been achieved in one round.

A trading rule is a function that tells each pair what trade to make. The inputs for the decision are not only what they have on hand – which defines what they can do – but what they know. Define a trading rule as a function

$$\rho(w_i^t, w_j^t \mid L^t) = (a_i^t, a_j^t),$$

where L^t is the set of information, beyond their current holdings, available to the pair at date t.

A rule is thought of as *decentralized* if it does not require more information than i, j are likely to possess. More precisely, varying degrees of modest informational requirements are characterized as

(D.1) $L^t = \{(v_i^t, v_j^t)\},$

(D.2) $L^t = \{(v_i^t, v_j^t), (i, j)\},$

(D.3) $L^t = \{(v_i^t, v_i^{t-1}, ..., v_i^1; v_j^t, v_j^{t-1}, ..., v_j^1), (i, j)\}.$

A trading rule is *centralized* if it requires more information than (D.1)–(D.3) can provide.

It is shown in Ostroy and Starr (1974) and Starr (1976) that:

(i)   There is a centralized (i.e., not decentralized) procedure that achieves the equlibrium allocation for an arbitrary economy in one round.

(ii)   It is not in general possible to find a decentralized procedure that achieves the equilibrium allocation for an arbitrary economy in one round.

(iii) In a monetary economy with sufficiently large stocks of the monetary good, there is a decentralized procedure that achieves the equilibrium allocation in one round. Money allows the decentralization of trade.

(iv)   There is a decentralized trading procedure for an arbitrary (non-monetary) economy that converges geometrically to full execution as the number of rounds increases.

2   Decentralized monetary trade with bank credit

To discuss trade with bank credit, we shall distinguish a single agent as the bank, β, and two commodities: debt d and bank notes c. The notes are understood to be redeemable at par for one unit of good m, the monetary commodity. Their price is $p_c = p_m$. The convention on d is that agents may hold negative amounts of d (unlike other goods), but d is traded only with the bank, β. The bank is unique in being allowed to hold (i.e., to issue) negative amounts of bank notes c. If we lacked a convention of this form to augment the stock of good m, the speed of execution of monetary trade would depend on the physical volume of m available and the efficacy of its transfer among a succession of debtors and creditors. The rationalization for the convention is behavioral; though the promissory notes of individual agents may not be reliable, those of the bank are known to be so.

Monetary trade then proceeds as follows: During the first round, agents go to the bank to sell good m and personal debt for bank notes c to finance their planned trades. During the next round, they use monetary trade with c as money to fulfill all outstanding excess demands except those for m, which is still held by the bank. In a third round, all trades are again with the bank. Debt is paid off by return of c, and demands for m can be satisfied.

This process requires two conventions: The nonnegativity restriction is relaxed with regard to debt issued by individuals to the bank and with regard to bank notes issued by the bank, (A.1.BC) below; full execution requires three rounds, (E.3) below, the first and last devoted to financial transactions only. The nonnegativity restriction (A.1) then becomes

(A.1.BC)
$$w_{in}^t + a_{in}^t \geq 0, \qquad w_{jn}^t + a_{jn}^t \geq 0$$
$$(n = 1, \ldots, N, \; n \neq d; \; j, i \neq \beta),$$
$$w_{\beta n}^t + a_{\beta n}^t \geq 0 \qquad (n = 1, \ldots, N, \; n \neq c).$$

The full execution criterion then is

(E.3) $\displaystyle\sum_{t=1}^{3\tau} a_i^t = z_i, \quad$ for all $i \in I$.

Debt-financed monetary trade is then characterized by *trading rule* δ: For $\pi^t(i) = j$, let

$$a_i^t = x_i^t + y_i^t, \qquad a_j^t = x_j^t + y_j^t,$$

where:

Round 1. $1 \le t \le \tau$:
For $i \ne \beta \ne j$,

$$a_i^t = 0.$$

For $i = \beta$,

$$x_{jn}^t = 0, n \ne m, d, c,$$

$$x_{\beta m}^t = -x_{jm}^t = b_{jm},$$

$$x_{\beta d}^t = -x_{jd}^t = \max\left[0, \frac{1}{p_m}(p \cdot [z_j]^+) - b_{jm}\right],$$

$$x_{jc}^t = -x_{\beta c}^t = (x_{jm}^t + x_{jd}^t),$$

$$y_i^t \equiv y_j^t \equiv 0.$$

Round 2. $\tau + 1 \le t \le 2\tau$:

$$x_{in}^t = -x_{jn}^t = \begin{cases} 0 & \text{if } v_{in}^t v_{jn}^t \ge 0, \\ \min(|v_{in}^t|, |v_{jn}^t|) & \text{if } v_{jn}^t < 0, \ v_{in}^t > 0, \\ -\min(|v_{in}^t|, |v_{jn}^t|) & \text{if } v_{jn}^t > 0, \ v_{in}^t < 0, \end{cases}$$

$$y_{in}^t = -y_{jn}^t = \begin{cases} 0 & \text{if } n \ne c, \\ -\dfrac{1}{p_m} p \cdot x_i^t & \text{if } n = c, \end{cases}$$

Round 3. $2\tau + 1 \le t \le 3\tau$:
For $i \ne \beta \ne j$,

$$x_j^t = y_j^t = x_i^t = y_i^t = 0.$$

For $i = \beta$,

$$x_{\beta m}^t = -x_{jm}^t = -v_{jm}^t,$$

$$x_{\beta d}^t = -x_{jd}^t = x_{jm}^t + v_{jc}^t,$$

$$x_{\beta c}^t = -x_{jc}^t = -w_{jc}^t,$$

$$y_\beta^t = 0 = y_j^t.$$

Theorem 1. Let (p, Z, B) satisfy (U) and let trade proceed according to trading rule δ. Then (A.1.BC), (A.2), (A.3), (D.3), and (E.3) are fulfilled. That is, the rule is decentralized and achieves full execution in three rounds.

Proof: At $t = \tau + 1$ (beginning of the second round), the assumptions of Ostroy and Starr (1974, Theorem 4) are fulfilled with good c acting in place of good m. Rule δ for $\tau+1 \leq t \leq 2\tau$, $n \neq c, d, m$, coincides with rule μ of Ostroy and Starr. Hence $\sum_{t=1}^{2\tau} a_{in}^t = z_{in}$ for all $i, n \neq c, d, m$. Thus (A.1.BC), (A.2), (A.3) are all fulfilled for $1 \leq t \leq 2\tau$. Further, $v_{in}^{2\tau+1} = 0$, $n \neq m, c, d$ for all i. This follows from Ostroy and Starr, Theorem 4. Hence, if no further trade is pursued in these goods, (E.3) will be fulfilled in $n \neq c, d, m$. Finally, rule δ requires no more information than is embodied in (D.3), which includes the names of i, j, current excess demands and their trading histories (from which the trading date can be inferred).

We must now demonstrate (A.1.BC), (A.2), and (A.3) with regard to m, d, and c in $2\tau+1 \leq t \leq 3\tau$; we must also demonstrate (E.3) for these goods. For $i \neq \beta$, $\pi^t(j) = \beta$, $2\tau+1 \leq t \leq 3\tau$, we have $v_{jm}^t = z_{jm} + b_{jm}$:

$$v_{jd}^t = \max\left[0, \frac{1}{p_m}(p \cdot [z_j]^+) - b_{jm}\right],$$

$$v_{jc}^t = \min\left[-b_{jm}, -\frac{1}{p_m}(p \cdot [z_j]^+)\right] - z_{jm}.$$

The last expression follows since $p_c = p_d = p_m$ and $p \cdot z_j = 0$ [by (U.1)]. But

$$v_{\beta m}^{\tau+1} = -\sum_i b_{im} + z_{\beta m} + b_{\beta m},$$

$$v_{\beta d}^{\tau+1} = -\sum_{i \neq \beta} \max\left[0, \frac{1}{p_m}(p \cdot [z_i]^+) - b_{im}\right],$$

$$v_{\beta c}^{\tau+1} = \sum_{i \neq \beta} \left\{b_{im} + \max\left[0, \frac{1}{p_m}(p \cdot [z_i]^+) - b_{im}\right]\right\}.$$

Hence following rule δ, $v_i^{3\tau+1} = 0$ for all i.   Q.E.D.

The theorem says that a relatively plausible decentralized trading process making active use of bank credit can achieve full execution of the equilibrium allocation in three rounds. There is one round of active trade. The first and third rounds are devoted to financial transactions. In the first round, agents go to the bank and arrange sufficiently large bank note balances (in exchange for debt) so that they are sure to be able to pay for all their purchases in the succeeding round. In the second round, bank notes act as money. Conventional monetary trade is used: Real goods go from net suppliers to net demanders and payment is made in bank notes. In the third round, individuals repay their bank debt; those who have surplus bank notes receive payment in specie (commodity m).

Commodity credit, the uniqueness of "money" and of the bank

The simplicity introduced by the use of a single bank or single medium of exchange shortens the time required for full execution. The greater flexibility that may be provided by multiple media of exchange or multiple sources of credit can be shown to result in corresponding greater complexity.

The simplicity of monetary trade with a single medium of exchange (rule μ of Ostroy and Starr) comes essentially from Walras' law. A general equilibrium system is typically overdetermined by one equation; if all but one market clears, the one remaining clears as well. The monetary trade rule (rule μ of Ostroy and Starr or the second round of rule δ above) assures market clearing on all of the goods markets but one. Hence the final market, for money, clears as a residual. This simplification, of course, is lost if more than one market is left uncleared at the end of the round of monetary trade. Hence the greater time and complexity required of rule γ in Starr (1976) where all goods act as money.

In the study of credit arrangements, two alternative modes show up: promissory notes payable in money and promises to deliver specified commodities. We can think of the first as trade credit and the second as commodity credit. The difficulty here is that credit is necessarily a named good. The promissory notes of David Rockefeller are distinct from those of Billy Sol Estes. Thus, though promises to pay will typically sum to zero, they will need to be executed separately. This amounts to a substantial increase in the dimension of the goods space with a corresponding added complexity. Thus, in a trade credit regime, after the completion of trade in nonmonetary goods, many rounds may be spent in completion of the financial transactions the prior trade has engendered: A will pay B when he receives payment from C who is waiting for D, and so on. The amount of physically available monetary commodity suitable for delivery on the promissory notes may itself constitute an impediment to the speedy execution of the financial obligations. It is, after all, the lack of sufficiently abundant conveniently distributed monetary commodity that generates the need for credit in the first instance. Hence trade credit or multiple sources of credit, for example, multiple banks lacking a central clearing house, generate complexity and delay in the trading process. Indeed, I conjecture below that successful decentralized trade in a trade credit economy is not generally possible.

Commodity credit is essentially subject to some of the same objections with the added complexity of promissory notes issued for many goods but without the difficulty of a shortage for the underlying good backing the credit instrument. A round of trade will be spent in a commodity credit world while debtors search for excess supplies of commodities with which to make good on their previously contracted promises to deliver goods. They will generally pay for these supplies with further debt instruments whose repayment will generate further delay. Nevertheless, it is shown below that full execution can be achieved in two (very busy) rounds of trade. It follows that a significant simplification and abbreviation of the trading process is introduced through the uniqueness of the medium of exchange and uniqueness of the credit instrument.

3   Commodity credit economy

In the commodity credit economy, we augment the N-good commodity space by $N \times J$ credit instruments, one for each agent and commodity. Each credit instrument is a promissory note by the issuer to deliver a unit of the named good. The nonnegativity condition on agents' trades [(A.1)] is relaxed to accommodate the issue of the commodity-specific IOUs. Each agent is required to hold nonnegative quantities of all goods, except that he may hold negative quantities (i.e., be a net issuer) of his own IOUs. This is formalized as assumption (A.1.CC), which replaces (A.1) in this model. Each good name is indexed by the issuer's name, the issuer 0 being the spot commodity. For example, good $0n$ is the spot good n; good in is a note for good n issued by i. The IOUs are valued at the price of the underlying commodity, that is,

$$p_{kn} = p_{0n}, \qquad k = 0, \dots, J.$$

The nonnegativity condition in this model then becomes

(A.1.CC)

$$w_{i,kn}^t + a_{i,kn}^t \geq 0, \qquad k \neq i,$$

$$w_{j,kn}^t + a_{j,kn}^t \geq 0, \qquad k \neq j.$$

Agent's i's estimate of unsatisfied demands and supplies is modified to include his net promissory note position. Thus we redefine v_{in}^{t+1} as

$$v_{in}^{t+1} = v_{in}^t - \sum_{k=0}^{J} a_{i,kn}^t.$$

That is, agents count as satisfied in making their own trading decisions a demand for which they hold a corresponding promise to deliver and as excess demands goods they have promised to deliver in the future for which they do not currently possess sufficient supplies or promissory notes. A workable trading rule for this economy is for two agents, when they meet, to scan their list of demands and supplies currently unsatisfied by actual holdings or promissory notes. Should one possess an unsatisfied excess supply for which the other has a corresponding demand, goods go from the supplier to the demander until the smaller of the two is exhausted. Accounts are settled by payment from the debtor to the creditor of promissory notes for goods of which the creditor has outstanding excess demand. The notes are fulfilled by delivery of spot goods at the meeting of issuer and holder of the notes, when the issuer has acquired spot goods to deliver. This is described more formally as trading rule θ (below). The rule consists of three parts: primary trade for fulfillment of outstanding excess demands, x; repayment of old notes, u; and issue of new notes, y. The issuer of promissory notes acquires the goods to fulfill them in trade and then delivers on them in his next meeting with the holder.

Trading rule θ (commodity credit economy):

For $\pi^t(i) = j$ let

$$a_i^t = x_i^t + y_i^t + u_i^t \quad \text{and} \quad a_j^t = x_j^t + y_j^t + u_j^t,$$

where

(1)
$$x_{i0n}^t = -x_{j0n}^t = \begin{cases} 0 & \text{if } v_{in}^t v_{jn}^t \geq 0 \text{ or if } n = m, \\ \min(|v_{in}^t|, |v_{jn}^t|) & \text{if } v_{in}^t > 0 \text{ and } v_{jn}^t < 0, \\ -\min(|v_{in}^t|, |v_{in}^t|) & \text{if } v_{in}^t < 0 \text{ and } v_{jn}^t > 0, \end{cases}$$

and

(2)
$$u_{i0n}^t = -u_{j0n}^t = \begin{cases} 0 \\ -\max[w_{jin}, w_{i0n}] & \text{if } w_{jin} > 0 \text{ and } w_{i0n} > 0, \\ \max[w_{ijn}, w_{j0n}] & \text{if } w_{ijn} > 0 \text{ and } w_{j0n} > 0, \end{cases}$$

$$u_{iin}^t = -u_{jin}^t = -u_{i0n}^t, \qquad u_{jjn}^t = -u_{ijn}^t = -u_{j0n}^t.$$

(3)
$$y_{ijn}^t = -y_{jjn}^t = \begin{cases} 0 & \text{if } p \cdot x_j^t \leq 0; \\ \text{if } p \cdot x_j^t > 0, & \text{then} \\ p \cdot y_{ij}^t = -p \cdot x_i^t & \text{and } \text{sign } y_{ijn}^t = \text{sign } v_{in}^t. \end{cases}$$

$$y_{jin}^t = -y_{iin}^t = \begin{cases} 0 & \text{if } p \cdot x_i^t \leq 0; \\ \text{if } p \cdot x_i^t > 0, & \text{then} \\ p \cdot y_{ji}^t = -p \cdot x_j^t & \text{and } \text{sign } y_{jin}^t = \text{sign } y_{jn}^t. \end{cases}$$

The effectiveness of trading rule θ is summarized in the following theorem.

Theorem 2. Let (p, Z, B) satisfy (U), and let trade proceed according to trading rule θ. Then (A.1.CC), (A.2), (A.3), (D.3), and (E.2) are fulfilled. That is, the rule is decentralized and achieves full execution in two rounds.

Proof: Without loss of generality, consider the case $v_{i0n}^1 < 0$, that is, agent i starts trade with an excess supply of good n. We claim that $v_{i0n}^{2\tau} = 0$, that is, the excess supply has been sold and delivered by the end of two rounds. We will show that by the end of two rounds, it has been delivered to a demander of n. By (U), $\sum_i v_{i0n}^1 = 0$, for every supplier there is a demander and vice versa. Hence we will claim that at the end of two rounds, full execution is achieved. Under rule θ, every trader has met every other trader twice in two rounds, and the second time the two meet, they have each met all the others at least once. Hence for j so that $v_{j0n}^1 > 0$, either i meets j at t so that $\pi^t(i) = j$ and $v_{j0n}^t > 0$ or j has previously $(t' < t)$ received a note for n. Hence in two rounds, $v_{i0n}^1 > 0$ will be reduced to $v_{i0n}^{2\tau} \leq 0$ by trade with a demander of n or an indebted note issuer of n. But the note issuer's meeting with his creditor precedes his meeting with i during the round so, under rule θ, the note issuer will deliver the promised goods on his subsequent meeting with j. Hence $v_{j0n}^{2\tau} = 0$. By quid pro quo this will be true for all i, j.   Q.E.D.

4   Trade credit economy

In the model of trade credit, we augment the N-good commodity space by the addition of J credit instruments (J is the number of agents). Each credit instrument is named, that is, it is a signed IOU issued by its signator. It is denominated in units of good m, the monetary commodity. The non-negativity restriction on agents' trades [(A.1)] is relaxed to accommodate issue of IOUs. Each agent is required to hold nonnegative quantities of all goods, except that he may hold negative quantities (i.e., be a net issuer) of his own IOUs. This is formalized as assumption (A.1.TC), which replaces (A.1) in this model. Good $N+i$, $i = 1, \ldots, J$, then is the IOU issued by agent i. The IOUs trade at par, that is,

$$p_{N+j} = p_m.$$

The nonnegativity condition in this model then becomes,

$$w_{in}^t + a_{in}^t \geq 0, \qquad n = 1, \ldots, N+J, \; n \neq N+i,$$

$$w_{jn}^t + a_{jn}^t \geq 0, \qquad n = 1, \ldots, N+J, \; n \neq N+j.$$

Full execution of the equilibrium allocation may not be achieved in a single round of trade in which each trader meets every other trader. We define full execution in K rounds of trade by

(E.K) $\displaystyle\sum_{t=1}^{K\tau} a_i^t = z_i$ for all i.

where τ is the number of trading periods in a round of trade:

$$\tau = \begin{cases} J-1 & \text{if } J \text{ even}, \\ J & \text{if } J \text{ odd}. \end{cases}$$

When the endowment of commodity m is insufficient to allow monetary trade to full execution in one round, we might suppose that the extra flexibility of using trade credit would allow decentralized trade to achieve full execution in a larger number of rounds, K. Full execution can trivially be achieved in the first round for all goods other than m and the credit instruments. The difficulty comes in achieving clearing of the debt instruments in a decentralized fashion. That it should be achievable in a nondecentralized fashion is a consequence of Ostroy and Starr (1974, Theorem 1).

More formally, we may posit a trading mechanism where the first round of trade is spent fulfilling excess demands and supplies of nonmonetary goods, payment being made in money, good m, or in promissory notes, goods $N+i$. Subsequent rounds would be spent in acquiring money to fulfill on the promissory notes and fulfilling thereon. Define monetary trade with trade credit by trading rule η.

Trading rule η (trade credit economy):
For $\pi^t(i)=j$, let

$$a_i^t = x_i^t + y_i^t \quad \text{and} \quad a_j^t = x_j^t + y_j^t,$$

where

(1) $\quad x_{in}^t = -x_{jn}^t = \begin{cases} 0 & \text{if } v_{in}^t v_{jn}^t \geq 0 \text{ or if } n=m, \\ \min(|v_{in}^t|, |v_{jn}^t|) & \text{if } v_{in}^t > 0 \text{ and } v_{jn}^t < 0, \\ -\min(|v_{in}^t|, |v_{jn}^t|) & \text{if } v_{in}^t < 0 \text{ and } v_{jn}^t > 0. \end{cases}$

Define

$$\ell_j^t \equiv w_{jm}^t + y_{jN+j}^t, \qquad \ell_i^t \equiv w_{im}^t + y_{iN+i}^t.$$

$$x_{im}^t = -x_{jm}^t = \begin{cases} 0 & \text{if } \ell_i^t \ell_j^t \geq 0, \\ -\min(|\ell_i^t|, |\ell_j^t|) & \text{if } \ell_i^t < 0 \text{ and } \ell_j^t > 0, \\ \min(|\ell_i^t|, |\ell_j^t|) & \text{if } \ell_i^t > 0 \text{ and } \ell_j^t < 0. \end{cases}$$

(2) *Case a.* $p \cdot x_i^t > 0 > p \cdot x_j^t$:

$$y_{im}^t = -\min\left[w_{im}^t, \frac{p \cdot x_i^t}{p_m}\right],$$

$$y_{iN+i}^t = -\left(\frac{p \cdot x_i^t}{p_m} - y_{im}^t\right),$$

$$y_{jn}^t = -y_{in}^t.$$

(3) *Case b.* $p \cdot x_i^t < 0 < p \cdot x_j^t$:

$$y_{jm}^t = -\min\left[w_{jm}^t, \frac{p \cdot x_j^t}{p_m}\right],$$

$$y_{jN+i}^t = -\left(\frac{p \cdot x_j^t}{p_m} - y_{jm}^t\right),$$

$$y_{in}^t = -y_{jn}^t.$$

(4) *Case c.* $p \cdot x_i^t = 0 = p \cdot x_j^t$:

$$y_{in}^t = 0 = y_{jn}^t \quad \text{for all } n.$$

Trading rule η represents one formalization of decentralized trade in a trade credit economy. Its speed of execution depends on the volume of good m available and the distribution of m in each round. I have not been able to demonstrate full execution in general in finite time – indeed, I expect this to be false. All trade in goods other than money, good m, and credit, goods $N+i$, $i=1, \ldots, J$, is completed in the first round. Subsequent trade involves the settlement of accounts by repayment of IOUs in money. To accomplish this, holders of good m who do not need it as a transactions balance trade the good away to those who need it in exchange for IOUs subsequently to be repaid. This arrangement appears, however, to lead to the possibility of successive reshuffling of debt with no net extinction of aggregate debt. Hence, we are led to

Conjecture: Let K be a positive integer. There is no trading rule fulfilling (A.1.TC), (A.2), (A.3), (D.3), and (E.K) for arbitrary (p, Z, B) satisfying (U) with $\sum_i p_m b_{im} > 0$.

Plausibility argument: Full execution in goods other than money and debt can be achieved in one round. This will typically result in an array for each agent of debt held and debt owed. Restrictions on the array are primarily from (A.1.TC) and (A.3). To the extent that financing the repayment of old debt requires floating new debt, there may be no net extinction of debt in trade. Though the models are not identical, there appears to be a formal equivalence between the debt repayment model here and the Ostroy–Starr (1974) model. Hence the impossibility result of Theorem 2 there should apply. It is shown there that execution cannot be achieved in a decentralized fashion in one round. A similar proposition in the present model would be the impossibility of assuring in any single round of decentralized trade a predetermined level of debt extinction equivalent, for example, to the amount of m outstanding. Hence, the level of debt extinction in one round cannot be bounded away from zero. Repeated application should result in the impossibility of assuring decentralized trade to achieve full debt repayment in a finite number of rounds, which was to be demonstrated.

5 Conclusion

It is argued in Ostroy and Starr (1974) that monetary trade is distinctive in providing a decentralized trading process that achieves full execution of an equilibrium allocation in one round of trade. Alternative methods for effecting the allocation require more elaborate organization or more time. The initial condition that allows the use of monetary trade is that all agents must hold sufficiently large stocks of the monetary commodity, good m. Each agent's holdings have to be sufficiently large to finance his planned purchases. Unfortunately, there is no fundamental reason why we should expect this assumption in general to hold as an initial condition.

It is precisely because of the difficulty of arranging sufficient timely stocks of media of exchange that credit and financial intermediation arise. In this essay, we characterize a bank as an agent that buys personal debt and specie (good m), issuing its own notes in payment. There is no limit in the model on the real value this note issue can achieve. In particular, each agent can be issued (in exchange for his personal debt) sufficient notes to finance all of his desired purchases (which necessarily cannot exceed his net worth). Hence the institution of bank credit can provide sufficient media of exchange in the form of bank notes c to allow decentralized monetary trade to take place effectively in a relatively short time.

More flexible credit arrangements – trade credit and commodity credit – though apparently equally simple in any single trade, result in significantly more complex coordination problems. The use of a single bank and a unique medium of exchange are effective simplifications of the trading process.

REFERENCES

Ostroy, J. M. and R. M. Starr (1974), "Money and the decentralization of exchange," *Econometrica,* 42(6): 1093–1113.

Starr, R. M. (1976), "Decentralized nonmonetary trade," *Econometrica,* 44(5): 1087–89.

Townsend, R. and N. Wallace (1984), "Circulating private debt: An example with a coordination problem," May, duplicated.

CHAPTER 5

Lump-sum taxes and transfers: public debt in the overlapping-generations model

Yves Balasko and Karl Shell

1 Introduction, summary, and reader's guide

Americans are hearing a lot these days about the government deficit and its integral, the public debt. The subject is hardly new for students of public finance and macroeconomics. In this chapter, we return to square one. We examine the nature of the intertemporal consistency restrictions imposed on the government's fiscal policy. In particular, we evaluate the basis for the current ("neo-Ricardian") fixation with long-run debt retirement.

Our analysis is cast in terms of the standard overlapping-generations model of exchange. Consumers are assumed to possess perfect foresight. The government commits itself to a full intertemporal fiscal policy, which it announces at the beginning of time. There is assumed to be neither intrinsic uncertainty nor extrinsic uncertainty. The spot markets and the borrowing-and-lending markets are complete and competitive. Participation in these markets is restricted only by the natural lifetimes of the consumers. Since sunspot equilibria are ruled out by assumption, the restrictions on market participation are not essential.

Trading is assumed to be costless. Financial assets have only two roles. They are potential value stores. They can also be used by consumers in paying their taxes (and by the government in distributing transfers). In this environment, financial instruments are in essence identical. We can assume, therefore, that there is only one type of instrument, called "money."

This research was supported by National Science Foundation Grant SES-83-08450 at the Center for Analytical Research in Economics and the Social Sciences, University of Pennsylvania, by National Science Foundation Grant BNS-80-11494 to the Center for Advanced Study in the Behavioral Sciences, and by National Science Foundation Grant SES-83-20464 at the Institute for Mathematical Studies in the Social Sciences, Stanford University. The authors thank Dave Cass, Walt Heller, Jim Peck, Andy Postlewaite, and David Schmeidler for helpful comments.

121

(Since it serves no special role in facilitating exchange, you might prefer to think of this instrument as a "bond," a bond that does not pay nominal interest but can appreciate in value relative to commodities. The absence of nominal interest is a pure technicality; nothing of substance is lost by its exclusion.)

It is assumed for simplicity that the government makes no expenditures on goods and services. The government is assumed to have the power to levy costless lump-sum taxes (and distribute costless lump-sum transfers) *in terms of money*. In this respect, that is, in couching the analysis in terms of nominal taxes rather than in terms of real taxes, the present study is a companion to our analysis of money taxation in the static economy (Balasko and Shell 1983). Recall that a tax-transfer policy is said to be *bonafide* (for a given economy) if it is consistent with some competitive equilibrium in which the goods price of money is nonzero (i.e., in which the general price level is finite). If money is a free good, then the money tax is no burden to the taxed consumer (nor is the money transfer any benefit to the subsidized consumer). Hence, if a fiscal policy is not bonafide, it cannot possibly affect the allocation of resources.

In the static economy, a tax-transfer (or fiscal) policy is said to be *balanced* if the algebraic sum of the transfers is zero. We have established elsewhere (Balasko and Shell 1983) that for the static economy the government fiscal policy is bonafide if and only if it is balanced. In this chapter, we extend this result to the finite-horizon, overlapping-generations economy. Balanced policies are then interpreted as those having the property that the public debt is retired at the terminal date. If the world is known to end with certainty on a given date, the following are true: (1) If the debt is not perfectly retired on the terminal date, then money must be worthless at each date, and (2) if the debt is perfectly retired on the terminal date, then there is a range of positive goods prices of money consistent with competitive equilibrium.

We use our results for finite-horizon economies to establish our basic theorem for infinite-horizon, overlapping-generations economies: *Strongly balanced tax-transfer policies,* policies for which the public debt is forever zero after some finite date, *are always bonafide.* It does not appear to be possible to strengthen this theorem in any interesting way. Without restricting preferences and endowments, weaker notions of balancedness do not necessarily imply bonafidelity. Hence, if the public debt is retired by some finite date, after which time the government neither taxes nor makes transfers, then there are positive goods prices of money consistent with competitive equilibrium. Nonetheless, even if the public debt vanishes asymptotically, money is necessarily worthless if debt retirement is too slow for the given economy.

Furthermore, the government can select a fiscal policy for which the debt is not retired in any sense, yet there can be positive goods prices of money consistent with competitive equilibrium. Indeed, it is well known that infinite-horizon economies can be constructed so that the obviously nonbalanced, constant-public-debt policy is bonafide.

The overlapping-generations model is described in Section 2. We employ notation that allows us to present the finite-horizon version and the infinite-horizon version simultaneously. The infinite-horizon version reduces to the model used in Balasko and Shell (1981).

The finite-horizon version of the overlapping-generations model is analyzed in Section 3. The identity between the set of bonafide tax-transfer policies and the set of balanced tax-transfer policies is established through an analysis of an associated no-taxation economy. The set of tax-transfer policies consistent with equilibrium in which the price of money is 1 is shown to be bounded and arc connected and to contain zero in its relative interior. There is a continuum of equilibria for each balanced tax-transfer policy. In the set of equilibrium money prices, zero is not isolated.

The infinite-horizon version of the overlapping-generations model is analyzed in Sections 4 and 5. This analysis can be taken as an extension of our earlier work (Balasko and Shell 1981). In Section 4, we use the central result of Section 3 to show that strongly balanced tax-transfer policies are bonafide. In Section 5, we construct two examples. The first example establishes that asymptotically balanced tax-transfer policies are not necessarily bonafide. The second example establishes that recurrently balanced tax-transfer policies, policies for which the public debt is zero infinitely often, are not necessarily bonafide. Even recurrently balanced policies with the further property that the *limit superior* of the public debt vanishes are not necessarily bonafide.

Two important points emerge from our analysis. First, it matters if taxes are set in money terms rather than in real terms. Even in the case of perfect lump-sum *money* taxation, the government does not have full fiscal potency because it cannot determine the general price level. Second, it matters if the economic horizon is essentially infinite rather than being based on some known finite date. For the finite-horizon case, we know that a fiscal policy is bonafide if and only if the debt is perfectly retired on the terminal date. For the infinite-horizon case, there are examples of economies and fiscal policies for which there is asymptotic debt retirement but not bonafidelity, and there are cases without debt retirement that, nonetheless, exhibit bonafidelity.

2   The overlapping-generations model with lump-sum taxes and transfers

We summarize here some essential elements of the overlapping-generations model. Our model is based on that of Balasko and Shell (1981), but there is one very important difference: Here we allow for the possibility of a finite-time horizon as well as an infinite horizon.

We postulate a very simple demographic pattern, but this causes no loss in generality. Consumer h $(h=0,1,...,T)$ is indexed by his place in the birth order. He is either present at the beginning of the economy $(h=0)$ and lives out the balance of his life in period 1 or he is born in the beginning of period t $(h=t; t=1,...,T)$ and lives out his life in periods t and $t+1$. For the finite-horizon variant of the model, T is a (finite) positive integer. For the infinite-horizon variant, we take $T=+\infty$ in a way that makes the model identical to that presented in Balasko and Shell (1981).

In each period t $(t=1,...,T+1)$, there are ℓ perishable commodities. The government creates and destroys otherwise imperishable fiat money. There is no other production. Let $x_t^{s,i}$ be the consumption of commodity i $(i=1,...,\ell)$ by consumer t in period s. The preferences of consumer t are described by the utility function

$$u_t(x_t) \quad \text{for} \quad t=0,1,...,T,$$

where

$$x_0 = x_0^1 = (x_0^{1,1},...,x_0^{1,\ell}) \in \mathbb{R}_{++}^\ell$$

and

$$x_t = (x_t^t, x_t^{t+1}) = (x_t^{t,1},...,x_t^{t,\ell}, x_t^{t+1,1},...,x_t^{t+1,\ell}) \in \mathbb{R}_{++}^{2\ell} \quad \text{for} \quad t=1,...,T.$$

Also denote by x_0 and x_t the respective vectors in $(\mathbb{R}_{++}^\ell)^{T+1}$, $x_0 = (x_0^1,0,...,0)$ and $x_t = (0,...,0,x_t^t,x_t^{t+1},0,...,0)$ for $t=1,...,T$. [If $T=\infty$, then under this latter interpretation we have, for example, that x_t is the sequence $(0,...,0,x_t^t,x_t^{t+1},0,...)$ in $(\mathbb{R}_{++}^\ell)^\infty$. See Balasko and Shell (1981), especially Section 2.] Let $x = (x_0,x_1,...,x_T)$ be the commodity allocation vector and $X = \mathbb{R}_{++}^{\ell(2T+1)}$ be the commodity space. The utility function u_0 (respectively u_t, $t=1,...,T$) is assumed to be strictly increasing, smooth, and strictly quasiconcave on $\mathbb{R}_{++}^\ell$ (respectively, $\mathbb{R}_{++}^{2\ell}$). To avoid messy boundary problems, we also assume that the closure of each indifference surface in $\mathbb{R}^\ell$ (respectively, $\mathbb{R}^{2\ell}$) is contained in $\mathbb{R}_{++}^\ell$ (respectively, $\mathbb{R}_{++}^{2\ell}$).

Commodity endowments are given by

$$\omega_0 = \omega_0^1 = (\omega_0^{1,1}, \ldots, \omega_0^{1,\ell}) \in \mathbb{R}_{++}^\ell$$

and

$$\omega_t = (\omega_t^t, \omega_t^{t+1}) = (\omega_t^{t,1}, \ldots, \omega_t^{t,\ell}, \omega_t^{t+1,1}, \ldots, \omega_t^{t+1,\ell}) \in \mathbb{R}_{++}^{2\ell} \quad \text{for } t = 1, \ldots, T.$$

Also denote by ω_0 and ω_t the respective vectors in $(\mathbb{R}_{++}^\ell)^{T+1}$, $\omega_0 = (\omega_0^1, 0, \ldots, 0, \ldots)$ and $\omega_t = (0, \ldots, 0, \omega_t^t, \omega_t^{t+1}, 0, \ldots, 0)$ for $t = 1, \ldots, T$. Let $\omega = (\omega_0, \omega_1, \ldots, \omega_T) \in X$ denote the commodity endowment vector.

Let $\mu_t \in \mathbb{R}$ be the nominal (money) lump-sum transfer to consumer t $(t = 0, 1, \ldots, T)$. Let the tax-transfer vector be denoted by

$$\mu = (\mu_0, \mu_1, \ldots, \mu_t, \ldots, \mu_T) \in \mathbb{R}^{T+1} = \mathfrak{M},$$

the space of lump-sum tax-transfer policies.

Let $p^{t,i} \in \mathbb{R}_{++}$ be the price of commodity i $(i = 1, \ldots, \ell)$ in period t, and define $p^t \in \mathbb{R}_{++}^\ell$ by $p^t = (p^{t,1}, \ldots, p^{t,i}, \ldots, p^{t,\ell})$. Then define the commodity price vector $p \in \mathbb{R}_{++}^{\ell(T+1)}$ by $p = (p^1, \ldots, p^t, \ldots, p^{T+1})$. Let $p^m \in \mathbb{R}_+$ be the price of money, so that the wealth of consumer t is given by

$$w_t = p \cdot \omega_t + p^m \mu_t$$

for $t = 0, 1, \ldots, T$. Let $w = (w_0, w_1, \ldots, w_T) \in W = \mathbb{R}_{++}^{T+1}$ be the vector of consumer incomes (or, more accurately, consumer wealths). Let $\mathcal{P}$ be the set of present prices, $\mathcal{P} = \{p \in (\mathbb{R}_{++}^\ell)^{T+1} \mid p^{1,1} = 1\}$. Define the demand functions $f_t : (p, w_t) \mapsto x_t$ for $t = 0, 1, \ldots, T$. Thus, we have $f_t : \mathcal{P} \times \mathbb{R}_{++} \to (\mathbb{R}_{++}^\ell)^{T+1}$ for $t = 0, 1, \ldots, T$.[1]

2.1. Definition. For the given commodity endowments $\omega \in X$ and the given tax transfer policy $\mu \in \mathfrak{M}$, a *competitive equilibrium* is a price system $(p, p^m) \in \mathcal{P} \times \mathbb{R}_+$ that solves the equations

$$\sum_{t=0}^T f_t(p, w_t) = \sum_{t=0}^T \omega_t = r$$

and

$$w_t = p \cdot \omega_t + p^m \mu_t \quad \text{for } t \geq 0,$$

where $r = (r^1, \ldots, r^t, \ldots, r^{T+1}) \in (\mathbb{R}_{++}^\ell)^{T+1}$ is the vector of aggregate resources.

Let $q = (p, p^m)$ and $\mathcal{Q} = \mathcal{P} \times \mathbb{R}_+$.

2.2. Definition. Let $\mathcal{Q}(\omega, \mu)$ denote the *set of competitive equlibria* for $\omega \in X$ and $\mu \in \mathfrak{M}$. Thus, we have $\mathcal{Q}(\omega, \mu) = \{q \in \mathcal{Q} \mid$ Definition 2.1 is satisfied for $\omega \in X$ and $\mu \in \mathfrak{M}\}$. The price system $q = (p, p^m)$ is said to define a *proper monetary equilibrium* for $\omega \in X$ and $\mu \in \mathfrak{M}$ if we have $q = (p, p^m) \in \mathcal{Q}(\omega, \mu)$ and $p^m > 0$.

2.3. Proposition. For each positive scalar λ, we have

$$\mathcal{Q}(\omega, \lambda\mu) = \{(p, p^m/\lambda) \mid (p, p^m) \in \mathcal{Q}(\omega, \mu)\}.$$

Proof: From the definition of wealth, we have $w_t = p \cdot \omega_t + p^m \mu_t$ for $t = 0, 1, \ldots, T$. Since the only effect of μ or p^m on f_t is through w_t, the result follows immediately.   Q.E.D.

2.4. Definition. The tax-transfer policy $\mu \in \mathfrak{M}$ is said to be *bonafide* [for the economy defined by the demand functions $f = (f_0, \ldots, f_t, \ldots, f_T)$ and endowments $\omega \in X$] if there is a *proper* monetary equilibrium associated with (ω, μ), that is, there is a $q = (p, p^m) \in \mathcal{Q}(\omega, \mu)$ such that $p^m \neq 0$.

2.5. Proposition. The set of bonafide tax-transfer policies is a cone in $\mathfrak{M}$.

Proof: The proof follows directly from Definition 2.4 and Proposition 2.3.   Q.E.D.

Following Balasko and Shell (1981), we go on to study a "cross section" of the cone of bonafide tax-transfer policies. This is the purpose of the next definition.

2.6. Definition. The *bonafide tax-transfer policy* $\mu \in \mathfrak{M}$ is said to be *normalized* if $(p, 1)$ is a (proper) monetary equilibrium associated with (ω, μ). Let $\mathfrak{M}_B(\omega) \subset \mathfrak{M}$ denote the *set of normalized bonafide tax-transfer policies*. [The set of bonafide tax-transfer policies is the positive cone in $\mathfrak{M}$ generated by $\mathfrak{M}_B(\omega)$.]

We next define the set of equilibrium money prices for the economy defined by (ω, μ) and proceed to establish its close relationship with the set $\mathfrak{M}_B(\omega)$.

2.7. Definition. The set of equilibrium money prices $\mathcal{P}^m(\omega, \mu) \subset \mathbb{R}_+$ is defined by

$$\mathcal{P}^m(\omega, \mu) = \{p^m \mid (p, p^m) \in \mathcal{Q}(\omega, \mu) \text{ for some } p \in \mathcal{P}\}.$$

2.8. Proposition. (i) The set $\mathcal{P}^m(\omega, \mu)$ is not empty. (ii) $\mathcal{P}^m(\omega, \mu) \neq \{0\}$ if and only if μ is a bonafide tax-transfer policy. (iii) Fix $\mu \in \mathfrak{M}$ and define $L(\mu) \subset \mathfrak{M}$, the nonnegative ray generated by μ, by $L(\mu) = \{\lambda\mu \mid \lambda \in \mathbb{R}_+\}$. The set $\mathcal{P}^m(\omega, \mu)$ is related to the set $(\mathfrak{M}_B(\omega) \cap L(\mu))$ by a one-to-one mapping.[2]

Proof: (i) Consider the economy without taxes and transfers, $\mu = 0$. (a) First, consider the finite case, $1 \leq T < +\infty$. Consumers are indirectly resource related in the no-taxation economy. Clearly, an ordinary competitive equilibrium price vector $p \in \mathcal{P}$ exists. (b) Second, consider the infinite case, $T = +\infty$. From Proposition 3.10 (Balasko and Shell 1980, p. 289), we know that a competitive equilibrium price sequence $p \in \mathcal{P}$ exists for the no-taxation economy. Therefore, for T finite or infinite, we know there is a $p \in \mathcal{P}$ such that $(p, 1) \in \mathcal{Q}(\omega, 0)$ and $(p, 0) \in \mathcal{Q}(\omega, \mu)$ (using Proposition 2.3). Hence, we have $0 \in \mathcal{P}^m(\omega, \mu)$ (from Definition 2.7). (ii) The proof of (ii) follows directly from Definitions 2.4 and 2.7 and Proposition 2.8.i. (iii) From Definitions 2.4 and 2.7 and Proposition 2.3, the mapping defined by $p^m \mapsto p^m\mu$ is clearly a bijection from $\mathcal{P}^m(\omega, \mu)$ to $\mathfrak{M}_B(\omega) \cap L(\mu)$.   Q.E.D.

3   The finite-horizon, overlapping-generations model

Throughout this section, T is assumed to be a positive finite integer. There are then $T+1$ consumers, $h = 0, 1, \ldots, T$, and $T+1$ periods, $t = 1, \ldots, T+1$. Perfect foresight is assumed. Balanced fiscal policies play a central role in finite economies; the formal definition is given next.

3.1. Definition. Let T be finite. The tax-transfer policy

$$\mu = (\mu_0, \ldots, \mu_t, \ldots, \mu_T) \in \mathbb{R}^{T+1}$$

is said to be *balanced* if we have $\sum_{t=0}^T \mu_t = 0$. The set of balanced tax-transfer policies is $\{\mu \in \mathbb{R}^{T+1} \mid \sum_{t=0}^T \mu_t = 0\}$.

The amount of outstanding government debt at the end of the last period is equal to $\sum_{t=0}^T \mu_t$. Hence, there is an equivalent definition of balancedness applicable to finite-horizon dynamic economies: *The government's tax-transfer policy is said to be balanced if the outstanding debt of the government is zero on the terminal date.*

The next proposition provides the first step in our program of analyzing the relationships between bonafide and balanced tax-transfer policies.

3.2. Proposition. Let T be finite. If the tax-transfer policy $\mu \in \mathbb{R}^{T+1}$ is bonafide (Definition 2.4), then μ is balanced (Definition 3.1).

Proof: Let $q = (p, p^m)$ be a competitive equilibrium for the economy defined by (ω, μ); hence we have $q \in \mathcal{Q}(\omega, \mu)$. Since utility functions are increasing, it follows that $p \cdot f_t(p, w_t) = w_t = p \cdot \omega_t + p^m \mu_t$ for $t = 0, 1, \ldots, T$. Summing these equalities yields

$$p \cdot \sum_{t=0}^{T} f_t(p, w_t) = p \cdot \sum_{t=0}^{T} \omega_t + p^m \sum_{t=0}^{T} \mu_t.$$

But we know from Definition 2.1 that

$$\sum_{t=0}^{T} f_t(p, w_t) = \sum_{t=0}^{T} \omega_t.$$

Therefore, we have $p^m \sum_{t=0}^{T} \mu_t = 0$. Thus, if μ is bonafide [i.e., if there is a proper competitive equilibrium $q = (p, p^m)$], then μ is balanced.

$$\text{Q.E.D.}$$

For finite economies, Proposition 3.2 is an immediate consequence of Walras' law. The converse of Proposition 3.2 is also true, but its proof is not so straightforward. In what follows, we show that each balanced policy is bonafide. Our strategy of proof is based on that of Balasko and Shell (1983, Proposition 3.6). We construct an associated no-taxation economy in which endowments of the first commodity have been reallocated. For the static economy (Balasko and Shell 1983), sufficiently small reallocations can be made while retaining the property that individual endowments lie within the consumption set. This is not in general possible in the dynamic economy because of the nature of generational overlap. Hence, in the analysis of the associated economy, we must expand the consumption sets and extend the preferences to be defined over the expanded consumption sets.

We proceed to the construction of the associated no-taxation economy. Let $\mu = (\mu_0, \mu_1, \ldots, \mu_t, \ldots, \mu_T)$ be a vector in $\mathbb{R}^{T+1}$ that satisfies $\sum_{t=0}^{T} \mu_t = 0$, where T is finite. Let $\tilde{\omega} = (\tilde{\omega}_0, \tilde{\omega}_1, \ldots, \tilde{\omega}_t, \ldots, \tilde{\omega}_T)$ be the vector of endowments for the associated economy that satisfies

$$(3.3) \qquad \tilde{\omega}_0 = (\omega_0^{1,1} + \mu_0, \omega_0^{1,2}, \ldots, \omega_0^{1,\ell}, 0, \ldots, 0),$$

$$\tilde{\omega}_1 = (\omega_1^{1,1} + \mu_1, \omega_1^{1,2}, \ldots, \omega_0^{1,\ell}, \omega_1^{2,1}, \ldots, \omega_1^{2,\ell}, 0, \ldots, 0),$$

$$\vdots$$

$$\tilde{\omega}_t = (\mu_t, 0, \ldots, 0, \omega_t^{t,1}, \ldots, \omega_t^{t,\ell}, \omega_t^{t+1,1}, \ldots, \omega_t^{t+1,\ell}, 0, \ldots, 0),$$

$$\vdots$$

$$\tilde{\omega}_T = (\mu_T, 0, \ldots, 0, \omega_T^{T,1}, \ldots, \omega_T^{T,\ell}, \omega_T^{T+1,1}, \ldots, \omega_T^{T+1,\ell}),$$

where the omegas on the right side are the endowments

$$\omega = (\omega_0, \omega_1, \ldots, \omega_t, \ldots, \omega_T) \in X$$

for the original (tax-transfer) economy described in Section 2. Notice that by construction we have $\tilde{\omega}_t \in \mathbb{R}^{\ell(T+1)}$ for $t = 0, 1, \ldots, T$, and

$$\sum_{t=0}^{T} \tilde{\omega}_t = \sum_{t=0}^{T} \omega_t = r \in \mathbb{R}_{++}^{\ell(T+1)},$$

even though some of the $\tilde{\omega}_t$ may have nonpositive first components.

In Section 2, the preferences of consumer $t = 1, \ldots, T$ are defined only on $\mathbb{R}_{++}^{2\ell}$ and those of consumer 0 only on $\mathbb{R}_{++}^{\ell}$. Here we extend preferences so that they are defined on all of $\mathbb{R}^{\ell(T+1)}$. This is done in two steps. In the first step, preferences are extended from the positive orthant, $\mathbb{R}_{++}^{2\ell}$ or $\mathbb{R}_{++}^{\ell}$, to the whole Euclidean space, $\mathbb{R}^{2\ell}$ or $\mathbb{R}^{\ell}$. In the second step, preferences are extended from $\mathbb{R}^{2\ell}$ or $\mathbb{R}^{\ell}$ to $\mathbb{R}^{\ell(T+1)}$.

Step 1: Consider consumer t ($t = 1, \ldots, T$). Through each point (x_t^t, x_t^{t+1}) in $\mathbb{R}_{++}^{2\ell}$ passes an indifference surface that is a level set to $u_t(\cdot)$. First, extend the preference map to $\mathbb{R}_{+}^{2\ell}$. The set $\mathbb{R}_{+}^{2\ell} \setminus \mathbb{R}_{++}^{2\ell}$ is assumed to be an indifference surface. Each point in $\mathbb{R}_{++}^{2\ell}$ is preferred to any point in $\mathbb{R}_{+}^{2\ell} \setminus \mathbb{R}_{++}^{2\ell}$. Then construct a family of piecewise linear indifference surfaces in $\mathbb{R}^{2\ell} \setminus \mathbb{R}_{+}^{2\ell}$, where each indifference surface in $\mathbb{R}^{2\ell} \setminus \mathbb{R}_{+}^{2\ell}$ is parallel to the indifference surface $\mathbb{R}_{+}^{2\ell} \setminus \mathbb{R}_{++}^{2\ell}$. Preferences on $\mathbb{R}^{2\ell}$ are thus monotonic (although not strictly monotonic) and exhibit local nonsatiation. Also, preferred sets in $\mathbb{R}^{2\ell}$ are convex. [The logic of this extension is illustrated in Figure 1. The solid curves depict indifference surfaces generated by the utility function $u_t(\cdot)$. The dashed curves represent the new indifference surfaces, which expand the preference relation to all of $\mathbb{R}^{2\ell}$.] In like fashion, extend the preferences of consumer 0 from $\mathbb{R}_{++}^{\ell}$ to all of $\mathbb{R}^{\ell}$.

The extended preferences can be represented by continuous utility functions $\phi_0 : \mathbb{R}^{\ell} \to \mathbb{R}$ and $\phi_t : \mathbb{R}^{2\ell} \to \mathbb{R}$ for $t = 1, \ldots, T$, where

(3.4) $\quad \phi_0(x_0) = u_0(x_0) \quad$ for $x_0 \in \mathbb{R}_{++}^{\ell}$,

$$\phi_0(x_0) = \min_{i=1,\ldots,\ell} (x_0^{1,i}) \quad \text{for } x_0 \in \mathbb{R}^{\ell} \setminus \mathbb{R}_{++}^{\ell},$$

and

$$\phi_t(x_t) = u_t(x_t) \quad \text{for } x_t \in \mathbb{R}_{++}^{2\ell},$$

$$\phi_t(x_t) = \min_{\substack{s=t,t+1 \\ i=1,\ldots,\ell}} (x_t^{s,i}) \quad \text{for } x_t \in \mathbb{R}^{2\ell} \setminus \mathbb{R}_{++}^{2\ell},$$

$$\text{for } t = 1, \ldots, T.$$

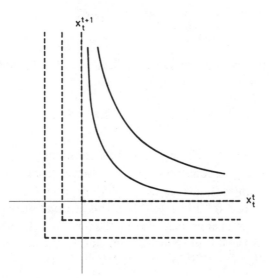

Figure 1. Extension of preferences from $\mathbb{R}^{2\ell}_{++}$ to $\mathbb{R}^{2\ell}$.

For purposes of the construction in equations (3.4), the functions u_t have been scaled so that

(i) $u_0(x_0) \in \mathbb{R}_{++}$ for each $x_0 \in \mathbb{R}^{\ell}_{++}$, and $u_t(x_t) \in \mathbb{R}_{++}$ for each $x_t \in \mathbb{R}^{2\ell}_{++}$ $(t = 1, \ldots, T)$,

and

(ii)   if $\{x_0^{\nu}\}$ (respectively, $\{x_t^{\nu}\}$) is a sequence with $x_0^{\nu} \in \mathbb{R}^{\ell}_{++}$ (respectively, $x_t^{\nu} \in \mathbb{R}^{2\ell}_{++}$) for each ν and $\lim_{\nu \to \infty} x_0^{\nu} \in \mathbb{R}^{\ell}_+ \setminus \mathbb{R}^{\ell}_{++}$ (respectively, $\lim_{\nu \to \infty} x_t^{\nu} \in \mathbb{R}^{2\ell}_+ \setminus \mathbb{R}^{2\ell}_{++}$), then $\lim_{\nu \to \infty} u_0(x_0^{\nu}) = 0$ (respectively, $\lim_{\nu \to \infty} u_t(x_t^{\nu}) = 0$ for $t = 1, \ldots, T$).

Step 2: Let $\tilde{x}_t = (x_t^1, \ldots, x_t^t, x_t^{t+1}, \ldots, x_t^{T+1}) \in \mathbb{R}^{\ell(T+1)}$ be consumer t's extended consumption vector. Let his preferences on $\mathbb{R}^{\ell(T+1)}$ be represented be the continuous utility function $v_t: \mathbb{R}^{\ell(T+1)} \to \mathbb{R}$, which is defined by

(3.5) $v_t(\tilde{x}_t) = \phi_t(x_t) - b \displaystyle\sum_{\substack{s \neq t, s \neq t+1 \\ i = 1, \ldots, \ell}} |x_t^{i,s}|$ for $t = 1, \ldots, T$

and

$$v_0(\tilde{x}_0) = \phi_0(x_0) - b \sum_{\substack{s = 2, \ldots, T \\ i = 1, \ldots, \ell}} |x_0^{i,s}|,$$

where b is a positive scalar and $|\ |$ denotes absolute value. The utility function v_t is nondecreasing in each of the commodities available during consumer t's lifetime and is strictly decreasing in the absolute value of consumptions outside his lifetime. Preferences defined on $\mathbb{R}^{\ell(T+1)}$ are continuous, convex, and exhibit local nonsatiation. Notice also that the preorderings defined by equations (3.4) on $\mathbb{R}^{2\ell}$ or $\mathbb{R}^{\ell}$ are preserved on $\mathbb{R}^{\ell(T+1)}$ [cf. (3.5)]; in particular, we have

(3.6) $(0, ..., 0, x_t^t, x_t^{t+1}, 0, ..., 0)$ is preferred to (respectively, indifferent to) $(0, ..., 0, y_t^t, y_t^{t+1}, 0, ..., 0)$ on $\mathbb{R}^{\ell(T+1)}$ if and only if (x_t^t, x_t^{t+1}) is preferred to (respectively, indifferent to) (y_t^t, y_t^{t+1}) on $\mathbb{R}^{2\ell}$ for consumer $t = 1, ..., T$,

and

$(x_0^1, 0, ..., 0)$ is preferred to (respectively, indifferent to) $(y_0^1, 0, ..., 0)$ on $\mathbb{R}^{\ell(T+1)}$ if and only if x_0^1 is preferred to (respectively, indifferent to) y_0^1 on $\mathbb{R}^{\ell}$ for consumer 0.

Other things equal, consumer t prefers zero consumption outside his lifetime to nonzero consumption outside his lifetime; that is, we have, from equation (3.5),

(3.7) $(0, ..., 0, x_t^t, x_t^{t+1}, 0, ..., 0) \gtrsim_t (x_t^1, ..., x_t^t, x_t^{t+1}, ..., x_t^{T+1})$ with strict preference when the two vectors are unequal for consumer $t = 1, ..., T$,

and

$(x_0^1, 0, ..., 0) \gtrsim_0 (x_0^1, ..., x_0^{T+1})$ with strict preference when the two vectors are unequal for consumer 0.

Because of property 3.7, we know that consumers will not choose positive consumptions outside their natural lifetimes as long as prices are nonnegative. They might, however, choose some negative consumptions outside their lifetimes in order to finance increased consumption during their natural life spans.

This bizarre behavior will eventually be ruled out by specifying a sufficiently large value for the scalar b. Until this is accomplished, we must restrict consumer t's consumption to K_t, a compact subset of $\mathbb{R}^{\ell(T+1)}$, defined as follows: Given a positive scalar ϵ, define the negative scalar a by

(3.8) $a = \min_{t = 0, ..., T} (\mu_t) - \epsilon.$

It follows from equation (3.3) that $\tilde{\omega}_t^{i,s} > a$ for $i = 1, \ldots, \ell$; $s = 1, \ldots, T+1$; and $t = 0, \ldots, T$. Next define the positive scalar c by

$$(3.9) \qquad c = \max_{\substack{i=1,\ldots,\ell \\ s=1,\ldots,T+1}} (r^{i,s}) + \epsilon - Ta.$$

Then define the set $K_t \subset \mathbb{R}^{\ell(T+1)}$ by

$$(3.10) \qquad K_t = \{\tilde{x}_t \in \mathbb{R}^{\ell(T+1)} \mid a \le x_t^{i,s} \le c$$
$$\text{for } i = 1, \ldots, \ell \text{ and } s = 1, \ldots, T+1\},$$

for $t = 0, \ldots, T$. The set K_t is obviously compact (and independent of t). We restrict $\tilde{x}_t$ to K_t. This restriction is essential in the associated no-taxation economy because without it there could be the possibility of negative consumptions that are unbounded.

Let $p = (p^1, \ldots, p^{T+1})$ be the commodity price vector. Restrict prices in the associated economy to the normalized set

$$\tilde{\mathcal{P}} = \left\{ p \in \mathbb{R}_+^{\ell(T+1)} \,\middle|\, \sum_{t,i} p^{t,i} = 1 \right\}.$$

Let $w_t = p \cdot \tilde{\omega}_t \in \mathbb{R}$ be the wealth of consumer t, $t = 0, 1, \ldots, T$. Consumer t is assumed to maximize $v_t(\tilde{x}_t)$ subject to the constraints $\tilde{x}_t \in K_t$ and $p \cdot \tilde{x}_t \le p \cdot \tilde{\omega}_t = w_t$. This consumer's demands can then be described by the upper hemi-continuous correspondence $\tilde{f}_t : (p, w_t) \mapsto \tilde{x}_t$ so that $\tilde{f}_t : \tilde{\mathcal{P}} \times \mathbb{R} \to K_t \subset \mathbb{R}^{\ell(T+1)}$.

We next define competitive equilibrium for the associated no-taxation economy.

3.11. Definition. Competitive equilibrium for the associated (finite) economy with endowments $\tilde{\omega} \in \mathbb{R}^{\ell(T+1)(T+1)}$ is a price vector $p \in \tilde{\mathcal{P}}$ satisfying

$$\sum_{t=0}^{T} \tilde{f}_t(p, p \cdot \tilde{\omega}_t) \le \sum_{t=0}^{T} \tilde{\omega}_t$$

with strict equality for component (t, i) if $p^{t,i} > 0$, $t = 1, \ldots, T+1$ and $i = 1, \ldots, \ell$.

3.12. Lemma. Consider the associated economy with endowments $\tilde{\omega} \in \mathbb{R}^{\ell(T+1)(T+1)}$ satisfying the system (3.3). There is a price vector $p \in \tilde{\mathcal{P}}$ that is a competitive equilibrium for the associated economy (Definition 3.11).

Proof: First, we use the theorem in Debreu (1962, pp. 259–260) to establish the existence of a compensated equilibrium (or quasiequilibrium), $p \in \tilde{\mathcal{P}}$.

(i) The set K_t is closed, convex, and bounded by construction (3.8)–(3.10). (ii) Because of (3.5) and (3.8)–(3.10), we know that for each attainable $\tilde{x}_t$ in K_t there is a $\tilde{y}_t$ in K_t that is preferred by consumer t to $\tilde{x}_t$. (iii) Also, for every $\tilde{y}_t$ in K_t, the set $\{\tilde{x}_t \in K_t \mid \tilde{x}_t \gtrsim_t \tilde{y}_t\}$ is closed in K_t and is convex. We have thus established the existence of a compensated equilibrium.

Second, observe that each individual endowment vector lies in the interior of the consumption set. In particular, $\tilde{\omega}_t$ is in the interior of K_t for $t = 0, 1, ..., T$. Thus, consumers are (directly) resource related to one another (cf. Arrow and Hahn 1971, Chapter 5). Thus the compensated equilibrium $p \in \tilde{\mathcal{P}}$ is a competitive equilibrium (Definition 3.11).

Q.E.D.

In equilibrium, some (but not all) of the components of the price vector $p \in \tilde{\mathcal{P}}$ may be zero. The corresponding consumption allocation vector $\tilde{x} = (\tilde{x}_0, ..., \tilde{x}_T) \in (\tilde{f}_0(p, p \cdot \tilde{\omega}_0), ..., \tilde{f}_T(p, p \cdot \tilde{\omega}_T))$ contains components that are nonpositive. (In particular, we have as a consequence of the nonnegativity of prices, Property 3.7 and Definition 3.11 that $x_t^s \leq 0$ for $t = 1, ..., T$; $s \neq t$, $s \neq t+1$, and $x_0^s \leq 0$ for $s \neq 1$.) The corresponding vector of individual wealths $w = (w_0, ..., w_T)$ may contain some zero components and some negative components. We next establish that the first component of p is necessarily positive.

3.13. Lemma. Let p be a competitive equilibrium for the associated economy (Definition 3.11). Then the first component of p is positive; that is, $p^{1,1} \in \mathbb{R}_{++}$.

Proof: Assume otherwise; that is, assume that $p^{1,1} = 0$. This implies that $p^1 = 0$ and $p^2 = 0$; otherwise, w_1 would be positive, which implies that $x_1 = (x_1^1, x_1^2)$ would in equilibrium be a strictly positive vector. Then (p^1, p^2) would be proportional to $\operatorname{grad} u_1(x_1^1, x_1^2)$. Because of the assumptions made on u_1, if any component of (p^1, p^2) is positive, all components must be positive.

Assume that $p^t = 0$ for some t ($t = 2, ..., T$). Under the assumption that $p^{1,1} = 0$, we have that unless (p^t, p^{t+1}) is identically zero, then w_t is positive and thus (x_t^t, x_t^{t+1}) is strictly positive. Hence, (p^t, p^{t+1}) must be proportional to $\operatorname{grad} u_t(x_t^t, x_t^{t+1})$. Therefore, $p^t = 0$ implies $p^{t+1} = 0$ for $t = 2, ..., T$.

We have established that $p^{1,1} = 0$ implies $p = 0$. The zero vector does not belong to $\tilde{\mathcal{P}}$ because $0 + \cdots + 0 \neq 1$. We have a contradiction. Hence, we have established that $p^{1,1}$ is positive. Q.E.D.

Nonpositive wealths and zero prices must be allowed for in the associated economy because negative endowments of commodity $(1, 1)$ are permitted. Hence, in equilibrium, nonpositive consumptions during consumers' natural life spans are possible. If, however, the balanced tax-transfer vector $\mu = (\mu_0, \ldots, \mu_T)$ were sufficiently close to zero, then one would expect equilibrium prices to be strictly positive, equilibrium wealths to be strictly positive, and hence equilibrium consumptions during consumers' lifetimes to be strictly positive. Having found a set of balanced tax-transfer vectors sufficiently close to zero, one could then choose a sufficiently large value for the scalar b so that in equilibrium consumption of goods outside the consumers' lifetimes is zero (and so that in equilibrium the restrictions to the sets K_t are inessential). These ideas are formalized in the next proposition, which can be taken as an extension of Proposition 3.6 in Balasko and Shell (1983).

Define the sequence $\{\mu^\nu\} = \{(\mu_0^\nu, \ldots, \mu_T^\nu)\}$ where $\mu^\nu \in \mathbb{R}^{T+1}$ and $\sum_{s=0}^{T} \mu_s^\nu = 0$. Assume that μ^ν converges pointwise to 0 as $\nu \to \infty$. Let $p^\nu \in \tilde{\mathscr{P}}$ be the equilibrium price vector for the associated economy (Definition 3.11) when $(\mu_0, \ldots, \mu_T) = (\mu_0^\nu, \ldots, \mu_T^\nu)$ and ω is fixed. Define in the natural way the corresponding endowment vector $\tilde{\omega}^\nu = (\tilde{\omega}_0^\nu, \ldots, \tilde{\omega}_T^\nu) \in \mathbb{R}^{\ell(T+1)(T+1)}$, the corresponding equilibrium consumption allocations $\tilde{x}^\nu = (\tilde{x}_0^\nu, \ldots, \tilde{x}_T^\nu) \in \mathbb{R}^{\ell(T+1)(T+1)}$ and $x^\nu = (x_0^\nu, \ldots, x_T^\nu) \in \mathbb{R}^{\ell(2T+1)}$ and so forth.

3.14. Proposition. Consider the sequence of vectors $\{\mu^\nu\} = \{(\mu_0^\nu, \ldots, \mu_T^\nu)\}$ satisfying $\sum_{t=0}^{T} \mu_t^\nu = 0$ for each $\nu = 1, 2, \ldots$ and that converges pointwise to zero as $\nu \to +\infty$. Then there is a ν^* such that for $\nu \geq \nu^*$, the corresponding equilibrium price vector p^ν and consumption allocation vector x^ν in the associated economy are each strictly positive. Thus, we have $p^\nu \in \mathbb{R}_{++}^{\ell(T+1)}$ and $x^\nu \in \mathbb{R}_{++}^{\ell(2T+1)}$ for $\nu \geq \nu^*$. Furthermore, if the scalar b [defined in property (3.5)] is sufficiently large, then the corresponding equilibrium extended allocation vector $\tilde{x}^\nu$ is zero on all but $\ell(2T+1)$ components for $\nu \geq \nu^*$.

Proof: As $\nu \to +\infty$, $\omega_0^{1,1} + \mu_0^\nu \to \omega_0^{1,1}$. Hence, there is a ν_0 such that for $\nu \geq \nu_0$, $(x_0^1)^\nu$ belongs to X_0, a nonempty, compact subset of $\mathbb{R}_{++}^\ell$ defined by

$$X_0 = \{x_0^1 \mid x_0^{1,i} \leq c \text{ for } i = 1, \ldots, \ell \text{ and } u_0(x_0^1) \geq u_0(\omega_0^1/2)\},$$

where $c \in \mathbb{R}_{++}$ is defined in equation (3.9). For $\nu \geq \nu_0$, the price vector $(p^1)^\nu$ is proportional to $\operatorname{grad} u_0((x_0^1)^\nu) \in \mathbb{R}_{++}^\ell$. By Lemma 3.12, $(p^{1,1})^\nu \in \mathbb{R}_{++}$ for each ν. Hence, we have $(p^1)^\nu \in \mathbb{R}_{++}^\ell$ for $\nu \geq \nu_0$. Furthermore, since u_0 is strictly quasiconcave, we know that there are vectors $\alpha^1 =$

$(\alpha^{1,1}, ..., \alpha^{1,\ell}) \in \mathbb{R}^{\ell}_{++}$ and $\beta^1 = (\beta^{1,1}, ..., \beta^{1,\ell}) \in \mathbb{R}^{\ell}_{++}$ with the property

$$0 < \alpha^1 \le (p^1)^{\nu}/(p^{1,1})^{\nu} \le \beta^1 < +\infty$$

for $\nu \ge \nu_0$ [cf. Arrow and Hahn (1971, pp. 29–30, 101–104) and Balasko and Shell (1980, Lemma 3.4, pp. 287–288)].

As $\nu \to +\infty$, $\omega_1^{1,1} + \mu_1^{\nu} \to \omega_1^{1,1}$. Hence, there is $\nu_1 \ge \nu_0$ such that for $\nu \ge \nu_1$, $((x_1^1)^{\nu}, (x_1^2)^{\nu})$ belongs to X_1, a nonempty, compact subset of $\mathbb{R}^{2\ell}_{++}$ defined by

$$X_1 = \{(x_1^1, x_1^2) \mid x_1^{s,i} \le c \text{ for } s = 1, 2; \ i = 1, ..., \ell, \text{ and}$$

$$u_1(x_1^1, x_1^2) \ge u_1(\omega_1^1/2, \omega_1^2)\},$$

where $c \in \mathbb{R}_{++}$ is defined in equation (3.9). For $\nu \ge \nu_1$, the price vector $((p^1)^{\nu}, (p^2)^{\nu})$ is proportional to grad $u_1((x_1^1)^{\nu}, (x_1^2)^{\nu}) \in \mathbb{R}^{2\ell}_{++}$. Since $(p^1)^{\nu} \in \mathbb{R}^{\ell}_{++}$, we have that $(p^2)^{\nu} \in \mathbb{R}^{\ell}_{++}$ for $\nu \ge \nu_1$. Furthermore, there are vectors $\alpha^2 = (\alpha^{2,1}, ..., \alpha^{2,\ell}) \in \mathbb{R}^{\ell}_{++}$ and $\beta^2 = (\beta^{2,1}, ..., \beta^{2,\ell}) \in \mathbb{R}^{\ell}_{++}$ with the property

$$0 < \alpha^2 \le (p^2)^{\nu}/(p^{1,1})^{\nu} \le \beta^2 < +\infty$$

for $\nu \ge \nu_1$.

Assume that for some particular t $(t = 2, ..., T)$ there is ν_{t-1} such that for $\nu \ge \nu_{t-1}$ we have

$$0 < \alpha^t \le (p^t)^{\nu}/(p^{1,1})^{\nu} \le \beta^t < +\infty,$$

where $\alpha^t = (\alpha^{t,1}, ..., \alpha^{t,\ell}) \in \mathbb{R}^{\ell}_{++}$ and $\beta^t = (\beta^{t,1}, ..., \beta^{t,\ell}) \in \mathbb{R}^{\ell}_{++}$. Wealth of consumer t is given by

$$w_t^{\nu} = (p^{\nu}) \cdot (\tilde{\omega}_t^{\nu}) = (p^{1,1})^{\nu} \mu_t^{\nu} + (p^t)^{\nu} \cdot \omega_t^t + (p^{t+1})^{\nu} \cdot \omega_t^{t+1}$$

$$\ge (p^t)^{\nu} \cdot (\omega_t^{t,1} + \min(0, \mu_t^{\nu}/\alpha^{t,1}), \omega_t^{t,2}, ..., \omega_t^{t,\ell}) + (p^{t+1})^{\nu} \cdot \omega_t^{t+1}$$

for $\nu \ge \nu_{t-1}$. Hence there is a $\nu_t \ge \nu_{t-1}$ such that $((x_t^t)^{\nu}, (x_t^{t+1})^{\nu})$ belongs to X_t, a nonempty, compact subset of $\mathbb{R}^{2\ell}_{++}$ defined by

$$X_t = \{(x_t^t, x_t^{t+1}) \mid x_t^{s,i} \le c \text{ for } s = t, t+1, \ i = 1, ..., \ell, \text{ and}$$

$$u_t(x_t^t, x_t^{t+1}) \ge u_t(\omega_t^t/2, \omega_t^{t+1})\}$$

for $\nu \ge \nu_t$, where $c \in \mathbb{R}_{++}$ is defined in equation (3.9). It follows that $(p^{t+1})^{\nu} \in \mathbb{R}^{\ell}_{++}$ for $\nu \ge \nu_t$ and furthermore that there are vectors $\alpha^{t+1} = (\alpha^{t+1,1}, ..., \alpha^{t+1,\ell}) \in \mathbb{R}^{\ell}_{++}$ and $\beta^{t+1} = (\beta^{t+1,1}, ..., \beta^{t+1,\ell}) \in \mathbb{R}^{\ell}_{++}$ with the property

$$0 < \alpha^{t+1} \le (p^{t+1})^{\nu}/(p^{1,1})^{\nu} \le \beta^{t+1} < +\infty$$

for $\nu \ge \nu_t$.

Let $\nu^* = \nu_T$. The proof by induction is complete. We have established that there is a ν^* with the property that $x^\nu \in \mathbb{R}_{++}^{\ell(2T+1)}$, $p^\nu \in \mathbb{R}_{++}^{\ell(T+1)}$, and $w^\nu \in \mathbb{R}_{++}^{T+1}$ for $\nu \geq \nu^*$.

Since grad u_t is a continuous function of x_t on the compact set X_t, we can provide an upper bound on marginal utilities. In particular, we know there is a positive scalar γ with the properties

(i) $\gamma > \dfrac{\partial u_t(x_t^l, x_t^{l+1})}{\partial x_t^{s,i}}$ for $s = t$, $s = t+1$; $i = 1, \ldots, \ell$;

$$(x_t^l, x_t^{l+1}) \in X_t; \ t = 1, \ldots, T$$

and

(ii) $\gamma > \dfrac{\partial u_0(x_0^1)}{\partial x_0^{1,i}}$ for $i = 1, \ldots, \ell$; $x_0^1 \in X_0$.

Let $\alpha^{t,i}$ and $\beta^{t,i}$ be the upper and lower bounds on the price ratio $p^{t,i}/p^{1,1}$ that were derived in the first part of the proof. Choose positive scalars α and β that satisfy $\alpha < \alpha^{t,i}$ and $\beta > \beta^{t,i}$ for $i = 1, \ldots, \ell$; $t = 1, \ldots, T+1$. Then define the scalar b by

(3.15) $b = \gamma\beta/\alpha$.

Let the extended utility functions v_t defined in equations (3.5) satisfy the restriction (3.15). Then for $\nu \geq \nu^*$, equilibrium consumptions outside natural life spans are zero. Hence, in equilibrium, the extended allocation vector $\tilde{x}^\nu$ is zero on $\ell(T+1)(T+1) - \ell(2T+1)$ components and is strictly positive on the remaining $\ell(2T+1)$ components for $\nu \geq \nu^*$.   Q.E.D.

In the next lemma, we formalize the relationship between competitive equilibrium in the original economy (with taxation) and competitive equilibrium in the associated (no-taxation) economy.

3.16. Lemma. Let T be finite.

(i) Consider the associated no-taxation economy defined by the extended endowment vector $\tilde{\omega} \in \mathbb{R}^{\ell(T+1)(T+1)}$, which is consistent with the construction in (3.3). Assume that there is a competitive equilibrium price vector $p \in \tilde{\mathcal{P}}$ (Definition 3.11). Assume further that p is strictly positive, that is, $p \in \tilde{\mathcal{P}} \cap \mathbb{R}_{++}^{\ell(T+1)}$, equilibrium wealths are strictly positive, that is, $w = (p \cdot \tilde{\omega}_0, \ldots, p \cdot \tilde{\omega}_t, \ldots, p \cdot \tilde{\omega}_T) \in \mathbb{R}_{++}^{T+1}$, and the equilibrium allocation vector x is strictly positive, that is, $x = (x_0, \ldots, x_t, \ldots, x_T) \in \mathbb{R}_{++}^{\ell(2T+1)}$, but that the extended equilibrium allocation vector $\tilde{x} = (\tilde{x}_0, \ldots, \tilde{x}_t, \ldots, \tilde{x}_T) \in \mathbb{R}^{\ell(T+1)(T+1)}$ is zero on all but $\ell(2T+1)$ components. Define the price vector $p' \in \mathcal{P}$ by $p' = p/p^{1,1}$. Then $q = (p', 1) \in \mathcal{Q}$ is a competitive equilibrium for the taxation economy (Definition 2.1), where the endowments $\omega \in \mathbb{R}_{++}^{\ell(T+1)}$ together with the balanced tax-transfer policy $\mu \in \mathbb{R}^{T+1}$ satisfy equations (3.3); thus, we have $q = (p', 1) \in \mathcal{Q}(\omega, \mu)$.

(ii) Consider the taxation economy defined by the endowment vector $\omega \in \mathbb{R}_{++}^{\ell(2T+1)}$ and the balanced tax-transfer policy $\mu \in \mathbb{R}^{T+1}$. Assume that there is an equilibrium in which the price of money is unity; that is, assume there is $p \in \mathcal{P}$ with the property $(p, 1) \in \mathcal{Q}(\omega, \mu)$ (Definition 2.1). Define the price vector p' by $p' = p / \sum_{t,i} p^{t,i}$ so that $p' \in \tilde{\mathcal{P}} \cap \mathbb{R}_{++}^{\ell(T+1)}$. Then p' is a competitive equilibrium for the associated economy (Definition 3.11), where the extended endowment vector $\tilde{\omega} \in \mathbb{R}^{\ell(T+1)(T+1)}$ is related to the balanced tax-transfer vector $\mu \in \mathbb{R}^{T+1}$ by equation (3.3), and the scalar b [equation (3.5)] is sufficiently large.

Proof: (i) Fix $\tilde{\omega}$, the extended endowment vector for the associated economy. Choose $\omega \in \mathbb{R}_{++}^{\ell(2T+1)}$ and $\mu = (\mu_0, \ldots, \mu_t, \ldots, \mu_T) \in \mathbb{R}^{T+1}$, which together satisfy equations (3.3) and $\sum_{t=0}^{T} \mu_t = 0$. Let $p^m = 1$, and define the vector of wealths

$$w' = (p' \cdot \omega_0 + \mu_0, \ldots, p' \cdot \omega_t + \mu_t, \ldots, p' \cdot \omega_t + \mu_t)$$

$$= (p' \cdot \tilde{\omega}_0, \ldots, p' \cdot \tilde{\omega}_t, \ldots, p' \cdot \tilde{\omega}_T)$$

$$= (1/p^{1,1})(p \cdot \tilde{\omega}_0, \ldots, p \cdot \tilde{\omega}_t, \ldots, p \cdot \tilde{\omega}_T) = (1/p^{1,1})w.$$

Since (p', w') is proportional to (p, w), it follows that $f_0^{1,i}(p', w_0') = \tilde{f}_0^{1,i}(p, w_0) \in \mathbb{R}_{++}$ for $i = 1, \ldots, \ell$ and $f_t^{s,i}(p', w_t') = \tilde{f}_t^{s,i}(p, w_t) \in \mathbb{R}_{++}$ for $s = t, t+1; \; i = 1, \ldots, \ell; \; t = 1, \ldots, T$. It follows from definitions 2.1 and 3.11 that $q = (p', 1) \in \mathcal{Q}(\omega, \mu)$. (ii) Let

$$x = (x_0, \ldots, x_t, \ldots, x_T) = (x_0^1, \ldots, x_t^t, x_t^{t+1}, \ldots, x_T^T, x_T^{T+1}) \in \mathbb{R}_{++}^{\ell(2T+1)}$$

be the competitive allocation in the taxation economy with $p^m = 1$. Define the scalar b [cf. equation (3.5)] as in equation (3.15) except that the sets X_t $(t = 0, \ldots, T)$ are replaced by the sets Y_t $(t = 0, \ldots, T)$ where

$$Y_0 = \{y_0^1 \in \mathbb{R}_{++}^{\ell} \mid y_0^{1,i} \leq c \text{ for } i = 1, \ldots, \ell \text{ and } u_0(y_0^1) \geq u_0(x_0^1/2)\}$$

and

$$Y_t = \{(y_t^t, y_t^{t+1}) \in \mathbb{R}_{++}^{2\ell} \mid y_t^{s,i} \leq c \text{ for } s = t, t+1; \; i = 1, \ldots, \ell$$

$$\text{and } u_t(y_t^t, y_t^{t+1}) \geq u_t(x_t^t/2, x_t^{t+1})\}$$

for $t = 1, \ldots, T$. Define w', the vector of wealths in the associated economy, by

$$w' = p' \cdot \tilde{\omega} = (p' \cdot \tilde{\omega}_0, \ldots, p' \cdot \tilde{\omega}_t, \ldots, p' \cdot \tilde{\omega}_T)$$

$$= (1/(p^{1,1})')(p \cdot \tilde{\omega}_0, \ldots, p \cdot \tilde{\omega}_t, \ldots, p \cdot \tilde{\omega}_T)$$

$$= (1/(p^{1,1})')(p \cdot \omega_0 + \mu_0, \ldots, p \cdot \omega_t + \mu_t, \ldots, p \cdot \omega_T + \mu_T) = w/(p^{1,1})',$$

where $w \in \mathbb{R}_{++}^{T+1}$ is the vector of wealths in the taxation economy. Because (p', w') is proportional to (p, w) and b is sufficiently large, we have

$$\tilde{f}_0^{i,1}(p', w_0') = f_0^{1,i}(p, w_0) \in \mathbb{R}_{++} \quad \text{for } i = 1, \ldots, \ell,$$

$$\tilde{f}_t^{s,i}(p', w_t') = f_t^{s,i}(p, w_t) \in \mathbb{R}_{++} \quad \text{for } s = t, s = t+1;$$

$$i = 1, \ldots, \ell; \ t = 1, \ldots, T,$$

and

$$\tilde{f}_t^{s,i}(p', w_t') = 0 \quad \text{otherwise.} \qquad \text{Q.E.D.}$$

In the next three propositions, we complete our analysis (for the finite-horizon taxation economy) of the set of normalized bonafide tax-transfer policies, $\mathfrak{M}_B(\omega)$.

3.17. Proposition. Fix resources $r \in \mathbb{R}_{++}^{\ell(T+1)}$. Any Pareto-optimal allocation is a competitive equilibrium allocation associated with the fixed endowment vector $\omega = (\omega_0, \ldots, \omega_t, \ldots, \omega_T) \in \mathbb{R}_{++}^{\ell(2T+1)}$ satisfying $\sum_{t=0}^{T} \omega_t = r$ and some tax-transfer policy $\mu = (\mu_0, \ldots, \mu_t, \ldots, \mu_T) \in \mathfrak{M}_B(\omega)$.

Proof: Let $\mathcal{P} \subset \mathbb{R}_{++}^{\ell(2T+1)}$ be the set of Pareto-optimal allocations $x = (x_0, \ldots, x_t, \ldots, x_T)$ defined by the given consumer preferences and the given resources r. Let $g : \mathcal{P} \to \mathcal{P}$ be the mapping that associates the Pareto-optimal allocation with the unique price vector that supports x. Define $\psi(x)$ by $\psi(x) = g(x) \cdot ((x_0 - \omega_0), \ldots, (x_t - \omega_t), \ldots, (x_T - \omega_T))$. We have $\psi(x) \in \mathbb{R}^{T+1}$. Let $\mu = (\mu_0, \ldots, \mu_t, \ldots, \mu_T) = \psi(x)$. Because $\sum_{t=0}^{T} x_t = r = \sum_{t=0}^{T} \omega_t$, it follows that $\sum_{t=0}^{T} \mu_t = 0$. Observe that if $q = (p, 1) \in \mathcal{Q}(\omega, \mu)$ is a competitive equilibrium price system, then the competitive equilibrium allocation vector is $(f_0(p, p \cdot \omega_0 + \mu_0), \ldots, f_t(p, p \cdot \omega_t + \mu_t), \ldots, f_T(p, p \cdot \omega_T + \mu_T))$. Hence, $\mu = \psi(x)$ is the unique normalized tax-transfer policy that decentralizes the Pareto-optimal allocation x.   Q.E.D.

Proposition 3.17 is the lump-sum taxation version of the second fundamental theorem of welfare economics. It is given for completeness and because its proof is useful for the proof of the following proposition, which along with Corollary 3.19 completes our analysis for the finite-horizon economy of the set of normalized bonafide tax-transfer policies.

3.18. Proposition. Let T be finite. The set of normalized bonafide tax-transfer policies, $\mathfrak{M}_B(\omega)$, is bounded, arc connected, and 0 is contained in its relative interior.

Proof: The ambient space is

$$\left\{ \mu = (\mu_0, \ldots, \mu_t, \ldots, \mu_T) \in \mathbb{R}^{T+1} \,\middle|\, \sum_{t=0}^{T} \mu_t = 0 \right\}.$$

   (i) *Interiority of* 0. If $\mu = 0$ and $p^m = 1$, then $w_t = p \cdot \omega_t$ for $t = 0, 1, \ldots, T$. Hence the equations in Definition 2.1 reduce to those for a standard exchange economy without taxation (cf., e.g., Arrow and Hahn 1971, Chapter 5). Thus, there is $p \in \mathbb{R}_{++}^{\ell(T+1)}$ such that $(p, 1) \in \mathfrak{Q}(\omega, 0)$. From Proposition 3.14 and Lemma 3.16, there is a ball $\mathfrak{B}$ of balanced tax-transfer policies containing 0 such that for each $\mu \in \mathfrak{B}$ there is some p with $(p, 1) \in \mathfrak{Q}(\omega, \mu)$: that is, $0 \in \text{int } \mathfrak{B}$ and $\mathfrak{B} \subset \mathfrak{M}_B(\omega)$. Hence, 0 is contained in the relative interior of $\mathfrak{M}_B(\omega)$.

   (ii) *Boundedness.* Let ψ and g be the continuous mappings defined in the proof of Proposition 3.16. Let $\bar{\mathfrak{P}}$ be the closure of the set of Pareto-optimal allocations $\mathfrak{P}$. The mappings g and ψ have continuous extensions from $\mathfrak{P}$ to $\bar{\mathfrak{P}}$. The image $\psi(\bar{\mathfrak{P}})$ is compact and hence bounded. Since we have $\psi(\mathfrak{P}) \subset \psi(\bar{\mathfrak{P}})$, it follows that $\psi(\mathfrak{P})$ is bounded.

   (iii) It is well known that the set of Pareto-optimal allocations is arc connected (cf. e.g., Balasko 1979, Appendix 3, pp. 378–379). Hence, $\mathfrak{M}_B(\omega)$ is arc connected as the image by the continuous mapping ψ of the set $\mathfrak{P}$.   Q.E.D.

3.19. Corollary. Let T be finite. The tax-transfer policy

$$\mu = (\mu_0, \ldots, \mu_t, \ldots, \mu_T)$$

is bonafide (Definition 2.4) if and only if it is balanced (Definition 3.1). That is, we have $\{\lambda\mu \mid \mu \in \mathfrak{M}_B(\omega) \text{ and } \lambda \in \mathbb{R}_+\} = \{\mu \in \mathbb{R}^{T+1} \mid \sum_{t=0}^{T} \mu_t = 0\}$.

Proof: From Proposition 3.2, we have that if μ is bonafide, then μ is balanced.

   From Proposition 3.18, it follows that if μ is balanced so that $\sum_{t=0}^{T} \mu_t = 0$, then for each sufficiently large scalar θ, (μ/θ) belongs to $\mathfrak{M}_B(\omega)$. Hence, from Proposition 2.3, it follows that μ is bonafide (although not necessarily normalized).   Q.E.D.

Corollary 3.19 is our central result for the finite-horizon economy. It extends our result for the static economy (see Balasko and Shell 1983, Corollary 3.7) to the perfect-foresight dynamic economy.

That bonafidelity entails balancedness in finite models (including finite overlapping-generations models) is obvious; see Proposition 3.2. The converse is not obvious. Indeed, if our regularity assumptions are relaxed, it is no longer true that balancedness entails bonafidelity. This is illustrated by the next example.

3.20. Example. Let there be two consumers ($t = 0, 1$), two time periods ($s = 1, 2$), and only one commodity ($\ell = 1$). Assume that consumer 0 has only endowment of and taste for the commodity in period 1 and that consumer 1 has only endowment of and taste for the commodity in period 2. Let $p = (p^1, p^2) \in \tilde{\mathcal{P}} = \{(p^1, p^2) \in \mathbb{R}^2_+ \mid p^1 + p^2 = 1\}$, and let $p^m \in \mathbb{R}_+$ be the price of money. Consider the balanced fiscal policy $\mu = (\mu_0, \mu_1) \in \{(\mu_0, \mu_1) \in \mathbb{R}^2 \mid \mu_0 + \mu_1 = 0\}$. Equilibrium $(p^1, p^2, p^m) \in \tilde{\mathcal{P}} \times \mathbb{R}_+$ is a solution to the system

(3.21) $\max u_0(x_0^1)$ subject to $p^1 x_0^1 \le p^1 \omega_0^1 + p^m \mu_0$,

$\quad\quad\quad \max u_1(x_1^2)$ subject to $p^2 x_1^2 \le p^2 \omega_1^2 + p^m \mu_1$,

and

$\quad\quad\quad x_0^1 \le \omega_0^1$ and $x_1^2 \le \omega_1^2$.

The competitive equilibrium allocation is always autarkic, $x_0^1 = \omega_0^1$ and $x_1^2 = \omega_1^2$, for every $\mu \in \mathbb{R}^2$. Furthermore, p^m must be zero in equilibrium unless $\mu = (0, 0)$. Nontrivial tax-transfer policies μ (whether balanced or not) are not bonafide.

In Example 3.20, consumers are not resource related (cf. Arrow and Hahn 1971, Chapter 5, Section 4), but here this is no bar to existence. Competitive equilibrium always exists; indeed, with $p^m = 0$, *any* $(p^1, p^2) \in \tilde{\mathcal{P}}$ solves (3.21). Nonetheless, only the trivial fiscal policy is bonafide. The reasoning for this is simple. Nonbalanced policies are not bonafide. Focus then on nontrivial balanced fiscal policies. For one h ($h = 0, 1$), we have $\mu_h < 0$. Consumer h must pay a positive money tax, but he has nothing interesting to exchange with the other consumer, who has received a positive money transfer. Only with $p^m = 0$ can consumer h meet his tax obligation.

Our colleague Dave Cass (in an as-yet unpublished work) has extended the results of this section and of Balasko and Shell (1983). He has weakened our regularity assumptions on individual consumers and added the weaker assumption that consumers are (at least) indirectly resource related. He goes on to establish the equivalence of balanced and bonafide tax-transfer policies in finite economies – whether static or dynamic. (This is to be compared with our Corollary 3.19 in this chapter and Corollary 3.7 in Balasko and Shell 1983.)

In the next proposition, we apply the results of Proposition 3.18 to the set of equilibrium money prices.

3.22. Proposition. Let T be finite and let $\mu = (\mu_0, \ldots, \mu_t, \ldots, \mu_T)$ be a nontrivial (not necessarily normalized) balanced tax-transfer policy; hence $\Sigma_{t=0}^{T} \mu_t = 0$. Then the set of equilibrium money prices $\mathcal{P}^m(\omega, \mu)$ (Definition 2.7) is bounded. Furthermore, 0 belongs to $\mathcal{P}^m(\omega, \mu)$ and there is $\bar{p}^m \in \mathbb{R}_{++}$ such that the interval $[0, \bar{p}^m)$ is included in $\mathcal{P}^m(\omega, \mu)$.

Proof: From Proposition 2.8, we know that there is a one-to-one mapping between $\mathfrak{M}_B(\omega) \cap L(\mu)$ and $\mathcal{P}^m(\omega, \mu)$, namely, one in which $p^m \mapsto p^m \mu$. Boundedness of $\mathcal{P}^m(\omega, \mu)$ is a consequence of boundedness of $\mathfrak{M}_B(\omega)$ (Proposition 3.18). Since $0 \in \mathfrak{M}_B(\omega) \cap L(\mu)$, we have $0 \in \mathcal{P}^m(\omega, \mu)$; also see Proposition 2.8.i. Since 0 belongs to the relative interior of $\mathfrak{M}_B(\omega)$ by Proposition 3.18, we have that 0 is not isolated in $\mathcal{P}^m(\omega, \mu)$.   Q.E.D.

For a diagrammatic illustration of the relationship between the sets $\mathfrak{M}_B(\omega)$ and $\mathcal{P}^m(\omega, \mu)$, the reader is referred to Balasko and Shell (1983, Figures 1 and 2).

This concludes our analysis of the finite-horizon economy, although we shall employ the results of this section in the following two sections, which are devoted to the infinite-horizon economy.

4   The infinite-horizon model: strongly balanced tax-transfer policies

Let $T = \infty$. The model described in Section 2 then reduces to the model described in Balasko and Shell (1981, especially Sections 2–4). Our goal is to analyze for this infinite-horizon economy the relationship between balanced tax-transfer policies and bonafide tax-transfer policies. For the static economy and the finite-horizon economy, there is no difficulty in defining balancedness of the government's fiscal policy μ. In the infinite-horizon model, the policy $\mu = (\mu_0, \ldots, \mu_t, \ldots)$ is a sequence in $\mathbb{R}^\infty = \mathfrak{M}$. Not surprisingly, our results are sensitive to the behavior as t becomes large of the sequence $\{\sum_{t=0}^T \mu_s\}$.

We begin with our strongest notion of balancedness. We establish that the corresponding tax-transfer policies are always bonafide.

4.1. Definition. The tax-transfer policy $\mu = (\mu_0, \ldots, \mu_t, \ldots) \in \mathfrak{M} = \mathbb{R}^\infty$ is said to be *strongly balanced* if there is t' ($t' = 0, 1, \ldots$) with the property $\sum_{s=0}^t \mu_s = 0$ for $t \geq t'$.

4.2. Remark. If μ is strongly balanced, then obviously $\mu_t = 0$ for $t > t'$.

Our first step in the program of establishing that strongly balanced policies are bonafide is to truncate the infinite economy at *period* τ and establish the existence of a normalized equilibrium ($p^m = 1$) for the truncated economy. This is made precise in what follows.

4.3. Definition. The sequence $p = (p^1, \ldots, p^\tau, p^{\tau+1}, \ldots) \in \mathcal{P} \subset (\mathbb{R}_{++}^\ell)^\infty$ is said to be a *normalized τ-equilibrium* if the following τ equations are satisfied:

$$(4.4) \qquad f_0^1(p^1, p^1 \cdot \omega_0^1 + \mu_0) + f_1^1(p^1, p^2, p^1 \cdot \omega_1^1 + p^2 \cdot \omega_1^2 + \mu_1) = r^1,$$

$$f_1^2(p^1, p^2, p^1 \cdot \omega_1^1 + p^2 \cdot \omega_1^2 + \mu_1) + f_2^2(p^2, p^3, p^2 \cdot \omega_2^2 + p^3 \cdot \omega_2^3 + \mu_2) = r^2,$$

$$\vdots \qquad\qquad\qquad \vdots$$

$$f_{\tau-1}^\tau(p^{\tau-1}, p^\tau, p^{\tau-1} \cdot \omega_{\tau-1}^{\tau-1} + p^\tau \cdot \omega_{\tau-1}^\tau + \mu_{\tau-1})$$

$$+ f_\tau^\tau(p^\tau, p^{\tau+1}, p^\tau \cdot \omega_\tau^\tau + p^{\tau+1} \cdot \omega_\tau^{\tau+1} + \mu_\tau) = r^\tau,$$

where $f_t^s \in \mathbb{R}_{++}^\ell$ is the vector of demands of consumer t in period s ($t = 0, \ldots, \tau$; $s = 1, \ldots, \tau$).

4.5. Remark. Definition 4.3 is motivated by Definition 3.1 in Balasko and Shell (1980). Clearly, if $p = (p^1, p^2, \ldots, p^t, p^{t+1}, \ldots) \in \mathcal{P}$ is a normalized τ-equilibrium price sequence, then so is $p' = (p'^1, p'^2, \ldots, p'^t, p'^{t+1}, \ldots) \in \mathcal{P}$ satisfying $p'^t = p^t$ for $t = 1, \ldots, t+1$. The components $(p^{\tau+2}, p^{\tau+3}, \ldots)$ are indeterminate in a normalized τ-equilibrium.

In what follows, fix t' ($t' = 0, 1, \ldots$). Consider the strongly balanced tax-transfer policy $\mu^\nu = (\mu_0^\nu, \ldots, \mu_t^\nu, \ldots) \in \mathbb{R}^\infty$ with the property

(4.6) $\displaystyle\sum_{s=0}^{t} \mu_s^\nu = 0$ for $t \geq t'$.

Then form a sequence $\{\mu^\nu\}$ $(\nu = 1, 2, \ldots)$ of such policies that converges pointwise to the zero sequence as $\nu \to \infty$, that is, $\lim_{\nu \to +\infty} \mu^\nu = 0$.

In the next proposition, we establish that there is a $\bar\nu$ with the property that when $\mu = \mu^\nu$ for $\nu \geq \bar\nu$, a normalized τ-equilibrium price sequence $p^\nu = ((p^1)^\nu, \ldots, (p^t)^\nu, \ldots) \in \mathcal{P}$ (Definition 4.3) exists for each $\tau \geq t'$.

4.7. Proposition. Fix t' and construct a sequence of (strongly balanced) tax-transfer policies $\{\mu^\nu\}$ that satisfies equation (4.6) for each ν and converges pointwise to zero as $\nu \to +\infty$. There is then a $\bar\nu$ with the property that for each $\nu \geq \bar\nu$ and each $\tau \geq t'$ there is a normalized τ-equilibrium price sequence $p^\nu \in \mathcal{P}$.

Proof: Append the following equation to the system (4.4):

(4.8) $f_\tau^{\tau+1}(p^\tau, p^{\tau+1}, p^\tau \cdot \omega_\tau^\tau + p^{\tau+1} \cdot \omega_\tau^{\tau+1} + \mu_\tau) = \omega_\tau^{\tau+1}.$

Consider

$$(p^1, \ldots, p^\tau, p^{\tau+1}) \in \{(p^1, \ldots, p^\tau, p^{\tau+1}) \in \mathbb{R}_{++}^{\ell(\tau+1)} \mid p^{1,1} = 1\},$$

which solves the completed system [(4.4) and (4.8)] where $(\mu_0, \ldots, \mu_\tau) = (\mu_0^\nu, \ldots, \mu_\tau^\nu)$ and $\tau \geq t'$ so that $\Sigma_{t=0}^{t=\tau} \mu_t = 0$.

The completed system [(4.4) and (4.8)] is a $(\tau+1)$-consumer general equilibrium system with a balanced tax-transfer policy. From Lemma 3.16 and Proposition 3.14, we have that there is a $\bar\nu$ with the property that for each $\nu \geq \bar\nu$ there is some $((p^1)^\nu, \ldots, (p^\tau)^\nu, (p^{\tau+1})^\nu) \in \mathbb{R}_{++}^{\ell(\tau+1)}$ such that $((p^1)^\nu, \ldots, (p^\tau)^\nu, (p^{\tau+1})^\nu, 1) \in \mathcal{Q}(\omega_0, \ldots, \omega_\tau; \mu_0^\nu, \ldots, \mu_\tau^\nu)$. For $\nu \geq \bar\nu$, construct the normalized τ-equilibrium price sequence $(p^1, \ldots, p^\tau, p^{\tau+1}, \ldots) \in \mathcal{P}$ by setting $p^t = (p^t)^\nu$ for $t = 1, \ldots, \tau+1$ and arbitrarily choosing $p^t \in \mathbb{R}_{++}^\ell$ for $t > \tau+1$. We have constructed a normalized τ-equilibrium price sequence.   Q.E.D.

In what follows, we establish that we can restrict attention to a subset of $\mathcal{P}$ that is compact in the product topology.

4.9. Lemma. Let $\tau \geq t'$ so that $\Sigma_{t=0}^\tau \mu_t^\nu = 0$ for each ν. There are vectors $\bar\alpha^t \in \mathbb{R}^\ell$ and $\bar\beta^t \in \mathbb{R}^\ell$, $t = 1, \ldots, \tau+1$, and an integer $\bar\nu$ with the property that for $\nu \geq \bar\nu$ each normalized τ-equilibrium

$$p^\nu = ((p^1)^\nu, (p^2)^\nu, \ldots, (p^\tau)^\nu, (p^{\tau+1})^\nu, \ldots) \in \mathcal{P}$$

satisfies

(4.10) $0 < \bar{\alpha}' \le (p')'' \le \bar{\beta}' < +\infty$

for $t = 1, \ldots, \tau + 1$. The bounds are independent of the truncation τ. (The integer t' is fixed.) Furthermore, if $q'' = (p'', 1) = ((p^1)'', \ldots, (p')'', \ldots; 1) \in \mathfrak{Q}(\omega_0, \omega_1, \ldots; \mu_0^\nu, \mu_1^\nu, \ldots, \mu_{t'}^\nu, 0, 0, \ldots)$, then the bounds (4.10) hold for $t = 1, 2, \ldots$.

Proof: For $t = 1, \ldots, \tau + 1$, the existence of the bounds in (4.10) follows from Lemma 3.16 and the proof of Proposition 3.14. Varying $\tau = t', t' + 1, \ldots$ completes the proof of Lemma 4.9.   Q.E.D.

Lemma 4.9 allows us to restrict attention to a compact subset of the set of price sequences.

4.11. Definition. Let $\bar{\mathcal{P}} \subset \mathcal{P}$ be defined by

$$\bar{\mathcal{P}} = \{ p = (p^1, \ldots, p^t, \ldots) \in \mathcal{P} \mid 0 < \bar{\alpha}' \le p^t \le \bar{\beta}' < +\infty \text{ for } t = 1, 2, \ldots \},$$

where $\bar{\alpha}'$ and $\bar{\beta}'$ are the bounds defined in Lemma 4.9 [inequalities (4.10)].

Define next $\mathcal{P}(\nu, \tau)$, the set of normalized τ-equilibrium prices sequences in $\bar{\mathcal{P}}$ when the tax transfer policy is μ^ν.

4.12. Definition. Fix $\omega \in X$ and let the balanced tax-transfer policy be $\mu^\nu = (\mu_0^\nu, \ldots, \mu_t^\nu, \ldots) \in \mathfrak{M}$. Then define $\mathcal{P}(\nu, \tau)$ by

$$\mathcal{P}(\nu, \tau) = \{ p \in \bar{\mathcal{P}} \mid p \text{ solves equations (4.4)} \}.$$

Fix t'. By construction, $\{\mathcal{P}(\nu, \tau)\}_{\tau = t'}^{\tau = \infty}$ is a nested, decreasing sequence of nonempty sets. The following two lemmas formalize this idea, which is motivated by Remark 4.2.

4.13. Lemma.

$$\mathcal{P}(\nu, t') \supset \mathcal{P}(\nu, t' + 1) \supset \cdots \supset \mathcal{P}(\nu, \tau) \supset \mathcal{P}(\nu, \tau + 1) \supset \cdots.$$

Proof: The proof follows immediately from Definitions 4.3 and 4.12.
                                                                                Q.E.D.

4.14. Lemma. Fix t'. There is then a $\bar{\nu}$ such that for $\nu \ge \bar{\nu}$ and $\tau \ge t'$, the set $\mathcal{P}(\nu, \tau)$ is nonempty and compact in the product topology.

Proof: (i) Nonemptiness is an immediate consequence of Proposition 4.7.

(ii) Compactness. We have from Definition 4.11 that $\bar{\mathcal{P}}$ is the infinite product of compact sets. Therefore, by Tychonoff's theorem (see, e.g., Bourbaki 1966, Book I, Section 9.5, Theorem 3, p. 88), $\bar{\mathcal{P}}$ is compact for the product topology. For $\nu \geq \bar{\nu}$ and $\tau \geq t'$, $\mathcal{P}(\nu, \tau)$ is a closed subset of $\bar{\mathcal{P}}$ and hence is compact.   Q.E.D.

4.15. Proposition. Let $\mu^\nu \in \mathfrak{M} = \mathbb{R}^\infty$ be a strongly balanced tax-transfer policy. Define $\bar{\nu}$ as in Lemma 4.9. Then for each $\nu \geq \bar{\nu}$, there is a price sequence $p^\nu = ((p^1)^\nu, ..., (p^t)^\nu, ...) \in \bar{\mathcal{P}} \subset \mathcal{P}$ such that $(p^\nu, 1) \in \mathcal{Q}(\omega, \mu^\nu)$.

Proof: Let $\mathcal{P}(\nu) \subset (\mathbb{R}^\ell_{++})^\infty$ be defined by $\mathcal{P}(\nu) = \{p \in \bar{\mathcal{P}} \mid (p, 1) \in \mathcal{Q}(\omega, \mu^\nu)\}$. We have $\mathcal{P}(\nu) = \bigcap_{\tau = t'}^{\tau = \infty} \mathcal{P}(\nu, \tau)$. For $\nu \geq \bar{\nu}$, $\mathcal{P}(\nu)$ is equal to the intersection of a nonincreasing sequence of nonempty compact sets (Lemmas 4.13 and 4.14) and is therefore nonempty (see, e.g., Bourbaki 1966, Book I, Section 9.1, pp. 83–84).   Q.E.D.

We conclude this section with our central result on strongly balanced tax-transfer policies.

4.16. Proposition. Consider the infinite-horizon $(T = +\infty)$ version of the overlapping-generations model presented in Section 2 (see also Balasko and Shell 1981). Each strongly balanced tax-transfer policy is bonafide.

Proof: Fix t' (Definition 4.1). For $\nu \geq \bar{\nu}$ (cf. Lemma 4.9), μ^ν is normalized bonafide (Definition 2.6); that is, $\mu^\nu \in \mathfrak{M}_B(\omega)$ for $\nu \geq \bar{\nu}$, because of Proposition 4.15. But $\{\mu^\nu\}$ is *any* sequence satisfying equation (4.6) and converging pointwise to zero as $\nu \to +\infty$, and hence 0 belongs to the relative interior of $\mathfrak{M}_B(\omega)$ [that is, $0 \in \mathrm{int}(\mathfrak{M}_B(\omega) \cap \{\mu = (\mu_0, ..., \mu_t, ...) \mid \Sigma_{s=0}^t \mu_s = 0$ for $t \geq t'\})$]. Thus, by Proposition 2.3, each $\mu = (\mu_0, ..., \mu_t, ...)$ satisfying $\Sigma_{s=0}^t \mu_s = 0$ for all $t \geq t'$ is bonafide.   Q.E.D.

In the next section, we consider two weaker notions of balancedness. Although these definitions of balancedness seem very natural, neither implies bonafidelity for all economies.

5   The infinite-horizon economy: possible extensions

The central result of Section 4 is that every strongly balanced tax-transfer policy is bonafide. Unless one is willing to severely restrict preferences and endowments, it appears that for the infinite-horizon economy there is no interesting weakening of the definition of balancedness, which necessarily implies bonafidelity. We present here two "conjectured" strengthenings of Proposition 4.16, that is, two weakenings of the hypothesis of Proposition 4.16, and construct counterexamples to each "conjecture."

5.1. Definition. The tax-transfer policy $\mu = (\mu_0, \ldots, \mu_t, \ldots) \in \mathfrak{M} = \mathbb{R}^\infty$ is said to be *asymptotically balanced* if

$$\lim_{t \to \infty} \sum_{s=0}^{t} \mu_s = 0.$$

5.2. "Conjecture." If $\mu \in \mathbb{R}^\infty$ is asymptotically balanced, then μ is bonafide.

Our counterexample to "Conjecture" 5.2 is motivated by the following proposition, which is a simple extension of Proposition 5.8 in Balasko and Shell (1981, p. 129).

5.3. Proposition. Assume that the sequence of aggregate resources $\{r^t\}$ is bounded from above so there is a scalar K $(0 < K < +\infty)$ such that $\|r^t\| < K$ for $t = 1, 2, \ldots$ ($\|\cdot\|$ denotes Euclidean norm). Let $\mu = (\mu_0, \ldots, \mu_t, \ldots) \in \mathbb{R}^\infty$ be a bonafide tax-transfer policy admitting a proper competitive equilibrium $q = (p, p^m) \in \mathfrak{Q}(\omega, \mu)$, with $p^m \neq 0$. Assume that for some scalar θ $(0 \le \theta < +\infty)$ we have

$$\lim_{t \to \infty} (1+\theta)^t \|p^t\| = 0.$$

Then μ necessarily satisfies the equation

$$\lim_{t \to \infty} \sum_{s=0}^{t} (1+\theta)^s \mu_s = 0.$$

Proof: If $\mu \in \mathfrak{M}_B(\omega)$ admits the equilibrium $q = (p, 1) \in \mathfrak{Q}$, then we have

$$-p^{t+1} \cdot f_{t+1}^{t+1}(p, w_{t+1}) < \sum_{s=0}^{t} \mu_s < p^{t+1} \cdot f_t^{t+1}(p, w_t)$$

for $t = 0, 1, \ldots$ (see Balasko and Shell 1981, Proposition 5.5, p. 126). Hence, we also have

$$\left\| \sum_{s=0}^{t-1} \mu_s \right\| < \max(\|p^t \cdot f_{t-1}^t\|, \|p^t \cdot f_t^t\|) \le \|p^t \cdot r^t\| \le \|p^t\| \|r^t\|,$$

and therefore we achieve

$$\|p^t\| > \frac{1}{\|r^t\|}\left\|\sum_{s=0}^{t-1}\mu_s\right\| > \frac{1}{K}\left\|\sum_{s=0}^{t-1}\mu_s\right\|,$$

or

$$(1+\theta)^{t-1}K\|p^t\| > (1+\theta)^{t-1}\left\|\sum_{s=0}^{t-1}\mu_s\right\|.$$

Since by hypothesis the left side of the above inequality approaches zero as t approaches infinity, we have that $(1+\theta)^t\sum_{s=0}^t\mu_s$ converges to zero as t approaches infinity. Proposition 2.3 allows this result to be extended to nonnormalized bonafide tax-transfer policies, in which p^m is not equal to unity.   Q.E.D.

5.4. Counterexample (to "Conjecture" 5.2). Consider the tax-transfer policy $\mu = (\mu_0, \ldots, \mu_t, \ldots) \in \mathbb{R}^\infty$ given by $\mu_0 = 1/(1-\delta)$ and $\mu_t = -\delta^{t-1}$ for $t = 1, 2, \ldots$. Let δ be a scalar with $0 < \delta < 1$. Then the policy μ is asymptotically balanced, since we have

$$(5.5) \quad \sum_{t=0}^\infty \mu_t = \mu_0 + \sum_{t=1}^\infty \mu_t = \frac{1}{1-\delta} - \frac{1}{1-\delta} = 0.$$

On the other hand, the public debt is only "retired at infinity" since

$$(5.6) \quad \sum_{s=0}^t \mu_s > 0 \quad \text{for } t = 0, 1, \ldots,$$

that is, at each date t ($t = 1, 2, \ldots$), the "supply of outside money" is positive; μ is not strongly balanced.

We proceed to construct an economy for which μ is not a bonafide policy. Take the one-commodity case, $\ell = 1$. Assume stationarity of commodity endowments, that is,

$$\omega_t = (\omega_t^t, \omega_t^{t+1}) = (a, b) \in \mathbb{R}^2_{++}$$

for $t = 1, 2, \ldots,$. We have

$$(5.7) \quad w_t = p^m\mu_t + p^t\omega_t^t + p^{t+1}\omega_t^{t+1}$$

$$= -p^m\delta^{t-1} + p^ta + p^{t+1}b$$

for $t = 1, 2, \ldots$. Define accordingly the nonmonetary equivalent endowment[3] ω_t' for consumer t ($t \geq 1$) by

$$(5.8) \quad \omega_t' = ((\omega_t^t)', (\omega_t^{t+1})') = (\omega_t^t - (p^m\delta^{t-1}/p^t), \omega_t^{t+1})$$

$$= (a - (p^m\delta^{t-1}/p^t), b).$$

Assume that $q = (p, p''') = (p^1, \ldots, p^t, \ldots; p''') \in \mathfrak{Q}(\omega, \mu)$ and $p''' \neq 0$. An immediate consequence of equilibrium [cf., e.g., Balasko and Shell 1981, equations (3.4.1), p. 120] is

$$(5.9) \quad x_t^t = a - \frac{p'''}{p^t} \left[\frac{1}{1-\delta} - \sum_{s=0}^{t-2} \delta^s \right].$$

That is, in equilibrium, consumer t sells period-t commodity to consumer $t-1$ in exchange for all of the money held by consumer $t-1$ (which is equal to $[1/(1-\delta) - \sum_{s=0}^{t-2} \delta^s] > 0$). We know that

$$\sum_{s=0}^{t} \mu_s = \frac{1}{1-\delta} - \sum_{s=0}^{t-1} \delta^s = \left[\frac{1}{1-\delta} - \sum_{s=0}^{t-2} \delta^s \right] - (\delta)^{t-1} > 0,$$

which implies

$$(5.10) \quad \frac{1}{1-\delta} - \sum_{s=0}^{t-2} \delta^s > \delta^{t-1}.$$

Combining equations (5.8)–(5.10) yields

$$(5.11) \quad \omega_t^t > (\omega_t^t)' > x_t^t,$$

which implies that $(\omega_t^t)' > 0$, since in equilibrium $x_t^t \in \mathbb{R}_{++}$.

Hence, in equilibrium, (x_t^t, x_t^{t+1}) must belong to $\mathfrak{X}$, a subset of $\mathbb{R}_{++}^2$ defined by

$$\mathfrak{X} = \{(x_t^t, x_t^{t+1}) \in \mathbb{R}_{++}^2 \mid x_t^t < a \text{ and } x_t^{t+1} > b\}.$$

Without violating our regularity assumptions, we can choose (stationary or nonstationary) utility functions $u_t(\cdot)$ with the property

$$(5.12) \quad \sup_{(x_t^t, x_t^{t+1}) \in \mathfrak{X}} \left(\frac{\partial u_t / \partial x_t^{t+1}}{\partial u_t / \partial x_t^t} \right) < \delta - \epsilon$$

for some positive scalar ϵ and for each $t \geq 1$. Thus, in equilibrium, we have

$$(5.13) \quad 0 < (p^{t+1}/p^t) < \delta - \epsilon.$$

From equations (5.8) and (5.13), we obtain

$$(5.14) \quad (\omega_t^t)' < a - \frac{p'''(\delta)^{t-1}}{(\delta - \epsilon)^{t-1}}.$$

From equation (5.14), we see that for t sufficiently large we have $(\omega_t^t)' < 0$, which by equation (5.11) contradicts the equilibrium requirement that $x_t^t \in \mathbb{R}_{++}$.

We have constructed a simple overlapping-generations economy in which the asymptotically balanced (but not strongly balanced) tax-transfer policy μ is not bonafide.

In the following definition, we present our third notion of balancedness for the infinite-horizon economy.

5.15. Definition. The tax-transfer policy $\mu = (\mu_0, \ldots, \mu_t, \ldots) \in \mathbb{R}^\infty$ is said to be *recurrently balanced* if there is a sequence of positive integers $\{t^\nu\}$ approaching $+\infty$ as ν approaches $+\infty$ with the property that for each ν,

$$\sum_{t=0}^{t^\nu} \mu_s = 0.$$

If μ is recurrently balanced (or, alternatively, balanced infinitely often), then for each t^ν (Definition 5.15) there is a corresponding finite-horizon economy that admits a positive equilibrium price of money. This suggests the following "conjecture."

5.16. "Conjecture." If $\mu \in \mathbb{R}^\infty$ is a recurrently balanced tax-transfer policy, then μ is bonafide.

In the following, we sketch a counterexample to "Conjecture" 5.16; we rely on the approach used in Counterexample 5.14.

5.17. Counterexample (to "Conjecture" 5.16). First, we choose $\mu \in \mathbb{R}^\infty$ that is recurrently balanced (Definition 5.15). Let there be a sequence of positive integers $\{t^\nu\}$ such that $t^{\nu+1} > t^\nu$ and

$$\sum_{s=0}^{t^\nu} \mu_s = 0$$

for each t^ν. Let $m^\nu \in \mathbb{R}_+$ be defined by

(5.18) $\quad m^\nu = \max_{t^k \in T^\nu} \sum_{s=0}^{t^k} \mu_s,$

where $T^\nu = \{t^\nu, t^\nu+1, \ldots, t^{\nu+1}\}$. Define t_*^ν as the argmax of the right side of equation (5.18) so that

(5.19) $\quad m^\nu = \sum_{s=0}^{t_*^\nu} \mu_s.$

Let δ be a positive fraction. Choose $\mu = (\mu_0, \ldots, \mu_t, \ldots) \in \mathbb{R}^\infty$ to be recurrently balanced (Definition 5.15) with the following additional properties:

$$(5.20) \quad \mu_{t^\nu_* + 1} = -(\delta)^{t^\nu_*}$$

and

$$(5.21) \quad m^\nu > \delta^{t^\nu_*}$$

for $\nu = 1, 2, \ldots$. By construction, we have $t^\nu_* \in (t^\nu + 1, \ldots, t^{\nu+1} - 2\}$, that is, $t^\nu_* \neq t^\nu$, $t^\nu_* \neq t^{\nu+1} - 1$, and $t^\nu_* \neq t^{\nu+1}$, for $\nu = 1, 2, \ldots$. Consider next consumer $t^\nu_* + 1$. An immediate consequence of equilibrium in this model is

$$(5.22) \quad (x^{t^\nu_* + 1}_{t^\nu_* + 1}) = a - \frac{p^m m^\nu}{p^{t^\nu_* + 1}}$$

(see Balasko and Shell 1981, equations (3.4.1), p. 120). There are only two consumers alive in period $t^\nu_* + 1$. In equilibrium, consumer $t^\nu_* + 1$ sells period-$(t^\nu_* + 1)$ commodity to consumer t^ν_* in exchange for all his money, m^ν.

As in equation (5.8), we calculate the no-taxation equivalent endowment for consumer $t^\nu_* + 1$,

$$(\omega_{t^\nu_* + 1})' = ((\omega^{t^\nu_* + 1}_{t^\nu_* + 1})', b),$$

where from equation (5.20) we have

$$(5.23) \quad (\omega^{t^\nu_* + 1}_{t^\nu_* + 1})' = a - \frac{p^m (\delta)^{t^\nu_*}}{p^{t^\nu_* + 1}}.$$

Combining equation (5.20)–(5.23) yields

$$(5.24) \quad (\omega^{t^\nu_* + 1}_{t^\nu_* + 1})' > x^{t^\nu_* + 1}_{t^\nu_* + 1}.$$

As before, the utility functions $u_t(\cdot)$ can be chosen so that inequality (5.12) is satisfied on $\mathfrak{X} = \{(x^t_t, x^{t+1}_t) \in \mathbb{R}^2_{++} \mid x^t_t < a \text{ and } x^{t+1}_t > b\}$ for $t = 1, 2, \ldots$. Thus, for a given $\epsilon > 0$, in equilibrium, commodity prices $\{p^t\}$ must satisfy

$$(5.25) \quad 0 < (p^{t+1}/p^t) < \delta - \epsilon$$

for $t = 1, 2, \ldots$. But $p^1 = 1$, and thus for ν sufficiently large, $(\omega^{t^\nu_* + 1}_{t^\nu_* + 1})'$ is negative by equations (5.23) and (5.25). Therefore, using equation (5.24), we have $(x^{t^\nu_* + 1}_{t^\nu_* + 1})$ is also negative for ν sufficiently large, which is a contradiction to the equilibrium conditions (Definition 2.1).

We have constructed a simple overlapping-generations economy in which the recurrently balanced (but not strongly balanced) tax-transfer policy μ is not bonafide.

5.26. Remark. Counterexample 5.17 shows that not all recurrently balanced tax-transfer policies are bonafide. Close reading of the argument in the counterexample [see especially equations (5.20) and (5.21)] shows that if we restrict attention to recurrently balanced policies $\mu = (\mu_0, \dots,$ $\mu_1, \dots) \in \mathbb{R}^\infty$ with the additional property $m^\nu \to 0$ as $\nu \to +\infty$, we can still construct economies for which μ is not bonafide. Policies with the property that the limit superior of the outside money supply is zero are not necessarily bonafide even if we restrict attention to recurrently balanced tax-transfer policies.

Finally, we remind the reader of the well-known fact that there are economies for which nonbalanced tax-transfer policies are bonafide.

5.27. Definition. A tax-transfer policy $\mu = (\mu_0, \dots, \mu_t, \dots) \in \mathfrak{M} = \mathbb{R}^\infty$ is said to be *passive* if $\mu_t = 0$ for $t \geq 1$.

5.28. Observation. Consider the passive tax-transfer policy

$$\mu = (1, 0, \dots, 0, \dots) \in \mathbb{R}^\infty.$$

The policy μ is obviously not balanced in any relevant sense, since $\sum_{s=0}^{t} \mu_s = 1$ for $t = 0, 1, \dots$. Nonetheless, there exist (stationary) economies for which μ is bonafide.

Proof: See, for example, Samuelson (1958, especially pp. 477–482) and Gale (1973, Figure 1, p. 20).   Q.E.D.

6   Concluding remarks

Perfectly foreseen, nondistorting government fiscal policy matters in the overlapping-generations economy. Taxes and transfers are the means of effecting interpersonal and intergenerational redistribution. The only neutrality result relevant to fiscal policy in the overlapping-generations model is the independence of the timing of taxes and tranfers for a *given* individual consumer (see our note 1).

This chapter can be taken in part as a response to the current (neo-Ricardian) fixation with repaying the public debt. Debt retirement is central to fiscal policy in finite perfect-foresight models; see, for example, Balasko and Shell (1983) and Section 3 of this chapter. (There have also been claims that the centrality of debt retirement extends to the popular macroeconomic model based on a finite number of infinitely lived families.[4]) For the infinite overlapping-generations model, Samuelson (1958) has taught us that there are environments in which fiscal policy can be effective without debt retirement; see Observation 5.28. The Samuelson example answers only one side of the debt retirement issue. In Sections 4 and 5, we investigate the other side. We establish that if the debt is retired in finite time, then fiscal policy can be effective (for every environment); see Proposition 4.16. On the other hand, we also show that if debt retirement in the infinite-horizon economy does not proceed at a sufficiently rapid rate for the given environment, then fiscal policy is necessarily ineffective; see Proposition 5.3, Counterexamples 5.4 and 5.17, and Remark 5.26.

NOTES

1   It is implicitly assumed that each consumer faces perfect borrowing and lending markets during his lifetime. An immediate consequence of overall equilibrium is that the *present* price of money, $p^{m,t}$, is independent of date t, i.e., $p^{m,t} = p^m \in \mathbb{R}_+$ for $t = 1, 2, ..., T+1$. It also follows from equilibrium considerations that consumer t's opportunities depend only on his lifetime transfer μ_t (and are independent of the time profile of his transfers). These "arbitrage" arguments are carefully spelled out in Balasko and Shell (1981, Sections 2–3). One interpretation of our model is that the markets for inside money are perfect and that the price of inside money is positive even when the price of outside money is zero. At any rate, by assumption no Clower (or Clower-like) constraints are binding in this chapter.
2   A representation of this important isomorphism is given in Balasko and Shell (1981, Fig. 7.1, Erratum), in which the emphasis is on the infinite horizon. See also Balasko and Shell (1983, Figs. 2 and 3), in which the (finite) static economy is analyzed.
3   Compare the definition of nonmonetary equivalent endowment, ω_t', [equation (5.8)] with that of adjusted endowment, $\bar{\omega}_t$, in the associated no-taxation economy [equations (3.3)]. Notice that $\bar{\omega}_t \in \mathbb{R}^{\ell(T+1)}$ is constructed from ω_t by adjusting commodity 1 *in period* 1, whereas $\omega_t' \in \mathbb{R}^2$ is constructed from ω_t by adjusting the single commodity *in period* t.
4   We have seen some of these claims, but we have seen no proof of them. It is our belief that the model with infinitely lived consumers is in fact more complicated than most users of the model imagine.

REFERENCES

Arrow, K. J. and F. H. Hahn (1971), *General competitive analysis,* San Francisco: Holden-Day.
Balasko, Y. (1979), "Budget-constrained and Pareto-efficient allocations," *Journal of Economic Theory,* 21: 359–79.

Balasko, Y. and K. Shell (1980), "The overlapping-generations model, I: the case of pure exchange without money," *Journal of Economic Theory,* 21: 281–306.

Balasko, Y. and K. Shell (1981), "The overlapping-generations model, II: the case of pure exchange with money," *Journal of Economic Theory,* 24: 112–42; see also Erratum, *Journal of Economic Theory,* 24: 471.

Balasko, Y. and K. Shell (1983), "Lump-sum taxation: The static economy," CARESS Working Paper #83-08RR, University of Pennsylvania, Philadelphia, August 1, 1983; see also Y. Balasko and K. Shell, "On taxation and competitive equilibria," in *Optimalité et structure* (G. Ritschard and D. Royer, Eds.), Paris: Economica, 1985, Chapter 5, 69–83.

Bourbaki, N. (1966), *Elements of mathematics: General topology, Part I,* Reading, Mass.: Addison-Wesley.

Debreu, G. (1962), "New concepts and techniques for equilibrium analysis," *International Economic Review,* 3: 257–73.

Gale, D. (1973), "Pure exchange equilibrium of dynamic economic models," *Journal of Economic Theory,* 6: 12–36.

Samuelson, P. A. (1958), "An exact consumption-loan model of interest with or without the social contrivance of money," *Journal of Political Economy,* 66: 477–82.

CHAPTER 6

Coordination failure under complete markets with applications to effective demand

Walter P. Heller

1 Introduction

Arrow (1969) refined the idea [implicit in Meade (1952), for example] that missing markets were at the foundation of market failure in perfectly competitive economies. He also advanced the notion that nonexistence of complementary markets could explain why economic agents might have no incentive to open missing markets. Heller and Starrett (1976) developed the idea that the nonexistence of complementary markets could be mutually reinforcing, thereby providing a more complete explanation for the nonexistence of markets. Hart (1980) and Makowski (1980) give fairly general treatments of these ideas in the context of product innovation.

In this essay, I show that even when all markets exist, there can be a coordination failure of a type similar to that which occurs with missing markets. There is no missing market here, nor is there any element of uncertainty or time. Instead, there are multiple, Pareto-ranked equilibria in a simple general equilibrium model with a noncompetitive sector. There is, of course, a Pareto inefficiency that results from imperfect competition, but there are additional inefficiencies of the same type that arise in a modified Prisoners' Dilemma game: There is no incentive for any player to unilaterally change his strategy to that associated with a Pareto-superior equilibrium, but coordination among agents could move the economy to the superior equilibrium. Strictly because of noncompetitive behavior, there is also incentive for the players to move away from a Pareto-efficient allocation (viz., the Walrasian allocation).

Acknowledgments: Support from the National Science Foundation is gratefully acknowledged. I am especially indebted to Frank Hahn, Donald Saari, and Joaquim Silvestre for their extensive and very helpful suggestions. I have also benefited from comments from William Brock, Douglas Gale, Jean-Michel Grandmont, Ted Groves, Bengt Holmstrom, Taka Ito, Mark Machina, Louis Makowski, Eric Maskin, Michael Rothschild, Robert Solow, Richard Startz, David Starrett, and James Tobin.

There are several recent strands of the general equilibrium literature that bear on this chapter. One strand is found in Hart's (1982) study of underemployment with perfectly flexible prices on oligopolistic markets. Hart also has complete markets in his 1982 model. The major differences with Hart's model follow.

1. The labor market in Hart's model is syndicalized (mine is competitive).
2. Consumers have preferences over three commodities (consumers in this essay have only consumption and leisure in utility, but there are different types of consumers).
3. For simplicity, Hart imposes assumptions that guarantee there is a unique equilibrium for any level of the unproduced good.
4. The degree of underemployment in Hart's paper has little to do with what I have called coordination failure; rather, it has to do with the impact on demand for the produced good of changes in the endowment of the nonproduced good. I focus on coordination inefficiencies brought about by multiple bootstrap equilibria.

The similarities are these: A major objective of both essays is to provide an explanation of how unemployment might be sustained in general equilibrium even if there is perfect price flexibility and rational demand perceptions. An intended mechanism in both cases is the direct entrance of income as a separate variable in demand functions. The entrance of income as a separate variable comes about because wage and nonwage income may not be determined by prices alone. In addition, markets always clear in both models, which means that there is no involuntary unemployment, only underemployment.

In the presence of perfect wage flexibility, changes from a high-level equilibrium to a low-level equilibrium are accompanied by changes in employment, but there is never unemployment. A story could be told that with various wage rigidities in the labor market (e.g., implicit contracts), changes in the level of economic activity show up as involuntary unemployment at a roughly constant wage level. But I have no comprehensive model that melds wage rigidities with the other economic forces present in this chapter.

Another relevant strand of the literature is exemplified by the recent work of Diamond (see, e.g., 1982). He also shows the existence of multiple, Pareto-ranked equilibria, which also arise because of pecuniary externalities. His work is complementary to mine in that he examines search theory models where prices are fixed between buyers and sellers, but there is no well-organized anonymous market on which buyers and sellers can frictionlessly carry out transactions.

Finally, there are the recent papers of Cooper and John (1985) and Roberts (1984), which also examine low-level equilibria caused by externalities. Cooper and John assume linear utility functions but do admit involuntary unemployment. In addition, their oligopolists do not perceive the demand effect of (their own) changes in hours worked that are induced by a change in price of the (consumption) good. Roberts models the economy as a game in which some of the strategies are quantity offers as well as prices. The economy looks much like the one below except that, as in Hart (1982), there is a third endowed good. He shows that there can be a continuum of equilibria because a consumer must forecast the demand for his labor, which in turn depends on the expectation of the demand for output by another consumer.

I begin, in the next section, with a general discussion about pecuniary externalities and coordination problems with complete and incomplete markets. Next is presented a simple general equilibrium model in which equilibria are Pareto ranked. The coordination difficulties that sustain "bad" equilibria are discussed, as are policy remedies. Conditions for existence and multiplicity of equilibria are developed. Finally, some extensions are discussed.

2   Pecuniary externalities on complete markets*

The essentials of a Scitovsky (1954) pecuniary externality can be summarized as follows: Consider the markets for two complementary goods, x_1 and x_2. Demand in each industry is conditional on the equilibrium output of the other industry. There are two equilibrium output pairs: a low-level equilibrium $(\hat{x}_1, \hat{x}_2)$ and a high-level equilibrium $(\hat{\hat{x}}_1, \hat{\hat{x}}_2)$. If each industry were unaware of the demand conditions in the other industry, then each industry uses the demand function conditional on existing levels of output in the other industry. If initial conditions are such that production levels are near $\hat{x}_1$ and $\hat{x}_2$, the situation settles down to the low-level equilibrium.

If the producers in the x_1 industry had full general equilibrium knowledge of the repercussions on the x_2 industry of an expansion in the output of x_1, then the more profitable (and presumably Pareto-superior) equilibrium $(\hat{\hat{x}}_1, \hat{\hat{x}}_2)$ would occur if the x_1 producers cooperated. Without such coordination of effort, expansion by a single x_1 producer might not result

*May be skipped at first reading.

in increased demand for his product but rather in increased demand for some other producer's products. This failure of private return to match social return could occur if the factor owners who are enriched by the x_1 expansion are not customers of the firm that expanded.[1]

The conditional demands $D_1(p_1 | x_2), D_2(p_2 | x_1)$ can be thought of as effective demands in the sense that variables such as quantities or incomes enter in an essential way that cannot be captured by a price vector. This could never happen with complete Arrow–Debreu markets, where demand and supply can always be written as functions of prices alone. But as seen below, effective demands are quite possible with some kinds of market imperfections.

A major difference between, on the one hand, the model presented here and Scitovsky (1954) and, on the other hand, the 1980 innovation papers of Hart and Makowski is that here (and in Scitovsky) market failure is not caused by the absence of any spot market. All spot markets are open here, but the price system on spot markets fails to signal correct long-run responses to a firm's action in the present. Pecuniary externalities may be far more extensive than those encountered in the innovation process, where markets are incomplete. Although markets seem to be complete in Scitovsky, Arrow pointed out (in footnote 16 of Scitovsky's paper) that futures markets in the two outputs could provide the proper signals. No market could provide the appropriate signals in the model presented below.

What is common to all of the above situations is that producers' condition their expectations of demand on some nonprice variable of the economic system. In the Hart–Makowski–Scitovsky papers, that variable is current sales (in the producers' own and related markets). Producers in the simple model presented in the next sections must make forecasts of nonwage income of their buyers in order to determine their best output and price. In equilibrium, these forecasts are fulfilled. However, there may be many equilibria, and some of these equilibria are worse than others.

Producers in all cases considered here are trying to forecast demand conditions. Recall that, by contrast, in a purely competitive Arrow–Debreu world, a complete price vector fully coordinates the economy: It yields all the information about the economy any agent needs for efficient decentralization.

Another significant difference between the model presented here (and Scitovsky's as well) and the models of Hart and Makowski is that the decision makers have only partial equilibrium knowledge here. Market-by-market behavior is, of course, in the spirit of the perfectly competitive paradigm. It is also a property that Keynes believed was responsible for the failure of markets to avoid business cycles. [Compare Grandmont, Laroque, and Younès (1978), for example.] It is quite likely that purely partial equilibrium knowledge is common when there are many markets intertwined, with long and complicated chains of interaction. For example, an expansion in x_1 increases the demand for x_2, and so on, until finally the resulting expansion in x_n increases the demand for x_1.

3   The model

To keep things very simple, suppose that there are just two consumption outputs, two types of labor skills, two types of firms, and two types of consumers. The question of generalizations will be discussed later. Furthermore, a consumer with type 1 labor only desires type 2 consumption goods. Similarly, a type 2 consumer only desires type 1 goods. A firm in industry 1 uses only type 1 labor to produce type 1 goods, and similarly for a firm in industry 2. Moreover, all firms have the same productivity parameter.

There are m firms in each industry. The technologies are for type 1 (identical firms):

$$y_1^j = \alpha L_1^j \quad (j = 1, \ldots, m), \quad \text{with } \alpha > 0.$$

Similarly, type 2 technology (identical firms) is constant returns with the same marginal product parameter α:

$$y_2^j = \alpha L_2^j \quad (j = 1, \ldots, m).$$

Here y_1, y_2 are two different consumption goods and L_1, L_2 are two different kinds of labor. The two types of competitive consumers (n identical consumers of each type) are each endowed with one unit of their kind of labor and have utility functions

$$U^1(c_2^i, 1 - L_1^i), \qquad U^2(c_1^i, 1 - L_2^i), \qquad i = 1, \ldots, n.$$

Further assume that the functions are identical, $U_1 = U_2 = U$, and are thrice continuously differentiable, strictly quasiconcave, and for which the indifference curves never touch the axes. Again, for simplicity, suppose type 1 consumers own only equal shares in type 1 firms, so that total profits going to the representative type 1 consumer are $r_1 = \Pi_1/n$, where Π_1 is total industry 1 profits. A similar property holds for type 2 consumers. Then, the budget constraint for a representative type 1 consumer is $p_2 c_2 \le w_1 L_1 + r_1$. Let the type 1 consumer choice functions for leisure and consumption be denoted $1 - L_1^s(p_2, w_1, r_1) \equiv \ell_1^s(p_2, w_1, r_1)$ and $c_2^d(p_2, w_1, r_1)$. Similar notation holds for type 2. Industry aggregates are denoted $C_1(p_1, w_2, r_2)$ and $C_2(p_2, w_1, r_1)$.

I will exploit symmetry so that, for example, $c_2 = C_2/n$, where the capital letters without the superscript denote industry aggregates. Similarly, for type 2, the budget constraint is $p_1 c_1 = w_2 L_2 + r_2$.

I now specify industry demand perceptions and market structure. Each type 1 firm is a Cournot oligopolist in the sense that it takes the quantities produced by other firms as given when making its own output and price decisions, and it assumes price-matching behavior on the part of the other firms. Each firm also knows the *true* industry demand curve $C_1(p_1, w_2, r_2)$ derived from consumer behavior above. (It would not be too surprising that there are Pareto-ranked outcomes if demand misperceptions were the chief culprit.) The firm must forecast and take as given outside the industry the nonwage income (r_2 in the case of industry 1) and the wage rate (w_2 in the case of industry 1) of its buyers.

The firm's problem is then to choose p_1 to maximize its profit

$$\pi_1(p_1, w_2, r_2, Y_1') \equiv (p_1 - 1/\alpha)[C_1(p_1, w_2, r_2) - Y_1'],$$

given Y_1', the output of the rest of the industry. Standard calculations show that a firm in industry 1 chooses output y_1^j so that

$$p_1[1 - 1/(m\epsilon_p^1)] = w_1/\alpha \tag{1}$$

in any symmetric industry Cournot equilibrium (i.e., where $y_1^j = Y_1/m$). As usual, ϵ_p^1 is the ordinary price elasticity of demand,

$$\epsilon_p^1(p_1, w_2, r_2) = -\frac{p_1}{c_1} \frac{\partial C_1(p_1, w_2, r_2)}{\partial p_1}. \tag{2}$$

A similar formula holds for industry 2. There may be nonsymmetric equilibria as well, but these are ignored here. As is well known (McManus 1964, Roberts and Sonnenschein, 1976), the profit function may not be concave, but an industry Cournot equilibrium will exist in the case of decreasing demand and identical firms with constant costs. Therefore, it is assumed that the consumption good is not Giffen.

It should be pointed out that under these conditions (firms large relative to consumers) one should also allow firms to exploit monopoly power in the labor market. Doing so would add a markup term to the left side of equation (1). The greater complexity might perhaps make the multiplicity property (cf. below) even more likely, but this case has not been examined.

Symmetry is now exploited still further to conclude that in a general symmetric Nash equilibrium for this economy (if one exists), it must be the case that $w_1 = w_2 = 1$ (a normalization of prices), $Y_1 = Y_2 \equiv Y$, $L_1^j = L_2^j$, and $\pi_1 = \pi_2 \equiv \pi$ in each industry. Thus, at the individual consumer level, $c_1 = c_2 \equiv c$, $L_1 = L_2 \equiv L$, and $r_1 = r_2 \equiv r$. Note that $r = (m/n)\pi$.

Define leisure to be $\ell = 1 - L$. In consumption–leisure space, we will look for general equilibrium points on the symmetric feasibility frontier (SFF):

$$\text{SFF} = \{(c, \ell) \mid \ell = 1 - c/\alpha\}. \tag{3}$$

A *general Nash equilibrium (GNE)* for this economy is one in which, subject to consumer and producer optimizing behavior as given above, producer and consumer plans are consistent; the consumption goods and labor markets must all clear, and forecast nonwage incomes must be realized. In view of all the symmetry that has been imposed, a GNE has the property that $\ell^s(p, r) = 1 - (1/\alpha)c^d(p, r)$ for some (p, r) such that an industry Cournot equilibrium is realized at p for nonwage income level r.

Denote by $p(c, \ell)$ the demand price, then

$$p(c, \ell) \equiv u_c(c, \ell)/u_\ell(c, \ell) = p, \tag{4}$$

where u_c and u_ℓ are the partial derivatives of u.

Lemma 1. Any point (c', ℓ') of the feasibility frontier (3) satisfying the industry first-order condition (1) and the consumer choice first-order condition (4) is a general Nash equilibrium provided the profit function for each firm satisfies the local second-order condition for maximization [$\pi_{pp} < 0$ at all points where it satisfies the first-order condition (1)].

Proof: See Appendix.

The hypothesis about local second-order conditions in Lemma 1 needs to be derived from conditions on the primitives: Lemma 2 does this by giving conditions on the curvature of the utility function that imply the needed local second-order conditions. Let $p = f(c, r)$ be the inverse demand function so that $f(c^d(p, r), r) \equiv p$. Define the elasticity operator for any function $y = g(x, z)$:

$$\frac{Ey}{Ex} \equiv -\frac{x}{y} \frac{\partial y}{\partial x}.$$

Further define

$$\eta \equiv \frac{Ep}{Ec} \equiv -\frac{c}{p}\frac{\partial f}{\partial c},$$

where $\eta \equiv \eta(c, r)$ is the inverse of the price elasticity of demand, ϵ. Graphically, η is a measure of the speed with which the marginal rate of substitution changes per increment of c as one moves up the offer curve determined by nonwage income r. The greater is η, the less the willingness to consume more as price decreases. There is a formula given in Lemma 3 that relates η to the second partial derivatives of the utility function.

The second-order sufficiency condition given in Lemma 2 actually involves $E\eta/Ec$, which is a condition on the third derivatives of the utility function. Recall that a critical point of a function is a point such that the first derivative is zero. Roughly, condition (5) of Lemma 2 says that at the critical points of the profit function, η cannot be decreasing too rapidly.

Lemma 2. Let u satisfy

$$E\eta/Ec < 2m - (1 + \eta) \tag{5}$$

at all critical points of $\pi(\cdot)$. Then at those critical points, $\pi_{pp} < 0$. [A sufficient condition for equation (5) is $E\eta/Ec < m - 1$.]

Proof: See Appendix.

4   Multiple equilibria and coordination failure

Conditions under which there exist multiple equilibria are provided in the next section. Here I note the economic consequences of multiplicity. In this simple model, Theorem 1 is almost immediate:

Theorem 1. All general Nash equilibria are Pareto ranked. Equilibria that have greater economic activity are unambiguously better.

Proof: See Appendix.

Figure 1 illustrates the coordination problem with multiple equilibria. The point W is Walrasian equilibrium, that is, if all firms were perfect competitors. Points E_1 and E_2 are general Nash equilibria with E_1 Pareto superior to E_2. [There is no way I know of to represent the elasticity ϵ_p on the diagram, but we know that solutions $\hat{p}$ to equation (1) are such that $\hat{p} > 1/\alpha$ unless $\epsilon_p = \infty$.] The diagram illustrates the conjecture that

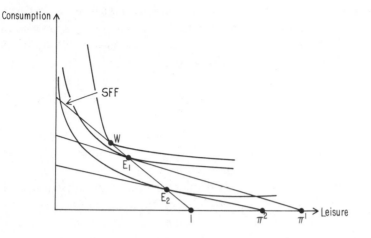

Figure 1. Multiple Pareto-ranked equilibria.

higher nonwage income $r = \pi$ is related to higher levels of economic activity and economic welfare. However, there seems to be no reason it could not happen that high profits could be made on low activity levels if prices were sufficiently above marginal cost (i.e., demand is relatively inelastic at the lower equilibrium point).

One may interpret the Pareto inefficiency of E_1 as representing a classic monopoly power market failure. Market failure caused by the coordination problem is illustrated by E_2. There would be unanimous agreement to move to E_1 from E_2, yet no agent would unilaterally move an E_1 strategy from E_2 (for reasons that are spelled out below). There is a coordination failure in the sense that these are all Nash equilibria. Only if all other firms agree to move to a different equilibrium strategy will any one firm choose to change its strategy.

If there were complete knowledge, full communication, and the possibility of making binding agreements, then all firms might settle on E_1 strategies at the Pareto-dominant equilibrium.[2] However, if π_2 were greater at E_2 than π_1 at E_1, then managers would actually prefer the inferior equilibrium and would never choose to coordinate with each other to move to E_1 from E_2. In either case, we argue below that only government policy can remedy the situation.

These equilibria are stable under experimentation. Suppose a manager of a firm in the c_2 industry contemplated a unilateral expansion away from a low-level equilibrium. The manager would expand output and would lose profits in the short run (with an eye on the long run). The resultant increase in income of workers associated with the type 2 firm might lead to increased demand in industry 1. Workers and owners in industry 1 would then have greater income, which they would dutifully spend on c_2. But the original c_2 firm would receive only a small fraction (say, $1/m$) of the burst in demand for c_2, which is spread uniformly across industry 2. The manager therefore chooses to remain at his initial equilibrium strategy.

Any firm suffers an externality in that the social return of its expansion exceeds its private return. However, if there were a monopoly in both industries, there would be no such externality. Any gain in income of the monopolist's buyers is spent on his product. In this case, the importance of the market-by-market partial equilibrium thinking on the part of the participants comes to the fore. If a monopolist had knowledge of how the other market responds to his actions, he could lead the economy away from a less profitable (not necessarily Pareto-inferior) equilibrium. If, on the other hand, the monopolist was only aware of relationships within his own market, then there would be no such bootstrapping.

This myopic mode of thought is one level higher feedback awareness than competitive conjectures. Price setters in this essay are aware of their influence on demand in their own markets. If producers are small in their markets, or if the interaction between the firm's output decisions and the income of its buyers is filtered through many markets, the effect is so small in the short run that it cannot be discovered (or does not seem worth the calculation costs).

As in all cases of coordination failure, there is a role for collective action. In this case, policy can be especially simple. For example, consider a remedy for moving from E_2 to E_1 in Figure 1. The government could announce a one-shot burst of demands for each of the two consumption goods in amount ΔC, corresponding to the gap between the two equilibria in Figure 1. But how does the government know what consumption is in each of the two equilibrium states? One answer is that state E_1 is a high-level equilibrium state that obtained in a previous time period. An external shock pushed the economy toward the low-level state, and adjustment dynamics then placed the economy at E_2.

How would the government achieve budget balance while undertaking this expenditure policy? It could do so by egalitarian lump-sum taxation in the amount $2p^1 \Delta C$ where p^1 is the equilibrium price in E_1. Payment would be one shot and in units of account. The mere announcement of an increase in government demand could suffice so long as all agents believed and acted in anticipation of the greater demand for output. The resulting consumer income would then suffice to purchase the output if the government reneged on its plans.[3]

Notice that unlike the case of property right externalities, there is no missing spot market here. There is an absent set of futures markets, but these would not suffice here (unlike the Scitovsky concept of pecuniary externality). Because of noncompetitive market demand perceptions, a change in expected price is not the key here; what is needed is a change in perceived demand schedules. As above, such changes could be effected by government policy. Alternatively, some nongovernment device to increase expected consumer income might be found.

Cooperation among all consumers and firms could induce a move to a Pareto-efficient allocation under ideal circumstances, but this ignores the administrative costs of coalition formation and the policing costs of monitoring and enforcing agreements. It is perhaps easier to imagine the two industries getting together and coordinating on strategies at the highest-level equilibrium. This is why I call the latter kind of failure a coordination failure, so as to distinguish it from the former kind of failure, which requires a change in the industrial structure of the economy rather than a change in strategies.

5   Analysis of existence and multiplicity of equilibria

An example that has multiple, Pareto-ranked equilibria is given by $U(c, \ell) = \ln(c-1) + 2\ln \ell$, $m = 2$, $n = 1$, and $\alpha = 20$. There are two general Nash equilibria, one with $c_1 = 4.204$ and the other with $c_2 = 1.395$. For comparison, Walrasian equilibrium entails $c^* = 7.333$. This can be checked by substituting equations (3) and (4) into (1) and rewriting (1) as

$$Ep/Ec = m[1 - (1/\alpha p)], \tag{6}$$

where $Ep/Ec(\cdot)$ and $p(\cdot)$ are both functions of $(c, 1-(c/\alpha))$, as shown in Lemma 3 below. The left-hand side (LHS) of equation (6) is given by $3c/3c - 2$, and the right-hand side (RHS) is $2[(2+\alpha-3c)/(\alpha-c)]$. The LHS is convex in c, whereas the RHS is concave (see Fig. 2).

We know that the RHS of equation (6) always intersects the horizontal axis at c^*. But it is clear that for α small, the RHS never intersects the LHS at all. Indeed, a condition to rule this out is needed for existence. One can also see on this diagram the arguments presented below for multiplicity. Let $\underline{c}$ be the lower bound of definition for the utility function. If at $\underline{c}$, $EP/Ec < 1 - 1/\alpha p$, then the number of equilibria is even, except for degeneracies. If the reverse inequality holds, the number of equilibria is

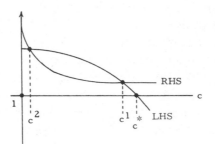

Figure 2. Multiple solutions to equation (6).

odd. In the latter case, one can impose a condition that guarantees that at least one of the intersections occurs with the RHS cutting the LHS from below, and this guarantees multiplicity.

The first order of business is to establish existence of a GNE.

Theorem 2. Let α, the common marginal product of labor, be sufficiently large that marginal revenue is above marginal cost for some feasible output less than Walrasian c^*: There exists $c' < c^*$ such that

$$p\left(c', 1 - \frac{c'}{\alpha}\right)\left[1 - \frac{1}{m}\frac{Ep[c', 1 - (c'/\alpha)]}{Ec}\right] > \frac{1}{\alpha}. \tag{7}$$

Then there exists a nonautarkic general Nash equilibrium.

Remarks: If condition (7) failed to be true, then marginal cost is always above marginal revenue [since $p(\cdot) < 1/\alpha$ for $c > c^*$ on the SFF] and autarky is an equilibrium. One might think that the assumption that indifference curves never touch axes is sufficient to guarantee condition (7). But so far as has been determined, it could happen that the markup term in square brackets in condition (7) is negative whenever p is large.

Proof: See Appendix.

Lemma 3 presents a handy formula for Ep/Ec in terms of various elasticities of the marginal utility. These elasticities can be interpreted as measures of curvature of the utility function in various directions. For example, $EU_c/Ec \equiv -cU_{cc}/U_c$ (relative risk aversion in uncertainty theory) is the percentage rate of change at which marginal utility of consumption decreases as consumption increases. Similar interpretations can be given to $EU_\ell/Ec \equiv -cU_{c\ell}/U_\ell$, $EU_c/E\ell \equiv -\ell U_{c\ell}/U_c$, and $EU_\ell/E\ell \equiv -\ell U_{\ell\ell}/U_\ell$.

Lemma 3. If U is C^2 and $p(c, 1 - pc + r)$ is the inverse demand function,

$$\frac{Ep(c,r)}{Ec} = \frac{\left[\dfrac{EU_c}{Ec} - \dfrac{EU_\ell}{Ec}\right] + \dfrac{cU_c}{\ell U_\ell}\left[\dfrac{EU_\ell}{E\ell} - \dfrac{EU_c}{E\ell}\right]}{1 + \dfrac{cU_c}{\ell U_\ell}\left[\dfrac{EU_\ell}{E\ell} - \dfrac{EU_c}{E\ell}\right]}. \tag{8}$$

Accordingly, the price elasticity of demand is

$$\epsilon_p(p,r) = \frac{1 + \dfrac{pc^d}{\ell^s}\left[\dfrac{EU_\ell}{E\ell} - \dfrac{EU_c}{E\ell}\right]}{\left[\dfrac{EU_c}{Ec} - \dfrac{EU_\ell}{Ec}\right] + \dfrac{pc^d}{\ell^s}\left[\dfrac{EU_\ell}{E\ell} - \dfrac{EU_c}{E\ell}\right]}, \tag{9}$$

where the various elasticities of marginal utility are functions of (p, r) through the substitutions $c = c^d(p, r)$, $\ell = \ell^s(p, r)$.

Proof: See Appendix.

The next result provides a method for constructing multitudinous examples of economies with multiple equilibria, but it is local in nature and somewhat difficult to interpret economically (i.e., it does not say what sorts of economies have multiplicity). However, the method has the virtue that it is easily generalized to many dimensions and nonsymmetric economies.[4]

The method consists of picking arbitrary isolated points on the SFF in Figure 1 to the southeast of the Walrasian equilibrium. Let p be given by equation (4), and let r be such that the budget equation allows consumption of a given point on the SFF. One alters the second partials of the utility function at each selected point so that equation (1) is satisfied at those points. The necessary alterations to the second partials are given by solving equation (1) for $1/\epsilon \equiv Ep/Ec$, thereby obtaining equation (6) again. The RHS of equation (6) is $m[1 - (1/\alpha p)]$, a given quantity at this stage of the construction. The second partials of the utility function under construction are now given by equations (6) and (8), and the first partials are given by equation (3). Since the selected points are isolated and equation (1) is only a point condition (and not an open condition), there is no conflict with any of the other restrictions except possibly the second-order condition on profits. But Lemma 2 gives a local property of the utility function that is sufficient for the second-order condition and involves third partial derivatives. This introduces enough degrees of freedom to ensure that second-order conditions remain satisfied without altering the values of the second partials needed to satisfy equation (1). Finally, by using Lemma 1, one is assured that each of the points is indeed a GNE. Summarizing:

Theorem 3. Any configuration of isolated points on the symmetric feasibility frontier with consumption and labor below competitive levels can be general Nash equilibria for some utility function.

The next step is to search for a general condition that would characterize a class of economies that possess multiple equilibria. The basic idea that is pursued now is to give a condition on the utility function that ensures that at the lower bound to consumption, $\underline{c}$, the LHS of equation (6) is greater than the RHS. There is then a general analytic counterpart to Figure 2, as the discussion accompanying Figure 2 makes clear.
For convenience, define $\eta(c) \equiv Ep(c, 1 - c/\alpha)/Ec$ and $\underline{\eta} \equiv \eta(\underline{c})$.

Theorem 4. If the utility function U is such that conditions (7) and

$$\lim_{c \to \underline{c}_+} \frac{Ep(c)}{Ec} \equiv \underline{\eta} > m \tag{10}$$

hold, then there are multiple Pareto-ranked equilibria.

Remarks: Condition (10) says that demand for consumption is highly inelastic ($\epsilon = 1/\eta$ is less than $1/m$) when consumption is near survival levels. This seems perfectly reasonable. From equation (8), it is seen that the example $\log(c - 1) + 2 \log \ell$ satisfies conditions (10) and (7). Equation (8) also shows that utility functions for which EU_c/Ec is large relative to EU_ℓ/Ec will satisfy condition (10).

Proof: See Appendix.

6   Extensions

The previous discussion was carried out in an economy with only two types of consumers and two types of firms. This was done partly to show that coordination failure arising from equilibrium multiplicity can arise even in this restricted context with relatively few free parameters. If a general economy is considered and only aggregate demand functions are specified, then there are considerably more possibilities for multiple Pareto-ranked equilibria. This follows from the Sonnenschein (1974) and Debreu (1974) results on the unrestrictedness of aggregate demand functions.

To see this, the first step is to develop equilibrium conditions in the case of nonidentical consumers. Let $C_1(p_1, w_2, r_2)$ and $C_2(p_2, w_1, r_1)$ be aggregate demands for consumption of the two types; we retain the assumptions that consumers of good i own one unit of labor and $1/n$ of the profits associated with the other industry. Similarly, let $L_1(p_2, w_1, r_1)$ and $L_2(p_1, w_2, r_2)$ be supplies of labor by consumers owning type 1 and type 2 labor. For given levels of nonwage income r_1, r_2 and wages w_1, w_2, let $p_1(w_1, w_2, r_1)$ and $p_2(w_1, w_2, r_2)$ be the Cournot equilibrium prices in the two industries [i.e., prices satisfying equation (1)]. Then a general Nash equilibrium will occur if

$$C_1(p_1(w_1, w_2, r_2), w_2, r_2) = \alpha L_1(p_2(w_1, w_2, r_1), w_1, r_1),$$
$$C_2(p_2(w_1, w_2, r_1), w_1, r_1) = \alpha L_2(p_1(w_1, w_2, r_2), w_2, r_2). \tag{11}$$

The $p_1(\cdot)$ and $p_2(\cdot)$ functions in general will not be continuous, and so the usual existence arguments will not work in these cases. However, we can still construct examples where there are a multiplicity of equilibria. One example with a continuum of equilibria is the following: Let $C_1(\cdot)$ and $C_2(\cdot)$ be given downward-sloping aggregate demand functions. The functions $p_1(\cdot)$ and $p_2(\cdot)$ are then given by equation (1). Define the aggregate supply functions $L_1(\cdot)$ and $L_2(\cdot)$ so as to satisfy equation (11) for all values of (w_1, w_2, r_1, r_2) such that $w_1 = w_2$ and $r_1 = r_2$. This latter requirement is needed because the RHS of equation (11) involves (w_i, r_i), whereas the corresponding LHS involves (w_j, r_j).[5] Then any point on the two-dimensional manifold consisting of pairs $(w, r) \gg 0$ with $w_1 = w_2 = w$ and $r_1 = r_2 = r$ is an equilibrium, since the equilibrium equation (11) holds for all such pairs.

The conditions developed in the previous sections for the case of two types can be immediately extended to the case of a chain of markets. Let there be T types of consumption goods and T types of labor skills. Suppose a consumer of type t owns only labor skills of type t and profits in industry t and cares only for consumption goods of type $t+1$ (or type 1, if $t = T$). So long as the functional form of the utility and production functions remain the same (only the names of the variables change), the previous results extend to an economy with T oligopolistic goods markets and T competitive labor markets.

The question sometimes arises: What does all this have to do with business cycles? At this point, I will resort to a dynamic story. Initially, the economy is at a high-level equilibrium. An exogenous shock comes along and dislodges the economy away from high-level equilibrium into the neighborhood of a low-level equilibrium. Local stability of some of the equilibria takes over from there. If one thinks of significant shocks in various directions as occurring repeatedly but infrequently, one could trace out a business cycle in which the economy is usually near an equilibrium of one sort or another.

It would be desirable to eliminate the enormous amount of symmetry among agents assumed in this chapter. The mathematics of obtaining conditions for multiplicity is the equilibrium set of a considerably higher order than that used here. It is possible to generate examples of multiplicity in nonsymmetric economies by appealing to Sonnenschein–Debreu results on aggregate demand functions. The more difficult task is, again, to give conditions that would enable one to test any given nonsymmetric economy for multiple equilibria, at least some of which are dominated by other equilibria.

7   Conclusions

The existence of multiple, Pareto-ranked Nash equilibria gives rise to a kind of market failure that resembles both underconsumptionist doctrines (of Keynes 1936; Kalecki 1954; and others) for advanced economies and the pecuniary externality theories (of Rosenstein-Rodan 1943; Scitovsky 1954; and others) that are frequently applied to less-developed countries. Unlike this latter literature, however, there seems to be no missing market in the present case. The failure arises from the absence of a global auctioneerlike mechanism with simultaneous price announcements for all markets. Here price determination occurs market by market, and advantageous cross-market decisions cannot be readily coordinated. This kind of coordination failure may arise quite naturally in economies that are not perfectly competitive, even when they have complete markets.

Appendix: Proofs

Proof of Lemma 1: Let $p' \equiv p(c', r')$. By hypothesis, p' satisfies equation (1). It will first be shown that p' is a global maximum for $\pi(p, r', Y') \equiv (p - 1/\alpha)[C(p, r') - (m - 1/m)Y']$, where $Y' \equiv C(p', r')$. This will show that p' is a Cournot equilibrium for r'. If not, there exists a $\hat{p}$ such that $\pi(\cdot, r', Y')$ is maximized at $\hat{p}$ and so $\hat{\pi} > \pi'$. Suppose $\hat{p} > p'$ (the other case is similar). Then $\pi_p < 0$ in a neighborhood to the right of p', whereas

$\pi_p > 0$ in a neighborhood to the left of $\hat{p}$. By continuity of derivatives, there exists a point p'' between p' and $\hat{p}$ such that $\pi_p'' = 0$ and $\pi_{pp}'' > 0$. (If $\pi_{pp}'' < 0$ for all p'' such that $\pi_p'' = 0$, the partial derivative function could never enter the region $\pi_p > 0$.) But this contradicts the hypothesis that the second-order conditions are satisfied at every critical point. By construction, each firm is producing the same level of output at p', so p' is a symmetric Cournot equilibrium.

Next is shown that forecast nonwage income is realized, $r' = (m/n)\pi'$. Now $nr' = n(p'c' - (1 - \ell')) = p'C' - (1/\alpha)C'$, using equation (3). But the RHS is total industry profits $\Pi' = (p' - 1/\alpha)C'$.

Finally, the labor market clears since supply per household is $(1 - \ell') = (1/\alpha)C'$, and the latter is the demand for labor per household at (p', r').

∎

Proof of Lemma 2: The fact that the elasticity of the aggregate inverse demand function equals the elasticity of the individual inverse demand function is used throughout. To see this fact, let $P(Y, r) \equiv f((1/n)Y, r)$ be the aggregate inverse demand function (recall that f is the individual inverse demand function). Then

$$\frac{EP}{Ey} = -\frac{Y}{p} \frac{1}{n} \frac{\partial f}{\partial y} = \eta.$$

Let $\phi(y, Y', r) \equiv [P(y + Y', r) - 1/\alpha]y$, and define $\pi(p, Y', r) \equiv [p - (1/\alpha)](C(p, r) - Y')$. Then

$$\phi(C(p, r) - Y', Y', r) = [P(C(p, r), r) - 1/\alpha](C(p, r) - Y')$$

$$= (p - 1/\alpha)(C(p, r) - Y') = \pi(p, Y', r).$$

Therefore, $\partial\phi/\partial p = (\partial\phi/\partial y)(\partial C/\partial p) = \partial\pi/\partial p$. Then $\partial\phi/\partial y = 0$ at critical points of the profit function, and so

$$\frac{\partial^2 \pi}{\partial p^2} = \frac{\partial^2 \phi}{\partial y^2}\left(\frac{\partial c}{\partial p}\right)^2 + \frac{\partial\phi}{\partial y}\frac{\partial^2 c}{\partial p^2}$$

$$= \phi_{yy}(c_p)^2,$$

where the usual compact notation has been substituted for the partial derivatives.

It now suffices to show that $\phi_{yy} < 0$ at critical points. But

$$\phi_{yy} = 2(\partial P/\partial Y) + y(\partial^2 P/\partial Y^2)$$

where $Y = y + Y'$. Thus

$$(Y/p)\phi_{yy} = -2\eta + (Yy/p)(\partial^2 P/\partial Y^2).$$ (12)

Using symmetry $y = Y/m$, the second term equals

$$\frac{Yy}{p}\frac{\partial^2 P}{\partial Y^2} = \frac{c^2}{mp}\frac{\partial^2 p}{\partial c^2}$$

$$= \frac{\eta}{m}\left(\frac{E\eta}{Ec} + 1 + \eta\right).$$ (13)

This latter equality follows from

$$\frac{E\eta}{Ec} = -\frac{c}{\eta}\frac{\partial\eta}{\partial c} = -1 - \eta + \frac{c^2}{\eta p}\frac{\partial^2 p}{\partial c^2}.$$

Substituting equation (13) into (12) yields

$$(Y/p)\phi_{yy} = (\eta/m)[-2m + 1 + \eta + (E\eta/Ec)].$$ (14)

Thus, $\phi_{yy} < 0$ if and only if equation (5) holds.

In any industry equilibrium, $1 - (1/m)\eta > 0$, so $\eta < m$, and $E\eta/Ec < m - 1$ implies equation (5).   ∎

Proof of Theorem 1: All GNEs lie on the linear SFF (cf. Figure 1). By equation (1), $p > 1/\alpha$ in any GNE. But the Arrow–Debreu–Walras equilibrium for this economy is $p^* = 1/\alpha$, with $r^* = \pi^* = 0$. By strict quasiconcavity of U, this equilibrium is unique, and so all GNEs lie below the point W on Figure 1 on the line SFF. Thus, any GNE point $q = (c, \ell)$ can be represented by a convex combination of $W = (c^*, \ell^*)$ and $(0, 1)$, $q^\lambda = \lambda W + (1 - \lambda)(0, 1)$, with $U(W) > U(0, 1)$. By quasiconcavity of the utility function, $U(q^\lambda)$ is increasing in λ, so GNEs are Pareto ranked, with $U(W) > U(q^\lambda)$.

Also, GNEs that are represented by a higher value of λ are those that involve more production and greater volume of transactions on both the labor and goods markets.   ∎

Proof of Theorem 2: The Walrasian price $p^* = 1/\alpha$, so the LHS of condition (7) is less than the RHS at p^*, since the markup term in brackets is less than unity (the absence of Giffen goods has been assumed). But condition (7) plus continuity then implies the existence of a $\hat{c}$ such that equations (1), (3), and (4) are simultaneously satisfied. Lemma 1 now implies existence.   ∎

Proof of Lemma 3: First write (recalling that the budget constraint is $1 - \ell + r - pc = 0$)

$$p(c,r) = \frac{U_c(c, 1+r-pc)}{U_\ell(c, 1+r-pc)}.$$

Next compute

$$\partial(\ln p)/\partial c = \partial(\ln U_c)/\partial c - \partial \ln(U_\ell)/\partial c,$$

where

$$\left.\frac{dU_c}{dc}\right|_r = U_{cc} - U_{c\ell}(p + c\,\partial p/\partial c),$$

$$\left.\frac{dU_\ell}{dc}\right|_r = U_{\ell c} - U_{\ell\ell}(p + c\,\partial p/\partial c).$$

So

$$\frac{1}{p}\frac{\partial p}{\partial c} = \frac{U_{cc} - U_{c\ell}[p + (c\,\partial p/\partial c)]}{U_c} - \left[\frac{U_{c\ell} - U_{\ell\ell}[p + (c\,\partial p/\partial c)]}{U_\ell}\right],$$

or

$$-\frac{c}{p}\frac{\partial p}{\partial c}\left[1 + pc\frac{U_{c\ell}}{U_c} - pc\frac{U_{\ell\ell}}{U_\ell}\right] = \left[\frac{-cU_{cc}}{U_c} + \frac{pcU_{c\ell}}{U_c} + \frac{cU_{c\ell}}{U_\ell} - \frac{pcU_{\ell\ell}}{U_\ell}\right],$$

or

$$-\frac{c}{p}\frac{\partial p}{\partial c}\left[1 - \frac{pc}{\ell}\frac{EU_c}{E\ell} + \frac{pc}{\ell}\frac{EU_\ell}{E\ell}\right] = \left[\frac{EU_c}{Ec} - \frac{EU_\ell}{Ec} + \frac{pc}{\ell}\left(\frac{EU_\ell}{E\ell} - \frac{EU_c}{E\ell}\right)\right].$$

Dividing through both sides by the term in brackets on the LHS and substituting $p = U_c/U_\ell$ yields expression (11). Equation (12) now follows, or it can be derived directly (as a check) from differentiating the first-order conditions for utility maximization. ∎

Proof of Theorem 4: The objective is to show that the LHS of equation (6) is less than the RHS at very low values of c and also at high values of c. But then if there is any transverse intersection of the two curves, there must be an even number (cf. Fig. 2) of intersections. A single tangency of the two curves is a degeneracy ruled out by the strict inequality (7).

We first show that the LHS of equation (6) is greater than the RHS. By the assumption that the indifference curves never touch axes,

$$\underline{p} \equiv \lim_{c \to \underline{c}_+} p(c, 1 - c/\alpha) = \infty.$$

So by (13),

$$\eta > [1 - (1/\alpha\underline{p})]m = m.$$

At c^*, $p^* = 1/\alpha$, so the RHS of equation (6) is zero. But $\eta > 0$ at c^*, so that the LHS of equation (6) is greater than the RHS for larger values of c as well.

Condition (7) may be rewritten as $[1 - (1/\alpha p')]m > \eta'$; that is, the LHS of equation (6) is less than the RHS for the value c' between $\underline{c}$ and c^*. By continuity, there is first an equilibrium between $\underline{c}$ and c' and also an equilibrium between c' and c^*.   ■

NOTES

1 Note that the example suggests Pareto superiority of one equilibria over another, but there is no clear proof of it. We can only conclude with certainty that one is more profitable than the other.
2 The efficient equilibrium W is unreachable with oligopoly market structure because profit-seeking managers have no loyalty to their (e.g., type 2) customers, only to their owners (e.g., type 1 consumers).
3 Indeed, government policy must be contingent on realized aggregate demand. If the dynamics of expectations adjustment were very fast, enactment of the announced increase in government spending would change the equilibrium set.
4 I am indebted to Don Sarri for this observation.
5 If the aggregate demand function were identical across the two sectors (i.e., $C_1 = C_2$, etc.), then the $w_1 = w_2$ and $r_1 = r_2$ requirements would be satisfied automatically.

REFERENCES

Arrow, K. J. (1969), "The organization of economic activity: Issues pertinent to the choice of market vs. non-market allocation," in Joint Economic Committee, *The analysis of public expenditure: The PPB system,* Washington, D.C., Government Printing Office, 47–64.

Cooper, R. and A. John (1985), "Coordinating coordination failures in Keynesian models," Cowles Foundation D.P. #745.

Debreu, G. (1974), "Excess demand functions," *Journal of Mathematical Economics,* 1: 15–23.

Diamond, P. A. (1982), "Aggregate demand management in search equilibrium," *Journal of Political Economy,* 90: 881–94.

Grandmont, J.-M., G. Laroque, and Y. Younès (1978), "Equilibrium with quantity rationing and recontracting," *Journal of Economic Theory,* 19: 84–102.

Hart, O. (1980), "Perfect competition and optimal product differentiation," *Journal of Economic Theory,* 22: 279–312.

Hart, O. (1982), "A model of imperfect competition with Keynesian features," *Quarterly Journal of Economics,* 97: 109–38.

Heller, W. P. and D. A. Starrett (1976), "On the nature of externalities," in S. Lin (Ed.), *Theory and measurement of economic externalities,* New York: Academic Press.

Kalecki, M. (1954), *Theory of economic dynamics. An essay on cyclical and long-run changes in a capitalist economy.* London: Allen & Unwin.

Keynes, J. M. (1936), *The general theory of employment, interest and money,* New York: Harcourt Brace.

McManus, M. (1964), "Equilibrium, numbers and size in Cournot oligopoly," *Yorkshire Bulletin,* 16: 68–75.

Makowski, L. (1980), "Perfect competition, the profit criterion and the organization of economic activity," *Journal of Economic Theory,* 22: 222–42.

Meade, J. E. (1952), "External economies and diseconomies in a competitive situation," *Economic Journal,* 62: 54–67.

Roberts, J. (1984), "General equlibrium analysis of imperfect competition: An illustrative example," Stanford University, mimeo.

Roberts, J. and H. Sonnenschein (1976), "On the existence of Cournot equilibrium without concave profit functions," *Journal of Economic Theory,* 13: 112–17.

Rosenstein-Rodan, P. (1943), "Problems of industrialization of eastern and southeastern Europe," *Economic Journal,* 53: 202–11.

Scitovsky, T. (1954), "Two concepts of external economies," *Journal of Political Economy,* 62: 70–82.

Sonnenschein, H. (1974), "Market excess demand functions, *Econometrica,* 40: 459–63.

PART II

Microfoundations of macroeconomics

Arrow was among the first to call for a rigorous microfoundation for the major questions arising in macroeconomics (1967). He was also the first to point out (1959) that when markets are in disequilibrium, agents are in a position to affect their own terms of trade. This point is frequently raised in objection to the fixed price approaches of Bennassy, Dreze, and Malinvaud (for example) as well as the voluminous search theory literature.

It is therefore of real interest to uncover evidence as to whether or not quantities adjust faster than prices. Some evidence that quantity adjustment is faster is given in the paper by Koenig and Nerlove using French and West German industry data.

Modern "rational expectationists" (e.g., Lucas and Sargent) have argued that there is significant doubt as to whether there is any long-term disequilibrium; in particular, they question the existence of involuntary unemployment: Workers, in a variety of contexts, rationally take their chances in the labor market and occasionally lose, that is, are voluntarily (ex ante) unemployed. In response to this view, Kurz presents a model in which the worker does not know his or her own quality, even after the firm discovers it. A low-quality worker is fired and enters the labor market, demanding the same wage as high-quality workers. This situation is both one of involuntary unemployment and is also ex ante rational for the worker. This is so because there are high-quality workers looking for a job (some of them may have missed the entrance requirements for the firm to which they applied).

Weiss argues in his contribution that a firm experiences asymmetric adjustment costs in changing its labor force: An increase in employment is more costly than a decrease. Thus, sectors that experience temporary negative shocks will lay off more workers than firms that experience an equal and opposite positive shock. The result is that there can be an aggregate increase in unemployment even when there is no corresponding net increase in adverse exogenous shocks.

Ito analyzes the implicit contracts labor market setting in more general contexts. He shows, among other things, that a laid-off worker with

177

optimal severance pay can be better off than a fully employed worker if and only if absolute risk aversion is decreasing.

Hahn addresses the point that Arrow raised in his 1959 paper. Even when rational firms recognize that they have market power, disequilibrium can persist because wages will be sticky downward even in the presence of unemployed workers. One reason is that a firm cannot perfectly observe whether or not there is full employment. The firm may not decrease wages with some unemployment around because to do so would be to risk losing all its workers to another firm on the chance that there is full employment.

Solow works with a particular case of general equilibrium monopolistic competition with increasing returns. He shows that any level of unemployment is possible, even when firms have rational perceptions of their output markets. Standard fiscal policy is shown to work.

CHAPTER 7

Price flexibility, inventory behavior, and production responses

Heinz Koenig and Marc Nerlove

1   Introduction

Two paradigms based on different assumptions about the response of economic agents to disturbances in markets have characterized the debate in macroeconomics of the past decade. In one paradigm, originating in the work by Patinkin (1965), Clower (1965), and Leijonhufvud (1968), the main conceptual framework of Keynesian theory has been substantially reconsidered. In view of sluggish price movements in most Western economies, a number of short-run macroeconomic models have been developed that assume that prices adjust only after quantities have fully adjusted. Malinvaud (1977, 1980) argues that such sluggish adjustment is more than a purely institutional fact and that, due to uncertainty and to information and transactions costs, the first reaction of firms to changes in demand is more often a revision of quantities than a revision of prices. This new *disequilibrium macroeconomics,* therefore, posits fixed prices (and price expectations) for the short run; movement in prices between two periods is treated as autonomous and "it is not significantly influenced... by the formation of demands and supplies" (Malinvaud 1977, p. 12).

A second paradigm has been evolved by supporters of the *new classical equilibrium economics,* especially in the context of rational expectations. Here it is assumed that universal auction markets allow economic agents to adjust instantly to perceived nominal demand changes and that only

The research on which this paper is based has been supported by the U.S. National Science Foundation and the Deutsche Forschungsgemeinschaft. We are indebted for helpful comments to two anonymous referees and for able research assistance to G. Flaig and K. Zimmermann, University of Mannheim, to A. Schirm, University of Pennsylvania, and to D. Ross, Williams College, who also made numerous helpful expository suggestions. Our colleague G. Oudiz generously provided access to the French data. We are also greatly indebted to Eugenia Grohman of the U.S. National Academy of Sciences for her editorial assistance.

imperfect information prevents economic agents from selecting the quantity that would maintain an aggregate equilibrium. [For a discussion, see Gordon (1981).]

The question of whether real-world adjustment processes are better described by the paradigm of neo-Keynesian disequilibrium or that of new classical equilibrium theory is most important for the question of the effectiveness of macroeconomic policy and cannot be answered a priori. [See, e.g., Barro (1976), Gordon (1981), and Laidler (1981).] Moreover, as implicit in the work of Arrow, Karlin, and Scarf (1958) and made explicit in recent papers by Blinder (1981, 1982) and Blinder and Fischer (1981), it is entirely possible to devise a neoclassical model of the optimizing firms with inventories in which markets are always in equilibrium but in which quantities adjust more fully or more often than do prices.

This chapter brings some new empirical evidence to bear in order to shed some light on these paradigms. It analyzes, at the microlevel, firms' reactions in terms of production plans and price anticipations to expected demand changes and to surprises in demand, that is, deviations of expected from actual demand during the previous period, and of the effects of such demand shocks on deviations of ex post prices and production from their ex ante values. We also examine the evidence of changes in reaction patterns over time. Although we do not have data on costs, it can plausibly be argued that omission of such information should bias our results in a way that only strengthens our conclusions.

2   A simple theoretical model of a firm with inventories

2.1   Basic relations and dynamic optimization

The basic framework for analyzing the production and pricing decisions of a firm with inventories of finished products have been set forth by Arrow, Karlin, and Scarf (1958). They write, "Basically, inventories constitute an alternative to production in the future. To have available one unit of product tomorrow, we may either produce (or purchase) it then or produce it today and store it until tomorrow. The choice between the two procedures depends on their relative profitability" (p. 19). Optimal production and inventory policy therefore involves a comparison of current production costs and revenues from sales with the value to the firm of holding a unit of inventory, and "For most purposes, it is...appropriate to assign the inventories a...value which is equal to their value to the firm itself in its future operations" (p. 22). Following this simple framework, Blinder and Fischer (1981) have proposed a theoretical model of the firm, further elaborated by Blinder (1982), that emphasizes the role of inventories and order backlogs for production smoothing and for damping price adjustment processes. [See also Blinder (1981), Maccini (1981), and Reagan (1982).] Our development of a theoretical framework for the empirical analysis that follows closely parallels the Blinder–Fischer model. Since, however, we have direct observations on some of the expectations that determine behavior, we do not have to assume anything about how they are generated but can analyze directly the ways in which changing short-term and long-term expectations affect prices, production, and inventories.

Assume that in the short run the firm operates in an imperfectly competitive market and that the demand function is of a form that ensures that the elasticity does not change as the function shifts vertically, for example,

$$P_t = \Pi_t D(X_t) u_t, \tag{2.1}$$

where P_t is the firm's absolute price, Π_t is the general price level, and u_t is a shift variable that may reflect both factors specific to the firm and those other than general price level changes affecting all firms in the economy. In principle, both Π_t and u_t are random variables for the firm at the time it formulates price anticipations, production plans, and planned changes in inventory or order backlog levels, but the analysis in this section assumes that Π_0 and u_0 are known with certainty.[1] The function $D(X)$ is, in general, downward sloping.

Nominal production costs are assumed to be homogeneous of degree 1 in the general price level and a convex function of output or production Q_t. To provide an additional rationale for carrying inventories or order backlogs, we also assume that *changing* the rate of production causes the firm to incur additional costs over and above the costs associated with a steady rate of production.[2] Specific supply shocks not associated with changes in the general price level, v_t, are assumed to enter multiplicatively as in the demand function (2.1). The cost function is thus of the form

$$C_t = \Pi_t \{ c(Q_t) + d(Q_t - Q_{t-1}) \} v_t, \tag{2.2}$$

where $c' > 0$, $c'' > 0$, and $d' > 0$ if $Q_t > Q_{t-1}$ but ≤ 0 if $Q_t \leq Q_{t-1}$. Assume that $c' \to 0$ as $Q_t \to 0$ and $c' \to \infty$ as $Q_t \to \infty$, whereas $d' \to 0$ as $Q_t - Q_{t-1} \to 0$ and $d' \to \pm\infty$ as $Q_t - Q_{t-1} \to \pm\infty$, so that an interior solution for Q_t always exists.

We assume that the costs of adjusting prices are negligible. Dropping this assumption only strengthens our conclusions.

More than two-thirds of the firms whose behavior we examine here carry both inventories of finished products and backlogs of unfilled orders simultaneously for what is identified as the same product. Presumably, this is the result of some product inhomogeneity. In our empirical analysis, we treat order backlogs and inventories as two separate variables, but in this theoretical treatment, it is convenient to regard unfilled orders as negative inventories. Thus, with no nonnegativity constraint, we have

$$L_t - L_{t-1} = Q_t - X_t, \tag{2.3}$$

where L_t is the beginning of the period stock of finished goods, or the backlog of unfilled orders, according as $L_t > 0$ or $L_t < 0$. In addition to interest costs, which we will take into account later through a discount factor, there is a cost of carrying a unit of inventory from one period to the next or holding an unfilled order for one unit for one period. These costs are storage costs, including deterioration, in the case of positive inventories, and the costs of, for example, losing customers in the case of unfilled orders. We do not model the latter explicitly but merely assume that the costs are given by

$$B_t = \Pi_t B(L_t), \tag{2.4}$$

where $B(\ )$ is a convex function with $B' > 0$ for $L_t > 0$ and $B' < 0$ for $L_t < 0$. Here $B(\ )$ need not be symmetric about zero. [The existence of two branches for $B(\ )$ may cause certain difficulties in the analysis that we ignore.] Inventory holding costs are also assumed to be homogeneous of degree 1 in the general price level but not subject to random shocks.

The firm is assumed to maximize the expected discounted present value of its future net revenues in choosing the first-period values of production and sales or inventories. Let E_t denote the expectation operator *conditional* on information available up to time t, and let r denote a constant rate of discount (we could assume r to vary with time also in a random way, but this would only complicate the analysis without adding anything essential to the framework of the empirical analysis).[3] Thus, the firm wishes to choose L_1, X_0, and Q_0 subject to equation (2.3) to find

$$\Omega_0 = \max_{L_1, X_0, Q_0} E_0 \left[\sum_{t=0}^{\infty} \left(\frac{R(X_t, \Pi_t, u_t)}{(1+r)^t} - \frac{C(Q_t, \Pi_t, v_t)}{(1+r)^t} - \frac{\Pi_t B(L_{t+1})}{(1+r)^{t+1}} \right) \right], \tag{2.5}$$

where

$$R(X_t, \Pi_t, u_t) = \Pi_t D(X_t) u_t X_t$$

is assumed to be convex and bounded from above with $R \to 0$ as $X_t \to \infty$, and where

$$C(Q_t, \Pi_t, v_t) = \Pi_t[c(Q_t) + d(Q_t - Q_{t-1})]v_t.$$

The conditions on R and C assure that as long as the rate of change in the absolute price level is below r, interior solutions for X_0 and Q_0 exist for this problem.

The problem may be simplified by eliminating the constraint (2.3) and working with L_1 and Q_0 as the decision variables. The problem may be treated as a dynamic programming problem by writing

$$\omega_0 = R(X_0, \Pi_0, u_0) - C(Q_0, \Pi_0, v_0) - \frac{\Pi_0 B(L_1)}{1+r} \tag{2.6}$$

and

$$\Omega_1 = \max_{L_2, Q_1} E_1\left[\sum_{t=1}^{\infty} \left(\frac{R(X_t, \Pi_t, u_t)}{(1+r)^t} - \frac{C(Q_t, \Pi_t, v_t)}{(1+r)^t} - \frac{\Pi_t B(L_{t+1})}{(1+r)^{t+1}} \right) \right] \tag{2.7}$$

so that equation (2.5) becomes

$$\Omega_0 = \max_{L_1, Q_0} \left(\omega_0 + \frac{E_0(\Omega_1)}{1+r} \right), \tag{2.8}$$

where Π_0, u_0, v_0 are assumed to be known in period 0 and

$$X_0 = Q_0 + L_0 - L_1.$$

As in the Blinder–Fischer formulation, it is clear that the functions Ω_t depend only on the initial inventory stock, the initial realizations of the random variables u_t, v_t, and Π_t, and the joint distribution of future values. Since the inventory variable is the only state variable for the firm, we can suppress the random variables and write

$$\Omega_t = \Omega_t(L_{t+1}). \tag{2.9}$$

Note that L_{t+1} enters here since it is the inventory at the *end* of period t.

Although it is not true in general that certainty equivalents exist for the random variables in this formulation, a theorem of Malinvaud (1969) may be invoked to demonstrate the existence of approximate first-period certainty equivalents, which correspond roughly to the expectations reported in the survey data analyzed below. The assumptions made ensure that the Ω_t are concave bounded continuous functions and that, under some regularity conditions on the distributions of future u_t, v_t, and Π_t, an optimal policy exists. Moreover, Ω_t is a concave function of L_{t+1} with $\Omega_t' < 0$.

The first-order conditions for an interior maximum are

$$R_X(X_0, \Pi_0, u_0) - C_Q(\Pi_0, v_0) = 0, \tag{2.10}$$

and

$$\frac{E_0(\Omega_1') - \Pi_0 B'}{1+r} - R_X(X_0, \Pi_0, u_0) = 0. \tag{2.11}$$

Given first-period certainty equivalents, the random variables in Ω_1' may be replaced by their conditional expectations at time zero.

The expression

$$\lambda(L_1) = \frac{E_0(\Omega_1') - \Pi_0 B'}{1+r} \tag{2.12}$$

may be interpreted as the "shadow price" of carrying over one unit of inventory from period 0 to period 1. Thus the first-order conditions state

marginal revenue from sales = marginal cost of production
                             = the shadow price of a unit of inventories.

2.2   Comparative statics of the first period

The usual comparative statics techniques together with the various assumptions made about convexity and concavity permit us to sign various derivatives and thus to discuss the effects of changes in the general price level, specific demand and cost shocks, and interest rates. However, a graphical analysis may be more revealing intuitively. For this purpose, assume that the demand function is linear, that the steady-state production cost function $c(\ )$ is also quadratic, and that $d' = 0$ for $Q_t \le Q_{t-1}$. Given expectations of future demand and cost shocks and price level changes, the function $\lambda(L_1)$ will be downward sloping to the right. There is no direct connection between this function, however, and the marginal costs of production. As we shall see, the effects of some changes depend on the relative slopes of λ and C_Q.

The equilibrium of the firm is depicted in Figure 1, which also illustrates the effect of a one-time shock to the firm's demand function $u_1 > u_0$. A one-time shock clearly does not affect the shadow price of inventory schedule, $\lambda(L_1)$; demand shifts upward, parallel to the curve in the initial period, and the firm expands along the marginal cost schedule, which includes adjustment costs, until marginal cost equals marginal revenue, at which point the firm produces Q_1. However, inventories will be drawn down to L_1 since the shadow price of inventories at L_0 is now lower

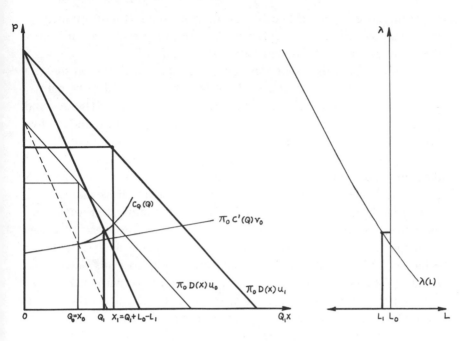

Figure 1. Effect of one-time firm-specific demand shock.

than marginal revenue. The new level of inventories will be L_1 so that sales
will be

$$X_1 = Q_1 + L_0 - L_1$$

and the new price, although it is higher than P_0, is not as high as it would
have been if the increase in demand had been met entirely out of current
production.

A specific demand shock that is expected to be permanent has more
complicated effects since such a shock also shifts the shadow price of inventories function upward by an amount that depends on u_1 relative to
u_0, the rate of discount, and future sales relative to current sales. Since
these will not be constant over time even if the demand shock is expected
to persist, it is not possible to give an explicit expression for the size of
the shift unless the functions are specified exactly. Clearly, however, the
level of inventories must fall less than in the case of a one-time shock and
may even increase. In this case, production will exceed sales, despite adjustment costs, as the firm builds up its inventory level to the point at
which marginal revenue is equal to the new shadow price of inventories.
If nothing further changes, there will still be more complicated effects

over time since adjustment costs vary along the time path of production. But we are concerned here only with first-period effects, since it is only these that are relevant from an econometric point of view.

It is clear from the first-order conditions and the definition of $\lambda(L)$ that a change in the general price level, which is expected to be permanent, will affect nothing except the price of the product: The demand function, marginal revenue function, marginal cost functions, and shadow price of inventories schedule all shift up by exactly equal amounts; production, sales, and inventories remain exactly the same, but the price of the firm's product rises exactly in proportion to the general price level. A change in the general price level that is not expected to be permanent has more complicated effects: Although it is true that marginal revenue and marginal costs shift upward by equal amounts so that production remains unchanged, the shadow price of inventories schedule does shift. From equations (2.7) and (2.12), we see that the marginal cost of storage rises. Because the rise in the price level is not expected to be permanent, however, $E_0(\Omega_1')$ does not change; thus, the $\lambda(L)$ curve shifts down by an amount equal to the discounted change in the marginal cost of storage. Thus, production is unchanged, but sales increase as inventories are run down both to take advantage of temporarily higher prices as well as because it is now temporarily more expensive to carry over a unit of inventories from this period to the next.[4] If the marginal costs of storage are relatively small, the latter effect will be small relative to the former. Figure 2 illustrates these remarks for a doubling of the general price level expected to be only temporary: The firm's specific price rises by much less, the level of production remains unchanged, but a large volume of inventories is disgorged, leading to a substantial increase in sales and only a small increase in product price. Conversely, when the general price level falls and the decline is expected to be only temporary, production will not change, but firms will build up inventories so that product prices will fall only by a fraction of the general decline.

An important theme in the literature on response to demand shocks concerns firms' difficulties in distinguishing specific demand shocks from general price level increases. In the model outlined here, the important difference lies in the fact that general price level changes affect both the location of the marginal revenue and marginal cost schedules and, if expected to be permanent, the shadow price of inventory schedule, all equally, whereas a specific demand shock affects only the marginal revenue schedule, if temporary, but may also raise the shadow price of inventories schedule if expected to be permanent. (Because of the multiplicative

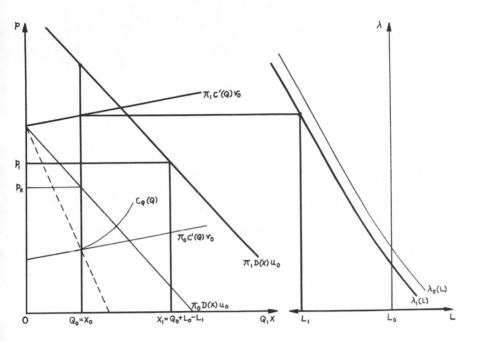

Figure 2. Effect of temporary rise in general price level.

form of the revenue function, the proportional effect will be identical to that of the revenue function itself.) Figure 3 shows the effect of a specific demand shock, expected to be permanent, on first-period production, sales, and inventories. Depending on the slope of the shadow price schedule, inventories may increase by a lot or by very little (the more rapidly the marginal costs of storage are rising, the steeper the shadow price schedule). The figure shows a case in which sales actually fall below the previous level, although production rises substantially, because inventories are built up to such a degree. Clearly, firms' inability to distinguish between general price level changes and specific demand shocks will mitigate this sort of behavior since if firms expect the changes to be permanent, expected costs rise as well as revenues, and the shadow price of inventories schedule shifts upward by still less (the term $\Pi_1 B'$ has the effect of shifting the schedule *downward* in an offsetting manner, in addition to the effect of rising costs of future as well as present production).

A firm-specific shift (fall) in costs that is expected to be only temporary is illustrated in Figure 4. If costs fall temporarily, the shadow price of inventories schedule is unaffected. Unless adjustment costs are rising

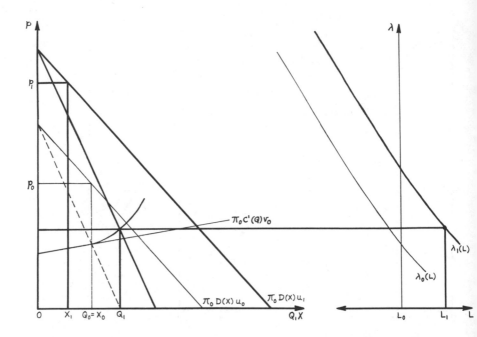

Figure 3. First-period effect of permanent firm-specific demand shock.

sharply and/or the shadow price of inventories is falling sharply, there is a possibility for such large shifts in costs that the firm chooses to build up inventories to such an extent that sales fall and prices actually rise despite an increase in production. Clearly, the general conclusion that in the short run the presence of inventories induces greater flexibility in production and inventories than in prices in response to cost shocks as well as demand shocks, expected to be only temporary, is sustained. If the shift in costs is expected to be permanent, however, the shift also enters the shadow price of inventories in a complicated manner. From equation (2.7), a permanent fall in the costs of production, holding sales, production, and inventories constant, reduces the expectation on the right. But inventories can be changed only by changing sales or production or both; a fall in the marginal cost of production makes it relatively cheaper to add to inventories by increasing production than by reducing sales: Hence, inventories that can be used to increase sales without additional production must be reduced in value on net balance. The shadow price of inventory schedule thus shifts downward, reducing the buildup of inventories, so that the increase in production is translated into an increase (or smaller fall) in sales and a fall (or smaller increase) in price.[5]

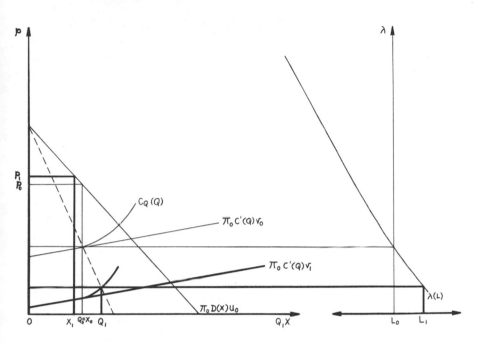

Figure 4. Effect of temporary fall in firm-specific costs of production.

Although there is no reason to expect firm-specific shifts in demand to be correlated with firm-specific shifts in costs, changes in the general price level increase marginal revenue, marginal cost, and the shadow price of inventories and may induce other changes in the shadow price of inventories if such price level changes are expected to be only temporary. To the extent, however, that firms are unable to distinguish positive demand shocks, permanent or temporary, from changes in the general price level in the short run, *perceived* shocks in demand and costs should be positively correlated. The effect of such a positive correlation should be to reduce the positive production response to a positive demand shock, increase the positive price response, and reduce inventory reductions.[6]

Whereas the precise conclusions of our analysis depend heavily on whether changes are expected to be temporary or permanent and the extent to which firms have difficulty in distinguishing firm-specific demand shocks from general changes in prices, the general thrust is that quantities, production, sales, and inventories will generally be more responsive than prices to all but general price level changes. If, in addition, there are nonnegligible price adjustment costs, perhaps of a fixed sort not depending on the size of the price change, these conclusions are further strengthened. Some firms will not adjust prices at all and some will adjust them fully, so that, observing a cross section of firms, we would expect the extent and prevalence of price adjustments to be further reduced.

3   Testing the model empirically

In the remainder of this chapter, we test the simple model elaborated above using data on individual firms drawn from so-called business tests for France and Germany. Microeconomic data have rarely been used to test hypotheses about the relative response of price and output to disequilibria, and, then, not within the context of an integrated model of response. [See, however, Kawasaki, McMillan, and Zimmerman (1982, 1983) and Ottenwaelter and Vuong (1984).]

3.1   *The French and German business test data*

For France, data are available for twenty-nine surveys conducted by the Institut Nationale de la Statistique et des Etudes Economiques (INSEE) between June 1974 and June 1982. The surveys were conducted three times per year until June 1978 (March, June, and November) and four times a year thereafter (January, March, June, and October) and cover approximately 3,000 firms. For Germany, data collected by the Ifo Institut für Wirtschaftsforschung are available for two periods, from January 1975 to December 1979 and from June 1980 to September 1982. The data are collected monthly, for about 5,000 firms in the early period and about 8,000 in the later period, with respect to eleven basic questions; they are collected quarterly, on a rotating basis, for the so-called *Sonderfragen.* For the *Sonderfragen,* we have the responses for only a few months in 1977 (January, March, April, May, and June) of the first period, but the data are complete in 1980–2.

Although the French and German economies are similar in many ways (level of industrialization, concentration, product mix, openness), it is believed by knowledgeable observers that there are important structural and institutional differences, particularly with respect to the way in which prices and production respond to various shocks (de Menil and Westphal 1982). Consequently, we believe that a comparative study of the French and German surveys may be especially illuminating with respect to the effects of demand shocks and, inferentially, factors affecting costs on changes in prices and in production. We show, indeed, that there are significant differences between the two countries.[7]

The basic data for our analysis consist of answers to questions regarding ex ante plans, anticipations and expectations of business conditions or product demand, production and prices, and ex post realized values of these, inventory and order backlogs, and incoming new orders. We also have appraisals of the levels of inventories and order backlogs. The exact questions on which our analyses are based are reproduced in the appendix.

Both the French and German economies experienced inflation during the period in question. Yet a significant number of responses reflect falling product prices for individual German firms. For France, which has experienced a relatively higher rate of inflation since the mid-1970s, continuous data on price anticipations and realizations are available, and these have been used to recategorize the responses so as to correct the relatively lesser presence of reported decreases.[8]

In the analyses reported in this chapter, we use data on German establishments only at three-month intervals, corresponding to the dates of the Sonderfragen concerning inventories. Moreover, the ex ante variables report anticipations during a three- to six-month period, whereas realizations are reported only for the previous month. The French responses refer to anticipated changes until the date of the next survey or to realized changes since the date of the last survey; our analyses use data at intervals corresponding to the intervals between surveys.

The theoretical model presented in the preceding section does not distinguish between ex ante and ex post variations in production, prices, and inventories or order backlogs, but it can be adapted to use this information available from the surveys to shed further light on the decision-making process of the firm. Appraisals of inventory and order backlog levels in relation to expected and unanticipated changes in demand offer some opportunity to make some inferences about whether these changes are expected to be temporary or permanent, although the surveys themselves contain no direct information on this matter.

3.2   *Statistical formulation of the model*

Relating theoretical constructs to empirical observation is the most difficult part of any econometric analysis and can never be carried out perfectly due to the complexity and ambiguity of the data and the simplicity of the theoretical model. We formulate a series of conditional probability statements relating realized changes in prices and production for French and German firms to a number of other variables such as previously anticipated price changes, changes in demand, changes in inventories, and appraisals of finished products and order backlogs. Data on changes in costs are not available in the Ifo and INSEE business test surveys on which we base our analysis. Omission of a variable reflecting cost changes will tend to bias our results with respect to the effects of demand shocks; however, we can infer the directions of bias and thus the effect of such omission on our conclusions.

The data with which we deal are almost all categorical, consisting of trichotomous responses of individual firms to survey questions. The data can be cross-classified for each respondent by question so that, for example, it is possible to see whether a firm that reports on one survey that it plans to increase its production over the coming months in fact does so as reported in a subsequent survey.[9] Methodological problems related to the analysis of cross-classified data, particularly of the kind one encounters in the German and French business tests, are dealt with elsewhere at some length [see Nerlove (1983) for references]. In subsequent work, we intend to develop models in which continuous latent variables trigger categorical responses, but it is not anticipated that such refinements will substantially alter the conclusions reported here.

A log-linear probability model represents a particular parameterization of a set of discrete probabilities (a priori positive) characterizing counts in a multidimensional contingency table. The logarithms of the probabilities are represented as the linear sum of terms analogous to the main and interaction effects of standard analysis of variance models. The importance of this parameterization to the analysis of ordinal categorical data of the sort found in many economic surveys lies in the following characteristics:

1. Because the relation between two or more variables is characterized by interactions of successively higher order, it is possible to eliminate some parameters in a way that still allows two or more variables to be related to one another.

2. The bivariate interaction effects may be used to construct a measure of partial bivariate association between pairs of ordinal variables, for example, as a suitable generalization of the Goodman–Kruskal gamma coefficient γ (Kawasaki 1979; Goodman and Kruskal 1979) and to formulate a chi-square test for the significance of association between pairs of variables (γ ranges between $+1$ for perfect positive association and -1 for perfect negative association).

3. The model also lends itself to a convenient parameterization of conditional probabilities in terms of a subset of main and interaction effects parameters that characterize the joint probabilities.

Systems of probability statements relating a number of categorical variables have been considered by Maddala and Lee (1976), Lee (1981), Ottenwaelter and Vuong (1981), and Vuong (1981). Vuong (1981) considers the most general case and derives conditions for the identification of systems of conditional probability statements in which conditional variables in some probability statements are conditioning in others. His work is summarized and extended in Ottenwaelter and Vuong (1981). The conditions are similar to those for the identification of a recursive system of simultaneous equations in econometric theory but somewhat less restrictive.[10]

Such a system of conditional probability statements is formulated here to describe the probability law governing changes in prices and in production as reported in the Ifo and INSEE business test surveys. This model represents a step in an ongoing effort to study the formation and revision of firms' plans and anticipations at a highly disaggregated level.[11]

The notation adopted in this formulation is as follows:

Ex ante variables
D^*: expected future demand
P^*: anticipated price changes
Q^*: planned changes in production

Ex post or realized variables
D: demand
L: changes in inventories of finished products
S: changes in order backlogs
P: realized price changes
Q: realized changes in production

Appraisal variables
L^a: appraisal of inventory levels[12]
S^a: appraisal of order backlogs

The appendix contains the original questions on which these variables are based.

Demand D is taken to be purely exogenous. The observed variable that "drives" our system is not D itself but rather unexpected changes in demand. Unexpected changes in demand, denoted ϕD, are defined by the entries in the following contingency table relating previous anticipations, D^*_{-1}, and current realizations, D:

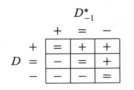

In earlier work on the German data, we found expected business conditions to be a plausible measure of expected future demand but incoming orders to be a better measure than business conditions of the realized state of demand. Consequently, ϕD is constructed using lagged expected business conditions for German respondents but current incoming orders for the realized values. Unexpected changes in prices, ϕP, and in production, ϕQ, may be similarly defined.

In our implementation of the theoretical model described in Section 2, we focus on the determination of price anticipations and production plans and on the reasons that the ex post values differ from the ex ante values of prices and production, that is, ϕP and ϕQ. There are, however, two implicit "identities" in the model relating previous anticipations or plans to their ex post values reported on a subsequent survey:

$$P \equiv P^*_{-1} \text{ "+" } \phi P, \qquad Q \equiv Q^*_{-1} \text{ "+" } \phi Q. \tag{3.1}$$

It is obvious that because of the categorical nature of the variables, these are not identities in the usual sense. It is clear, however, that if we had quantitative data, the identity

$$\text{actual} \equiv \text{anticipated} + \text{surprise}$$

would hold.

It is interesting to note that about two-thirds of all firms surveyed simultaneously carry both inventories of finished product and backlogs of unfilled orders for what is reputedly the same product. Presumably this is the result of some product inhomogeneity. Whereas the theoretical model treats backlogs as negative inventories, in the statistical formulation we must, perforce, deal with the two variables simultaneously. To do so, we restrict the sample for the estimation of relationships containing these variables or appraisals thereof to firms responding to both sets of questions.

The model we formulate is recursive in the sense defined previously. Expectations of future demand are determined by past unexpected changes and in turn affect changes in inventory levels and order backlogs, which, together with expectations of future demand, are reflected in appraisals of these variables. Appraisals, expectations of future demand, and perceptions of capacity constraints determine price anticipations and production plans, which by the implicit identities (3.1) determine realized changes in prices and production. In addition to (3.1), the model contains five more probability statements:

Determination of expectations of future demand:

$$\text{Prob}\{D^* \,|\, D^*_{-1}, D\}. \tag{3.2}$$

Unanticipated changes in production and prices:

$$\text{Prob}\{\phi P, \phi Q \,|\, \phi D, D^*, L, S\}. \tag{3.3}$$

Changes in inventories and order backlogs:

$$\text{Prob}\{L, S \,|\, \phi D, D^*\}. \tag{3.4}$$

Inventory and order backlog appraisals:

$$\text{Prob}\{L^a, S^a \,|\, D^*, L, S\}. \tag{3.5}$$

Production plans and price anticipations:

$$\text{Prob}\{P^*, Q^* \,|\, D^*, L^a, S^a\}. \tag{3.6}$$

A detailed justification of these relationships in terms of the theoretical model of Section 1 is given in the next section.

3.3 *Relation of the statistical formulation to the theoretical model*

In Section 2, we explored the comparative statics of the optimal first-period responses of a firm with inventories to demand and cost changes. Ex ante and ex post magnitudes were not distinguished, as they are in the data at hand, nor were a firm's appraisals of the current situation treated explicitly. On the other hand, expectations beyond the immediate future of demand and cost changes, neither of which are directly available in the data, were found to be important. Thus, we must try to use appraisals and differences of ex post magnitudes from ex ante magnitudes to infer what we may about current expectations in relation to longer-term expectations and, in particular, to infer what biases may result from the lack of cost data in our source.

The theoretical model does not specify how expectations of future demand are determined. Since we have responses concerning D^* directly from the surveys, there is no need, as there is when expectations are not directly observed, to introduce a model of expectation formation. In previous analyses (reported in Nerlove 1983), we found that a simple error-learning, or "adaptive," expectations model explained changes in all three ex ante variables better than a number of other simple mechanical models we estimated. The results were highly stable over time and showed a large and very significant positive association between changes in an ex ante variable and previously unexpected changes. For completeness, we adopt a similar but somewhat more flexible formulation here for D^* but formulate in (3.6) an explanation of P^* and Q^* with greater economic content.

Although the data do not give us any information about firms' long-run expectations, we do have information about how short-term expectations differ from what actually happened in the immediately preceding time period and how the firm responded. Rather than simply assume static expectations (i.e., whatever is expected for the immediate future is expected indefinitely), we make some inferences with respect to the determination of P^* and Q^* by using the information on the relation of ϕP and ϕQ to ϕD. It is common sense that a firm's plans and expectations will be revised when unexpected events occur. For changes in demand or costs expected to be only temporary, the theory predicts that a portion of the shock will be absorbed by changes in prices and production and a portion by inventories/backlogs. Now consider a relationship that conditions on both the current value of D^* and the unexpected change in demand this period, ϕD. Expected demand D^* contains information about the effects of factors expected to influence future demand both in the coming period and in the more distant future, but analogous to the standard regression result, ϕD given D^* reflects factors the influence of which is judged to be only temporary, since anything else will be incorporated in D^*. Thus in (3.3) and (3.4), we interpret the relation between ϕP, ϕQ, and ϕD or L, S, and ϕD holding D^* constant as the effect of a demand shock expected to be only temporary.

In general, positive firm-specific demand shocks result in smaller (or fewer) price adjustments than production adjustments. However, such firm-specific shocks may not be readily distinguishable from variations in the general rate of inflation. Temporary variations in the rate of change of the general price level should be reflected mainly in prices rather than in production, but these will also be damped by inventory changes (since the shadow price of inventory schedule is plausibly only slightly affected by temporary general price level variations). More importantly, inability to distinguish may lead to interpretation of firm-specific demand shocks as positively correlated with firm-specific variations in cost. Since these are not included in the analysis, bias may result.

Recent work by Lee (1982) sheds some light on the direction of this potential bias. Lee's results are somewhat complicated to interpret because he deals with the full parameterization of relationships among variables rather than scalar measures of partial association (similar to regression coefficients); we conjecture, however, that his results may be extended, although not trivially, to show the following: Consider three variables all of which are positively associated ($\gamma > 0$); if one of the three is omitted, the relationship between the two remaining will be biased upward toward a higher degree of positive association than the true one. Similarly, if the relationship between the omitted variable is one of positive association with one of the included variables and negative with the other, the association between the remaining two will be biased toward zero. Thus, since positive cost changes expected to be temporary are associated positively with price changes and negatively with production changes, omitting cost variations biases the association between temporary demand shocks and production adjustments downward. But since cost changes and demand changes are both positively associated with price adjustments, omission of costs should lead to a misleadingly high association between demand shocks and price adjustments.[13]

One further troublesome difficulty should be mentioned. We are dealing with a cross section of firms; in general, the elasticities of demand facing individual firms will differ. Under perfect competition with homogeneous products, firms will not adjust their own relative prices to firm-specific demand shifts. To the extent that German and French industry contain different mixtures of firms, they may be competitive to different degrees, and this difference may affect the results. Such problems could be handled by disaggregating into different industry groups. Such disaggregation, however, raises difficult statistical issues in this context (see Nerlove and Press 1976).

In the statistical model, the joint relation between production, prices, and inventories and backlogs is separated into two conditional statements in order to relate the latter separately to appraisals, which are not related to the effects of temporary demand or cost changes. Changes in inventories and backlogs reflect the way in which firms buffer price and production adjustments both to temporary changes and permanent ones. How inventories and backlogs change, for whatever reason, clearly affects ϕP and ϕQ: The larger the change in inventories and backlogs, the smaller the necessary price and production adjustments. But, in addition, we expect the association between L and ϕD to be negative and between S and ϕD to be positive (i.e., a fall in inventory levels or an increase in order backlogs is associated with an unexpected increase in demand).

How a firm appraises its current inventory and backlog level gives us some indication of its long-term expectations with respect to demand and

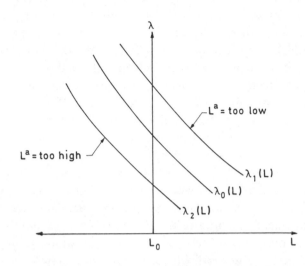

Figure 5. Effects of shifts in shadow price of inventory schedule on appraisal of current level of inventory.

cost changes relative to short-term expectations and responses, since the former primarily affect the shadow price of inventory schedule whereas the latter do so relatively little. The effect of short-term expectations may be expected to be felt primarily through what has just happened to inventories and backlogs (although these changes, of course, must depend partly on the location of the schedule). Holding expectations of future demand constant, if the schedule shifts little (i.e., most changes are expected to be only temporary), a recent negative change in inventories should be followed by the appraisal that they are too low (or order backlogs are too high) and conversely for a positive change. (The effects of recent changes in order backlogs should, of course, be reversed in sign.) Permanent increases in demand should shift the schedule upward so that any given level of inventories would then be regarded as too low. This is illustrated in Figure 5.

Finally, bearing in mind the previous caveats with respect to omission of cost variations, we come to the key relationship of the model, the relation between the ex ante variables, price anticipations and production plans. Inclusion of L^a and S^a is an attempt, as indicated, to fix the location of the shadow price of inventory schedule. In this case, expected changes in demand should be positively associated with both production plans and price anticipations, but less so for prices than for production. Interpretation of L^a and S^a in terms of the location of the shadow price of inventory schedule leads to the expectation that too low a level of

Table 1. *Model* Prob$\{D^* \mid D^*_{-1}, D, CS, SAI\}$.

Configuration	German firms		French firms	
	γ^a	$\chi^{2\,b}$	γ^a	$\chi^{2\,b}$
(D^*, D^*_{-1})	0.838	5,920.	0.380	423.
	(104)	(0.000)	(14.1)	(0.000)
(D^*, D)	0.523	1,770.	0.242	270.
	(32.3)	(0.000)	(9.41)	(0.000)
(D^*, CS)		233.		6.78
		(0.000)		(0.034)
(D^*, SAI)		58.4		21.0
		(0.000)		(0.002)
(D^*, D^*_{-1}, CS)		12.7		7.20
		(0.013)		(0.126)
(D^*, D^*_{-1}, SAI)		11.4		9.06
		(0.495)		(0.698)
(D^*, D, CS)		16.5		7.91
		(0.002)		(0.095)
(D^*, D, SAI)		13.5		3.94
		(0.333)		(0.984)
No. of observations		24,027.		6,507.

[a] Numbers in parentheses are *t* values.
[b] Numbers in parentheses are probabilities.

inventories or too high a level of order backlogs should be associated with planned increases in production and, perhaps, with some anticipated upward adjustment in prices. The effect of perceived constraints to the expansion of production depends on whether such constraints are expected to persist in the future: If they are not expected to persist, current constraints should be associated with planned increases in production, but not with anticipated changes in prices; if they are expected to persist, no planned increases in production should be anticipated, but prices should be expected to increase.

4 Estimates of parameters of the statistical model

The results of estimating the five conditional probabilities using a conditional log-linear probability model for each are presented in summary in Tables 1–6. The estimates are restricted to main effects and bivariate

Table 2. *Model* Prob$\{L, S \mid D^*, \phi D, \text{CS}, \text{SAI}\}$.

Configuration	German firms		French firms	
	γ^a	$\chi^{2\,b}$	γ^a	$\chi^{2\,b}$
(L, S)	0.098 (6.01)	61.0 (0.000)	0.044 (1.69)	17.4 (0.002)
(L, D^*)	0.010 (0.580)	16.6 (0.002)	0.025 (0.754)	43.5 (0.000)
$(L, \phi D)$	0.030 (2.14)	21.7 (0.000)	0.276 (9.61)	141.0 (0.000)
(S, D^*)	0.675 (47.5)	2,040. (0.000)	0.217 (8.76)	79.3 (0.000)
$(S, \phi D)$	0.735 (64.5)	2,340. (0.000)	0.176 (7.55)	83.5 (0.000)
(L, CS)		22.6 (0.000)		2.31 (0.315)
(L, SAI)		7.68 (0.262)		9.56 (0.144)
(S, CS)		51.0 (0.000)		0.790 (0.674)
(S, SAI)		7.65 (0.265)		6.65 (0.355)
(L, S, CS)		13.0 (0.011)		1.56 (0.815)
(L, S, SAI)		12.9 (0.375)		13.2 (0.351)
(L, D^*, CS)		8.9 (0.062)		2.06 (0.724)
(L, D^*, SAI)		15.4 (0.220)		15.8 (0.202)
$(L, \phi D, \text{CS})$		7.1 (0.130)		0.534 (0.970)
$(L, \phi D, \text{SAI})$		5.64 (0.933)		14.4 (0.274)
(S, D^*, CS)		4.29 (0.368)		6.55 (0.162)
(S, D^*, SAI)		29.6 (0.003)		19.3 (0.081)

Table 2 *(cont.)*

Configuration	German firms		French firms	
	γ^a	$\chi^{2\,b}$	γ^a	$\chi^{2\,b}$
$(S, \phi D, CS)$		34.9 (0.000)		7.30 (0.121)
$(S, \phi D, SAI)$		24.6 (0.017)		8.31 (0.760)
No. of observations		17,451.		4,911.

[a] Numbers in parentheses are t values.
[b] Numbers in parentheses are probabilities.

interaction configurations (except for the estimates on which the tests of seasonality and cyclical stability are based). Estimates are made for eight survey dates covering a recovery period of a full year and a recession period of a year for each country, as follows:

France
    Recession: October 1979, January 1980, March 1980, June 1980
    Recovery: June 1978, October 1978, January 1979, March 1979

Germany
    Recession: November 1980, February 1981, May 1981, August 1981
    Recovery: February 1983, May 1983, August 1983, November 1983

To account for cycle phase and seasonality, two new variables were introduced: a dichotomous variable for cycle phase, CS, and a four-category variable for season, SAI, the definition of which depends on whether we are considering France or Germany. SAI is 1, 2, 3, or 4 for the months of October, January, March, and June in that order for France and for November, February, May, and August in that order for Germany.

For each bivariate configuration of the conditional probability, we report a component γ-coefficient, an asymptotic t-statistic, the chi square for the entire configuration, and its associated upper-tail probability. Except for cases in which a configuration involving two trichotomous variables has been estimated only partly, due to an empty cell in the marginal

Table 3. *Model* Prob$\{L^a, S^a \mid D^*, L, S, CS, SAI\}$.

Configuration	German firms		French firms	
	γ^a	$\chi^{2\,b}$	γ^a	$\chi^{2\,b}$
(L^a, S^a)	0.847	2,940.	-0.530	313.0
	(66.6)	(0.000)	(14.2)	(0.000)
(L^a, D^*)	0.069	44.3	0.032	2.64
	(1.80)	(0.000)	(0.624)	(0.620)
(L^a, L)	0.250	247.	-0.905	1,650.
	(10.0)	(0.000)	(63.8)	(0.000)
(L^a, S)	0.084	62.2	0.026	7.12
	(2.41)	(0.000)	(0.675)	(0.130)
(S^a, D^*)	0.184	230.	0.534	385.
	(4.64)	(0.000)	(19.5)	(0.000)
(S^a, L)	0.022	18.2	0.054	11.8
	(0.805)	(0.001)	(1.30)	(0.019)
(S^a, S)	0.688	1,710.	0.191	67.4
	(30.8)	(0.000)	(7.35)	(0.000)
(L^a, CS)		6.25		0.222
		(0.044)		(0.895)
(L^a, SAI)		14.5		11.7
		(0.024)		(0.069)
(S^a, CS)		16.4		26.0
		(0.000)		(0.000)
(S^a, SAI)		12.0		12.8
		(0.061)		(0.046)
(L^a, S^a, CS)		12.9		5.56
		(0.012)		(0.234)
(L^a, S^a, SAI)		13.9		18.8
		(0.307)		(0.093)
(L^a, D^*, CS)		2.00		4.00
		(0.735)		(0.406)
(L^a, D^*, SAI)		10.8		7.70
		(0.549)		(0.808)
(L^a, L, CS)		14.3		1.50
		(0.006)		(0.827)
(L^a, L, SAI)		15.4		16.4[c]
		(0.220)		(0.037)

Table 3 *(cont.)*

Configuration	German firms		French firms	
	γ^a	$\chi^{2\,b}$	γ^a	$\chi^{2\,b}$
(L^a, S, CS)	2.44 (0.655)		1.00 (0.909)	
(L^a, S, SAI)	17.9 (0.117)		8.59 (0.738)	
(S^a, D^*, CS)	5.68 (0.225)		1.46 (0.834)	
(S^a, D^*, SAI)	31.9 (0.001)		10.6 (0.564)	
(S^a, L, CS)	3.45 (0.485)		4.25 (0.374)	
(S^a, L, SAI)	8.64 (0.734)		14.1 (0.295)	
(S^a, S, CS)	6.25 (0.181)		4.03 (0.402)	
(S^a, S, SAI)	13.1 (0.362)		15.1 (0.234)	
No. of observations	18,273.		4,866.	

[a] Numbers in parentheses are t values.
[b] Numbers in parentheses are probabilities.
[c] Partially estimated, eight degrees of freedom.

table corresponding to the configuration, there are four degrees of free-dom associated with the chi-square value. For such partially estimated configurations, there are two associated degrees of freedom. Bivariate configurations involving the dichotomous or four-category variables, CS or SAI, and one of the trichotomous variables have two and six asso-ciated degrees of freedom, respectively. Trivariate configurations with two trichotomous variables have four associated degrees of freedom with CS and twelve degrees of freedom with SAI. For configurations with CS and SAI, we report only the chi-square value and its associated upper-tail probability.[14]

In interpreting Tables 1–6, it is important to note the difference be-tween the phrasing of the questions for L^a and S^a in the French and in

Table 4. *Model* $\text{Prob}\{P^*, Q^* \mid D^*, L^a, S^a, \text{CS}, \text{SAI}\}$.

Configuration	German firms		French firms	
	γ^a	$\chi^{2\,b}$	γ^a	$\chi^{2\,b}$
(P^*, Q^*)	0.344	113.	0.031	4.43
	(5.37)	(0.000)	(0.206)	(0.351)
(P^*, D^*)	0.475	194.	0.218	9.45
	(8.43)	(0.000)	(1.50)	(0.051)
(P^*, L^a)	0.206	44.3	−0.088	4.40
	(2.85)	(0.000)	(0.527)	(0.354)
(P^*, S^a)	0.092	3.61	0.173	11.7
	(1.13)	(0.462)	(1.20)	(0.020)
(Q^*, D^*)	0.877	4,800.	0.907	1,370.
	(107.)	(0.000)	(65.2)	(0.000)
(Q^*, L^a)	0.304	161.	−0.237	27.8
	(7.63)	(0.000)	(4.06)	(0.000)
(Q^*, S^a)	0.457	426.	0.502	164.
	(12.8)	(0.000)	(12.0)	(0.000)
(P^*, CS)		53.2		2.66
		(0.000)		(0.265)
(P^*, SAI)		167.		14.3
		(0.000)		(0.027)
(Q^*, CS)		2.19		2.51
		(0.335)		(0.285)
(Q^*, SAI)		16.4		4.71
		(0.012)		(0.582)
(P^*, Q^*, CS)		8.81		4.72
		(0.066)		(0.317)
(P^*, Q^*, SAI)		2.67[c]		3.81[c]
		(0.953)		(0.874)
(P^*, D^*, CS)		15.6		1.32
		(0.004)		(0.859)
(P^*, D^*, SAI)		10.6		6.49[c]
		(0.565)		(0.593)
(P^*, L^a, CS)		7.12		3.94
		(0.130)		(0.414)
(P^*, L^a, SAI)		11.9		5.74[c]
		(0.454)		(0.677)

Table 4 (cont.)

	German firms		French firms	
Configuration	γ^a	$\chi^{2\,b}$	γ^a	$\chi^{2\,b}$
(P^*, S^a, CS)		6.36 (0.174)		2.11 (0.716)
(P^*, S^a, SAI)		23.0 (0.028)		8.68 (0.730)
(Q^*, D^*, CS)		6.48 (0.166)		1.36 (0.851)
(Q^*, D^*, SAI)		22.1 (0.037)		17.8 (0.122)
(Q^*, L^a, CS)		6.18 (0.186)		4.12 (0.390)
(Q^*, L^a, SAI)		22.9 (0.028)		6.21 (0.905)
(Q^*, S^a, CS)		8.11 (0.088)		5.76 (0.218)
(Q^*, S^a, SAI)		6.69 (0.877)		12.3 (0.422)
No. of observations		23,099.		4,082.

[a] Numbers in parentheses are t values.
[b] Numbers in parentheses are probabilities.
[c] Partially estimated, eight degrees of freedom.

the German questionnaire. The questions related to each variable used in the two surveys are reproduced in the original languages in the appendix. In the *French* questionnaire, the order of responses is greater than normal, normal, and less than normal for L^a and ample, normal, and insufficient for S^a. Thus, L^a and S^a should be negatively associated for French firms if indeed order backlogs function as negative inventories. On the other hand, in the *German* questionnaire, the order of responses is too small, sufficient, and too large for L^a (i.e., exactly the opposite of the French order) and comparatively large, sufficient, and too small for S^a. Thus, the relation between L^a and S^a should be positive if order backlogs function as negative inventories. Finally, we should expect the effects of L^a on other variables to be exactly the opposite in sign for French and for German firms.

Table 5. *Model* Prob$\{\phi P, \phi Q \mid D^*, \phi D, \text{CS}, \text{SAI}\}$.

	German firms		French firms	
Configuration	γ^a	$\chi^{2\ b}$	γ^a	$\chi^{2\ b}$
$(\phi P, \phi Q)$	0.185 (6.09)	55.2 (0.000)	0.063 (1.31)	3.08 (0.544)
$(\phi P, D^*)$	−0.012 (0.356)	24.8 (0.000)	0.037 (0.821)	12.4 (0.014)
$(\phi P, \phi D)$	0.191 (7.07)	74.0 (0.000)	0.093 (2.15)	12.8 (0.012)
$(\phi Q, D^*)$	0.060 (2.65)	162. (0.000)	−0.083 (2.17)	15.9 (0.003)
$(\phi Q, \phi D)$	0.672 (59.1)	2,650. (0.000)	0.740 (40.2)	1,100. (0.000)
$(\phi P, \text{CS})$		39.9 (0.000)		4.19 (0.123)
$(\phi P, \text{SAI})$		179. (0.000)		13.5 (0.036)
$(\phi Q, \text{CS})$		3.18 (0.204)		2.54 (0.280)
$(\phi Q, \text{SAI})$		22.8 (0.001)		3.48 (0.747)
$(\phi P, \phi Q, \text{CS})$		9.75 (0.045)		4.31 (0.366)
$(\phi P, \phi Q, \text{SAI})$		23.1 (0.027)		5.38 (0.944)
$(\phi P, D^*, \text{CS})$		0.297 (0.990)		5.22 (0.265)
$(\phi P, D^*, \text{SAI})$		22.7 (0.030)		20.2 (0.064)
$(\phi P, \phi D, \text{CS})$		4.11 (0.391)		2.56 (0.634)
$(\phi P, \phi D, \text{SAI})$		4.53 (0.972)		20.2 (0.064)
$(\phi Q, D^*, \text{CS})$		0.297 (0.990)		0.959 (0.916)
$(\phi Q, D^*, \text{SAI})$		23.1 (0.027)		7.40 (0.830)

Table 5 *(cont.)*

| | German firms | | French firms | |
Configuration	γ^a	$\chi^{2\,b}$	γ^a	$\chi^{2\,b}$
$(\phi Q, \phi D, \text{CS})$		9.87		2.04
		(0.043)		(0.729)
$(\phi Q, \phi D, \text{SAI})$		8.79		15.5
		(0.721)		(0.213)
No. of observations		18,498.		4,551.

^{a} Numbers in parentheses are t values.
^{b} Numbers in parentheses are probabilities.

Component γ-coefficients are sometimes not significantly different from zero (judged by the associated t-statistics), whereas the chi-square statistic for the configuration is significant. Such a result is an indication of a nonmonotonic relation between the two variables, since the γ-coefficient measures the strength of monotonic association only.

When the chi-square value for a bivariate configuration involving CS or SAI and a conditional variable is highly significant, as is often the case in the results reported, it means that the main effect corresponding to the conditioned variable varies cyclically or seasonally. Thus, for example, at certain times of the year or in the recovery phase of the cycle, firms generally expect increases in demand, *ceteris paribus*. When the chi-square value for the trivariate configuration involving two variables, both conditioned or one conditioned and the other conditioning, and either CS or SAI is highly significant, as fortunately is not often the case, it means that the *bivariate relation* between the former variables varies with cycle phase or with season.

Unfortunately, the relationship of the full model connecting unanticipated changes in prices and production to unanticipated changes in demand, anticipated changes in demand, and changes in order backlogs and inventory levels was too large to estimate with seasonal and cyclical effects given the available computer programs and speeds. Hence, this relationship was estimated without L and S, but with CS and SAI, and also with L and S for one survey date each for French firms and for German firms. The two sets of results are presented in Tables 5 and 6, respectively.

Table 6. *Model* Prob$\{\phi P, \phi Q \mid D^*, \phi D, L, S\}$.

	German firms		French firms	
Configuration	γ^a	$\chi^{2\,b}$	γ^a	$\chi^{2\,b}$
$(\phi P, \phi Q)$	0.148	7.54	0.082	2.25
	(1.78)	(0.106)	(0.652)	(0.690)
$(\phi P, D^*)$	0.008	5.29	−0.066	1.75
	(0.105)	(0.259)	(0.531)	(0.781)
$(\phi P, \phi D)$	0.170	9.94	0.012	11.8
	(2.18)	(0.042)	(0.091)	(0.019)
$(\phi P, L)$	0.024	5.58	0.110	3.16
	(0.416)	(0.232)	(0.852)	(0.531)
$(\phi P, S)$	−0.031	0.463	0.147	2.76
	(0.396)	(0.977)	(1.49)	(0.598)
$(\phi Q, D^*)$	0.052	28.8	−0.050	10.2
	(0.927)	(0.000)	(0.492)	(0.037)
$(\phi Q, \phi D)$	0.674	345.	0.741	152.
	(21.6)	(0.000)	(15.0)	(0.000)
$(\phi Q, L)$	0.113	11.7	−0.115	10.3
	(2.72)	(0.020)	(1.05)	(0.035)
$(\phi Q, S)$	0.136	32.8	0.020	0.701
	(2.07)	(0.000)	(0.240)	(0.951)
No. of observations		2,417.		619.

[a] Numbers in parentheses are *t* values.
[b] Numbers in parentheses are probabilities.

Although our model is very simple compared to a large-scale econometric model, it is nonetheless quite complex. That the model is couched in probability statements rather than more familiar equations does not make interpretation of the results easier. To aid the reader, we have held the number of parameters to a minimum and present below a brief summary of the main results. Were we dealing with a large-scale econometric model, we might resolve some similar expository problems by presenting a few policy simulations. Unfortunately, that is not possible in this case.

5   Summary of the main results

As in previous studies, we find highly significant positive associations between anticipated changes in future demand and past demand anticipations and realizations. In the case of both French firms and German firms, the strength of the association between past realizations and future anticipations is about 60 percent of the strength of the association between past anticipations and newly formed ones. This confirms all previous findings generally regarding the apparent adaptive nature of expectation formation. In addition, we find quite significant bivariate interactions of demand expectations with both cyclical and seasonal indicators, which suggests, not surprisingly, that firms anticipate demand increases more frequently at certain times of the year than at others, or in the recovery phase of the business cycle than in the recession phase. We find no seasonal effects, however, on the relation between D^* and D^*_{-1} or between D^* and D. There are significant, but not highly so, cyclical effects on these relations.

Turning first to the model for price anticipations and production plans, we find, as previously, that production plans for both French and German firms are significantly related to demand expectations and appraisals of order backlogs. Both French and German firms that evaluate their backlogs of orders as higher than normal or inventories of finished goods as too small exhibit a higher probability of reporting planned increases in production. Omission of cost variables, to the extent that they are positively associated with demand changes, will bias the association of production adjustments with expected changes in demand downward so our conclusion is robust.

For German firms, there exists a positive association between price anticipations and production plans, but a significant relationship is not found for the French firms. Also, for German firms, in terms of t-ratios and chi-square statistics, price anticipations are positively related to the appraisals of inventories, implying that firms that evaluate their inventories as too low (compared with normal) exhibit a higher probability of anticipated price increases. For French firms, however, a significant relationship is not observed. The model of Section 2 predicts a lesser response of prices to expected changes in demand that are not expected to be permanent. Our results are consistent with that hypothesis, as well as with the hypothesis that appraisals of inventories and backlogs reflect changes in demand or costs that are expected to be permanent and therefore shift the shadow price of inventory schedule. That we do observe some response of prices for German firms but not for French firms may reflect a greater degree of association between unobserved cost changes and demand shifts. As we have noted above, this would tend to bias upward the association between price adjustments and demand shifts.

For both German and French firms, we find highly significant seasonal effects on price anticipations, but only for German firms do there appear to be such effects in production plans. For German firms, there are significant cyclical effects on prices but not, surprisingly, on production; for French firms, we find neither. There are a few significant trivariate interactions for German firms suggesting that the relations between P^* and Q^*, between P^* and D^*, between P^* and S^a, between Q^* and D^*, and between Q^* and L^a may depend on seasonal or cyclic factors.[15]

Appraisals of order backlogs and inventory levels are conditionally highly dependent; moreover, given the ordering of the questions, the direction of association is exactly as expected if backlogs function as negative inventories. Previous changes in inventory levels are significantly associated with inventory appraisals for both French and German firms, that is, firms that have just experienced an increase in stocks report their stocks as too high. Anticipated changes in future demand do not appear to be associated with inventory appraisals for either French or German firms. But such anticipations are significantly associated with order backlog appraisals: For both French and German firms, an expected increase in demand is associated with an appraisal of an insufficient order backlog. The effect is more than twice as large for French as for German firms. Recent increases in order backlogs are associated with appraisals suggesting levels are too high for both groups of firms. There are significant seasonal and cyclic effects on appraisals and, for German firms, on the relation between L^a and L and S^a and D^*.

Both anticipated and unanticipated changes in demand are positively and significantly associated with increases in the backlog of orders for French and German firms, but the relationship of changes in inventory levels appears nonmonotonic. Cyclical and seasonal factors significantly affect changes in both inventories and order backlogs and the relation of these variables to demand for German firms but not for French firms. The inventory and backlog associations with unexpected changes in demand strongly support the conclusions drawn from the theoretical model in Section 2 that changes in demand expected to be only temporary will result in price and production adjustments damped to a great extent by inventory adjustments. That the responses of French firms appear weaker, but nonetheless in the right direction, may be due in part to a greater degree of association of firm-specific demand shocks with permanent overall price level changes.

The results for unanticipated changes in prices and production are somewhat difficult to interpret because we were not able to estimate full models for either French or German firms. Moreover, there are many significant seasonal and cyclical effects, so that the results reported in Table 6 for a particular month in the recession phase may be sensitive to the choice. Perhaps the most interesting finding is robust. Unanticipated changes in prices depend on unanticipated changes in demand but very little, if at all, or nonmonotonically on anticipated changes in demand. The most striking and robust finding is the positive relation between unanticipated changes in demand and unplanned increases in production. For German firms, changes in order backlogs and inventories display the relationship to unexpected changes of production we expected a priori. Firms that report increases in back orders exhibit a higher probability of reporting increases in actual production above that which had been planned; firms that experience a decrease in inventory levels show a similar response. For French firms, these reaction patterns are not observed. There is no way to know, however, if these results are significantly affected by omission of seasonal or cyclical factors, but they are consistent with the predictions of the theoretical model of Section 2 and the directions of bias that may be introduced by omission of cost variables.[16]

Chi-square values for each probability model against the null hypothesis of independence are uniformly high (in excess of 200–300), as are Goodman R^2's. For this reason, neither are presented. Nerlove and Press (1976) argue that none of the currently available measures of goodness of fit of the overall model are informative; under typical econometric circumstances, all will tend to be very high.

6   Concluding remarks

From the theoretical model presented in Section 2, we concluded that firm-specific demand shocks expected to be only temporary would affect both prices and production but that these effects would be damped by inventory adjustments and more damped for prices than for production. To the extent that the firm is (partly) unable to distinguish firm-specific demand shocks from general price level changes, price adjustments should be greater and inventory and production adjustments less. Changes in costs specific to the firm and expected to be only temporary also result in price and production adjustments that are damped, or even perversely affected, by inventory adjustments. The data used do not contain information on cost changes. Changes in costs specific to the firm might be expected to be independent of changes in demand specific to the firm. To the extent that perceived demand shifts and cost changes are due to changes in the overall economic situation, they should tend to be positively associated. However, omission of cost variables, in this case, should bias the positive association of production and inventory adjustments and demand shifts predicted by the theory toward zero and the positive association of price adjustments and demand shifts upward. Thus the conclusion that production and inventory adjustments predominate and that price adjustments are significantly less or absent is robust to omission of costs. These results support the position taken by Malinvaud (1977, 1980; see also Kawasaki et al. 1982). Thus the empirical evidence provides support for the hypothesis that is central to disequilibrium economics for French firms and to a somewhat lesser extent for German firms.

The data are richer than this fairly straightforward conclusion suggests: Unexpected changes in demand can be interpreted, given demand expectations proper, as temporary. Thus we can analyze the effects of temporary changes independently of assumptions about how much of a given expected change in demand is expected to be permanent. Moreover, inventory level and backlog appraisals give us information about the location of the shadow price of inventory schedule, which permanent changes in demand or costs may be expected to shift. The relationship of the model explaining ϕP and ϕQ even more clearly supports the basic conclusion that quantity adjustments are more important than price adjustments in the short run.

The way in which demand expectations and unexpected changes in demand work through changes in inventories and backlogs and appraisals thereof are not, of course, part of the formal theoretical model but give some indirect evidence on the effects of cost considerations.

As noted in previous work (*inter alia,* Nerlove and Press 1976, Nerlove 1983), main effects reflect factors affecting all or most firms at the same time. We have found significant seasonal and cyclic bivariate interactions with most of the variables in the model (suggesting cyclic or seasonal variation in main effects) but relatively few significant trivariate interactions. This finding suggests that the relationships among firm-level variables may be quite stable when account is taken of macroeconomic and seasonal factors affecting most firms in the economy at the same time.

A final caveat is in order: Firms are considered to be homogeneous in forming anticipations and plans as well as in their reactions to demand shocks. As is well known, market structure may be of considerable importance for pricing behavior. Differences in the market structure may not only affect the pricing policy of a firm but may also result in different reaction patterns in production, investment plans, and so forth (Monopolkommission 1976). Preliminary studies taking into account the degree of concentration of specific industry groups, however, did not yield significant results with respect to the estimated interaction effects.

Appendix: Questions from the French and German surveys used in the analyses

INSEE survey (relation of variables and questions)

D Evolution de la demande – tendance au cours des 3 ou 4 derniers mois: + = −.

D^* Evolution de la demande – tendance probable au cours des 3 ou 4 prochains mois: + = −.

P Veuillez indiquer la variation de vos prix de vente (hors taxes): +_____% = −_____%.

P^* Quelle sera la variation probable de vos prix de vente (hors taxes): +_____% = −_____%.

Q Evolution de votre production – tendance au cours des 3 ou 4 derniers mois: + = −.

Q^* Evolution de votre production – tendance probable au cours des 3 ou 4 prochains mois: + = −.

L Evolution de vos stocks de produits fabriqués (produits prêts pour la vente) – tendance au cours des 3 ou 4 derniers mois.

S Sur la base des commandes enregistrées restant à exécuter et du rythme actuel de fabrication, pour combien de semaines estimez-vous que votre activité est assurée? environ _____ semaines.

L^a Evolution de vos stocks de produits fabriqués (produits prêts pour la vente) – considérez-vous que, compte tenu de la saison, vos stocks actuels de produits fabriqués sont: supérieurs à la normale, norm, aux inférieurs à la normale.

S^a La notion de carnet de commandes a-t-elle une signification pour votre production? Si oui, considérez-vous que, compte tenu de la saison, votre carnet de commandes est actuellement bien garni, normal, peu garni?

Ifo survey (relation of variables and questions)

D Die Nachfragesituation (In- und Ausland) für XY hat sich bei uns gegenüber dem Vormonat – gebessert, nicht verändert, verschlechtert.

D^*　Unsere Geschäftslage für XY wird in den nächsten 6 Monaten in konjunktureller Hinsicht – also unter Ausschaltung rein saisonaler Schwankungen – eher günstiger, etwa gleich bleiben, eher ungünstiger.

P　Unsere Inlandsverkaufspreise (Nettopreise) für XY wurden – unter Berücksichtigung von Konditionsveränderungen – gegenüber dem Vormonat – erhöht, nicht verändert, gesenkt.

P^*　Unsere Inlandsverkaufspreise (Nettopreise) für XY werden – unter Berücksichtigung von Konditionsveränderungen – voraussichtlich im Laufe der nächsten 3 Monate – steigen, etwa gleich bleiben, fallen.

Q　Unsere inländische Produktionstätigkeit bezüglich XY war gegenüber dem Vormonat – lebhafter, unverändert, schwächer.

Q^*　Unsere inländische Produktionstätigkeit bezüglich XY wird voraussichtlich im Laufe der nächsten 3 Monate in konjunktureller Hinsicht – also unter Ausschaltung rein saisonaler Schwankungen – steigen, etwa gleich bleiben, abnehmen.

L　Unsere Bestände an unverkauften Fertigwaren von XY entsprechen z. Z. – weniger als 0.5, 0.5, 1, 2, 3, 4, 5, 6, mehr als 6, und zwar – Produktions*wochen* (gemessen am gegenwärtigen Produktionsumfang). Lagerhaltung nicht üblich.

S　Unser Auftragsbestand (wertmäßig, In- und Ausland) für XY ist z. Z. gegenüber dem Vormonat – höher, etwa gleich groß, niedriger. Auftragsbestand nicht üblich.

L^a　Unser Lager an unverkauften Fertigwaren von XY empfinden wir z. Z. als – zu klein, ausreichend (saisonüblich), zu groß. Lagerhaltung nicht üblich.

S^a　Unseren Auftragsbestand (In- und Ausland) für XY empfinden wir z. Z. als – verhältnismäßig groß (z. B. verlängerte Lieferzeiten), ausreichend (saisonüblich) bzw. zu klein. Auftragsbestand nicht üblich.

NOTES

1　In a partial equilibrium framework Π_0 and u_0 may be treated as exogenous to the firm, at least to a first order of approximation. Of course, in a dynamic, general equilibrium context, these variables must be treated endogenously.

2　As long as marginal production costs are rising, as is well known, it always pays to smooth production if storage and interest costs are sufficiently low. Hence, strictly speaking, the additional costs of varying rates of production are unnecessary to our further development. If, however, our analyses were to be extended to the case of falling marginal costs of production (in the long run), rising short-run costs associated with variations in the rate of production would be essential to avoid discontinuous inventory policy at the level of the individual firm.

3   Blinder and Fischer assume the firm maximizes the discounted value of *real* net revenues; that is, they divide everything through by Π_t. However, in the present formulation, it can easily be seen that changes in the general price level, provided they are perceived as such, will affect nothing. Our formulation has the advantage of allowing for effects on all costs, including inventory holding costs, and effects specific to production costs or revenues. The same analysis could be equivalently carried out using real rates of interest to discount the future and making future values of these random variables for the firm. Blinder (private correspondence, 1984) points out that our treatment implies real rates of interest, which vary dramatically. Since the interest rate, however, enters only via the shadow price of a unit of inventory and since *current* marginal revenue and marginal production costs are homogeneous of degree 1 in absolute prices, the asymmetric effects of price level variations considered to be only temporary and those considered permanent can be viewed alternatively as the effects of variations in the real rate of interest on the shadow price of inventory. This, however, does not in our view affect the desirability of separating factors affecting current marginal revenues and marginal production costs and those affecting future costs and revenues as summarized in the shadow price of a unit of inventory.

4   If the reader finds the notion of a temporary increase in the general price level bizarre, let these results be interpreted in terms of steady rates of change temporarily altered.

5   The possibility of an actual decline in specific product prices cannot be ruled out but is implausible unless the marginal costs of storage are rising extremely rapidly.

6   Presumably, costs refer to nominal adjustments rather than real ones, which will lead, in times of general inflation, to asymmetries in the effects of such costs. However, our general conclusions are based on analyses in which prices are perfectly and costlessly flexible and thus continue to hold.

7   In previous analyses, we have disaggregated by industry group to the extent possible given data limitations. We have, however, found no significant differences among firms in different industries. Consequently, we believe that the differences between France and Germany found in this research do not reflect differences in the mix of industries within the samples for the two countries.

8   The categories used for both anticipated and realized price changes for French firms are

"+" $\equiv\ >5\%$,

"=" $\equiv\ >0\%$ and $\leq 5\%$,

"−" $\equiv\ \leq 0\%$.

9   Corresponding to the values of the ex ante variables, in contrast to our previous work in which a complicated aggregation scheme was adopted, we simply chose the second month following the month for which the anticipation is reported. This method has the advantage of retaining more firms in the sample, particularly those firms that exhibit a great deal of variability over time.

10 This is a consequence of the fact that a complete set of univariate conditional probabilities derived from an underlying joint probability law uniquely determines the joint probability law and is determined by it; see Nerlove and Press (1976). As a consequence of (3) below, no restrictions need be imposed on the "structural" probabilities in (2) below in order to ensure that they are derivable from the same underlying joint distribution.

For simplicity, consider the case of three categorical variables A_1, A_2, A_3 the distribution of which is characterized by some joint probability law:

(1) $\text{Prob}\{A_1, A_2, A_3\}$.

Suppose that for theoretical reasons we believe that underlying the joint probability is a structural system of conditional probability laws:

(2) $\text{Prob}\{A_1 \mid A_2, A_3\}$, $\quad \text{Prob}\{A_2 \mid A_3\}$, $\quad \text{Prob}\{A_3\}$.

Provided that

(3)
$$\text{Prob}\{A_2 \mid A_1, A_3\} = \text{Prob}\{A_2 \mid A_3\},$$
$$\text{Prob}\{A_3 \mid A_1, A_2\} = \text{Prob}\{A_3\},$$

it is possible to estimate each of the structural probabilities separately. Moreover, the system of conditional probabilities uniquely determines the joint probability law (1).

11 In most macroeconomic models and other studies involving time series data, one can infer how expectations are formed and how they influence plans and behavior only indirectly by observing the outcomes of decisions made by the firms and the values of variables representing external forces affecting these firms. Such inferences can be tested only indirectly within the context of the behavioral model assumed. This means that errors in the formulation of a behavioral model affect conclusions regarding expectation formation and plans and vice versa. Therefore, it is essential to obtain independent evidence on the actual microdata themselves, i.e., on expectations and plans at the firm level.

12 In the case of Germany, the interpretation of L^a, inventory appraisals, is reversed in sign: For the French data, the first category is greater than normal, the second normal, etc., whereas for the German data the first category is too small, the second sufficient, etc.

13 The usual complications that occur in regression analysis when more than three variables are present and are mutually correlated also occur here. We neglect these complications as being of the second order with respect to the primary conclusion.

14 Strictly speaking, these probabilities are not correct because the observations from successive surveys are not independent. To estimate our models, we need a sample of firms responding on two successive survey dates; moreover, many firms respond throughout the two-year period. Any factors that affect the behavior of the firm in a manner that persists over time and are not captured by the variables explicitly included in the analysis will introduce a time

dependence among the observations and render the assumptions invalid on which the asymptotic chi-square result depends.

15 For example, during the recovery phase, the positive association between price anticipations and expected changes in future demand rises by more than 10 percent.

16 It is interesting to note that when the unconditional relationship between unanticipated changes in prices and in production is estimated, a strong positive association between ϕP and ϕQ is found, but that when this relationship is conditioned on ϕD, the association all but disappears, i.e., the two variables are nearly conditionally independent given unanticipated changes in demand.

REFERENCES

Arrow, K. J., S. Karlin, and H. Scarf (1958), "The nature and structure of inventory problems," in K. J. Arrow, S. Karlin, and H. Scarf (Eds.), *Studies in the mathematical theory of inventory and production,* Stanford: Stanford University Press.

Barro, R. J. (1976), "Rational expectations and the role of monetary policy," *Journal of Monetary Economics,* 2: 1–32.

Blinder, A. S. (1981), "Retail inventory behavior and business fluctuations," *Brookings Papers on Economic Activity,* 2: 443–505.

Blinder, A. S. (1982), "Inventories and sticky prices: More on the microfoundations of macroeconomics," *American Economic Review,* 72: 334–48.

Blinder, A. S. and S. Fischer (1981), "Inventories, rational expectations, and the business cycle," *Journal of Monetary Economics,* 8: 277–304.

Clower, R. W. (1965), "The Keynesian counterrevolution: A theoretical appraisal," in F. H. Hahn and F. Brechling (Eds.), *The theory of interest,* London: Macmillan.

Goodman, L. A. and W. Kruskal (1979), *Measures of association for crossclassifications,* New York: Springer-Verlag.

Gordon, R. J. (1981), "Output fluctuations and gradual price adjustment," *Journal of Economic Literature,* 19: 493–530.

Kawasaki, S. (1979), Application of log-linear probability models in econometrics, Ph.D. dissertation, Department of Economics, Northwestern University.

Kawasaki, S., J. McMillan, and K. F. Zimmermann (1982), "Disequilibrium dynamics: An empirical study," *American Economic Review,* 72: 992–1000.

Kawasaki, S., J. McMillan, and K. F. Zimmermann (1983), "Inventories and price inflexibility," *Econometrica,* 51: 599–610.

Laidler, D. (1981), "On Say's law, money and the business cycle," Research Report No. 8106, University of Western Ontario.

Lee, Lung-Fei (1981), "Fully recursive probability models and multivariate log-linear probability models for the analysis of qualitative data," *Journal of Econometrics,* 16: 15–69.

Lee, Lung-Fei (1982), "Specification error in multinomial logit models: Analysis of the omitted variable bias," *Journal of Econometrics,* 20: 197–209.

Leijonhufvud, A. (1968), *On Keynesian economics and the economics of Keynes: A study in monetary theory,* New York: Oxford University Press.

Maccini, L. J. (1981), "On the theory of the firm underlying empirical models of aggregate price behavior," *International Economic Review,* 22: 609–24.

Maddala, G. S. and Lung-Fei Lee (1976), "Recursive models with qualitative variables," *Annals of Economics and Social Measurement,* 5/4: 524–45.

de Menil, G. and U. Westphal (1982), "The transmission of international disturbances: A French–German cliometric analysis, 1972–80," *European Economic Review,* 18: 41–73.

Malinvaud, E. (1969), "First-order certainty equivalence," *Econometrica,* 37: 706–18.

Malinvaud, E. (1977), *The theory of unemployment reconsidered,* Oxford: Basil Blackwell.

Malinvaud, E. (1980), *Profitability and Unemployment,* Cambridge: Cambridge University Press.

Monopolkommission (1976), *Mehr Wettbewerb ist moeglich,* Hauptgutachten 1973/1975, Baden: Nomos Verlagsgesellschaft.

Nerlove, M. (1983), "Expectations, plans, and realizations in theory and practice," Presidential address to the Econometric Society. *Econometrica,* 51: 1251–79.

Nerlove, M. and S. J. Press (1976), "Multivariate log-linear probability models for the analysis of qualitative data," Discussion paper No. 1, Center for Statistics and Probability, Northwestern University.

Ottenwaelter, B. and Q. H. Vuong (1981), "Modèles conditionnele log-lineaires de probabilité et systèmes recursifs," *Annales de l'INSEE,* 44: 81–120.

Ottenwaelter, B. and Q. H. Vuong (1984), "An empirical analysis of backlog, inventory, production, and price adjustments: An application of recursive systems of log-linear models," *Journal of Business and Economic Statistics,* 2: 224–34.

Patinkin, D. (1965), *Money, interest, and prices: An integration of monetary and value theory,* 2nd ed., New York: Harper & Row.

Reagan, P. B. (1982), "Inventory and price behavior," *Review of Economic Studies,* 49: 137–42.

Vuong, Q. H. (1981), Conditional log-linear probability models: A theoretical development and an empirical application, Ph.D. dissertation, Department of Economics, Northwestern University.

CHAPTER 8

On asymmetric information, unemployment, and inflexible wages

Mordecai Kurz

1   Approaches to the theory of unemployment

Understanding the special features of the labor markets is crucial both for the understanding of the functioning of a market economy and for the formation of public policy. Although Keynes never explicitly assumed rigid wage rates, most of the interpretations of Keynesian economics suggest that the main cause for unemployment is rigid wage rates. Moreover, the various neo-Keynesian, non-Walrasian models of recent years intended to provide a microtheory for an economic system in which prices are either rigid or slow changing while quantities adjust rapidly. In such economies, markets cannot clear in the Walrasian sense, and equilibrium is attained through the formation of quantity constraints on economic agents. Market clearance in these economies means that, in general, rationing takes place; and in the particular case of the labor market, one would expect society to develop institutions that ration the relatively limited supply of jobs. Such unemployment is obviously not voluntary.

On the other extreme we have a rapidly growing literature based on the "market-clearing" hypothesis, which holds that all markets are cleared in the Walrasian sense and wage flexibility implies that observed unemployment is voluntary. This school of thought implies that a voluntary decision to be unemployed represents nothing but an intertemporal substitution of current leisure for future labor, which is expected to be provided at higher wage rates.

The two theories face serious empirical and conceptual challenges. Some historical evidence may be provided to support the hypothesis of wage

This research was supported by National Science Foundation Grant SES 82-01373 at the Institute for Mathematical Studies in the Social Sciences, Stanford University. The author thanks J. Stiglitz for stimulating discussions. He also thanks his student, Peter Streufert, for the calculations of Tables 1 and 2.

219

inflexibility. However, such hypothesis is difficult to reconcile with a comprehensive theory of markets. Why do the unemployed not offer to work for a lower wage rate while seeking employment? On the other side of this issue, it is hard to see how the observed unemployment in the Great Depression of the 1930s or even in the recession of 1981–3 represented a voluntary intertemporal substitution between labor and leisure. Such casual empirical observations may not be convincing and a recent paper by Bernanke (1983) raises exactly such a question. Bernanke uses microdata from the Great Depression to claim that the level of available public and private transfers to the unemployed was not significantly lower than the marginal wage rate. This would induce indifference, on the margin, between being currently employed and unemployed. Since we know that wage rates respond very little to unemployment, Bernanke seems to imply that it is the availability of public and private transfers that make workers voluntarily unemployed and indifferent between work and unemployment. It will be interesting to know if this hypothesis can withstand further scrutiny.

On the strictly theoretical level, the market-clearing hypothesis combined with rational expectations of economic agents faces the problem of explaining economic fluctuations. Apart from the excessive reliance on "monetary shocks," models of the business cycles employ various forms of rigidities. For example, Lucas uses either finite (1972) or a continuum (1975) of isolated markets among which workers and capital cannot move until the end of the period and across which information does not flow. It is the interaction of this rigidity with the accelerator that is the basis for the theory of the cycle proposed by Lucas.

The theory of *labor contracts* [see, e.g., Azariadis (1975), Baily (1974), and many subsequent contributions] has been developed in recent years as an intermediate hypothesis. From the non-Walrasian viewpoint, the theory of labor contracts is founded on the fact that markets fail to be complete. Due to well-known reasons, no adequate insurance against unemployment is available on the private markets. For this reason, labor contracts do not only cover work and wages but also provide insurance against unemployment. Trading of such "combinations" of commodities (insurance with labor services) means that the market mechanism cannot function in a Walrasian manner. The theory of labor contracts is thus able to explain the rigidity of wages and unemployment as a result of basic market failures, and to that extent, it supports the non-Walrasian approach to unemployment. However, the theory does not contradict the conclusions of the market clearance school. In most instances, unemployment that results from risk-sharing labor contracts is voluntary in the sense that it represents one possible outcome of the contract between the workers and the firm. Moreover, the voluntary nature of unemployment is highlighted by the fact that labor compensation (i.e., wage rates and unemployment compensation) is structured in such a way that in all states in which unemployment arises, the workers are indifferent between work and being unemployed.

Although somewhat appealing, the theory of labor contracts fails on three important counts. First, since the contracts are not enforceable, workers may violate the contract by moving to higher paying jobs, and the firm may renounce the contract if it is threatened by bankruptcy. Recent history of the 1981–3 recession shows how quickly contracts are renegotiated if either side feels injured enough to renounce the contract. With the ability to renegotiate, labor contracts may do no more than introduce minor rigidities in the rate of adjustment in the labor markets. Second, it is entirely unusual for firms to compensate workers who are being laid off. Moreover, all unemployment compensations come from public or union sources, and the contributions of workers and firms to state unemployment funds are mandated by law rather than by any voluntary arrangement between workers and firms. Although there is significant evidence for the existence of long-term attachment between firms and workers, there is almost no evidence that this attachment contains any significant insurance against utility loss due to temporary layoffs or unemployment. In addition, there are many other explanations for this attachment apart from the postulated long-term risk-sharing contract. Third, the supposition that unemployed workers are indifferent between work and unemployment seems to be contradicted by a great deal of evidence about the real welfare loss due to unemployment. This last point may not be so crucial since one may imagine equilibrium contracts in which such indifference is not exhibited. No doubt, this will require some additional imperfection and thus some form of market failure. A more comprehensive evaluation of the implicit contracts theory is provided in Stiglitz (1984b).

A different approach to a microtheory of wage rigidity and unemployment has been taken by the supporters of the efficiency wage hypothesis. In essence, this hypothesis holds that the productivity of labor varies with the wage rate, and such changes in productivity arise in many different forms. A few examples will illustrate the point. In less developed countries, lower wage rates may cause a reduction in the nutrition level of the workers (Stiglitz 1982). In advanced societies, a lower wage rate may cause workers to shirk on the job (Shapiro and Stiglitz 1982) or to increase their turnover rate (Stiglitz 1984a), which is costly to the firms. Other contributions include Stiglitz (1976), Weiss (1980), Calvo (1979), and Akerlof (1984). For further details, see Stiglitz (1984b) and Yellen (1984).

Our interest in this chapter concentrates on the effect of incomplete information in the labor markets. In Shapiro and Stiglitz (1982), incomplete monitoring of workers is essential to the theory and in the papers of Weiss (1980) and Guasch and Weiss (1980, 1982), incomplete information leads to the emergence of an equilibrium wage distribution. Such a distribution also arises in Stiglitz (1984a) due to the effect of wage rates on labor turnover. Incomplete information in the labor market makes information valuable, and since the acquisition of information may be costly, the amount of information acquired and the strategy of firms under such conditions are both central issues in this essay. This should also clarify the fact that our approach is close to Guasch and Weiss (1980, 1982) and to Stiglitz (1984a). However, we shall neglect any incentive effects that changes in the wage rate may have and concentrate mostly on the way the market adjusts to the environment of incomplete information.

In adopting the framework of asymmetric information in the labor market, we assume that initially neither workers nor the firms know the productivity level of an employee. A firm may learn something about the productivity of a worker by employing him for one period and evaluating him internally. This evaluation *is private information of the firm* and is unavailable to either the worker or to other firms. This asymmetry becomes even more important due to the fact that the evaluation of the firm is not precise and is subject to serious errors of measurement and judgment. Thus, even after the evaluation, there could be many employed workers whose true productivity level is below the required standards and many other workers who are being fired but their true productivity is above the required standards.

In this chapter, we shall maintain the assumption (contrary to Guasch and Weiss) that workers do not know their own productivity. A justification for this assumption is provided below. This assumption leads to a complication in the conceptualization of unemployment. Suppose a worker is evaluated to be below the productivity standard of an employing firm and for this reason loses his job. Not knowing his true efficiency level, the worker continues to search for employment. Is he unemployed? Under the informational conditions postulated, there is some justification for regarding this worker as involuntarily unemployed. This justification arises from the fact that in an equilibrium with unemployment there is a positive probability that very qualified workers are unemployed since they did not pass the qualification requirements of their employing firm. Using this probability with respect to his own situation, it is very reasonable for an unemployed worker to hold the view that there is a positive probability that he is as qualified as other people who are holding well-paying jobs, and for this reason he should continue to apply for the available jobs. Faced with the prospect of accepting an inferior job, it may be entirely rational for the worker to apply for higher paying jobs instead.

An important element in our modeling is the assumption that there is a continuum of labor qualities. In a world of complete information, an equilibrium would obviously call for a continuum of wage rates. We shall prove that because of lack of precision in the information, an equilibrium may entail only a finite number of wage rates. This actually proposes a more general principle that states that rising ignorance reduces the number of markets and the number of tradeable commodities. This analysis is completely missed in the Guasch–Weiss treatment where it is postulated that there are N distinct types of labor, and since the equilibrium is fully revealing, there are exactly N different wage rates in equilibrium. What is equally important in our analysis is the fact that due to the asymmetric and imprecise information, the finite wage structure is rigid, and to this extent, asymmetric information is held as a cause for wage inflexibility. Finally, our model admits unemployment in equilibrium.

2   A model of the labor market

We think of workers as divided into distinct "professions" or "jobs" each of which requires the worker to have some specified observable characteristics that are common knowledge. Each one of these professions will then constitute a labor market in which all workers appear identical but a firm may learn something about its workers if it employs them for a period. At any moment of time, a specified fraction of the aggregate labor force is identified as seeking employment in one of these finite number of jobs, and our analysis concentrates on one of these markets. We shall assume that these are large markets and express this assumption by postulating a continuum of workers in each market. With these introductory remarks, we may turn to the informational structure in the model.

2.1   *The informational structure*

Every worker is assumed to be characterized by an efficiency parameter θ that neither the worker nor a potential employer knows. It is important to state at the outset that θ is *not* a measure of ability nor is it a measure of intensity of effort. It is a synthetic measure that reflects both the characteristics of the worker as well as his suitability for the job at hand. A worker of medium intelligence who is endowed with extremely high discipline and with an ability to adapt to others on a team may have extremely high productivity on a monotonous assembly line. Equally so, a brilliant but careless and impatient worker may cause the destruction of valuable equipment (i.e., large *negative* θ) on a job where extreme care and patience are required for handling expensive but fragile equipment. We shall explicitly allow θ to take large negative values. Clearly, the firm has a vital interest in identifying the better workers.

A *labor force* of the firm is a measure $m(\theta)$ that specifies the "number" (density) of workers with each level of efficiency θ. The size of the labor force (S) and the effective labor input (L) are then defined in the natural way as

$$S = \int_{-\infty}^{\infty} dm(\theta), \tag{1a}$$

$$L = \int_{-\infty}^{\infty} \theta \, dm(\theta). \tag{1b}$$

Let $G(\theta)$ be the distribution and $g(\theta)$ the density of θ in the population. Both are common knowledge. Since θ is not observable, the firm cannot select the measure $m(\theta)$ at will. In fact, a typical way in which a firm selects its labor force is a two-step procedure. First it announces a wage rate and hires a random subset of the applicants. Having acquired some information about its employees, the firm can select, in the second period, a labor force from the set of workers at hand. The announced wage rate is an important strategic element for both the standard economic reasons and the informational considerations since it determines the set from which the firm can select its ultimate labor force. For example, if the firm announces the *highest* wage rate in the industry, then the applicants will be a random sample from the entire population, and if the firm wants to select a sample of size M, then

$$m(\theta) = MG(\theta).$$

The characteristics of the labor force are then

$$S = \int_{-\infty}^{\infty} Mg(\theta) \, d\theta = M, \tag{2a}$$

$$L = \int_{-\infty}^{\infty} M\theta g(\theta) \, d\theta = M\bar{\theta}, \qquad \bar{\theta} = \int_{-\infty}^{\infty} \theta f(\theta) \, d\theta. \tag{2b}$$

Now given a set of workers, the internal evaluation will aim to estimate the efficiency parameter of each worker. More specifically, the supervisors will provide an estimate, which we denote by μ, such that

$$\theta = \mu + \epsilon. \tag{3}$$

Clearly, μ is not a precise evaluation since

$$\mu = \theta - \epsilon,$$

where ϵ represent errors of judgment and errors of measurement. We denote by $\Gamma(\epsilon)$ the distribution and by $\gamma(\epsilon)$ the density of ϵ. We now specify the following restrictions:

Assumption 1. θ and ϵ are independent random variables with $E(\theta) = \bar{\theta}$ and $E(\epsilon) = 0$. The conditional expectations $E(\theta \mid \mu = x)$ is a continuous and strictly increasing function of x.

Assumption 1 specifies the quality of the estimated parameter μ. First, this assumption implies that

$$E(\theta) = E(\mu), \tag{4}$$

and this shows that on the average the internal evaluation is unbiased by providing for the mean value of θ. However, Assumption 1 also says that a higher observed μ would lead to a higher expected value of θ.

The analysis in this chapter is based on the supposition that θ is not known to anybody, whereas μ is observed by the firm. To explain this distinction, we think of μ as being synthesized by the firm from measured observables. Typical components that may enter the evaluation of μ are such observables as the IQ measurement of the worker, the speed of one's typing, measurement of the worker's eyesight, observations of the worker's speed, dexterity or physical strength in lifting weights, and so on. The common characteristic of such observations is that there is no point in taking a second set of observations in a later period since the readings will be the same. In addition, if an observation of μ is made by another firm, the reading is likely to be essentially the same.

It is reasonable to expect that some estimates of the worker's efficiency may be improved with repeated observations. However, we insist that it is unreasonable to assume that with repeated observations the firm can find out *exactly* what θ is and that a significant component of incomplete information will persist. This means that our model simplifies this transitory phase in which the firm can learn about the worker: It is compressed into a single period beyond which no additional learning can be accomplished.

Given that $G(\theta)$ and $\Gamma(\epsilon)$ are known and given the specification (3), if we denote by $F(\mu)$ and $f(\mu)$ the distribution and density of μ, we can show that they are defined by the convolutions

$$f(\mu) = \int_{-\infty}^{+\infty} g(\mu+\epsilon)\gamma(\epsilon)\,d\epsilon, \tag{5a}$$

$$F(\mu) = \int_{-\infty}^{\mu} \int_{-\infty}^{+\infty} g(x+\epsilon)\gamma(\epsilon)\,d\epsilon\,dx. \tag{5b}$$

Since μ is observed by the firm, this variable will be the basis for the firm's selection of its labor force. Of particular importance is the case in which the firm selects initially a random sample from the entire population and then selects the labor force such that the measured productivity μ satisfy $B_i^* \le \mu \le B_{i+1}^*$. We denote by

$f_{B_i^*}^{B_{i+1}^*}(y)$ – density of μ given $B_i^* \le \mu \le B_{i+1}^*$,

$F_{B_i^*}^{B_{i+1}^*}(y)$ – distribution of μ given $B_i^* \le \mu \le B_{i+1}^*$,

$g_{B_i^*}^{B_{i+1}^*}(y)$ – density of θ given $B_i^* \le \mu \le B_{i+1}^*$,

$G_{B_i^*}^{B_{i+1}^*}(y)$ – distribution of θ given $B_i^* \le \mu \le B_{i+1}^*$.

It is immediate that

$$f_{B_i^*}^{B_{i+1}^*}(y) = \frac{f(\mu)}{F(B_{i+1}^*) - F(B_i^*)}, \qquad B_i^* \le \mu \le B_{i+1}^*, \tag{6a}$$

$$F_{B_i^*}^{B_{i+1}^*}(y) = \frac{1}{F(B_{i+1}^*) - F(B_i^*)} \int_{B_i^*}^{y} f(\mu)\,d\mu, \qquad B_{i+1}^* \ge B_i^*. \tag{6b}$$

On the other hand, by definition,

$$G_{B_i^*}^{B_{i+1}^*}(y) = \text{Prob}\{\theta \le y \mid \theta = \mu+\epsilon,\ B_i^* \le \mu \le B_{i+1}^*\}$$

$$= \frac{\text{Prob}\{\theta \le y,\ B_i^* \le \theta - \epsilon \le B_{i+1}^*\}}{B^*(B_{i+1}^*) - F(B_i^*)} \qquad (B_{i+1}^* \ge B_i^*)$$

$$= \frac{1}{F(B_{i+1}^*) - F(B_i^*)} \int_{-\infty}^{y} \int_{\theta - B_{i+1}^*}^{\theta - B_i^*} g(\theta)\gamma(\epsilon)\,d\theta\,d\epsilon \qquad (B_{i+1}^* \ge B_i^*).$$

Hence, we finally have

$$G_{B_i^*}^{B_{i+1}^*}(y) = \frac{1}{F(B_{i+1}^*) - F(B_i^*)} \int_{-\infty}^{y} g(\theta)[\Gamma(\theta - B_i^*) - \Gamma(\theta - B_{i+1}^*)]\,d\theta$$

$$(B_{i+1}^* \ge B_i^*), \tag{7a}$$

$$g_{B_i^*}^{B_{i+1}^*}(y) = \frac{1}{F(B_{i-1}^*) - F(B_i^*)} g(y)[\Gamma(y - B_i^*) - \Gamma(y - B_{i+1}^*)]$$

$$(B_{i+1}^* \geq B_i^*), \qquad (7b)$$

where $\Gamma(x) = \int_{-\infty}^{x} \gamma(\epsilon) \, d\epsilon$, and in the case in which ϵ is a bounded random variable with support included in the interval $[\underline{\epsilon}, \bar{\epsilon}]$, then $\Gamma(x) = 0$ if $x \leq \underline{\epsilon}$ and $\Gamma(x) = 1$ if $x \geq \bar{\epsilon}$. Expressions (6a) and (6b) and (7a) and (7b) will be extensively used.

The final important informational condition relates to the *initial conditions*. Since the acquisition of information is costly, it is clear that firms will act differently given alternative initial states of information. Such differences in initial information may result in different equilibria, and to that extent, such differences in information may be perpetuated in equilibrium.

Although we concentrate in this chapter on stationary equilibria, we want to assume that initially the informational conditions are not stationary. This would happen if a significant portion of the workers are not known to any firm and if a significant fraction of the firms have no information. Failing to quantify *partial* ignorance, we shall postulate the more radical assumption:

Assumption 2. In the initial state, no firm has any information about any worker.

It will become clear that this assumption is not needed at all.

In evaluating the competitive nature of the industry, it is clear that there is asymmetry of information between incumbent firms and potential entrants. Naturally, such differences may provide some protection from entry. However, by insisting on the initial informational conditions specified in Assumption 2, we are assured that in the stationary equilibria that follow, the slight advantage of the incumbent firms arises from past expenditures on acquiring information.

2.2   Optimal behavior of firms

Our firms are assumed to have the simplest of all production technologies

$$Q(L) = \beta L, \qquad \beta > 0,$$

where L is *effective* labor input. The firm is assumed to hire workers and pay their wages at time t, but production and sale take place at time $t+1$. The price of output $q_{t+1}(s)$ that will prevail next period is a random variable depending on s, the state of the world; the probability distribution of s is known to all. If the interest rate is denoted by r_t, then in state s the one-period profit function has the form

$$\Pi'(s) = q_{t+1}(s)Q(L_t) - (1+r_t)W_t M_t, \tag{8a}$$

and its expectation is

$$E\Pi'(s) = \bar{q}_{t+1}Q(L_t) - (1+r_t)W_t M_t, \tag{8b}$$

where r_t is the interest rate at t, W_t is the single wage rate at t, and M_t is the size of the labor force at t. Taken over infinite number of periods, the present value of all future profits is defined by

$$\Pi(s) = \sum_{t=0}^{\infty} \frac{1}{(1+R_t)^t} \Pi'(s), \tag{9}$$

where R_t is the t-period interest rate.

It should be clear that the dynamic evolution of such a firm can be extremely complicated arising from several factors. First, the initial employment measures of different firms may constitute an unbalanced starting point. Second, nonstationarity of $q_{t+1}(s)$, r_t, and W_t may cause nonstationary evolution over time. Third, and this is perhaps the most important fact to notice, since this market has a continuum of distinct kinds of labor, there is no reason to assume that an equilibrium will entail a single wage rate. In a competitive equilibrium with complete information, we would certainly expect a continuum of wage rates, and for this reason, the number of distinct wage rates in equilibrium is of fundamental interest in this research. Now, given that one would expect an equilibrium wage distribution, we recall that without any internal evaluation, all workers are observationally identical. This means that the only basis for a firm to offer two workers distinct wage rates is that it has some private information about these two workers. Hence any wage function that differentiates among workers must be a function $W(\mu)$ of the observed values of μ. One also notes that the dynamics of the distribution of wages is intimately related to the dynamics of information acquisition by firms.

Our aims in this chapter are restricted to the study of stationary equilibria only. To facilitate the analysis of such equilibria, the following simplifications are made:

Assumption 3

(i)   The firms are assumed to be risk neutral, aiming to maximize $E\Pi(s)$.

(ii)   The distribution of $q_t(s)$ is independent of t; hence $Eq_t(s) = \bar{q} = 1$.

(iii) Interest rate $r_t = r$ for all t.

With the above in mind, the firm can select at any date a wage function $W_t(\mu)$ to depend on the information vector μ at time t. This would include a wage offer to workers about whom the firm knows nothing. We denote by $\mathbf{W}_t(\mu)$ the vector of wage functions offered by all firms. Associated with each wage function the firm will establish the following:

(i) $m_{t-1}(\theta)$, the measure of the labor force employed in period $t-1$;

(ii) $B_t(\mu)$, a censoring rule used by the firm at time t to select those of its workers at $t-1$ who are retained for employment at t; and

(iii) H_t, a hiring rule of new workers at time t.

Based on (i), (ii), and (iii) and given the entire vector $\mathbf{W}_t(\mu)$ of wage functions, an *outcome* at t is

(a)   a deduced density $f_t(\mu)$ of measured productivity of workers (deduction is made from the information available) and

(b)   a resulting labor force at t defined by

$$m_t(\theta \mid \mu) = m_t(m_{t-1}(\theta), B_t(\mu), H_t, \mathbf{W}_t(\mu)) \tag{10}$$

and $E_t(\theta \mid \mu)$ appropriately defined.

The *one-period payoff function* can now be defined in the natural way:

$$E\Pi^t = \beta \int_{-\infty}^{\infty} E_t(\theta \mid \mu) f_t(\mu)\, d\mu - (1+r) \int_{-\infty}^{\infty} W_t(\mu) f_t(\mu)\, d\mu. \tag{11}$$

The most crucial element in the construction above is the determination of the labor force function $m_t(\theta \mid \mu)$ in equation (10). It in fact specifies how labor gets allocated in response to wage offers by firms – a well known problem. Given our desire to provide as many competitive opportunities as possible, we shall study the problem under Bertrand-type assumptions. More specifically, we specify the competitive condition:

Assumption 4. Given wage offers by all other firms, a wage offer by a firm will draw a random sample of applicants from that segment of the population composed of the unemployed and those employed who are being paid a wage rate equal to or lower than the one offered.

This assumption needs some interpretation since its application depends on the information workers have. If workers are offered a job in the initial period, they accept it without any knowledge of their own productivity. However, after being employed for one period, they get a job offer from the employer, and as a result of this offer, they find out something about their own productivity. A worker indexed z gets a job offer $W_t(z)$ that specifies future wage rates depending on changing economic conditions. With the above in mind, we conclude that in the first period there would be a single uniform wage. Moreover, assuming that workers remember their wage rates, a new employer who would want to attract worker z will have to offer wage rate $\hat{W}_t(z)$ that satisfies $\hat{W}_t(z) \geq W_t(z)$.

Assumption 4 also implies that if a firm wishes to obtain a sample of workers with productivity drawn at random from the population distribution $G(\theta)$, it will have to offer the highest wage in the industry. Now let W be the initial wage paid by the firm, and let $W = W(B)$, where B is the cutoff point so that workers with $\mu \leq B$ apply. Then the present value of the profits of the firm can be written as

$$E\Pi = [\beta E(\theta \mid m \leq B) - (1+r)W]F(B)$$

$$+ \sum_{t=1}^{\infty} \int_{-\infty}^{\infty} \left(\frac{1}{1+r}\right)^t (\beta E_t(\theta \mid \mu) - (1+r)W_t(\mu)) f_t(\mu)\, d\mu. \tag{12}$$

With the objective (12) defined, we can think of our industry as being represented by a game. The *players* are the firms, and the *strategy* of every firm consists of a sequence of vectors

$$\{W_t(\mu), B_t(\mu), H_t\}_{t=0}^{\infty}$$

of wage offers, censoring rules of old workers, and hiring of new workers. At each t, the actions depend on the observed values of μ. The *outcome* of each play is a labor force $m_t(\theta \mid \mu)$ and an information density $f_t(\mu)$. The *payoff* of the game is defined by equation (12). To explain the equilibrium concept we shall adopt, note that one way to proceed is to assume that all players move simultaneously and thus seek a subgame perfect equilibrium. However, we shall also assume that firms have no memory, and all strategies are based on current information without reference to past moves. It is important to keep in mind that by including the nonactive firms who may enter at any time, we have an unlimited number of players. Since the exogenous conditions of the game are stationary, one reason a nonstationary policy may be followed is the acquisition of information. Thus, when the firms have as much information as they may wish to have, the natural strategies to consider are stationary. Thus, an equilibrium is said to be stationary if $W(\mu)$, $B(\mu)$, H, $m(\theta \mid \mu)$, and $f(\mu)$ are all constant over time. With

$$\sum_{t=1}^{\infty} \left(\frac{1}{1+r}\right)^t = \frac{1}{r},$$

the objective (12) can be written as

$$E\Pi = (\beta E(\theta \mid \mu \le B_0) - (1+r)W)F(B_0)$$

$$+ \frac{1}{r} \int_{-\infty}^{\infty} (\beta E(\theta \mid \mu) - (1+r)W(\mu))f_B(\mu)\,d\mu, \qquad (13)$$

where we write $f_B(\mu)$ to indicate that the stationary density may depend on the censoring rule adopted.

3   Stationary equilibria

Given that by Assumption 2 our firms start in a state of ignorance, it will be impossible for the industry to start from a stationary equilibrium. We shall seek, however, to characterize equilibria in which firms reach stationary strategies after a finite number of moves.

Suppose that in the first period firms draw a random sample of the entire population. Then, the expected gross revenue of the firm per unit of labor in the first period is simply $\beta\bar{\theta}$, and its cost per unit of labor is $(1+r)W$. This means that expected first-period profits must be

$$\beta\bar{\theta} - (1+r)W,$$

and we note that this quantity cannot be positive. If $\beta\bar{\theta} - (1+r)W > 0$, then firms will make profits regardless of what happens in all subsequent periods. At such a wage, the demand for labor will be unbounded. This leads to the conclusion that the initial wage must satisfy

$$W \ge \beta \frac{\bar{\theta}}{1+r}.$$

However, since wages in the first period cannot fall to zero, as a result of the initial state of ignorance, firms will continue to take samples of the available labor supply until the available supply is exhausted and *full employment* prevails in the first period. This implies, however, that at the end of the initial period firms will have as much information as they can ever have, and for this reason, the stationary phase can start from the second period on. We thus define the concept of a two-step stationary equilibrium as an equilibrium in which firms take an initial set of random samples from the population of workers and then follow it by offers of wage rates and output allocations that constitute a stationary equilibrium from the second period on. Since it is feasible to reach stationarity in a two-step equilibrium, and since stationary equilibria are the object of this chapter, we shall confine ourselves to two-step stationary equilibria.

3.1   *Two-step stationary equilibrium*

We start the study of stationary equilibria with the following result, which was discussed earlier.

Lemma 1. Let $(W_0, W(\mu))$ be the wage structure associated with a two-step stationary equilibrium. Then

(i) $$W_0 \geq \beta \frac{\bar{\theta}}{1+r},$$

(ii) $$W(z) \geq \beta \frac{E(\theta \mid \mu \leq z)}{1+r},$$

(iii) $$W(z) \leq \beta \frac{E(\theta \mid \mu = z)}{1+r}.$$

Proof: Equation (i) was proved in the foregoing. Equation (ii) follows from the fact that by Assumption 4 an entering firm must pay initially $W(z)$ in order to draw workers with $\mu \leq z$ to apply since all workers with $\mu \geq z$ will be employed. Equation (iii) follows from the fact that in equation (13) the firm may elect not to reemploy any worker with an observed μ in any arbitrary interval $\underline{z} \leq \mu \leq \bar{z}$.

The argument in Lemma 1 reveals two aspects of the role played by the inactive firms who may enter the industry at any stage. First, it suggests that firms who move first and enter the industry in the first period are likely to have advantages that will be explored later. The argument shows also that the workers in this market play a rather passive role, whereas the essential competition to firms in the industry comes from newly entering firms. It then follows that an important part of the equilibrium conditions require entering firms to make zero profits. To identify these conditions more precisely, let $W(\mu)$ be the wage function in the second period. Then, a newly entering firm must pay $W(B)$ in the first period in order to draw a sample of workers with $\mu \leq B$. Hence, by equation (13), the profit function of any firm that enters *from period 2 on* and offers $W(B)$ as the initial wage is

$$E\Pi^{(B)} = (\beta E(\theta \mid \mu \leq B) - (1+r)W(B))F(B)$$

$$+ \frac{1}{r} \int_{\underline{B}}^{B} (\beta E(\theta \mid \mu) - (1+r)W(\mu))f(\mu)\,d\mu, \tag{14}$$

where all $\mu \geq B$ are employed and B may be $-\infty$. In equilibrium,

$$E\Pi^{(B)} = 0 \quad \text{for all } B. \tag{15}$$

Conditions (15) and (14) imply that if $W(\mu)$ is an equilibrium wage function for employed workers with an observed value of μ and if it is differentiable, then

$$\frac{dW(\mu)}{d\mu} = \frac{f(\mu)}{rF(\mu)}[\beta E(\theta \mid \mu) - (1+r)W(\mu)]. \quad \text{Q.E.D.} \tag{16}$$

Lemma 2. If a two-step stationary equilibrium with a continuum of wage rates $W(\mu)$ exists, then there exists a finite maximal wage rate $W_M < \infty$ and two lower cutoffs B_0 and $\underline{B}$ such that

(i) $0 \leq W(\mu) < W_M$,
(ii) $W(\mu)$ is monotonically increasing for all μ,
(iii) $\underline{B}$ is defined by $E(\theta \mid \underline{B}) = 0$,
(iv) B_0 is defined by

$$\beta E(\theta \mid \mu \leq B_0) + \frac{\beta}{r}E(\theta \mid \underline{B} \leq \mu \leq B_0)\frac{F(B_0) - F(\underline{B})}{F(B_0)} \leq 0,$$

(v) for all μ in the interval $\underline{B} < \mu \leq B_0$, $E(\theta \mid \mu) > 0$ but $W(\mu) = 0$.

Proof: Let $W(\mu)$ be an equilibrium second-period wage function that is unbounded. By (iii) of Lemma 1, if $W(B) \to \infty$, then $B \to \infty$. Consider first the first term on the right side of equation (14):

$$\beta E(\theta \mid \mu \leq B)F(B) = \int_{-\infty}^{\infty} \theta g(\theta)[1 - \Gamma(\theta - B)]\, d\theta \to \bar{\theta}$$

as B tends to $+\infty$. Similarly, $W(B)F(B) \to \infty$ since $F(B) \to 1$. Turning now to the second expression, we have from (ii) of Lemma 1 that the expression is bounded by

$$\frac{1}{r}\int_{\underline{B}}^{B} \beta E(\theta \mid \mu) f(\mu)\, d\mu - \frac{1}{r}\int_{\underline{B}}^{B} \beta E(\theta \mid \mu \leq x) f(x)\, dx, \tag{17}$$

and both expressions are finite. Hence $\lim_{B \to \infty} E\Pi^{(B)} = -\infty$. This proves that there exists a W_M such that for all $W > W_M$ all entering firms will incur losses if they enter. It then follows that $W(\mu)$ is bounded.

To derive B_0 and $\underline{B}$, note first that $\underline{B}$ is the lowest value of the index μ that is still employed. Clearly $E(\theta \mid \mu = \underline{B}) = 0$. It then follows from (iii) of Lemma 1 that $W(\underline{B}) = 0$. Consider, however, a firm that enters at price $W(\underline{B}) = 0$. Its profits are calculated at

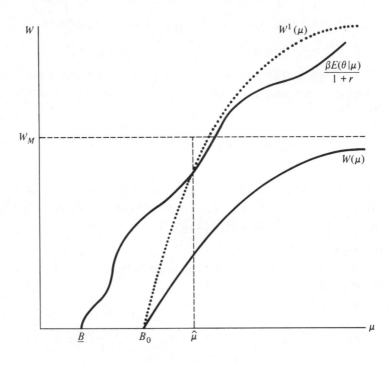

Figure 1.

$$E\Pi = \beta E(\theta \mid \mu \le \underline{B}) < 0,$$

and such a firm will not enter. If B_0 is the smallest μ index that would be the object of an entering firm, then $W(\mu) = 0$ for all $\underline{B} \le \mu < B_0$. Hence, if $W(B_0) = 0$, the profits of such an entering firm would be

$$E\Pi^{(B)} = \beta E(\theta \mid \mu \le B_0) + \frac{\beta}{r} E(\theta \mid \underline{B} \le \mu \le B_0) \frac{F(B_0) - F(\underline{B})}{F(B_0)} = 0, \qquad (18)$$

and given that $\underline{B}$ is defined by the equation $E(\theta \mid \underline{B}) = 0$, B_0 must satisfy $E\Pi^{(B)} = 0$.

To show that $W(\mu)$ is monotonic, we give a simple diagrammatic argument. From equation (16) and condition (iii) of Lemma 1, it follows that

$$W(\mu) \le \frac{\beta E(\theta \mid \mu)}{1 + r}.$$

In Figure 1, we draw two potential solutions to equation (16), denoted $W^1(\mu)$ and $W(\mu)$. We now show that $W^1(\mu)$ cannot be a solution. To see this, note first that it was earlier proved that $W(B_0) = 0$ and $E(\theta \mid B_0) > 0$.

If there is a $\hat{\mu}$ at which $\beta E(\theta \mid \hat{\mu}) = (1+r)W(\hat{\mu})$, then it follows from equation (16) that

$$\left. \frac{dW}{d\mu} \right|_{\mu = \hat{\mu}} = 0.$$

However, since $\beta E(\theta \mid \mu)/(1+r) \geq W(\mu)$ for $\mu = \hat{\mu}$, and since by Assumption 1 $E(\theta \mid \mu)$ is strictly monotonic in μ, the curve $W(\mu)$ must cross $\beta E(\theta \mid \mu)/(1+r)$ from below, and this contradicts the conclusion that

$$\left. \frac{dW}{d\mu} \right|_{\mu = \hat{\mu}} = 0.$$

The solution of equation (16) is a unique curve like $W(\mu)$ with $W(B_0) = 0$ and with an asymptotic value W_M.   Q.E.D.

We are now ready to state our first result.

Theorem 1. A two-step stationary equilibrium with a continuum of wage rates is characterized by a wage function $W^*(\mu)$ such that

   (i) $W^*(\mu)$ is a solution of the differential equation (16),
   (ii) $W^*(B_0) = 0$, and
   (iii) $\lim_{\mu \to \infty} W^*(\mu) = W_M$.

Such an equilibrium is unique.

   To proceed, let us first define the notion of a group wage strategy. A structure $W(\mu)$ of a second-period wage offered by a firm is said to be a *group wage strategy* if the firm subdivides the real line R into intervals $[B_i, B_{i+1}]$ such that

   (a) $\bigcup_{i=-\infty}^{+\infty} [B_i, B_{i+1}] = R$,
   (b) $B_i < B_{i+1}$, and
   (c)   if $\mu \in [B_i, B_{i+1})$, $W(\mu) \equiv W_i \leq W(B_i)$.

   A group wage strategy is immune to entry if any entrant *after period 2* cannot make profits. This specifically means that we can define a *type-k entrant* as a firm who offers initially the wage W_k aiming to attract applicants with $\mu \leq B_{k+1}$. The profit function of such a firm is

$$E\Pi^{(k)} = [\beta E(\theta \mid \mu \leq B_{k+1}) - (1+r)W_k]F(B_{k+1})$$

$$+ \sum_{i=-\infty}^{k} \frac{1}{r} \int_{B_i}^{B_{i+1}} [\beta E(\theta \mid \mu) - (1+r)W_i]f(\mu)\,d\mu. \qquad (19)$$

Thus, a group wage strategy with a wage structure $\{W_i\}_{i=-\infty}^{\infty}$ is immune to entry if $E\Pi^{(k)}=0$ for all k. Calculate from equation (19) $E\Pi^{(k)}-E\Pi^{k-1}$ to obtain that if $E\Pi^{(k)}=0$ for all k, then such a structure must satisfy the difference equation

$$W_{k-1}=W_k-\eta(B_k,B_{k+1},W_k),\tag{20}$$

where

$$\eta(B_k,B_{k+1},W_k)=\frac{1}{r}[\beta E(\theta\,|\,B_k\le\mu\le B_{k+1})-(1+r)W_k]\frac{F(B_{k+1})-F(B_k)}{F(B_k)}.$$

$$\tag{21}$$

Lemma 3. If a two-step stationary equilibrium with a group wage strategy exists, then there exists a finite maximal wage rate $W_M<\infty$, a finite maximal cutoff B_M, and two lower cutoffs $\underline{B}$ and B_0 such that

(i) $W_i\le W_M<\infty$ for $i=0,1,2,\dots,M$;
(ii) $\underline{B}$ is defined by $E(\theta\,|\,\underline{B})=0$ and B_0 satisfies

$$\beta E(\theta\,|\,\mu\le B_0)+\frac{\beta}{r}E(\theta\,|\,\underline{B}\le\mu\le B_0)\frac{F(B_0)-F(\underline{B})}{F(B_0)}\le 0;$$

(iii) for all μ with $\underline{B}\le\mu\le B_0$, $E(\theta\,|\,\mu)>0$, but if these workers are employed, they receive a wage rate of zero.

Proof: The proof of the existence of a finite pair (W_M,B_M), the definition of $\underline{B}$, and the condition of a zero wage for all workers with μ such that $\underline{B}\le\mu\le B_0$ is exactly the same as in Lemma 2. The definition of B_0 in (ii) is established with an inequality rather than an equality, as in Lemma 2.   Q.E.D.

In search of an equilibrium with a finite number of wage rates, we note that if $W(\mu)$ is a step function with a finite number of steps between $\underline{B}$ and B_M, then it must satisfy three conditions:

(a) $E\Pi^{(M)}=0$ where $E\Pi^{(M)}$ is defined in equation (19).
(b)   The difference equation

$$W_{k-1}=W_k-\eta(B_k,B_{k+1},W_k),$$

where $\eta(B_k,B_{k+1},W_k)$ is defined in equation (21).
(c) $(1+r)W_j\le\beta E(\theta\,|\,\mu)$ for all μ, which satisfies $B_j\le\mu\le B_{j+1}$.

In Figure 2, we illustrate how a wage structure with four wage rates is constructed. To further explain how an equilibrium is developed, note that from the recursive relation

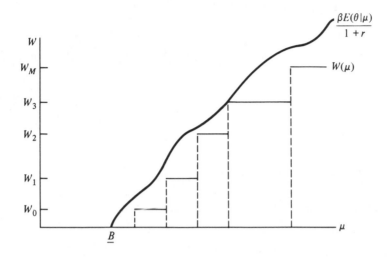

Figure 2.

$$W_{k-1} = W_k - \eta(B_k, B_{k+1}, W_k)$$

it is clear that the way to complete this construction is to select a sequence of continuous and monotonic functions

$$B_k = \Phi_k(W_k) \tag{22}$$

that satisfy the requirement

$$(1+r)\Phi_k^{-1}(B_k) \leq \beta E(\theta \mid B_k) \quad \text{for all } k. \tag{23}$$

When condition (22) is added to the first three conditions, it is then left to show that with (22) defined, the condition $E\Pi^{(M)} = 0$ is satisfied. Ignoring the issue of existence, we note that for condition (22) to be a viable definition, the implied difference equation

$$W_{k-1} = W_k - \eta(\Phi_k(W_k), \Phi_{k+1}(W_{k+1}), W_k) \tag{24}$$

must reach the value 0. We can thus define the notion of a *recursive wage structure starting at* B_M in the following way:

(i) Select B_M arbitrarily. Define W_M by

$$W_M = \Phi_M^{-1}(B_M).$$

(ii) Define $B_{M+1} = +\infty$, and for given W_M and B_M, let W_{M-1} be defined by

$$W_{M-1} = W_M - \frac{1}{r}[\beta E(\theta \mid \mu \geq B_M) - (1+r)\Phi_M^{-1}(B_M)]\frac{1-F(B_M)}{F(B_M)}$$

and B_{M-1} defined by

$$B_{M-1} = \Phi_{M-1}(W_{M-1}).$$

(iii)   For any (B_{k+1}, B_k, W_k), define (B_{k-1}, W_{k-1}) in the following way. First

$$W_{k-1} = W_k - \frac{1}{r}[\beta E(\theta \mid B_k \leq \mu \leq B_{k+1}) - (1+r)\Phi_k^{-1}(B_k)]\frac{F(B_{k+1}) - F(B_k)}{F(B_k)}$$

and B_{k-1} is defined by

$$B_{k-1} = \Phi_{k-1}(W_{k-1}).$$

Lemma 4. The recursive wage structure starting at B_M defines

$$(W_j(B_M), B_j(B_M))$$

for all j as continuous functions of B_M.

Proof: The continuity of W_{k-1} as a function of (W_k, B_k, B_{k+1}) follows directly from the continuity of $F(\cdot)$ and the continuity of the expectation operator $E(\theta \mid \cdot)$. On the other hand, the continuity of B_k as a function of W_k follows from Assumption 1 and from the continuity of Φ_k.   Q.E.D.

Lemma 5. In a recursive wage structure starting at B_M, $W_{M-j} < 0$ for some finite j.

Proof: By Assumption 1, there exists $\epsilon_k > 0$ such that $W_{k-1} \leq W_k - \epsilon_k$ and $B_k \leq B_{k+1} - \epsilon_k$. Moreover, since a recursive structure must reach zero, suppose, for some k, $W_k = 0$ and hence $E(\theta \mid B_k) = 0$. This implies

$$W_{k-1} = -\frac{\beta}{r}E(\theta \mid B_k \leq \mu \leq B_{k+1})\frac{F(B_{k+1}) - F(B_k)}{F(B_k)} < 0. \tag{25}$$

This proves that $W_k = 0$ is not an accumulation point of the recursive wage structure. In fact, there is no finite (W, B) that is an accumulation point, and this proves the lemma.   Q.E.D.

Now define

$$E(\theta \mid \underline{B}) = 0 \tag{26}$$

$$\zeta_i(B_M) = \max[0, \beta E(\theta \mid B_i(B_M)) \leq \mu \leq B_{i+1}(B_M)]. \tag{27}$$

Using the notation (26) and (27) and thinking of all $B_i(B_M)$ as functions of B_M, let

$$E\Pi^{(M)}(B_M) = \beta(E\theta - E(\theta \mid B_M))$$

$$+ \frac{1}{r}\left[\int_{\underline{B}}^{\infty} \beta E(\theta \mid \mu) f(\mu)\, d\mu - \sum_{i=-\infty}^{M} \zeta_i(B_M)\right].$$

It follows from Lemma 5 that $E\Pi^{(M)}(B_M)$ is well defined since only a finite number of the $\zeta_i(B_M)$ are nonzero. Lemma 4 implies that $E\Pi^{(M)}(B_M)$ is a continuous function of B_M. It is clear that for $B_M \to 0$,

$$\lim_{B_M \to 0} E\Pi^{(M)}(B_M) > 0,$$

and it follows from Lemma 3 that there is a finite $\bar{B}_M$ such that for all $B_M \geq \bar{B}_M$, $E\Pi^{(M)}(B_M) < 0$. Hence it follows that there is a unique maximal real number B_M^* such that

$$E\Pi^{(M)}(B_M^*) = 0,$$

$$E\Pi^{(M)}(B_M) < 0 \quad \text{for } B_M > B_M^*. \tag{28}$$

This proves Lemma 6 below.   Q.E.D.

Lemma 6. For any feasible map from W_k to B_k, there exists a unique (B_M^*, W_M^*) such that a recursive wage structure starting from B_M^* has only a finite number of positive wage rates denoted by $(W_M^*, W_{M-1}^*, \ldots, W_0^*)$ with the corresponding cutoffs $(B_M^*, B_{M-1}^*, \ldots, B_0^*)$.

Lemma 6 provides the basis for constructing an equilibrium with a finite number of wage rates. In Figure 2, we drew the curve $\beta E(\theta \mid \mu)/(1+r)$ and indicated the values of B_M^* and W_M^* obtained in equation (28). The structure $(W_M^*, W_{M-1}^*, \ldots, W_0^*)$ and $(B_M^*, B_{M-1}^*, \ldots, B_0^*)$ is that part of the recursive wage structure for which $W_j^* > 0$. This means three distinct facts. First, from the recursive structure, we have

$$\beta E(\theta \mid B_0^*) \geq (1+r)W_0^*.$$

Second, from the definition of $\underline{B}^*$, we have

$$\beta E(\theta \mid \underline{B}^*) = 0.$$

Third, if W_{-1}^* is the next wage from the recursive structure, then $W_{-1}^* < 0$, and if we paid a zero wage rate, profits will be

$$\beta E(\theta \mid \mu \leq B_0^*)F(B_0^*) + \frac{\beta}{r}E(\theta \mid \underline{B}^* \leq \mu \leq B_0^*)[F(B_0^*) - F(\underline{B}^*)] \leq 0.$$

Thus, no firm will enter to compete over workers with $\underline{B}^* \leq \mu \leq B_0^*$.

Theorem 2. A two-step stationary equilibrium with a group wage structure is characterized by a finite number of wage rates and cutoffs $\{B_j^*, W_j^*\}_{j=0}^M$, which is that part of a recursive wage structure that starts at W_M^* for which $W_j^* > 0$, $j = 0, 1, \ldots, \mu$. In addition,

    (i) W_M^* is maximal,

    (ii) $\beta E(\theta \mid B_j^*) \geq (1+r)W_j^*$, and

    (iii) all workers with $\underline{B}^* < \mu < B_0^*$ receive a wage rate of zero if they are employed, although $E(\theta \mid \mu) > 0$ for these workers.

It is important to remark that although it appears that a large number of equilibria may be generated by maps like (22), we have not examined what are the restrictions on (22) implied by the crucial requirement of feasibility, that is, reaching zero. Since it is this requirement that was used in the proof above, we need to demonstrate at least one wage recursion that does reach zero. The obvious one is

$$(1+r)W_k = \beta E(\theta \mid B_k).$$

By Assumption 1, this defines a monotonic and continuous map between W_k and B_k, and it is clear from Figure 2 that any recursion using this map is feasible.

To clarify the set of equilibria, we draw in Figure 3 the continuous wage structure $W(\mu)$ alongside a typical equilibrium with a finite number of wage rates W_i^*. What the diagram shows is that W_M^* of a finite wage structure does not have to be equal to the asymptotic value W_M of the continuous wage structure, and the number of steps used in the step function depends on the map between B_k and W_k. The equilibrium in which

$$\beta E(\theta \mid B_k) = (1+r)W_k$$

holds provides the highest possible wage rates from period 2 on, and due to the zero profit conditions, this would result in the smallest value of W_M^*. As we move to wage structures at which the profits in the second period are higher (so that the wage rates are lower), the initial wage rate W_M^* is larger and could thus exceed W_M.

3.2   Implications and interpretations

Apart from the characterization of equilibrium, the central issue examined in the previous section was the dimension of the active or traded commodity space. We conclude that although there is a continuum of

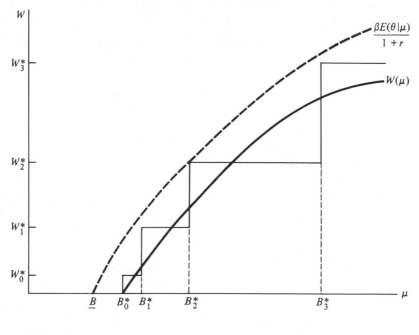

Figure 3.

distinct labor types identified by their productivity, in most equilibria there is only a finite number of wage rates. In some sense, the lack of information forces agents to redefine the commodities so that a commodity is identified with an interval $[B_i^*, B_{i+1}^*]$. Moreover, the number of active commodities is determined endogenously in the system. This suggests the conjecture of a general principle that would state that in markets with an infinite number of "basic" commodities whose characteristics are unknown and unobservable, the traded commodity space is often finite where each traded commodity represents a grouping of the basic commodities. The size of the commodity space is endogenously determined.

In the particular case of the labor market, the above principle is translated into a wage structure that assigns W_i^* to all workers with an observed measure μ in the interval $[B_i^*, B_{i+1}^*]$. We now turn to other important issues.

Unemployment and pareto optimality. Theorem 2 states that all workers with $\underline{B}^* \leq \mu \leq B_0^*$ are either not working or, if working, are being paid a zero wage. Moreover, any *entering* firm paying a zero wage would lose money, and the only way such a worker can be employed is that he or she accepted, at an earlier date, an offer for an initial positive wage. After the firm took a μ measure, the worker was reassigned to jobs "paying" zero wage. Are such workers unemployed? What is the unemployment rate in this economy?

Clearly, all workers with $\mu \le \underline{B}^*$ are unemployed and will not be assigned to any job. Technically speaking, if all workers with μ satisfying $\underline{B}^* \le \mu \le B_0^*$ are employed, they receive a zero wage and the equilibrium is pareto optimal. However, it is difficult to think of workers receiving a zero wage as being employed. From the point of view of the firm paying the zero wage, there is little chance that the worker will stay with the firm for very long since he or she will be constantly looking for higher paying jobs. In our stationary equilibrium, no new wage offers are made, and no worker applies to any new job. This is perhaps a weakness of our model since it forces workers who are paid a zero wage to stay with the employer. If any new job openings become available through the normal dynamics of the labor market (i.e., death, illness, retirement, new workers into the market, etc.), then the zero wage workers will always be seeking these new jobs. In a model like this, all workers with $\mu \le B_0^*$ will in fact be unemployed, and the equilibrium will not be pareto optimal. We may also note that the notion of unemployment in a market with incomplete information may be ambiguous. Recall that workers do not know their own productivity, and the measurements taken by the firms may be very unreliable. This means that if a worker is given a low wage offer, he cannot conclude that his true productivity is low. Even a worker with $E(\theta \mid \mu) < 0$ will continue to apply for jobs not knowing the true θ and hoping that some firm will take a measurement of μ that will be favorable. But should a worker with $E(\theta \mid \mu) < 0$ be regarded as unemployed?

We have defined the *gross unemployment rate* to be $F(B_0^*)$, indicating that all workers with $\mu \le B_0^*$ are unemployed. The problem is complicated by the fact that we may have workers with $\theta < 0$ and observed $\mu > B_0^*$ and also workers with $\theta > 0$ and $\mu < \underline{B}^*$.

Involuntary unemployment. A worker with $\theta < 0$ and $\mu \le \underline{B}^*$ may be regarded as unemployed, but it is not clear in what sense he is involuntarily unemployed. The reason is that the person is not qualified to hold a job in the industry under consideration, but the worker wishes to continue and apply for a job hoping that some firm will make an error and think he or she is qualified.

Consider, on the other hand, a person who is unemployed with $\mu < B_0^*$ who *is* unable to find a job with a positive wage although $\theta > B_0^*$. Since $\theta = \mu + \epsilon$, when $\mu = \beta_0^*$, then $\theta = B_0^* + \epsilon$, and if $\theta > B_0^*$, it means that $\epsilon > 0$, and thus the firm underestimated the productivity of the worker. In this case, it is reasonable to take the view that we have a qualified person who wants to work at the market wage rate. However, this person is unable to find a job since the firms regard him as too risky a prospect. It appears that such a person should be regarded as involuntarily unemployed, and this motivates the following:

Definition. A person with productivity θ is said to be *involuntarily unemployed* if he or she wishes to work at the market wage rate, is qualified for the jobs so that $\theta > B_0^*$, but the firm will not pay a positive wage since $\mu < B_0^*$.

In nonstationary conditions, a person may be caught without a work history and starting as unemployed will continue to be unemployed although his θ satisfied $\theta > B_0^*$. However, even in stationary conditions, involuntary unemployment arises. Denote by P_{IN} the probability of involuntary unemployment. Then under stationary conditions one may define P_{IN} to be

$$P_{\text{IN}} = \text{Prob}\{\theta \geq B_0^* \text{ and } \mu < B_0^*\}$$

$$= \text{Prob}\{\theta \geq B_0^* \text{ and } \theta - \epsilon < B_0^*\}$$

$$= \text{Prob}\{\epsilon > 0 \text{ and } B_0^* \leq \theta < B_0^* + \epsilon\}. \tag{29}$$

Assumption 1 together with equation (29) imply that

$$P_{\text{IN}} = \int_0^\infty \int_{B_0^*}^{B_0^* + \epsilon} g(\theta)\gamma(\epsilon)\, d\theta\, d\epsilon. \tag{30}$$

It is interesting that P_{IN} depends only on B_0^* and on the two distributions $\gamma(\epsilon)$ and $g(\theta)$. Recalling that B_0^* is determined by u, the observed unemployment rate, one should interpret P_{IN} as the fraction of u that should be regarded as involuntary. We shall use formula (30) below.

Wage rigidity. The step function in Figure 3 shows that firms in the industry respond to the competition of entering firms but are less responsive to excess supply of labor. If the supply of workers increases, firms will be reluctant to lower wages as long as the expected price of final output remains unaltered. In essence, firms are fearful that lowering the wage rate would cause them to lose their best employees since such departures would constitute serious capital losses to the firm.

New entrants into the labor market would attract additional job offers if the quality of the unemployed pool improves so that additional sampling is warranted.

Informational rent and collective bargaining. It is important to note that the firms who entered first – at an earlier age – have a significant advantage over potential entrants. This arises from the fact that regardless of what initial wage such a firm paid, in a two-step stationary equilibrium, an established firm has a rent that can be measured as follows. The best workers from B_M^* to $+\infty$ are being paid W_M^* and the rent per worker is

$$\beta E(\theta \mid \mu) - \beta E(\theta \mid B_M^*).$$

For workers with $\mu < B_M^*$, the rent is simply

$$\beta E(\theta \mid \mu) - \beta E(\theta \mid B_i^*), \qquad B_i^* \leq \mu \leq B_{i+1}^*.$$

Hence, total rent is (note $B_{M+1}^* = +\infty$)

$$\text{rent} = \sum_{i=-1}^{M} \int_{B_i^*}^{B_{i+1}^*} [\beta E(\theta \mid \mu) - \beta E(\theta \mid B_i^*)] f(\mu) \, d\mu.$$

These rents cannot be competed away by entering firms. A more important source of competition may come from the workers themselves. In equilibrium, every worker learns in what interval his μ estimate lies. However, an individual wage demand will not be effective. On the other hand, a threat of resignations by a group of workers may have a major impact on the firm. A union can be very effective if it is established in the entire industry and if it can prevent new workers from entering the market. Our objective here is not to analyze the entire bargaining process under the presumed conditions but rather to provide a general introduction to the simulations below. These simulations will be carried out under the assumption that the union aims only to resist wage decreases by threatening mass resignation of the workers. Under such conditions, the firm will be forced to hire the lower ranking workers in order to replace the resigning workers.

4   Simulation results

Most endogenous variables in the economy at hand are determined by the stochastic variables θ, μ, and ϵ. If, in addition, one uses the observed unemployment rate to deduce B_0^* from the relation

Table 1. *Simulated values of P_{IN}/u involuntarily unemployed.*[a]

u	$K=6$, $\sigma_\theta/\sigma_\epsilon=2.45$		$K=12.5$, $\sigma_\theta/\sigma_\epsilon=3.54$		$K=25$, $\sigma_\theta/\sigma_\epsilon=5$	
	ϵ normal	ϵ uniform	ϵ normal	ϵ uniform	ϵ normal	ϵ uniform
0.03	0.469	0.485	0.316	0.344	0.215	0.230
0.06	0.401	0.420	0.269	0.296	0.184	0.197
0.09	0.356	0.377	0.240	0.264	0.164	0.176
0.12	0.323	0.343	0.217	0.241	0.149	0.161
0.15	0.295	0.316	0.199	0.222	0.137	0.148
0.18	0.272	0.292	0.184	0.205	0.127	0.138
0.21	0.252	0.272	0.171	0.191	0.118	0.128
0.24	0.234	0.253	0.159	0.178	0.111	0.120

[a] θ is normal: $E\theta=1$, $\sigma_\theta^2=0.1$.

$$u = F(B_0^*),$$

then some interesting simulations can be carried out.

To carry out the simulations, we shall postulate reasonable distributions $g(\theta)$ and $\gamma(\epsilon)$ and compute some key variables for u ranging in value from 3 to 24 percent. We concentrate here on two variables: the fraction of involuntary unemployment and the range of wage change over over which collective bargaining could be effective.

4.1   Fraction of involuntary unemployment

In the simulations below, we shall assume that θ is normally distributed with $\bar\theta=1$ and $\sigma_\theta^2=0.1$. On the other hand, we shall postulate ϵ to be distributed either normally or uniformly. In both cases, $E\epsilon=0$, but the variances are selected so that the ratio $K=\sigma_\theta^2/\sigma_\epsilon^2$ takes various values between 1 and 25.

Note that since $\sigma_\theta=0.1$ and $E\epsilon=0$, the selection of K completely specifies σ_ϵ and the support of the uniform distribution. For example, if $K=10$, then $\sigma_\epsilon^2=0.01$ and $\sigma_\epsilon=0.1$; hence if ϵ is normal, then $E\epsilon=0$ and $\sigma_\epsilon=0.1$. On the other hand, if ϵ is uniform on $[-a,+a]$, it can be shown that

$$\sigma_\delta^2 = \tfrac{1}{3}a^2.$$

Hence if $\sigma_\epsilon^2=0.01$, then $a^2=0.03$ and $a=0.1732$.

The first calculations were made for θ distributed normally, and the results in Table 1 report the simulated values of P_{IN}/u for values of u

between 0.03 and 0.24 and for R taking the three values 6, 12.5, and 25.

We note first that the simulated numbers for uniform ϵ and for normal ϵ are rather similar. Concentrating on u between 6 and 12 percent, Table 1 shows that the fractions of involuntary unemployed are computed between 15 and 42 percent of the unemployed, and the majority of the simulated numbers reported in the table are above 24 percent. These numbers suggest that even under stationary conditions, it is not unreasonable to expect some one-fourth of the unemployed to be involuntarily unemployed.

The fact that P_{IN}/u declines with u is due to the fact that the involuntary aspect we are measuring is related to the informational structure, and this remains the same as u changes. However, as u arises, the amount of error in the system remains the same, and the ratio P_{IN}/u declines.

4.2   *Range of effective collective bargaining*

We have already commented on the informational rent that established firms have. Now suppose that the market is in a stationary equilibrium with a maximal wage W_M^* and cutoff at B_M^*. Note that since all workers with $\mu \geq B_M^*$ are being paid W_M^*, there may be a substantial rent above W_M^*. Now suppose that a union of the top workers is formed such that all union workers receive a wage W^* and members of the union have a μ value above B^*. The union may include only the top workers (thus $B^* = B_M^*$) or some lower ranking groups (such that $B^* < B_M^*$). The union is organized with the only objective of resisting wage decreases. The union thus issues a threat that if the firm attempts to lower the wage rate relative to the wage that prevailed at the initial date, then all the employees will go on strike. Since the firm can fire any worker, the union is in effect threatening an act of collective resignation. Without analyzing the entire bargaining process and its solution, do we want to establish here the range of the wage rate in which such a threat may be credible? Putting this question differently, suppose that relative to the initial situation all other conditions (distribution of q, value of r, etc.) remain identically the same. Then, by how much, on *the average,* would the wage rate on the open market need to fall before the firm will be prepared to let all the employees resign and hire new workers on the open market? This question has been extensively examined by many firms in recent years, since they faced situations in which their employees earned much more than their corresponding earning opportunities on the open market but the unions refused to allow significant wage decreases. In the case of some

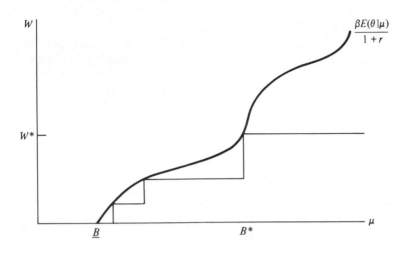

Figure 4.

airlines, the firms were prepared to let the employees go and hire new, nonunion workers on the open market at wages that were claimed to be 50–70 percent lower than the wages paid to the unionized employees. The question is: How reasonable or representative were these figures?

To analyze the question with the framework at hand, we draw in Figure 4 the assumed wage W^* to satisfy $\beta E(\theta \mid B^*) = (1+r)W^*$ while the productivity of the workers is measured by $\beta E(\theta \mid \mu \geq B^*)$. On the other hand, those with $\mu \leq B^*$ have productivity measured by $\beta E(\theta \mid \mu < B^*)$. If a union is established with the aim of preventing wage decreases, then a result of a collective resignation would be to force the firm to employ workers with $E(\theta \mid \mu \leq B^*)$. The per-worker loss to the firm from a mass resignation would be

$$E(\theta \mid \mu \geq B^*) - E(\theta \mid \mu \leq B^*),$$

and if C^* is the reduction of the wage that the firm will need to have in order to be indifferent to the resignation, then we must have

$$E(\theta \mid \mu \geq B^*) - E(\theta \mid \mu \leq B^*) = C^* W^* = C^* \frac{\beta E(\theta \mid \mu = B^*)}{1+r}.$$

Hence

$$C^* = \frac{E(\theta \mid \mu \geq B^*) - E(\theta \mid \mu \leq B^*)}{E(\theta \mid \mu = B^*)}(1+r).$$

Table 2. *Simulated values of* C^*.[a]

$F(B^*)$	$K=8$, $\sigma_\theta/\sigma_\epsilon=2.83$		$K=16\frac{2}{3}$, $\sigma_\theta/\sigma_\epsilon=4.08$	
	ϵ normal	ϵ uniform	ϵ normal	ϵ uniform
0.03	0.683	0.686	0.703	0.704
0.06	0.607	0.608	0.624	0.626
0.09	0.561	0.562	0.577	0.578
0.12	0.529	0.529	0.544	0.545
0.15	0.504	0.504	0.518	0.519
0.18	0.484	0.484	0.497	0.498
0.21	0.467	0.467	0.480	0.480
0.24	0.453	0.452	0.464	0.466

[a] θ is normal: $E\theta=1$, $\sigma_\theta^2=0.1$, $r=0$.

This expression measures the size of the decrease in wages over which the resistance of collective bargaining may be effective. The notation of C^* for this expression is used to remind the reader that this may be thought of as the potential range for collective bargaining.

The results of calculating C^* for various specifications of the size of the nonunionized sector $F(B^*)$ are reported in Table 2. Here θ is assumed normal and ϵ is either normal or uniform; K was assumed to be either 8 or $16\frac{2}{3}$. The calculations are made for $r=0$.

The surprising first conclusion one may draw from Table 2 is that the computed values of C^* are very large, ranging from 45 to 70 percent. The results are also little affected by the stochastic specifications of ϵ. Note also that the results in Table 2 are computed with $r=0$. If $r=2$, for example, all the C^* in the table have to be increased by the factor of 1.2, making the results even more significant. These calculations suggest that the figures cited earlier for the airlines may not be accidental.

The possibilities of informational rents must be evaluated with care. Recall that they arise since an entering firm must take a loss during the initial entry phase. In equilibrium, the informational rents must be equal to the initial loss at entry. This means that if a union tries to expropriate this rent at a later date, entry will be further restricted. Even if a union cannot expropriate the rent on a permanent basis, it is possible that collective bargaining may be capable of preventing short-term fluctuations of the wage rate paid by the firm although this may cause short-term declines in profits.

REFERENCES

Akerlof, G. (1984), "Gift exchange and efficiency wage theory: Four views," American Economic Review, Papers and Proceedings, May, pp. 79–83.

Azariadis, C. (1975), "Implicit contracts and underemployment equilibria," *Journal of Political Economy,* 83(6): 1183–1202.

Baily, M. N. (1974), "Wage and employment under uncertain demand," *Review of Economic Studies,* 41(January): 37–50.

Bernanke, B. S. (1983), "An equilibrium model of industrial employment, hours and earnings, 1923–1939." Mimeo, Graduate School of Business, Stanford University, August.

Calvo, G. (1979), "Quasi-Walrasian theories of unemployment," *American Economic Review,* papers and proceedings, 69(2): 102–108.

Guasch, L. J. and A. Weiss (1980), "Wages as sorting mechanisms in competitive markets with asymmetric information: A theory of testing," *Review of Economic Studies,* 149(July): 485–97.

Guasch, L. J. and A. Weiss (1982), "An equilibrium analysis of wage-productivity gaps," *Review of Economic Studies,* 158(October): 485–98.

Lucas, R. E., Jr., (1972), "Expectations and the neutrality of money," *Journal of Economic Theory,* 4(2): 103–23.

Lucas, R. E., Jr., (1975), "An equilibrium model of the business cycle," *Journal of Political Economy,* 83(6): 1113–44.

Shapiro, C. and J. E. Stiglitz (1982), "Equilibrium unemployment as a worker discipline device," Discussion Paper #28, Woodrow Wilson School, Princeton University, Princeton, April.

Stiglitz, J. E. (1976), "Price and queues as screening devices in competitive markets," IMSSS Technical Report No. 212, Stanford University.

Stiglitz, J. E. (1982), "The structure of labor markets in L.D.C.'s," in *Migration and the Labor Market in Developing Countries,* R. Sabot (Ed.), Boulder: Westview Press.

Stiglitz, J. E. (1984a), "Equilibrium wage distributions," National Bureau of Economic Research, Working Paper No. 1337, Cambridge, Mass., April.

Stiglitz, J. E. (1984b), "Theories of wage rigidity," Paper read at a conference on Keynes' Economic Legacy, University of Delaware, January, Mimeo.

Weiss, A. (1980), "Job queues and layoffs in labor markets with flexible wages," *Journal of Political Economy,* 88(3): 526–38.

Yellen, J. L. (1984), "Efficiency wage models of unemployment," *American Economic Review,* Papers and Proceedings, May, pp. 200–205.

CHAPTER 9

Asymmetric adjustment costs and sectoral shifts

Laurence Weiss

The purpose of this chapter is to formulate and empirically assess an aggregate economic model that displays the feature that *sectoral shocks* – changes in either relative demands or the technology that requires labor to be reallocated among various sectors – causes short-run changes in aggregate employment and output. The model emphasizes the costs to the firm of changing its labor force. Like the treatment of the costs of changing the capital shock in Eisner and Strotz (1963), Lucas (1967), and Gould (1968), these costs are assumed to increase rapidly with the absolute rate of employment changes so that the firm will never jump to its desired long-run employment levels. However, unlike those contributions, the cost of adjustment is assumed to be asymmetric – an increase in employment costs more than a decline of equal magnitude. It is this asymmetry that yields a temporary decline in aggregate employment in response to a sectoral shock. Firms that experience a decline in their relative position are quicker to fire workers than those firms that are expanding hire additional workers. Over time, firms asymptotically approach their long-run desired employment, which, by assumption, is invariant to the cross-sectional distribution of sectoral specific employment.

This chapter is motivated, in part, by recent work of Lilien (1982a, b), who has attempted to show empirically that a large part of fluctuations in measured unemployment in recent U.S. experience can be attributed to the unusually large structural shifts over this period. Although Lilien's empirical results are suggestive, his theoretical model is not spelled out, and it is not clear what structural features of the labor market would lead to behavior consistent with his hypothesis. The model presented in this chapter is an attempt to remedy this defect by showing how asymmetric

Research supported by grants from the National Science Foundation and the Alfred P. Sloan Foundation. Robert Lucas and Jose Scheinkman provided valuable assistance. Robert Litterman graciously furnished the empirical work.

251

costs can give rise to aggregate consequences of the type Lilien has documented. Somewhat unexpectedly, however, the model also implies that Lilien's results are consistent with the conventional view of business cycles, which emphasizes that output movements across broadly defined sectors move together. An attempt is made to assess empirically the importance of the sectoral shock hypothesis for causing aggregate movements in light of this alternative interpretation of Lilien's results. The result (which must be considered preliminary) is not overly encouraging.

This essay is organized as follows: Section 1 is a model of a representative firm's, or sector's, optimal employment time path when faced with a stationary distribution of exogenous shocks. In Section 2, it is shown that this leads to an explicit expression for the distribution of employment over time. Section 3 shows how this procedure can be modified for certain kinds of nonstationary exogenous shocks. Section 4 derives an interesting summary statistic that is easy to implement empirically. The fifth section shows how the model can give rise to aggregate consequences. The sixth section reviews Lilien's empirical work and shows how it is consistent with the conventional one-factor model of business cycles. In this section, some new empirical evidence is presented that supports the hypothesis of adjustment cost asymmetry. The seventh section is the conclusion.

1   The model of a representative firm

Consider a firm that seeks to maximize the expected present discounted value of profits: $E[\int_0^\infty e^{-\beta t} \pi(t)\, dt]$, where $\pi(t)$ is given by

$$\pi(t) = \eta(t)L(t) - \tfrac{1}{2}L^2(t) - \tfrac{1}{2}a_1 \max^2(0, \dot{L}) - \tfrac{1}{2}a_2 \max^2(0, -\dot{L}), \qquad (1)$$

where η_t is an exogenous random variable (most simply taken to be the technology). Assume η_t can take on two possible values $\eta_1 > \eta_2$. The duration of time over which the technological parameter is constant is assumed generated from a Poisson probability distribution with parameter λ_1 in state 1 and λ_2 in state 2. Thus, the transition probabilities of state changes is given by:

$$\Pr(S(t+dt) = S_2 \mid S(t) = S_1) = \lambda_1\, dt,$$

$$\Pr(s(t+dt) = S_1 \mid S(t) = S_1) = 1 - \lambda_1\, dt,$$

$$\Pr(S(t+dt) = S_1 \mid S(t) = S_2) = \lambda_2\, dt, \qquad (2)$$

$$\Pr(S(t+dt) = S_2 \mid S(t) = S_1) = 1 - \lambda_2\, dt.$$

Note that the objective function (1) penalizes the firm if it adjusts its labor input rapidly, since the total cost is proportional to $\dot{L}^2$. Also, adjustment costs are assumed to be asymmetrical; it is assumed that $a_1 > a_2 > 0$ – meaning that a rise in labor input costs more than a decline of equal magnitude.

Denote by $V_i(L)$ the value function in state i if the firm has L workers. By the optimum principle

$$V_i(L) = \max_{L(t)} [\eta_i L(t) - \tfrac{1}{2}L^2(t) - \tfrac{1}{2}a_1 \max^2(0, L) - \tfrac{1}{2}a_2 \max^2(0, -\dot{L})]\, dt$$

$$+ e^{-\beta\, dt}[(1 - \lambda_i\, dt)V_i(L)t) + \dot{L}(t)\, dt) + \lambda_i\, dt\, V_j(L(t) + \dot{L}(t)\, dt)]$$

$$(3)$$

such that $L(0) = L$.

Assume (tentatively) that $V_1' > 0$ and $V_2' < 0$; that is, the firm hires in the good state and lays workers off in the bad state. Maximizing equation (3) with respect to $\dot{L}$ yields

$$-a_1 \dot{L}_1(L) + V_1'(L) = 0, \tag{4}$$

$$-a_2 \dot{L}_2(L) + V_2'(L) = 0. \tag{5}$$

Inserting equation (4) into (3) for $s(t) = s_1$, expanding around $dt = 0$, and dropping terms of order dt^2 and higher and dividing by dt yields

$$(\beta + \lambda_1) V_1(L) = \eta_1 L - \frac{1}{2}L^2 + \frac{1}{2a_1}V_1'^2 + \lambda_1 V_2(L). \tag{6}$$

Similarly, inserting equation (6) into (3) yields

$$(\beta + \lambda_2) V_2(L) = \eta_2 L - \frac{1}{2}L^2 + \frac{1}{2a_2}V_2'^2 + \lambda_2 V_1(L). \tag{7}$$

Equations (6) and (7) comprise a pair of differential equations. It turns out that it is simpler to work directly with the derivatives of the value functions. Differentiating equations (6) and (7) with respect to L yields

$$(\beta + \lambda_1) V_1'(L) = \eta_1 - L + \frac{1}{a_1}V_1'V_1'' + \lambda_1 V_2'(L), \tag{8}$$

$$(\beta + \lambda_2) V_2'(L) = \eta_2 - L + \frac{1}{a_2}V_2'V_2'' + \lambda_2 V_2'(L). \tag{9}$$

To solve equations (8) and (9), posit a solution of the form $V_i' = x_i(y_i - L)$ for some values of x and y. This implies $V_i'' = -x_i$. Inserting the candidate solution back into the original functions yields

$$(\beta+\lambda_1)x_1(y_1-L)=\eta_1-L-\frac{x_1^2}{a_1}(y_1-L)+\lambda_1 x_2(y_2-L), \qquad (10)$$

$$(\beta+\lambda_2)x_2(y_2-L)=\eta_2-L-\frac{x_2^2}{a_2}(y_2-L)+\lambda_2 x_1(y_1-L). \qquad (11)$$

Since equations (10) and (11) must hold for every L, it must be the case that

$$-(\beta+\lambda_1)x_1-\frac{x_1^2}{a_1}+1+\lambda_1 x_2=0, \qquad (12)$$

$$-(\beta+\lambda_2)x_2-\frac{x_2^2}{a_2}+1+\lambda_2 x_1=0, \qquad (13)$$

$$(\beta+\lambda_1)x_1 y_1-\eta_1+\frac{y_1 x_1^2}{a_1}-\lambda_1 x_2 y_2=0, \qquad (14)$$

$$(\beta+\lambda_2)x_2 y_2-\eta_2+\frac{y_2 x_2^2}{a_2}-\lambda_2 x_1 y_1=0. \qquad (15)$$

It is straightforward to verify that there exists a unique solution to equations (12)–(15) with x_i's positive, which is necessary for concavity of the value function. To show that this candidate solution is, in fact, the unique optimum for the firm's problem, one appeals to a stochastic version of the well-known procedure of showing that if a path satisfies a Euler equation [in this case equations (6) and (7)] and satisfies a transversality condition (such as $\lim_{t\to\infty} E[e^{-\beta t} LV'(L)]=0$), then the path is a unique optimum if the objective function is concave. [See Scheinkman and Weiss (1986) for an example of this procedure.]

Of central interest is the implication of this solution for the speed of adjustment of desired labor. From equations (4) and (5), the optimal change in labor input is given by

$$\dot{L}=\frac{x_1}{a_1}(y_1-L) \quad \text{if } s(t)=s_1, \qquad (16)$$

$$\dot{L}=\frac{x_2}{a_2}(y_2-L) \quad \text{if } s(t)=s_2. \qquad (17)$$

Equations (6) and (7) have a straightforward interpretation. They imply that, in each state, the firm has a "target" level of employment, y_i, and that they approach this level asymptotically at a rate x_i/a_i. The following proposition shows that the qualitative relative speed of adjustment between hires and layoffs depends on the relative costs of adjustment.

Proposition 1. $x_1/a_1 < x_2/a_2 \Leftrightarrow a_1 > a_2$.

Proof: Subtracting equation (13) from (12) yields

$$\frac{x_2^2}{a_2} - \frac{x_1^2}{a_1} + (\beta + \lambda_1 + \lambda_2)(x_2 - x_1) = 0. \tag{18}$$

Since all of the variables are positive, it is immediate that $x_1 > x_2$ iff $a_1 > a_2$. Similarly, $x_2^2/a_2 > x_1^2/a_1$ iff $a_1 > a_2$. Combining these two relationships establishes the proposition.   Q.E.D.

The magnitude of the speed of adjustment depends also on the rate of discount β and the probability of state changes. It may be shown that an increase in β reduces both speeds of adjustment and lowers the difference between the speed of layoffs and hires. An increase in λ_1, the probability of exiting the good state, decreases the speed of adjustment in both states, and an increase in λ_2, the probability of exiting the bad state, increases the speed of adjustment in both states.

It may also be shown that $\eta_2 < y_2 < y_1 < \eta_1$. That is, the desired labor targets (y_2 and y_1) vary less than they would in the absence of adjustment costs. This is because the firm's decisions are forward looking and take into account the future costs incurred when reversing current labor changes.

2   The stationary distribution of employment

Starting from an initial distribution of employment and state of technological productivity at time t_0, the distribution of employment and technology at t_1 is random, as it depends on the realization of the random technology between t_0 and t_1. In this section, the stationary distribution of employment will be calculated. This distribution has the following interpretation: Suppose $\Pr(\ell < L)$ at t_0 is given by $F(L)$, then at any time $t_1 > t_0$, $\Pr(\ell < L)$ is also $F(L)$. Since the system is ergodic, it may be shown that, starting from an arbitrary initial state, the sample path will converge to this stationary distribution.

Consider time $t + dt$ when $s_{t+dt} = s_1$ and the firm's employment is $\ell \leq L$. There are two ways in which this state could have been reached: either $s_t = 1$ and $\ell \leq L - \dot{L}_1(L)\, dt$ or $s_t = s_2$ and $\ell \leq L - \dot{L}_2(L)\, dt$. Conditional on $s_{t+dt} = 1$, the probability of the latter is $\lambda_1\, dt$ and the former $1 - \lambda_1\, dt$. This implies

$$F_1(L, t+dt) = (1 - \lambda_1\, dt) F_1(L - \dot{L}_1(L)\, dt, t) + \lambda_1\, dt\, F_2(L - \dot{L}_2(L)\, dt, t), \tag{19}$$

where $F_s(L, t)$ is $\Pr(\ell < L)$ at t conditional on the state of technology. Similarly,

$$F_2(L, t+dt) = (1 - \lambda_2\, dt) F_2(L - \dot{L}_2(L)\, dt, t) + \lambda_2\, dt\, F_1(L - \dot{L}_1(L)\, dt, t).$$
(20)

Expanding around $dt = 0$ and dropping terms of order $(dt)^2$ and dividing by dt, the condition $F(L, s, t + dt) = F(L, s, t)$ implies

$$\dot{L}_1(L) f_1(L) = -\lambda_1 (F_1(L) - F_2(L)),$$
(21)

$$\dot{L}_2(L) f_2(L) = -\lambda_2 (F_2(L) - F_1(L)).$$
(22)

Differentiating equations (21) and (22) yields, after some manipulation,

$$\frac{f_1'}{f_1} = -\frac{\lambda_1}{\dot{L}_1} - \frac{\lambda_2}{\dot{L}_2} - \frac{\dot{L}_1'}{\dot{L}_1}.$$
(23)

Letting $b_i = x_i/a_i$, the $\dot{L}$ functions are [from equations (16) and (17)]

$$\dot{L}_1(L) = b_1(y_1 - L),$$
(16′)

$$\dot{L}_2(L) = -b_2(L - y_2).$$
(17′)

Integrating both sides of (23) yields

$$\log f_1(L) = \left(\frac{\lambda_1}{b_1} - 1\right) \log(y_1 - L) + \frac{\lambda_2}{b_2} \log(L - y_2) + \log k_1, \quad (24)$$

where k_1 is some constant such that $\int_{y_2}^{y_1} f(L)\, dL = 1$. Similarly,

$$\log f_2(L) = \frac{\lambda_1}{b_1} \log(y_1 - L) + \left(\frac{\lambda_2}{b_2} - 1\right) \log(L - y_2) + \log k_2. \quad (25)$$

Since the unconditional cumulative density is the sum of the conditional distributions weighted by the unconditional probability of the states,

$$F(L) = F_1(L)\pi_1 + F_2(L)\pi_2,$$
(26)

where

$$\pi_1 = \frac{\lambda_2}{\lambda_1 + \lambda_2} \quad \text{and} \quad \pi_2 = \frac{\lambda_1}{\lambda_1 + \lambda_2}.$$

The unconditional marginal density function is

$$f(L) = (y_1 - L)^{\lambda_1/b_1 + 1}(L - y_2)^{\lambda_2/b_2} \left[\frac{k_1\lambda_2}{y_1 - L} + \frac{k_2\lambda_1}{L - y_2}\right] \frac{1}{(\lambda_1 + \lambda_2)}. \quad (27)$$

3   The effects of time trends

The model presented in Section 1 assumes that the firms' desired "target" employment takes on one of two possible values. In this section, the effects of secular growth on desired labor input will be investigated to see how these affect the properties of the firms' optimal employment time path. Accordingly, let the exogenous technological process be given by

$$\eta_1(t) = gt + \eta_1 \quad \text{if } s(t) = s_1,$$

$$\eta_2(t) = gt + \eta_2 \quad \text{if } s(t) = s_2,$$

where g is some known arbitrary constant and η_1 and η_2 are as before. (Note that in the empirical work that follows, it is assumed that the model holds for L being the log of employment, so that a linear time trend in the exogenous forcing variable implies exponential growth in desired employment levels.)

Repeating the calculations in Section 1 shows that the firms' desired labor input in the face of secular growth is modified to be

$$\dot{L}(t) = \frac{x_1}{a_1}(y_1' + gt - L) \quad \text{if } s(t) = s_1,$$

$$\dot{L}(t) = \frac{x_2}{a_2}(y_2' + gt - L) \quad \text{if } s(t) = s_2,$$

where the x's are as before [implicitly determined in equations (12) and (13)] and the new y's are determined analogously to equations (14) and (15) by replacing η_1 by $\eta_1 + x_1 g$ in equation (14) and η_2 by $\eta_2 + x_2 g$ in equation (15). Note that since $x_1 > x_2$, secular growth *amplifies* the effects of an exogenous technological shock on the desired target employment level at a point in time but, because of the additive specification, does not affect the speeds of adjustment.

Since the desired labor target grows with time, there will be no stationary distribution of employment over time. However, detrended labor input, $\ell(t) - gt$, will have a stationary distribution. To derive this distribution, consider time $t + dt$ when $s(t + dt) = s$ and $\ell(t + dt) - g(t + dt) \leq L$ or $\ell(t + dt) \leq L + g(t + dt)$. Analogous to the previous derivation [equation (19)],

$$F_1(L + g(t + dt), t + dt) = (1 - \lambda_1 \, dt)F(L - \dot{L}_1(L + gt) \, dt + gt, t)$$

$$+ \lambda_1 F_2(L + gt, t). \tag{19'}$$

Expanding around $dt = 0$, dividing by dt, and dropping terms of order $(dt)^2$ and higher, the condition that $F_1(L + gt, t)$ is independent of its second argument yields

$$f_1(L + gt)(g + L_1(L + gt)) = -\lambda_1 F_1 + \lambda_1 F_2. \tag{20'}$$

Thus, the stationary distribution of detrended labor $\hat{L}(t) = L(t) - gt$ is given implicitly by

$$f_1(\hat{L})\left(g + \frac{x_1}{a_1}(y_1' - \hat{L})\right) = -\lambda_1 F_1(\hat{L}) + \lambda_1 F_2(\hat{L}), \tag{21'}$$

$$f_2(\hat{L})\left(g + \frac{x_1}{a_1}(y_2' - \hat{L})\right) = -\lambda_2 F_2(L) + \lambda_2 F_1(\hat{L}). \tag{22'}$$

The unconditional marginal density function is now the same functional form as equation (27) with y_1 replaced by $\hat{y}_1 = y_1' + g(a_1/x_1)$ and y_2 replaced by $\hat{y}_2 = y_2' + g(a_2 x_2)$.

4   Some implications

The model developed in Section 1 shows how firms respond more quickly to negative changes in desired long-run employment than to positive changes and only if the cost of fires is less than the cost of hires. In this section, a convenient summary statistic is derived that permits an empirical test of this asymmetry. This statistic is to compare the expected positive employment changes squared to expected negative employment changes squared. Denoting

$$\varphi = E(\dot{L}^2 \mid \dot{L} > 0)/E(\dot{L}^2 \mid \dot{L} < 0)$$

$$\equiv \frac{\int \dot{L}_1^2(L)\, df_1(L)}{\int \dot{L}_2^2(L)\, df_2(L)}$$

$$= \frac{\int_{y_2}^{y_1} b_1^2 (y_1 - L)^{\lambda_1/b_1 + 1}(L - y_2)^{\lambda_2/b} k_1\, dL}{\int_{y_2}^{y_1} b_2^2 (y_1 - L)^{\lambda_1/b_1}(L - y_2)^{\lambda_2/y_2 + 1} k_2\, dL}. \tag{28}$$

Now, using the fact that

$$\int_{y_2}^{y_1} \frac{\partial}{\partial L}\{(y_1 - L)^{\lambda_1/b_1}(L - y_2)^{\lambda_2/b_2}\}\, dL = 0,$$

it is easy to show that $k_1/k_2 = (\lambda_1/b_1)/(\lambda_2/b_2)$. Similarly, since

$$\int_{y_2}^{y_1} \frac{\partial}{\partial L}\{(y_1 - L)^{\lambda_1/b_1 + 1}(L - y_2)^{\lambda_2/b_1 + 1}\}\, dL = 0,$$

some manipulation is sufficient to show

$$\varphi = \frac{\lambda_1(\lambda_1 + b_1)}{\lambda_2(\lambda_2 + b_2)}. \tag{29}$$

This shows that if the mean duration of up runs and down runs are equal $(\lambda_1 = \lambda_2)$, φ will be less than 1 if and only if $b_1 < b_2$ or $a_1 > a_2$.

5   Aggregate implications

Consider an economy composed of several firms of the type described in Section 1. To justify the assumption of constant wage and interest rates, assume that all agents have linear utility functions of the form $\int e^{-\beta t}[c(t) - L(t)]\,dt$. (This is, of course, implausible, but, presumably, any specification emphasizing the role of substitution effects will give qualitatively similar results.)

Consider first an aggregate model in which all firms respond qualitatively similarly to a common shock; in other words, all firms expand or contract together. Formally, assume for each firm j, $\eta_1^j > \eta_2^j$. In this case, the preceding model permits aggregation over firms, $L^{A} = b_i(Y_i^{A} - L^{A})$, where $Y_i^{A} = \sum_{j=1}^{J} Y_i^j$ and $L^{A} = \sum_{j=1}^{J} L^j$. In this case, φ, the ratio of mean positive employment changes to mean negative employment changes, will be the same for aggregate data as for a representative firm.

To show how sectoral shocks can affect aggregate outcomes in this type of economy, consider the case where the exogenous technological shocks are perfectly negatively correlated; when firm I is "high," firm II is "low." In the absence of asymmetric adjustment costs, total employment from the declining firm would move instantly into the expanding firm. To show the aggregate effects of adjustment cost asymmetry, assume that layoffs are costless (which corresponds to setting a_2 in the previous model equal to zero). Under this polar case, the firms experiencing a low state move to their long-run level of employment instantly. However, firms in the high state would move to their target asymptotically. Thus, after a shock that reversed the relative positions of the two firms, aggregate employment would be temporally depressed.

In this economy, the variance of total employment about its mean equals the variance of the high firm's employment about its mean, since the low firm's employment is always constant. The variance of aggregate employment is thus equal the variance of L^h, where the distribution is given by equation (24) with $b_2 = \infty$. Thus, the density function is

$$f_1(L) = \frac{(y_1 - L)^{\lambda_1/b_1 - 1}}{(\lambda_1/b_1)(y_1 - y_2)^{\lambda/b_1}},$$

and hence the variance of aggregate outcomes equals

$$\frac{\lambda_1/b_1}{(\lambda_1/c_1 + 2)(\lambda_1/b_1 + 1)^2}(y_1 - y_2)^2.$$

This expression is maximized for intermediate values of λ_1/b_1.

6   Empirical evidence

The model developed in Section 4 shows how sectoral shocks in the presence of asymmetric adjustment costs can contribute to aggregate fluctuations. In this section, some issues pertinent to empirically assessing the importance of this phenomena will be discussed.

In a series of papers, Lilien (1982a, b) has attempted to show empirically that a large part of fluctuations in measured unemployment in recent U.S. experience can be attributed to the unusually large structural shifts over this period. Lilien's evidence for this proposition comes from several sources. First, he notes that there has been an unusually large decline in manufacturing employment during the seventies and that periods of greatest structural change coincide with peak measured unemployment. More formally, Lilien has shown that there is an empirically significant contemporaneous relationship between measured unemployment (alternatively, aggregate employment) and the cross-sectional standard deviation of sectoral employment growth rates.[1] Despite the lack of a formal model underlying this test, he interprets this result as confirmation of the hypothesis that an increase in the rate of sectoral shocks has contributed to measured employment.

However, the model developed in this chapter shows that this test has no power to discriminate against an alternative one-factor view of the business cycle. The basic idea is that employment changes are asymmetric – large deviations are more likely to be negative than positive. Given that the distribution of employment changes is negatively skewed, any random sample from this distribution will exhibit a statistical relationship between the mean and standard deviation. This relationship will be negative, as empirically documented by Lilien. Thus, even if all firms' employment respond qualitatively similarly to a common factor (the business cycle), Lilien's results will still be possible.

To show this possibility intuitively, consider a one-factor model of cycles where employment is the jth sector at time t and is given by

$$L_t^j = \beta^j x_t$$

where all β^j's are of the same sign and x_t is the common factor. In this economy, the average sectoral growth rate is given by

$$\Delta L = \bar{\beta} \Delta x,$$

where

$$\bar{\beta} = \frac{1}{J} \sum_{j=1}^{J} \beta^j,$$

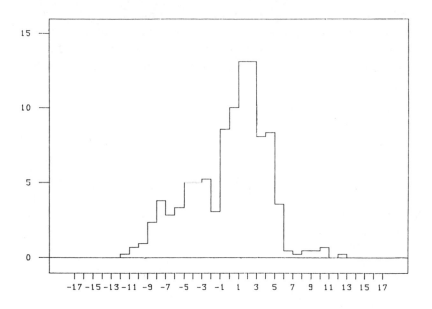

Figure 1. Histogram of aggregate monthly employment changes. Moments are 1.99, 2.54, −.76; significance = .000259. (Abscissa: 4 × standard deviation. Ordinate: percentages.)

and the cross-sectoral variance of growth rates is

$$\sigma = \sigma_\beta (\Delta x)^2,$$

where

$$\sigma_\beta = \frac{1}{J} \sum_{j=1}^{J} (\beta^j - \bar{\beta})^2.$$

A statistical relationship between σ and ΔL will arise if and only if there exists a statistical relationship between Δx and $(\Delta x)^2$, which is equivalent to showing that the distribution of employment changes is skewed. The possible importance of this argument is confirmed empirically by examining the frequency distribution of percentage of employment changes. In both aggregate data and in ten of the twelve sectors examined, this distribution is significantly negatively skewed.[2]

Figure 1 presents a histogram of aggregate monthly employment changes at annual rates. The test statistic is the probability, under the null hypothesis of zero skewness, of observing a coefficient of skewness – defined as the ratio of the third centered moment to the cube of the standard deviation – greater than or equal to that observed (the statistic treats observations as independent so that it probably overstates the true significance).

More precisely, the aggregate model developed in Section 5 can give rise to Lilien-type results even if all firms respond qualitatively similarly to the common factor. To see this, consider a two-firm world in which both firms expand or contract simultaneously. In this world, Lilien's σ is given by

$$\sigma^2 = \tfrac{1}{4}(\dot{L}^1 - \dot{L}^2)^2,$$

where $\dot{L}^j$ is firm j's instantaneous growth rate of labor input. If all firms expand or contract together,

$$\sigma_i^2 = \tfrac{1}{4}b_i^2(y_i^1 - y_i^2 - (L_i^1 - L_i^2))^2, \qquad i = 1, 2.$$

To see how the expected value of σ^2 will be higher in downturns than expansions define,

$$L_i(t) = L_i^1(t) - L_i^2(t), \qquad i = 1, 2;$$

$$y_i = y_i^1 - y_i^2.$$

Now, since

$$\dot{L}_i(t) = b_i(y_i - L), \qquad i = 1, 2;$$

which are precisely the same laws of motion as equations (16') and (17'), the state-dependent cumulative density function of the difference in labor between the two firms is the same functional form as equation (25). Since $\sigma^2 = \tfrac{1}{4}[\dot{L}_1(t)]^2$, the ratio of σ^2 in upturns to those in downturns will be exactly equal to φ, as defined in equation (29). Thus we can conclude the following.

Proposition 2. If all firms respond qualitatively similarly to a common shock but differ in their sensitivities, and if upturns last as long as downturns ($\lambda_1 = \lambda_2$), then the mean cross-sectional variance of employment growth rates will be higher in downturns than in upturns if and only if the cost of hires is greater than the cost of fires.

Table 1 reports the mean durations of runs of detrended positive and negative employment changes in ten broadly defined sectors of the U.S. economy and aggregate employment changes over the same period. Also shown is φ, the ratio of mean squared employment changes when positive to negative. The table shows that there is evidence of adjustment cost asymmetry since $\varphi < 1$ for the aggregate data and in seven of the ten sectors examined.

Table 1. *Length of runs in employment by industry.*

Industry	Mean positive run (months)	Mean negative run (months)	1983 Employment (millions)	$\dfrac{E[(\dot{L}^+)^2]}{E[(\dot{L}^-)^2]}$
Mining	6.7	9.3	1.0	0.54
Construction	8.5	7.1	3.9	0.52
Durable manufacturing	12.0	10.0	10.9	0.29
Nondurable manufacturing	13.4	12.4	7.7	0.51
Transport + public utilities	12.0	8.2	4.9	1.06
Wholesale + retail	12.8	13.2	20.5	0.57
Finance, insurance	14.6	18.9	5.5	1.03
Services	8.9	9.1	19.6	0.77
Government	8.1	9.7	15.7	1.3
Aggregate	13.0	11.0	90.0	0.52
Weighted average	10.9	11.0	90.0	0.75

Notes: The raw data in monthly employment levels from 1947 (6 months) to 1983 (12 months) transformed into logs and detrended with a cubic time trend. A run was defined by taking a seventh-month moving average with equal weights. A positive run is one in which this moving average increases, and a negative run is one in which this moving average decreases. The first and last observation of each run was dropped. The last column presents the ratio of the average change squared in detrended employment in up runs to downs runs.

Some preliminary evidence against Lilien's hypothesis that sectoral shocks cause aggregate employment changes comes from comparing the aggregate data with the weighted average across sectors. If Lilien's hypothesis were correct, it might be expected that aggregate employment changes would be more nearly symmetric than the individual components. If, however, the alternative one-factor model sketched in Section 5 were correct, the aggregate would be the same as representative sectors. The dates show that the aggregate φ is less than that of a representative sector.

7   Conclusions

This chapter has presented a model of asymmetric adjustment costs with the hope of showing how such costs can contribute to aggregate implications of sectoral shocks. This asymmetry has important applications for challenging previous empirical work that has attempted to quantify the magnitude of sectoral shocks for causing aggregate employment changes.

The preliminary empirical work shows that there is support for the hypothesis of asymmetric adjustment costs. However, it is unclear how important this phenomenon is for causing aggregate consequences from relative shocks.

NOTES

1   Lilien (1982a) defines the cross-sectional dispersion of industry growth rates as

$$
\sigma_t = \left[\sum_{L=1}^{11} \frac{x_{Lt}}{x_t} (\Delta \log x_{it} - \Delta \log x_t)^2 \right]^{1/2},
$$

where x_{Lt} is employment in sector i at time t and x_t is aggregate employment at t. He shows that this variable is positively related to measured unemployment and that this relationship is robust to the inclusion of other explanatory variables.
2   Neftci (1984) also finds evidence of asymmetry of aggregate unemployment changes.

REFERENCES

Eisner, R. and R. H. Strotz (1963), "Determinants of business investment" in *Impacts of Monetary Policy,* New York: Prentice Hall.
Gould, J. P. (1968), "Adjustment costs in the theory of the firm," *The Review of Economic Studies,* XXXV(1), No. 101: 47–56.
Lilien, D. M. (1982a), "Sectoral shifts and cyclical unemployment," *Journal of Political Economy,* 90(4): 777–94.
Lilien, D. M. (1982b), "A sectoral model of the business cycle" MRE Working Paper #8231.
Lucas, R. E. (1967), "Adjustment cost and the theory of supply," *Journal of Political Economy,* Part 1, 75(4): 321–24.
Neftci, S. (1984), "Are economic time series asymmetric over the business cycle," *Journal of Political Economy,* 92(2): 307–29.
Scheinkman, J. and L. Weiss (1986), "Borrowing constraints and aggregate economic activity," *Econometrica,* 54(1): 23–47.

CHAPTER 10

Implicit contracts and risk aversion

Takatoshi Ito

1   Introduction

There have been numerous contributions to economic theory of uncertainty and insurance. Despite well-developed theory in risk aversion in a complete market framework, economic behavior in an incomplete market case has not been investigated in sufficient depth. It was only recently that Ross (1981) showed that a basic theorem of Pratt (1964) about the relationship between the degree of risk aversion and the size of risk premium does not necessarily hold without a stronger condition in incomplete market situations.

Suppose that a risk-averse agent faces different amounts of income for different states of nature. It is well known that optimal risk sharing between a risk-averse agent and a risk-neutral agent (insurance company) results in equalization of net income (income after premium and coverage) across different states of nature, given that all states of nature are verifiable, that is, that markets are complete. Suppose now that a subset of states of nature are not verifiable individually, but only as a group of states, by an insurance (risk-neutral) agent. If uncertainty is additive to insurance coverage, then an optimal insurance policy is such that the *expected marginal utility* of net income over a group of unverifiable states of nature is equal to the marginal utility of the net (sure) income at a verifiable state of nature. If uncertainty is multiplicative, then an optimal insurance policy would equalize the expected marginal utility weighted

This chapter is an extension of the joint project with Mark Machina, to whom the author is very much indebted for stimulating discussions and insights. Discussions and comments at mathematical economics workshops at the California Institute of Technology, University of California, San Diego, and at the University of Minnesota were very helpful. Comments from K. J. Arrow, J. Geanakoplos, J. S. Jordan, L. L. Wilde, and an anonymous referee were especially appreciated. Financial support from National Science Foundation is gratefully acknowledged.

265

by the multiplicative stochastic yield to the marginal utility of a sure income at a verifiable state. It is of great interest to study a property of an optimal incomplete insurance policy. It is especially important to compare the *level* of utility of a verifiable state with that of expected utility of a group of unverifiable states because if the latter is higher than the former, it would introduce the moral hazard problem.

Which level of (expected) utility is higher depends crucially on the behavior of a degree of risk aversion. In the case of additive uncertainty, whether the absolute risk aversion is increasing or decreasing is a deciding factor, whereas in the case of multiplicative uncertainty, whether the relative risk aversion is increasing or decreasing along with the size of the degree of risk aversion influences the comparison of two levels of (expected) utility.

A role of severance payments in a model of implicit contracts is studied as an example of incomplete insurance. Since severance payments usually do not depend on outcomes at alternative opportunities after layoff, they are considered at best incomplete insurance for layoff. Suppose that if a worker is not laid off, then he is paid at a sure (deterministic) wage. But if a worker is laid off, then severance payments are made to him. When a worker leaves the firm, he proceeds to search an opportunity at other firms. A worker with such implicit contracts is covered against risk of layoff but not against risks over alternative opportunities outside the originally contracted firm. The first-order condition is given by an equality between the expected marginal utility of the case of layoff and the marginal utility of the case of retention. The problem can be viewed as a two-stage lottery with fair insurance policies available for the first stage only. Several results concerning comparative statics for this incomplete insurance are demonstrated. A crucial question, however, is whether an expected utility of a laid-off worker is greater or less than that of a retained worker, given the optimal amount of severance payments. If the former is the case, there is an apparent problem of moral hazard among workers. Since a probability of layoff is treated as fixed in our model, and severance payments are not paid for voluntary quits, moral hazard is ruled out. A model with an endogenous probability of layoff and an endogenous effort level is a possible topic for future research. The model and theorems in this chapter have a general property of incomplete insurance, so that interpretations and applications other than labor contracts will be suggested in the concluding section.

2   Two models of implicit contracts

Suppose a firm announces laying off a certain proportion $(1-p)$ of its labor force randomly. The rest are retained and paid the sure (deterministic) wage y. Assume the probability of retention, p, is fixed and known. Each worker has an identical monotone increasing, strictly concave, and thrice continuously differentiable, utility function $u(x)$, where x is the net monetary income. A laid-off worker proceeds to search an alternative opportunity and may be rehired at another firm. The rehiring wage, $\tilde{y}$, is stochastic before the search. Its probability distribution is identical for and known to all workers. Suppose that the firm is risk neutral and willing to offer fair insurance contingent on a verifiable state of nature for its workers. (You may assume that an outside insurance company or a labor union instead of the firm arranges a fair insurance.) By fair insurance, we mean a contingent contract with an expected payoff being equal to zero. A decision of layoff or retention is observable and verifiable by both parties. Therefore, the firm agrees to arrange severance payments to a laid-off worker. However, a fair insurance does not depend on a rehiring wage because it cannot be easily observable and verifiable by the original employer. Moreover, if the insurance were dependent on a rehiring wage, it causes a moral hazard in the worker's search for alternative employment. As Hall and Lilien (1979) observed, severance payments rarely depend on events outside the firm. We will investigate the properties of optimal severance payments as incomplete insurance of worker's net income. Two specifications of stochastic alternative wages are investigated. The first case is that uncertainty is *additive* to severance payments. The net (stochastic) income of a laid-off worker is $c + \tilde{w}$, where $\tilde{w}$ is a rehiring wage at another firm. The second case is one with a *multiplicative* uncertainty. The net income of a laid-off worker is proportional to severance payments made at the time of layoff, with a proportion being stochastic: $\tilde{y} = \tilde{r}c$. The first case is applicable if the search process does not require a substantial monetary input but rather luck in finding an opportunity. A typical case of multiplicative uncertainty is when a laid-off worker has to spend a portion of the severance payments to move and search for a new employer or to start a business. The net income of the laid-off worker will be proportional to how far search could be extended or how large scale is the business the worker starts, with a proportion being stochastic.

An extensive form of the model is illustrated in Figure 1. For the first stage of uncertainty, fair insurance is available. This is shown in payments of c for the upper branch and of $-(1-p)c/p$ for the lower branch. The payment for the upper branch is interpreted as severance payments as insurance coverage for layoff, and the cost for the lower branch is interpreted as an insurance premium for the above-mentioned insurance. The net income for a worker at the lower branch is a sure wage minus the insurance premium, $y - (1-p)c/p$. If a worker is laid off, that is, at the

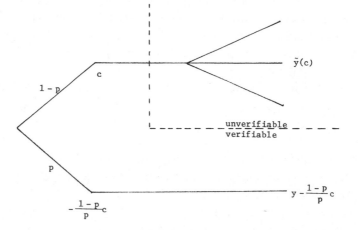

Figure 1. Model I (additive uncertainty): $\tilde{y}(c) = c + \tilde{w}$. Model II (multiplicative uncertainty): $\tilde{y}(c) = \tilde{r}c$.

upper branch, he is exposed to the second-stage uncertainty, which is not observable or verifiable by a risk-neutral agent (an insurance company). This net income, $\tilde{y}$, is stochastic and a function of severance payments. In the case of additive uncertainty, by being rehired, an income is added to severance payments. In the case of multiplicative uncertainty, the net income of the laid-off worker is proportional to severance payments. The level of optimal severance payments is determined by maximizing an ex ante (before the first-stage uncertainty is known) expected utility.

This is a logical point to comment on a difference between our model and the model proposed by Ross (1981) referring to Figure 1. An incomplete insurance model considered in Ross' paper can be identified as calculating a risk premium of the second uncertainty, which we classified as unverifiable, whereas the payments at the two branches of the first stage are different and fixed. Our problem is to find an optimal shift in payments at the first stage of uncertainty, whereas the second stage is not insurable.

A goal of this essay is to examine the properties of optimal severance payments for proposed implicit contract models. One of the questions asked is whether the level of utility in the retained worker given optimal severance payments is greater than the level of expected utility of the laid-off worker before search. This question is posed by Geanakoplos and Ito (1982) for the case of additive uncertainty, and the question about the level of expected utility is answered in Imai, Geanakoplos, and Ito (1981) without an extensive discussion. In the next two sections of this chapter, a theorem due to Imai, Geanakoplos, and Ito (1981) will be presented with a simpler proof with heuristic discussions. Moreover, a theorem for the case of multiplicative uncertainty, due to Ito and Machina (1983), will be proved in a manner parallel to a theorem for the case of additive uncertainty.

3   Theorems

In this section, we present three, of which one is well known, purely mathematical theorems relevant in solving questions posed in the preceding section. First, we prepare some notation and definition. Let us define a nonnegative random variable $\tilde{x}$ whose expected value exists and is denoted by $\bar{x}$: $E\tilde{x} \equiv \bar{x}$. A von Neumann–Morgenstern utility function of class C^3 is denoted by u: $\mathbb{R}_+ \to \mathbb{R}$. For all $y \in \mathbb{R}_+$, $u'(y) > 0$ and $u''(y) < 0$. Another von Neumann–Morgenstern utility function of class C^3 is denoted by v: $\mathbb{R}_+ \to \mathbb{R}$. For all $y \in \mathbb{R}_+$, $v'(y) > 0$. We do not necessarily impose concavity on v. Now, let us define the certainty equivalence level of $\tilde{x}$ with respect to utility function u by $\underline{x}^u$: namely, $Eu(\tilde{x}) = u(\underline{x}^u)$. A relationship between $\underline{x}^u$ and a risk premium, π_u, which is an amount a risk-averse agent with a utility function u is willing to pay to eliminate uncertainty, is calculated as follows: $\pi_u = \bar{x} - \underline{x}^u$. The Arrow–Pratt measures of risk aversion, investigated in Arrow (1965) and Pratt (1964), are defined as usual. The degree of absolute risk aversion of u is defined by

$$A_u(x) = -\frac{u''(x)}{u'(x)},$$

and the degree of relative risk aversion of u is defined by

$$R_u(x) = -\frac{xu''(x)}{u'(x)}.$$

Let us define two other functions and their "certainty equivalent" values with respect to a random variable $\tilde{x}$. A negative of marginal utility is defined by f: $f(x) \equiv -u'(x)$. By assumptions on utility function, $f'(x) > 0$. The certainty equivalence level with respect to a marginal utility function u' and random variable $\tilde{x}$ is denoted by $\hat{x}$: $Eu'(\tilde{x}) = u'(\hat{x})$ and $Ef(\tilde{x}) = f(\hat{x})$. Let us also define a weighted marginal utility, g: $g(x) \equiv xu'(x)$, and its certainty equivalence level with respect to g and $\tilde{x}$ by $x^\dagger$: $x^\dagger u'(x^\dagger) = E[\tilde{x}u'(\tilde{x})]$. Let us consider properties of g in relation to the degree of risk aversion:

$$g'(x) = u'(x) + xu''(x)$$
$$= u'(x)\{1 - R_u(x)\}.$$

Therefore,

for all x, $g'(x)\{\gtreqless\}0$,   iff, for all x, $R_u(x)\{\lesseqgtr\}1$, respectively.   (3.1)

Now let us recall a theorem proved by Pratt, which states that a person with a more risk-averse (in the sense of absolute risk aversion) utility function requires a larger risk premium, and vice versa.

Theorem 3.1 (Pratt 1964). Consider two utility functions u and v. For all x, $A_u(x)\{\lesseqgtr\}A_v(x)$, iff, for all probability distribution of $\tilde{x}$, $\underline{x}^u\{\gtreqless\}\underline{x}^v$, respectively.

Proof: Rewriting the second condition using the risk premium,

$$\underline{x}^u\{\gtreqless\}\underline{x}^v, \quad \text{iff } \pi_u\{\lesseqgtr\}\pi_v, \text{ respectively.}$$

Then, apply Pratt's Theorem 1, conditions (a) and (b).   Q.E.D.

The second theorem is the one previously proved by Imai et al. (1981). However, the following proof gives a better intuition of the theorem and is a step toward proving Theorem 3.3.

Theorem 3.2 (Imai et al. 1981). For any $\tilde{x}$, recall that $\hat{x}$ is defined by

$$u'(\hat{x}) = Eu'(\tilde{x}).$$

Then it is shown that

$$u(\hat{x})\{\lesseqgtr\}Eu(\tilde{x}), \quad \text{iff, for all } x, A'_u(x)\{\lesseqgtr\}0, \text{ respectively.}$$

Proof: Recall that $f(x) = -u'(x)$ and $f'(x) = -u''(x) > 0$. Compare the absolute risk aversion of f and u. That is, replace v by f in Pratt's theorem. Then

for all x, $A_u(x)\{\lesseqgtr\}A_f(x)$,   iff, for any $\tilde{x}, \underline{x}^u\{\gtreqless\}\hat{x}$.   (3.2)

Since the u is an increasing function,

$\underline{x}^u\{\gtreqless\}\hat{x}$,   iff, for any $\tilde{x}$, $u(\underline{x}^u)\{\gtreqless\}u(\hat{x})$,   where $u(\underline{x}^u) \equiv Eu(\tilde{x})$
and $u'(\hat{x}) \equiv Eu'(\tilde{x})$.   (3.3)

Now let us investigate that function u is more "risk averse" than f, if and only if u demonstrates an increasing risk aversion. Recalling that $f' = -u''$ and $f'' = -u'''$,

$$A_u(x) - A_f(x) = -\frac{u''(x)}{u'(x)} + \frac{u'''(x)}{u''(x)} = \frac{u'(x)u'''(x) - (u''(x))^2}{u'(x)u''(x)}. \qquad (3.4)$$

Now recall that

$$A_u'(x) = -\frac{u'(x)u'''(x) - (u''(x))^2}{(u'(x))^2}. \qquad (3.5)$$

Since $u' > 0$ and $u'' < 0$, for all x, expressions of (3.4) and (3.5) have the same sign:

for all x, $\quad A_u\{\lesseqgtr\}A_f$, iff, for all x, $A_u'(x)\{\lesseqgtr\}0$, respectively. $\qquad (3.6)$

Combining (3.2), (3.3), and (3.6), for any $\tilde{x}$, $Eu(\tilde{x})\{\gtreqless\}u(\hat{x})$, where $\hat{x}$ is defined by $u'(\hat{x}) \equiv Eu'(\tilde{x})$ iff, for all x, $A_u'(x)\{\lesseqgtr\}0$, respectively.

$$\text{Q.E.D.}$$

The next theorem extends the result of Theorem 3.2 to the case of relative risk aversion. Its proof proceeds in a similar manner, with one change that we have to differentiate two cases; one where $g'(x)$ is increasing and the other where it is decreasing.

Theorem 3.3 (Ito and Machina 1983). For any $\tilde{x}$, recall that $x^\dagger$ is defined by

$$x^\dagger u'(x^\dagger) = E[\tilde{x}u'(\tilde{x})].$$

(A)   If, for all x, $R_u(x)$ is strictly between 0 and 1, then, for any $\tilde{x}$,

$$u(x^\dagger)\{\lesseqgtr\}Eu(\tilde{x}), \quad \text{iff, for all } x, \; R_u'(x)\{\gtreqless\}0, \text{ respectively.}$$

(B)   If, for all x, $R_u(x)$ is strictly greater than 1, then, for any $\tilde{x}$,

$$u(x^\dagger)\{\gtreqless\}Eu(\tilde{x}), \quad \text{iff, for all } x, \; R_u'(x)\{\gtreqless\}0, \text{ respectively.}$$

Proof: First, consider case (A): $0 < R_u(x) < 1$. Recall that $g'(x) = u'(x)(1 - R_u(x)) > 0$ and, $g''(x) = u''(x)(1 - R_u(x)) - u'(x)R_u'(x)$. Compare the absolute risk aversion of u and g. That is, replace v by g in Pratt's theorem,

for any $\tilde{x}$, $\quad x^\dagger\{\lesseqgtr\}\underline{x}$, iff, for all x, $A_g(x)\{\gtreqless\}A_u(x)$, respectively.

$$(3.7)$$

Now check the difference in the degrees of absolute risk aversion in g and u:

$$A_g(x) - A_u(x) = \left(-\frac{g''(x)}{g'(x)}\right) - \left(-\frac{u''(x)}{u'(x)}\right)$$

$$= -\frac{u''(1-R) - u'R'}{u'(1-R)} + \frac{u''}{u'}$$

$$= \frac{R_u'(x)}{1 - R_u(x)}.$$

Since $0 < R_u(x) < 1$,

for all x, $\quad A_g(x)\{\lessgtr\}A_u(x)$, $\quad$ iff, for all x, $R_u'(x)\{\lessgtr\}0$, respectively.

(3.8)

Confirm that

$$x^\dagger\{\lessgtr\}\underline{x}^u, \quad \text{iff } u(x^\dagger)\{\lessgtr\}u(\underline{x}^u) \equiv Eu(\tilde{x}), \text{ respectively.} \tag{3.9}$$

Combining (3.7), (3.8), and (3.9), we have, for any $\tilde{x}$,

$u(x^\dagger)\{\lessgtr\}Eu(\tilde{x})$, $\quad$ where $x^\dagger u'(x^\dagger) = E[\tilde{x}u'(\tilde{x})]$, $\quad$ iff, for all x, $R_u'(x)\{\lessgtr\}0$, respectively.

For case (B), $R_u(x) > 1$. Equation (3.8) is modified since $1 - R_u(x) < 0$. Then

for all x, $\quad A_g(x)\{\lessgtr\}A_u(x)$, $\quad$ iff, for all x, $R_u'(x)\{\gtrless\}0$, respectively.

(3.8')

Combining (3.7), (3.8'), and (3.9), the desired outcome is obtained.

Q.E.D.

Two remarks are in order. First, if $R_u'(x)$ fluctuates between positive and negative, causing $R_u(x)$ to become larger and less than 1, over some range of x, then there is no unambiguous result obtained as for which is greater, $Eu(\tilde{x})$ or $u(x^\dagger)$. Second, if $R_u(x) = 1$ for all x, that is, implying $R_u'(x) = 0$ for all x, then $g'(x) = u'(x)\{1 - R_u(x)\} = 0$. Therefore, g is a constant function and $x^\dagger$ is not uniquely defined by its definition.

4   Properties of incomplete insurance

4.1   *Additive uncertainty*

Consider the model presented in Section 2 with additive uncertainty. An expected utility before the revelation of the first-stage uncertainty (layoff decision) is calculated as $V = pu(y - (1-p)c/p) + (1-p)Eu(c+\tilde{w})$. Maximizing V with respect to c gives the first-order condition

$$u'\left(y - \frac{1-p}{p}c^*\right) = Eu'(c^* + \tilde{w}). \qquad (4.1)$$

Note that the second-order condition is always satisfied because u'' is strictly negative by assumption. The above equation defines the optimal level of coverage c (severance payments) as incomplete insurance. The first question is whether the optimal coverage uniquely exits. With an appropriate assumption on $u'(0)$ and the range of $\tilde{w}$, the existence of the optimum c strictly between 0 and $py/(1-p)$ can be guaranteed.[1] Once it exists, it must be unique, because the left side of equation (4.1) is an increasing function of c, and the right side is a decreasing function of c. We assume the existence of such c^*. Now let us investigate how this c^* changes as some of the parameters change. First, the effects of an increase in probability of retention, p, on the size of optimal insurance coverage, c^*, and its premium $(1-p)c^*/p$ are analyzed. Taking total derivatives of equation (4.1) with respect to c^* and p, we have

$$-\frac{1-p}{p}u''\left(y - \frac{1-p}{p}c^*\right)dc^* + \frac{c^*}{p}u''\left(y - \frac{1-p}{p}c^*\right)dp = Eu''(c^* + \tilde{w})\,dc^*,$$

$$(4.2)$$

and rearranging terms, the following result of comparative statics is derived:

$$\frac{dc^*}{dp} = \frac{(c^*/p)u''(y - (1-p)c^*/p)}{((1-p)/p)u''(y - (1-p)c^*/p) + Eu''(c^* + \tilde{w})} > 0. \qquad (4.3)$$

The result implies that as the likelihood of retention increases, the size of severance payments increases. Since the insurance is restricted to a class of fair insurance, an increase in probability of retention can be thought of as a decrease in the price of an incomplete insurance. As the price of an insurance policy goes down, it is intuitively straightforward to have more demand for coverage. An effect of an increase in probability of retention on the size of premium, $(1-p)c^*/p$, has two channels: First, an effect through the amount of coverage, which we know is increasing, $dc^*/dp > 0$; second, the price of the coverage $(1-p)/p$ is decreasing with respect to p. By calculating a total effect, we derive the amount of premium decreases as the probability of retention increases.

$$\frac{d}{dp}\frac{1-p}{p}c^* = c^*\frac{d}{dp}\frac{1-p}{p} + \frac{1-p}{p}\frac{dc^*}{dp}$$

$$= c^* \left(-\frac{1}{p^2} \right) + \frac{c^*}{p} \frac{(1-p)u''(y-(1-p)c^*/p)}{(1-p)u''(y-(1-p)c^*/p)+pEu''(c^*+\tilde{w})}$$

$$= -\frac{c^*}{p} \cdot \frac{Eu''(c^*+\tilde{w})}{(1-p)u''(y-(1-p)c^*/p)+pEu''(c^*+\tilde{w})} < 0.$$

$$(4.4)$$

Therefore, an increase in the retention probability increases both sure income in the second branch (retention) and an income of every realization in the first branch (layoff) by increasing a coverage and reducing a premium. The incomplete insurance defined in this model is thus a normal good in the sense that a decrease in the relative price causes an increase in purchase.

Let us consider an income effect on this incomplete insurance. By taking total derivatives of equation (4.1) with respect to y and c^*, we find that an increase in sure income for the employed will lead to an increase in severance payments, that is, an increase in purchase of incomplete insurance.

$$\frac{dc^*}{dy} = \frac{u''(y-(1-p)c^*/p)}{((1-p)/p)u''(y-(1-p)c^*/p)+Eu''(c^*+\tilde{w})} > 0. \quad (4.5)$$

The effect of a change in the probability distribution of $\tilde{w}$ is difficult to analyze unless it is parameterized in some manner. We consider only a simple case here in which the "mean preserving spread" of the uncertain second-stage income can be defined. Suppose

$$\tilde{w} = \begin{cases} \bar{w}+\epsilon & \text{with probability } \frac{1}{2}, \text{ and} \\ \bar{w}-\epsilon & \text{with probability } \frac{1}{2}. \end{cases}$$

Thus, the first-order condition in this special case is written as

$$u'(y-(1-p)c^*/p) = \frac{1}{2}[u'(c+\bar{w}+\epsilon)+u'(c+\bar{w}-\epsilon)]. \quad (4.1')$$

After taking the total derivatives of (4.1') with respect to c^* and ϵ, the following expressions for an effect of the mean preserving spread, that is, a marginal change in ϵ, on the optimal incomplete insurance;

$$\frac{dc^*}{d\epsilon} = -\frac{[u''(c+\bar{w}+\epsilon)-u''(c+\bar{w}-\epsilon)]}{(2(1-p)/p)u''(y-(1-p)c^*/p)+u''(c+\bar{w}+\epsilon)+u''(c+\bar{w}-\epsilon)}.$$

$$(4.6)$$

Note that the denominator is always negative, because $u'' < 0$ for all x. Therefore, considering the negative sign in front, the sign of the equation is the same as the sign of the numerator, which is determined by the sign of the third derivative of the utility function. Hence, for any $\bar{w}$ and ϵ, $\dfrac{dc^*}{d\epsilon}\{\gtreqless\}0,$ iff, for all x, $u'''\{\gtreqless\}0$, respectively.

$$(4.7)$$

At first glance, it may seem counterintuitive to find a case where an optimal level of severance payments decreases in response to an increase in the variance of uncertainty in income of the laid off. Let us look closely at how this happens. When u' is concave, adding an uncertainty given the level of c^* decreases $Eu'(c^*+\tilde{w})$. That is, a mean preserving spread decreases the expected "marginal" utility. Recall that $Eu'(c+\tilde{w})$ is shown to be decreasing in c, and that $u'(y-(1-p)c/p)$ is increasing in c. An optimal response to a mean preserving spread, which has an effect of decreasing the expected marginal utility, should be a decrease in severance payments, which has an effect of increasing the expected marginal utility. In fact, the marginal effect of severance payments becomes more effective by more uncertainty in rehiring wages. Therefore, a lesser amount of severance payments is necessary to achieve the first-order condition. An intuition of increasing risk premium for more uncertainty comes from the equality of the levels of utility, whereas the first-order condition for an incomplete insurance is the equality of (expected) marginal utilities. However, this case of concave u' implies an increasing absolute risk aversion, which is not very likely.

Now we are ready to analyze a crucial question, whether the level of utility obtained by a retained worker is more or less than the expected utility of a laid-off worker before search, given the optimal level of severance payments. A question can be phrased in terms of Figure 1 as follows. At the time of first branching but before the full evolution of an event, which branch commands more (expected) utility, the first or the second? Although the expected marginal utility is equalized between the two branches, it is not clear how the levels of utility compare in the two branches. The following proposition gives the answer.

Proposition 4.1. For any uncertainty of rehiring wage, given the optimal incomplete insurance, that is, equation (4.1), the level of utility of a retained worker is higher than (equal to, or lowerer than, respectively) the level of expected utility of a laid-off worker before a search of rehiring wage if and only if the absolute risk aversion is increasing (constant, or decreasing, respectively) for all levels of income.

Proof: Define $\hat{x}$ by $y-(1-p)c^*/p$ and $\tilde{x}$ by $c^*+\tilde{w}$, and then apply Theorem 3.2.   Q.E.D.

The best way to understand this result is to recall the discussion of the effect of a mean-preserving spread, extending an analysis to its effect on $Eu(x)$ of the laid-off worker. When $u'(x)$ is concave, that is, $A'_u(x) > 0$, a mean-preserving spread has the effect of decreasing both $Eu'(x)$ and $Eu(x)$ for the laid-off worker given the level of severance payments. To keep the first-order condition, the level of severance payments has to be adjusted, and again the concavity of $u'(x)$ implies that the level of c has to be decreased, which also decreases the level of $Eu(x)$. These two effects on $Eu(x)$ reinforce each other and have a definite decreasing effect on the expected utility of the laid-off worker. Consider the conceptual experiment of mean-preserving spread for some interval, and the case of increasing absolute risk aversion is understood. For the case of decreasing absolute risk aversion, two channels of effect of a mean-preserving spread on $Eu(x)$ have opposite signs. Namely, a mean-preserving spread has a direct decreasing effect on $Eu(x)$ because of the concavity of $u(x)$. However, from an investigation of optimal adjustment of severance payments, we know that the convexity of $u'(x)$ implies that c^* increases for a mean-preserving spread. Then the total effect of a mean-preserving effect on $Eu(x)$ depends on the relative strengths of the two effects, namely, relative "concaveness" of $u(x)$ and $-u'(x)$.

4.2   Multiplicative case

Now let us investigate a case of multiplicative uncertainty. An expected utility before the layoff decision is $Z = pu(y - (1-p)c/p) + (1-p)Eu(\tilde{r}c)$. Maximizing Z with respect to severance payments c, we derive the first-order condition

$$u'\left(y - \frac{1-p}{p}c\right) = E[\tilde{r}u'(\tilde{r}c)]. \tag{4.8}$$

Multiplying c on both sides of the above equation yields

$$cu'\left(y - \frac{1-p}{p}c\right) = E(\tilde{r}cu'(\tilde{r}c)]. \tag{4.8'}$$

It is easy to find a condition on $u'(0)$ and on the range of r such that there exists a c that satisfies (4.8). Given that such a c exists, it is unique, because the left side of (4.8) is increasing in c, and the right side is decreasing in c.

Now let us investigate comparative statics questions. To that end, it is convenient to decompose a stochastic yield $\tilde{r}$ into a mean and disturbances around the mean,

$$\tilde{r} = \bar{r} + \tilde{\theta}, \qquad E\tilde{\theta} = 0.$$

Moreover, define a special case of a mean preserving spread as

$$\tilde{\theta} = \begin{cases} \theta & \text{with probability } \frac{1}{2}, \\ -\theta & \text{with probability } \frac{1}{2}. \end{cases}$$

First, let us check the effect of an increase of the mean yield on the optimal level of severance payments. Taking the total derivatives of the first-order condition, we obtain

$$-\frac{1-p}{p} u'' \left(y - \frac{1-p}{p} c \right) dc - E(\tilde{r})^2 u''(\tilde{r}c)\, dc$$

$$= E(\tilde{r}c) u''(\tilde{r}c)\, d\bar{r} + E u'(\tilde{r}c)\, d\bar{r}. \tag{4.9}$$

Noticing that $u'(\tilde{r}c) + (\tilde{r}c) u''(\tilde{r}c) = u'(\tilde{r}c)\{1 - R_u(\tilde{r}c)\}$,

$$\frac{dc^*}{d\bar{r}} = -\frac{E\{u'(\tilde{r}c)(1 - R_u(\tilde{r}c))\}}{((1-p)/p) u''(y - (1-p)c/p) - E\tilde{r}u''(\tilde{r}c)}. \tag{4.10}$$

Therefore, we derive that

if, for all x, $R_u(x)\{\lessgtr\}1$, then $\dfrac{dc^*}{d\bar{r}}\{\gtrless\}0$.

Second, let us investigate the effect of a mean-preserving spread on the optimal level of severance payments. Rewriting the first-order condition for the special case of a mean-preserving spread defined above,

$$u'\left(y - \frac{1-p}{p} c \right) = \tfrac{1}{2}(\bar{r}+\theta) u'((\bar{r}+\theta)c) + \tfrac{1}{2}(\bar{r}-\theta) u'((\bar{r}-\theta)c). \tag{4.11}$$

Taking the total derivative with respect to c and θ and rearranging terms, we have (denoting $\bar{r}+\theta$ by r^+ and $\bar{r}-\theta$ by r^-)

$$\frac{dc^*}{d\theta} = -\frac{u'(r^+c)[1 - R_u(r^+c)] - u'(r^-c)[1 - R_u(r^-c)]}{2\dfrac{(1-p)}{p} u''\left(y - \dfrac{(1-p)c}{p} \right) + (r^+)^2 u''(r^+c) + (r^-)^2 u''(r^-c)}. \tag{4.12}$$

Therefore, knowing $u'(x) > 0$, and $u''(x) < 0$, for all x,

if $R_u'(x)\{\lessgtr\}0$ and $R_u(x)\{\gtrless\}1$, then $\dfrac{dc^*}{d\theta}\{\gtrless\}0$.

Now we are interested in knowing whether the optimal severance payment exceeds an amount of the net (sure) income of the employed, namely, whether c^* or $y-(1-p)c/p$ is greater. The severance payment may seem too large an amount if it is larger than the net (sure) income. However, this is perfectly plausible, because severance payments are relevant only for the case of layoff with probability $1-p$, which may be very small. This question is not only interesting in itself but is also important for answering the crucial question of whether the retained or the laid-off worker has a higher (expected) utility given optimal severance payments. Two steps are needed to answer this question. First, consider the case of certainty; second, add the effect of a mean-preserving spread. Suppose that $\theta=0$ is always the case. Then the first-order condition is rewritten as

$$c^*u'(y-(1-p)c/p)=\bar{r}cu'(\bar{r}c). \tag{4.8''}$$

Recall that $g(x)=xu'(x)$ is increasing, constant, or decreasing depending on whether the degree of relative risk aversion is greater than, equal to, or smaller than 1, respectively. Therefore, defining $\bar{r}c=x$,

$$\frac{d(\text{RHS}(4.8''))}{d(\bar{r}c)}\{\lessgtr\}0, \quad \text{iff, for all } x,\ R_u(x)\{\gtrless\}0, \text{ respectively.}$$

where RSH(4.8″) refers to the right side of equation (4.8″). Now suppose $R_u(x)>1$ and $\bar{r}>1$. By $\bar{r}>1$, we know immediately $\bar{r}c>c$. By $R_u(x)>1$, we know $g'(x)<0$, which implies, in relation to (4.8″),

$$\bar{r}cu'(\bar{r}c)<cu'(c). \tag{4.13A}$$

Replace the left side of (4.13) by the left side of (4.8″):

$$cu'(y-(1-p)c/p)<cu'(c). \tag{4.13B}$$

Dividing both sides by $c>0$ yields

$$u'(y-(1-p)c/p)<u'(c). \tag{4.13C}$$

Since the marginal utility is a decreasing function,

$$(y-(1-p)c/p)>c, \tag{4.13D}$$

that is,

$$py>c. \tag{4.13E}$$

Let us consider a second case: $R_u>1$ and $\bar{r}<1$. This implies $\bar{r}c<c$. Then all the inequalities in (4.13A) through (4.13E) become opposite.

In the third case, $R_u(x)<1$ and $\bar{r}>1$, which implies $\bar{r}c>c$. But now $g'(x)>0$, so all the inequalities in (4.13A) through (4.13E) again become opposite.

Table 1. *Certainty case* $\theta = 0$.

	$\bar{r} < 1$	$\bar{r} = 1$	$\bar{r} > 1$
For all x, $R_u(x) > 1$	$c^* > py$	$c^* = py$	$c^* < py$
For all x, $R_u(x) = 1$	$c^* = py$	$c^* = py$	$c^* = py$
For all x, $R_u(x) < 1$	$c^* < py$	$c^* = py$	$c^* > py$

As may be easily guessed, in the fourth case,

$$R_u(x) < 1 \quad \text{and} \quad \bar{r} > 1.$$

All the inequalities in (4.13A) through (4.13E) hold true.

Lastly, if $R_u(x) = 1$ and/or $\bar{r} = 1$, then all the inequalities above become equalities. In summary, we have the classification in Table 1 for the question of whether severance payments are greater or smaller than net (sure) income.

It should be remembered that Table 1 is derived for the certainty case. Now let us consider the second effect, that is, an effect of uncertainty. For this exercise, it is enough to recall the result for the mean-preserving spread; that is,

$$\frac{dc^*}{d\theta} \{\gtreqless\} 0, \quad \text{iff, for all } x, \ R_u(x) \{\gtreqless\} 1, \text{ respectively.}$$

This uncertainty effect reinforces the case of certainty only in the case of $\bar{r} < 1$. If $\bar{r} = 1$, then $c^* > py$ for $R_u(x) > 1$, and vice versa. Note that for the case of $\bar{r} > 1$, the uncertainty effect and the case of certainty cancel each other, so that the total effect is ambiguous. The combined case is summarized in Table 2.

By continuity of functions involved, we can show that $\bar{r}^*$ such that $c = py$ has the following properties. As uncertainty becomes small, that is, $\theta \to 0$, $\bar{r}^*$ must converge to 1. If $R_u(x) > 1$ for all x, and it becomes larger everywhere, then $\bar{r}^*$ becomes further away from 1. By the same argument, if $R_u(x) < 1$, and it becomes smaller everywhere, then $\bar{r}^*$ becomes further away from 1.

Finally, we are ready to answer whether a laid-off worker is better or worse off in the expected utility sense than a retained worker in the multiplicative uncertainty case. As we have seen in answers to other questions, whether the degree of relative risk aversion is greater or smaller than 1

Table 2. *General case $\theta > 0$.*

			$\bar{r} > 1$		
	$\bar{r} < 1$	$\bar{r} = 1$	$\theta \gg 0$ $\bar{r} \approx 1$	For some combination of θ and $\bar{r}$	$\theta \approx 0$ $\bar{r} \gg 1$
For all x, $R_u(x) > 1$	$c^* > py$	$c^* > py$	$c^* > py$	$c^* = py$	$c^* < py$
For all x, $R_u(x) = 1$	$c^* = py$	$c^* = py$	$c^* = py$	$c^* = py$	$c^* = py$
For all x, $R_u(x) < 1$	$c^* < py$	$c^* < py$	$c^* < py$	$c^* = py$	$c^* > py$

makes a crucial difference. It is also important to classify whether c^* is greater or smaller than py.

We start with the case where $c^* > py$, that is, $c^* > y - (1-p)c/p$. Recall that this is likely if $R_u(x) > 1$ and $\bar{r} < 1$, or if $0 < R_u(x) < 1$, and $\bar{r}$ is sufficiently larger than 1. Multiplying $u'(\cdot)$ on both sides of $c > y - (1-p)c/p$, we have

$$c^* u'\left(y - \frac{1-p}{p} c^*\right) > \left(y - \frac{1-p}{p} c^*\right) u'\left(y - \frac{1-p}{p} c^*\right). \qquad (4.14)$$

By substituting the first-order condition (4.8′) into the left side of (4.14), it is shown that

$$E(\tilde{r}c^* u'(\tilde{r}c^*)) > \left(y - \frac{1-p}{p} c^*\right) u'\left(y - \frac{1-p}{p} c^*\right). \qquad (4.15)$$

Suppose that there exists an $x^\dagger$ such that

$$E(\tilde{r}c^* u'(\tilde{r}c)) = x^\dagger u'(x^\dagger). \qquad (4.16)$$

From (4.15) and (4.16),

$$x^\dagger u'(x^\dagger) > \left(y - \frac{1-p}{p} c^*\right) u'\left(y - \frac{1-p}{p} c^*\right). \qquad (4.17)$$

Now we come to the point of differentiating subcases, depending on the size of the degree of relative risk aversion. Recall that if for all x, $R_u(x) > 1$, then $g'(x) < 0$. Then applying this relationship to (4.17),

$$x^\dagger < y - (1-p)c/p.$$

On the other hand, if for all x, $0 < R_u(x) < 1$, then $g'(x) > 0$; that is,

$$x^\dagger > y - (1-p)c/p.$$

In sum, we have the following relationships:

if, for all x, $R_u(x) > 1$, then $u(x^\dagger) < u\left(y - \dfrac{1-p}{p}c^*\right)$, (4.18A)

and

if, for all x, $0 < R_u(x) < 1$, then $u(x^\dagger) > u\left(y - \dfrac{1-p}{p}c^*\right)$. (4.18B)

At this point we apply Theorem 3.3, which was proved in the last section. Regarding equation (4.16), suppose for all x, $R_u(x) > 1$. Then, for any $\tilde{r}$,

$$u(x^\dagger)\{\gtreqless\}Eu(\tilde{r}c^*), \quad \text{iff, for all } x, \ R'_u(x)\{\gtreqless\}0; \quad (4.19A)$$

and suppose for all x, $0 < R_u(x) < 1$. Then, for any $\tilde{r}$,

$$u(x^\dagger)\{\lesseqgtr\}Eu(\tilde{r}c), \quad \text{iff, for all } x, \ R'_u(x)\{\gtreqless\}0. \quad (4.19B)$$

By combining (4.18) and (4.19), we have a relationship between $Eu(\tilde{r}c^*)$ and $u(y - (1-p)c^*/p)$. Suppose for all x, $R_u(x) > 1$. If:

(i) for all x, $R'_u(x) \le 0$, then

$$Eu(\tilde{r}c^*) \le u(x^\dagger) < u\left(y - \frac{1-p}{p}c^*\right); \quad (4.20A)$$

(ii) for all x, $R'_u(x) > 0$, then it is ambiguous whether $Eu(\tilde{r}c^*)$ is greater or smaller than $u(y - [(1-p)/p]c^*)$ because both are greater than $u(x^\dagger)$.

Suppose for all x, $0 < R_u(x) < 1$. If:

(i) for all x, $R'_u(x) \ge 0$, then

$$Eu(\tilde{r}c^*) \ge u(x^\dagger) > u\left(y - \frac{1-p}{p}c^*\right); \quad (4.20B)$$

(ii) for all x, $R'_u(x) < 0$, then whether $Eu(\tilde{r}c^*)$ is greater or smaller than $u(y - [(1-p)/p]c^*)$ is ambiguous because both are smaller than $u(x^\dagger)$.

For the case of $c^* < y - (1-p)c/p$, that is, $c^* < py$, appropriate inequalities should be reversed, but an analysis works in the same manner. Ambiguous cases occur in the case of increasing relative risk aversion: $R'_u(x) > 0$.

Lastly, if $c^* = py$, then

$$c^*u'\left(y - \frac{1-p}{p}c^*\right) = \left(y - \frac{1-p}{p}c^*\right)u'\left(y - \frac{1-p}{p}c^*\right).$$

Table 3

			1. For all x, $R'_u(x) > 0$	2. For all x, $R'_u(x) = 0$	3. For all x, $R'_u(x) < 0$
1. For all x, $R_u(x) > 1$	$\bar{r} < 1$ / $\bar{r} = 1$	$c^* > py$		$Eu(\tilde{r}c^*) < u\left(y - \dfrac{1-p}{p}c^*\right)$	Ambiguous
		$c^* = py$		$Eu(\cdot) = u(\cdot\cdot)$	
	$\bar{r} > 1$	$c^* < py$	Ambiguous	$Eu(\tilde{r}c^*) > u\left(y - \dfrac{1-p}{p}c^*\right)$	
2. For all x, $0 < R_u(x) < 1$	$\bar{r} > 1$	$c^* > py$		$Eu(\tilde{r}c) > u\left(y - \dfrac{1-p}{p}c^*\right)$	Ambiguous
		$c^* = py$		$Eu(\cdot) = u(\cdot\cdot)$	
	$\bar{r} = 1$ / $\bar{r} < 1$	$c^* < py$	Ambiguous	$Eu(\tilde{r}c^*) < u\left(y - \dfrac{1-p}{p}c^*\right)$	
3. For all x, $R_u(x) = 1$	For any $\bar{r}$	$c^* = py$	Not possible	$Eu(\tilde{r}c^*) = u\left(y - \dfrac{1-p}{p}c^*\right)$	Not possible

Therefore, applying the first-order condition,

$$E[\tilde{r}c^*u'(\tilde{r}c^*)] = (y - (1-p)c^*/p)u'(\cdot).$$

Apply Theorem 3.3 by interpreting $\tilde{x} = \tilde{r}c^*$, and $x^\dagger = y - (1-p)c^*/p$.
   Suppose $R_u(x) > 1$. Then, for any $\tilde{r}$,

$$u(x^\dagger)\{\geqq\}Eu(\tilde{r}c^*), \quad \text{iff, for all } x, \ R'_u(x)\{\geqq\}0. \tag{4.21A}$$

Suppose $0 < R_u(x) < 1$. Then, for any $\tilde{r}$,

$$u(x^\dagger)\{\leqq\}Eu(\tilde{r}c^*), \quad \text{iff, for all } x, \ R'_u(x)\{\geqq\}0. \tag{4.21B}$$

   Suppose that the degree of relative risk aversion is equal to 1 for all x; namely, it is constant relative risk aversion, $R'_u(x) = 0$. Then $u(x^\dagger)$ is equal to $Eu(\tilde{r}x^*)$. Note that $x^\dagger$ is uniquely determined by the first-order condition.
   The results are summarized in Table 3.
   Let us consider whether this multiplicative uncertainty case has a moral hazard problem like the one in the additive uncertainty case. First, we

need a reasonable estimate of the degree and derivative of relative risk aversion. Although many economists agree that absolute risk aversion is decreasing, such consensus is not reached for the relative risk aversion. The degree of risk aversion seems to be more than 1, that is, $R_u(x) < 1$ for all x, according to Grossman and Shiller (1981) and Friend and Blume (1975).[2] In Friend and Blume (1975) and Blume and Friend (1975), they claim that their findings are consistent with decreasing or constant relative risk aversion. Cohn, Lewellen, Lease, and Schlarbaum (1975) conclude that relative risk aversion declines as wealth increases across households. However, Siegel and Hoban (1982) have recently issued a caution on the above-mentioned studies. The last finding suggests that relative risk aversion may be increasing in the less wealthy families and decreasing in the more wealthy ones, where wealth includes human capital as well as financial assets. These studies are not conclusive not only because they differ in conclusions but also because they are cross-sectional studies instead of, say, panel data analyses. But this essay is not an empirical analysis. All that is desired here is a reasonable estimate of the degree and derivative of relative risk aversion. It seems to us that the degree of relative risk aversion is greater than 1, and it may be decreasing or constant, or at least not strongly increasing. Suppose also that the mean of the stochastic yield on severance payments is larger than 1, that is, $\bar{r} > 1$. This assumption is very plausible if the laid-off worker is allowed to keep money and does not go on a costly search. The last assumption is that $c^* < py$, which can be justified by a sufficiently large r or by a sufficiently small θ. After all, a combination of these assumptions derived from evidence points to the case depicted in Table 3 enclosed by bold lines. In other words, with optimal severance payments, the laid-off worker is better off than the worker who is retained at the point of layoff and before search of rehiring: $Eu(\bar{r}c) > u(y - (1 - p)c/p)$.

5 Examples

In this section, two simple examples will be presented to illustrate some aspects of the basic framework described in Section 2. The first example shows what kind of model yields multiplicative uncertainty, and the second example clarifies the moral hazard problem.

5.1 Human capital investment

Suppose that human capital investment has multiplicative uncertainty in its outcome as productivity. Moreover, human capital is *firm specific*, so that investment has to be made again when the worker moves from one firm to another. There are two kinds of workers: those with high productivity and those with low productivity. Workers with high productivity can successfully invest the "seed money" z into human capital and yield $\tilde{r}_s z$, where $s = g, b$ and $r_s \in (r_s^{\min}, r_s^{\max})$. Workers with low productivity yield only $\bar{y}$, where $r_s^{\min} z > \bar{y}$.

Assume that each worker has a two-period life. The firm would recruit young workers with seed money z without knowing whether a particular worker is a high-productivity or low-productivity type. After one period, regardless of its state of nature, s, the firm can segregate low-productivity workers and fire them without severance payments. Those who proved to be high-productivity workers enter a second-period contract, which is described in Section 2.

It remains to be explained why the individual productivity risk can be insured in addition to the state-of-the-nature risk, and why those who are laid off (as opposed to fired) cannot get insurance on their individual productivity risk $\tilde{r}$.

Those who proved to be high-productivity workers can be insured by the firm they were attached to in the first period because the firm knows that the particular individual has invested in human (firm-specific) capital. Thus, the firm can expect the individual productivity to be $y_g = E_{\tilde{r}} \tilde{r}_g z$ in $s = g$, and $y_b = E_{\tilde{r}} \tilde{r}_b z$ in $s = b$, on average (as a result of the law of large numbers).

In the event of $s = b$, the proportion r of high-productivity workers are laid off. In the spot market of older workers (in the second period of their life cycle), there are many low-productivity workers and some high-productivity workers. Because of this adverse selection problem, it is straightforward that the firm hiring from this spot market would not insure the productivity risk $\tilde{r}$. The wage negotiated in the spot market is thus equal to the productivity found ex post. The laid-off worker uses the severance payment to invest in the new (firm-specific) human capital. Thus, the alternative income that the laid-off worker commands is $\tilde{r}c$.

In sum, a contract the older high-productivity worker negotiates before the state of the nature is known has the structure described in Section 2, the case of multiplicative uncertainty.

5.2   Disability insurance

In the model presented in Section 2, worker's separation from the firm is assumed to be initiated by the firm. Although the fact that the laid-off worker commands the expected utility higher than the retained worker poses a curious feature of the model, suggesting the moral hazard problem, the model is internally consistent in that the retained workers are not allowed to collect the severance payments if they choose to quit the firm voluntarily.

Let us describe an example that is slightly different from that in Section 2 in order to illustrate a moral hazard problem in action. Suppose a constant proportion p of workers are disabled by accidents in a period. Those who are disabled are sent home with severance payments c and earn an extra income $\tilde{y}$. Those who remain at the firm with no accident produce $\bar{y}$, where $E_{\tilde{y}} \tilde{y} < \bar{y}$. Suppose that disabilities (accidents) are observable and verifiable. Then the optimal contract between the risk-neutral firm and the risk-averse workers is obtained by solving

$$\max_{c} pu(\bar{y} - (1-p)c/p) + (1-p)E_{\tilde{y}}u(c + \tilde{y}).$$

The first-order condition is obtained as $u'(\bar{y} - (1-p)c^*/p) = E_{\tilde{y}}u'(c^* + \tilde{y})$. By Theorem 3.2, we know that $u(\bar{y} - (1-p)c^*/p) < Eu(c^* + \tilde{y})$, in case of decreasing absolute risk aversion. That is, the disabled is better off.

Suppose now that disability is not observable (e.g., headaches instead of a physical handicap). Obviously, the above solution would not be viable, because the not-disabled workers would claim that they had an accident.

In case of unobservable disabilities, the contract problem to be solved has to have the *incentive compatibility* constraint, that is, the not-disabled worker has an incentive to stay. The contract problem is formulated as

$$\max_{c} pu(\bar{y} - (1-p)c/p) + (1-p)E_{\tilde{y}}u(c + \tilde{y})$$

$$\text{subject to } u(\bar{y} - (1-p)c/p) \geq Eu(c + \tilde{y}).$$

By Theorem 3.2, the above constraint is always binding when absolute risk aversion is decreasing. Thus the optimal level of severance payments is determined by $Eu(\hat{c} + \tilde{y}) = u(\bar{y} - (1-p)\hat{c}/p)$. It is easy to verify $\hat{c} < c^*$. To prevent the moral hazard problem of falsely claiming disabilities, the level of severance payments has to be reduced, thus distorting first-best (full-information) risk sharing. With $\hat{c}$, the disabled and the not disabled are perfectly separated.

This example illustrates how Theorem 3.2 can be used to check whether the incentive compatibility constraint (preventing the moral hazard problem) is binding or not.

6   Concluding remarks

Our theoretical model predicts that both additive and multiplicative uncertainty that is not verifiable by an insurance company results in severance payments so high that the expected utility of the laid-off worker is higher than the sure utility of the retained, under reasonable assumptions on risk aversion. On the way to these results, we have proved a new theorem on incomplete insurance. There are two ways to interpret our counterintuitive results. First, severance payments cannot be so high in a real world in order to prevent an apparent moral hazard problem, which is assumed away in our model by a fixed p and no severance payments to voluntary quits. If this is a case, then it is of interest to investigate how severance payments have to be reduced to the second-best solution with a moral hazard constraint. It is also important to know whether there is any institutional device to prevent a moral hazard and thus to increase severance payments toward the level of the first-best solution. Second, severance payments defined in this model may be broadened to include human capital, which is increased through a tenure of employment before a layoff. Then it may be true that severance payments with human capital are indeed very large, so that the laid-off worker is as well off, if not better off, as the retained. However, these questions are beyond the scope of this chapter and should be investigated soon.

The models considered in this essay imply the general properties of incomplete insurance, not only for implicit contract models but also for any other applications. For example, it is possible to interpret two branches of an extensive form of our model as "accident" and "no accident" or as "sick" and "healthy," where the true costs, including psychological hardships, of accident or sickness are not observable and hence not insurable. These applications of incomplete insurance other than severance payments were briefly illustrated in Section 5. A full investigation of those models is on my agenda for future research, and the theorems proved in this essay will be relevant to those applications.

NOTES

1 The assumptions to guarantee the existence of c^* such that $0 < c^* < py/(1-p)$ are $-u'(y) + Eu'(\tilde{w}) > 0$ and $-u'(0) + Eu'(\tilde{w} + py/(1-p)) < 0$.

2 Grossman and Shiller (1981) restricted themselves to a class of utility functions with a constant risk aversion and measured the size of the degree of risk aversion. In that sense, it is not consistent to combine their work with that of others, which asserts decreasing or increasing relative risk aversion.

REFERENCES

Arrow, K. J. (1965), "The theory of risk aversion," in *Aspects of the theory of risk-bearing,* Helsinki: Yrjo Jahnssionin Saatio.

Blume, M. E. and I. Friend (1975), "The asset structure of individual portfolios and some implications for utility functions," *Journal of Finance* 30: 585–603.

Cohn, R. A., W. G. Lewellen, R. C. Lease, and G. G. Schlarbaum (1975), "Individual investor risk aversion and investment portfolio composition," *Journal of Finance* 30: 605–20.

Friend, I. and M. E. Blume (1975), "The demand for risky assets," *American Economic Review* 65: 900–22.

Geanakoplos, J. and T. Ito (1982), "On implicit contracts and involuntary unemployments," Discussion Paper No. 81-155R, Center for Economic Research, Department of Economics, University of Minnesota.

Grossman, S. and R. J. Shiller (1981), "The determinants of the variability of stock market prices," *American Economic Review* 71: 222–27.

Hall, R. E. and D. M. Lilien (1979), "Efficient wage bargains under uncertain supply and demand," *American Economic Review* 69: 868–79.

Imai, H., J. Geanakoplos, and T. Ito (1981), "Incomplete insurance and absolute risk aversion," *Economics Letters* 8: 107–12.

Ito, T. and M. J. Machina (1983), "The incentive implications of incomplete insurance: The multiplicative case," *Economics Letters,* 13: 319–23.

Pratt, J. W. (1964), "Risk aversion in the small and in the large," *Econometrica* 32: 112–36.

Ross, S. A. (1981), "Some stronger measures of risk aversion in the small and the large with applications," *Econometrica* 49: 621–38.

Siegel, F. W. and J. P. Hoban Jr. (1982), "Relative risk aversion revisited," *Review of Economics and Statistics* 64: 481–87.

CHAPTER 11

An exercise in non-Walrasian analysis

Frank Hahn

Kenneth Arrow "bestrides the world like a colossus," and in this instance that is a cause for celebration and not for conspiracy. There is hardly any area of our subject which he has not illuminated and often profoundly changed. But I hold it to be an almost equal claim on our admiration that he has always known what he is about. This is a surprisingly rare virtue among economists. By "knowing what he is about" I mean that he has always been as much aware of what has been left out as of what his virtuosity allowed him to include. That is why having (with Debreu) founded modern general equilibrium theory, we find him also active in information theory, organisation theory, and the theories of racial discrimination and of health insurance, to name only a few. There is no evidence that he has ever considered it satisfactory to assume actual economies to be (more or less) perpetually in Arrow–Debreu equilibrium. Indeed, his pioneering work with Hurwicz on stability suggests that he has very properly held the view that the triumph of the invisible hand in bringing about equilibrium, if indeed it does this, is something to be explained and not assumed. In other words, like all great theorists, he has always known precisely what the limits of applicability of any given theory are.

The present essay is written in what I hope is the Arrowian spirit although, alas, without Arrowian penetration and conclusiveness. Its theme is very simple. When we use an equilibrium concept, we are singling out a subset of possible states of the economy for special attention. To say that an economy is in equilibrium is only of interest if it excludes other *possible* states of the economy. That is why we need existence proofs and why it is not a fruitful use of equilibrium to assert that only equilibrium states are possible.

I owe much to discussions with Robert Solow who, however, is innocent of anything unfortunate in this essay. I have also had useful comments from Walter Heller.

For Walrasian economies, the equilibrium notion is motivated by an implicit dynamics (and *not* by the fundamental theorem of welfare economics that, after all, Arrow had to prove). This dynamics is the proposition that prices will change if the optimally formulated plans of agents are mutually incompatible. Or to look at the other side, we can think of no reason for prices to change (in the absence of unforeseen shocks) when an economy is in equilibrium.

Now it was Arrow (1959) who drew our attention to the difficulties with this notion when decisions to change price are as much a matter of rational calculation as are decisions to consume or produce. If one takes account of this observation, then it has consequences for the appropriate equilibrium notion. It must now include some explicit condition that it is not optimal for any agent to change price. This, one can argue, will still be true in states that are Walrasian equilibrium states. But there may also be others, and that is what this chapter is about.

I have, because that is where my present research interests lie, taken a simple general equilibrium model in which it is the price of labour alone that does not fit the implicit dynamics underlying the Walrasian equilibrium notion. Specifically, I consider a general equilibrium model in which the price of labour only falls if the Walrasian excess supply of labour exceeds a certain level in absolute value. There are three things to do with this hypothesis. First, one must formulate the appropriate equilibrium concept. Second, one must show that it is not vacuous and that besides containing the Walrasian equilibrium it has others. Third, one must offer some justification for the basic hypothesis I call limited downward flexibility of wages (LDFW). These three projects summarise the plan of this essay.

First, it will be obvious that if there are non-Walrasian equilibria, these will involve quantity constraints. But it is the virtue of the approach that *no* prices are set exogenously. It is therefore not a "fixed price" model I study. Second, it will transpire that there are, as expected, a continuum of these equilibria. Since I motivate my equilibrium concept by the absence of forces leading to a change in prices, an economy could be stuck away from Walrasian equilibrium. The welfare and policy implications of this I have regarded as too obvious to require elaboration. However, the following obvious point, in the light of the current literature, needs stressing. If market economies do not deliver their Arrow–Debreu fruits the explanation must be sought in those features of actual economies which do not appear in that construction or simply in the absence of equilibrium. I have here chosen the first route, which essentially is an absence of coordination that can arise when prices are not "called." It may be that this particular route will ultimately prove unpersuasive. But I am sure that it must be explored if one is to avoid the "ad hocery" of simply always taking prices to be Walrasian equilibrium prices.

There is one last remark. The "justifications" I offer for limited downward wage flexibility are as far as I know new but not necessarily the best. There are many others that come from bargaining theory, efficiency wage theory, concern with relative wages, and so on. The reason I do not discuss these is twofold: They are known and I do not at present see how to incorporate them into a general equilibrium model.

1   The model

I consider an economy of n goods and labour (goods are indexed by $i = 1, \ldots, n$, labour by 0). I am here concerned with an economy at one moment of time. Let $p \in R_+^{n+1}$ be the price vector. Let $x \in R_+^{n+1}$ be a household's consumption vector. All households have the same strictly concave utility function $u(x)$, each is endowed with one unit of leisure, and each is entitled to the same share of profits. The budget constraint is $p \cdot x \le p_0 + (1/m)\pi(p)$ when there are m households and $\pi(p)$ represents total profits at p. In addition, the household faces the constraint

$$x_0 - 1 \ge b \quad \text{where} \quad b < 0.$$

The vector of aggregate excess demand functions is $\xi(p)$ if the constraint is slack at p and $\hat{\xi}(p, b)$ if it is not. One calls the former the *Walrasian* and the latter the *labour-restricted* excess demand function vector. Notice that this formulation excludes the possibility of firms being quantity constrained [since b is the only argument of $\hat{\xi}(\cdot)$]. Hence, in what follows, the behaviour of the economy is only defined for a nonpositive Walrasian excess demand function for labour.

Definition 1.1. I shall say that (p^0, b^0) is an equilibrium if $b^0 < 0$, $p^0 \in \Delta$ (the simplex):

(a) $\qquad \hat{\xi}(p^0, b^0) = 0,$

$\hfill (1.1)$

(b) $\qquad \xi_0(p^0) + a(p^0) \ge 0,$

where $a(p) > 0$ for all $p \in \Delta$.

I shall now justify this definition in a preliminary way.

First notice that if p^* is the ordinary Walrasian equilibrium, $(p^*, -1)$ is an equilibrium according to Definition 1.1. For $\hat{\xi}(p^*, -1) = \xi(p)$. Now

(a) of equation (1.1) essentially says that a necessary condition for $\dot{p}_i' = 0$, $i = 1, ..., n$ is that all labour-constrained excess demands are zero. (I am here ignoring the case of some zero prices.) But a sufficient condition for $\dot{p}_0 = 0$ is the additional requirement that the excess Walrasian supply of labour be less in absolute value than $a(p)$. I call this the hypothesis of *limited downward flexibility of wages* (LDFW). I discuss this hypothesis and the function $a(p)$ in more detail below. Here we note that an equilibrium of Definition 1.1 is *not* a rationing equilibrium of the Belgian–French variety. It is not based on exogenously given prices but on direct postulates of some features of an adjustment process that in turn serves to motivate the equilibrium concept.

The story behind Definition 1.1 is this: Price changes are brought about by agents and not by an auctioneer. In the market for goods, firms observe the effective demand of agents, and their Walrasian demand can be of no interest to them as long as they are labour constrained. In the market for labour, however, their Walrasian supply of labour is certainly relevant to workers when considering wage changes. Moreover, it is also of interest to firms when making wage offers. The following two sections discuss a particular version of this story in some detail.

The following – in the light of what has already been said – is trivial.

Proposition 1.1. If (p, b) satisfying Definition 1.1 is called a LDFW equilibrium, then a LDFW equilibrium exists whenever a Walrasian equilibrium exists.

Proof: $(p^*, -1)$ satisfy Definition 1.1 if p^* is a Walrasian equilibrium. ∎

The question is whether there are LDFW equlibria that are not Walrasian. To answer that, note for fixed $b < 0$: $p \cdot \hat{\xi}(p, b) = 0$ for all $p \in \Delta$. Also, the set of x that is budget and constraint feasible for a given b is convex. Assuming now that all production sets are strictly convex, the set of feasible household choices has the origin in its interior. For, if $p_0 = 0$, it must be that some $p_i > 0$ ($p \in \Delta$), and households receive the profits of firms. The possibility $p_0 = 1$ leads to the same conclusion. If the household's consumption set is the positive orthant, then classic arguments (e.g., Debreu (1959)) establish

$$\hat{\xi}(p, b) \text{ is continuous on } \Delta \text{ with } b \text{ fixed.}$$

Note that $b < 0$ so that firms can never face a rationing constraint. Since the Walras law holds for a given b, one now has another proposition.

Proposition 1.2. Given $b < 0$, there exists $p(b)$ such that

$$\hat{\xi}(p(b), b) = 0. \tag{1.2}$$

Proof: Any traditional proof of the existence of competitive equilibrium will do, for example, Debreu (1959). ∎

I now introduce Assumption 1.1.

Assumption 1.1. For any $b < 0$, $p(b)$ satisfying Proposition 1.2 is unique; $p(b)$ is a function.

This assumption is stronger than I need. For instance, it could be replaced by the weaker postulate that for any $b < 0$, the set of $p(b)$ satisfying Proposition 1.2 has isolated elements (the economy for a given b is "regular"). But I stick to the simpler case.

Now let

$$\theta(b) = \xi_0(p(b)) + a(p(b)).$$

and postulate two more assumptions.

Assumption 1.2. The economy has a unique Walrasian equilibrium p^* with $x_0(p^*) < 1$.

Assumption 1.3. The function $a: \Delta \to R_{++}$ is continuous.

We can now proceed as follows. By Assumption 1.1 and the continuity of $\xi(\cdot)$, one has that $p(b)$ is continuous for $b < 0$. Let

$$b^* = \max\{b < 0 \mid p(b) = p^*\}.$$

By Assumption 1.2, this is well defined. Also $\theta(b^*) = a(p(b^*)) > 0$ (e.g., Hildenbrandt and Mertens 1972). Hence $\theta(b)$ is continuous by Assumption 1.3. But then there must exist $b > b^*$ such that $\theta(b) = \xi_0(p(b)) + a(p(b)) > 0$. Since $p(b)$ cannot by Assumption 1.2 be a Walrasian equilibrium, the transaction constraint cannot be slack. We therefore have the next proposition.

Proposition 1.3. There exists an equilibrium in which households are constrained in their sale of labour.

There will in general be a continuum of such labour-constrained equilibria all with different price systems. I reemphasise that prices are not here given from outside the model.

2   Justification of LDFW

The justification discussed is not meant to be *the* justification of possible limited downward flexibility in the world. I am looking for a justification that is consistent with the model of the previous section. That means that I cannot appeal to bargaining theory (with imperfect information), which I suspect would yield a very plausible justification. For bargaining situations would require a modification of the general equilibrium formulation, and I am quite unsure what this will have to be.

2.1   *Lack of coordination between firms*

I assume here that if wages change, then it is firms that change them.

A firm can plausibly be taken as knowing total employment (written as e) but not as knowing ξ_0. I accordingly define

$$\lambda(p,e) = \text{Prob}[\xi_0 < 0 \,|\, p, e].$$

The argument now proceeds as follows. If a firm offers a wage lower than that prevailing, then with probability $\lambda(p,e)$, its profits will increase since a Walrasian excess supply of labour means that it can retain its workers. However, with probability $1 - \lambda(p,e)$, it will lose all its workers. This latter assumption, which is in the spirit of perfect competition, is more drastic than one needs for the conclusion – it would be enough if a fraction of workers were lost if wages are lowered in the presence of a positive Walrasian excess demand for labour. In making its decision, the firm must therefore calculate the effect on expected profits.

To formulate this more precisely, let p^0 be the prevailing vector of prices including that of labour. Let $\bar{p}_0$ be the shadow wage of labour so that $p_0^0 > p_0$ implies $\xi_0(p^0) < 0$. Define

$$\mu(\epsilon \,|\, p^0, e) = \text{Prob}\{p_0^0 - \bar{p}_0 < \epsilon\}.$$

So $\mu(0 \,|\, p^0, e) = \lambda(p^0, e)$. If the firm offers a wage $p_0^0 - \epsilon$ and it can retain its workers and hire the optimum number of new workers, then $\Delta\pi_i(\epsilon)$ is its change in profits, and it is positive. However, with probability $1 - \mu(\epsilon \,|\, p^0, e)$, it will lose all its workers and hence the profit $\pi_i(p^0)$, which it was making before the wage was reduced. Hence the expected gain from lowering the wage, written as $g_i(\epsilon, p^0, e^0)$, is given by

$$g_i(\epsilon, p^0, e^0) = \mu(\epsilon \,|\, p^0, e^0)\Delta\pi_i(\epsilon) - (1 - \mu(\epsilon \,|\, p^0, e^0))\pi_i(p^0).$$

Let

$$\hat{g}_i(p^0, e^0) = \sup_{\epsilon < 0} g_i(e, p^0, e^0).$$

Then the firm will not lower its wage if

$$\hat{g}_i(p^0, e^0) < 0.$$

By our assumption of the relation between the probability estimate of an excess supply of labour and the observed level of employment, $g^*(\hat{p}^*, e^*)$ can be taken to be increasing in e. Let $\hat{e}(p^*)$ solve $g^*(\hat{p}^*, e) = 0$. Then when $e^* \geq \hat{e}(p^*)$, the firm has no incentive to lower wages.

Now let $e(p) = (1 - x_0(p))m$ be the Walrasian labour supply at p and let

$$a(p) = s(p) - \hat{e}(p).$$

Then

$$X(p) + a(p) = e(p) - \hat{e}(p).$$

If one now assumes $e(p^*) > \hat{e}(p^*)$ (where p^* is the Walrasian equilibrium price), then our argument is consistent with wages not changing in Walrasian equilibrium.

The probabilities which appear in the story are taken as exogenous. If one were to think of the economy as often repeated and allowed for experimentation, a theory of their formulation could be derived. Since experimentation is costly, there seems no reason to suppose that firms would learn the true relation between e and ξ_0. But that needs further study. If different firms have different beliefs but were otherwise symmetrical, it would be the firm with the largest $g^*(\cdot)$ which would determine $\hat{e}(p^*)$. Also, I have used a Bertrand-like approach. It *is*, of course, possible that there will be implicit coordination in wage reductions by each firm believing other firms to be like itself. Since the amount of the wage reduction would have to be the same over firms, I do not attach much weight to this argument. Lastly, my assumption that a firm that alone reduced its wage would, in the absence of $\xi_0 = 0$, not be able to employ all (or any) of the labour it wants is, of course, the same as that of the Walrasian model.

But I have said nothing about the unemployed reducing their wage. To that I now turn.

2.2   Fairness

To develop this part of the justification, the interpretation of the basic model must be changed.

I shall now think of labour input as consisting of "men" and hours per man. Assume that hours (h) worked by any man must exceed $\underline{h} > 0$ if there is to be any output at all. (One can index $\underline{h}$ by i, but I simplify.) It is in fact plausible to suppose that there will be a range of hours worked per man above $\underline{h}$ for which there are increasing returns to hours. But I shall neglect this possibility here so that output is concave increasing in $h > \underline{h}$. I shall also assume that all x with $(x_0 - 1) = \underline{h}$ and $x_i > 0$, $i > 0$, are in the interior of the consumption set of households.

The introduction of "setup costs" in hours makes the production set nonconvex over a range. I shall therefore now *assume* that the economy has a unique Walrasian equilibrium p^0 at which the profits of each firm are positive. Hence, in the neighbourhood of such an equilibrium, the excess demand functions are continuous.

Now let β be the proportion of households who face the constraint

$$x_0 - 1 \geq 0.$$

That is, β is the proportion of households who cannot work at all. One interprets $\hat{\xi}(p, 0)$ is the vector of Walrasian excess demand functions.

The second change is as follows. We now think of the economy being indefinitely repeated and that labour constrained for one period will, unless wages change, be also constrained in the second period. At the end of that period all workers again have the same probability of being constrained.

When prices are $p(\beta)$ and stay constant, then at the beginning of the period, all workers have the same probability β of being labour constrained when their utility per period is $\bar{V}(p(\beta))$ and probability $1 - \beta$ of not being constrained and enjoying utility $V(p(\beta))$. Let $W(p(\beta), \beta)$ be the expected utility of this gamble. If the worker looks ahead two periods, then (ignoring discounting) his expected utility is $2W(p(\beta), \beta)$ provided those who find themselves unemployed at the end of the first period do not reduce wages.

I now postulate that workers cannot set wages economywide by means of an explicit or implicit monopolistic agreement. Once a worker offers to work at a wage different from that prevailing, it is every man for himself. "Fairness" concerns the agreed rule when it is permissible to start such a process. The rule is, a la Rawls and Harsanyi, agreed upon before the economy opens. The rule may be against the self-interest of a worker at the beginning of the second period but he adheres to it because it could also have been in his interest to respect it, and when the rule was agreed upon, he did not know on which side he would be. So fairness here is a *trigger* rule: It decides when individuals can follow their self-interest in not adhering to the given wage.

Suppose the rule allows the unemployed to cut wages when at the end of the first period they are unemployed at $(p(\beta), \beta)$. Once the trigger has been released, classical arguments suggest that self-interest will drive the economy to the Walrasian equilibrium p^0 in the second period. Hence, before the economy opens, the expected utility of a worker is

$$W(p(\beta), \beta) + V(p^0).$$

So before knowing whether or not he will be employed, the worker will agree that the trigger should not be released as long as the above expectation is less than $2W(p(\beta), \beta)$, that is, as long as

$$W(p(\beta), \beta) > V(p^0).$$

If this inequality holds for some $\hat{\beta} < 1$ and all $\beta \leq \hat{\beta}$, then that is sufficient for LDFW.

But we must now also look for the trigger for wage increases. When this trigger is released at $(p(\beta), \beta)$, the self-interest of those unemployed is always to keep their wage fractionally below those who are employed. Any worker employed at the end of the first period who takes advantage of it being fair to raise his wage will lose his job because once the trigger is released, everyone is allowed to pursue his self-interest. Hence in fact wages will not rise as long as workers are constrained.

A good deal of the unrealism of this story comes from our present assumption that all workers are identical and that those who are employed in the first period do not acquire a certain amount of monopoly power by acquiring firm specific skills. Such considerations, of course, also endanger the permanence of a Walrasian equilibrium, and that is why they are not discussed in an essay which only seeks to depart from the Walrasian setting in a minimal way.

But I also want to defend the approach. The fairness argument appeals to a Gedanken experiment and not to any actual meeting of agents at which rules are laid down. To reach the conclusion that it is unfair to disrupt some particular status quo before my position in it is known to me is clearly much easier and *prior* to deciding what precise disruptions are fair assuming that any disruption is. For one thing, it requires a good deal more information. For another, it may put very great strain on the value of fairness, and this may be foreseen. For instance, if somehow workers could agree to set the wage at the end of the first period which maximises their expected utility from the point of view of the original position, then workers who find themselves unemployed will suffer more than in the status quo and yet will be expected to stick to the initial agreement. In other words, it may be unfair or impossible to put too much strain on the sense of fairness.

However, should the reader conclude that it is fair to set the wage which maximises expected utility, then of course the second period economy is a "fixed" wage one, and there is nothing more to discuss.

In any event, at least in Britain, arguments turning on fairness are often heard when it comes to wages. Often these turn on relative wages of different groups of workers, a matter I have not discussed. But certainly they also concern undercutting of wages. Imperfectly as the above captures the full situation, it seems to me to capture an important part of it and in so doing is another (partial) justification of LDFW.

3   Some remarks on involuntary unemployment

So far I have avoided the term *involuntary unemployment* because experience teaches that it causes anxiety and stress sufficiently strong to lead to incoherence. But modestly imitating Galileo, all I can say is: "Yet it exists," and if I do that, I had better elaborate.

In the model I have discussed, it is clear that in a labour-constrained equilibrium, the utility of being employed will generally exceed the utility of those who are quantity constrained. That is what for forty years was called involuntary unemployment. Now if, for instance, one adopts my fairness account of LDFW, then there will be the temptation to argue that since unemployed are unwilling to reduce wages, they are voluntarily unemployed. That is to substitute philosophy for economics. There is a technical definition of involuntary unemployment, and this should not be glossed further by a search for the "real" meaning of *voluntary*. Moreover, it is an interesting definition. First, because the economy *does* have an equilibrium in which there is no involuntary unemployment and, second, because the latter has important policy implications; for example, employment can be increased without the offer of a higher real wage.

Now, of course, the precise technical definition of the term will depend on the economy we study. For instance, sometimes it will be appropriate to compare the *expected* utility of the employed with that of the unemployed. Since, for some reason, this seems a difficult point, I shall illustrate from search theory.

One of the difficulties with that theory is that it is hard put to account for a wage distribution for homogeneous labour. But accept that such a distribution is consistent with equilibrium and that the distribution of wages paid is known to all. Suppose, however, that for every wage in that distribution there is a probability of being offered the job and that this for some wages at least is less than 1. Formally, of course, one can think of the case where a job is not offered as an offer of a zero wage. But it is more useful to consider search as finding a firm that pays the "right" wage *and* is willing to offer a job at that wage. For instance, we can imagine the worker first searching among the wages being paid to existing workers and asking whether there is a vacancy at the right wage.

This elementary setup leads the worker to set a reservation wage p_0^* so that if he finds $p_0 \geq p_0^*$ and there is a vacancy, he will accept the job. The reservation wage, of course, depends on the knowledge that there will be occasions when a satisfactory wage is found, but there is no vacancy. That is, the relevant probability is the product of the probability of finding a given wage and the probability of being offered a job at that wage. When the wage found exceeds p_0^* and no job is offered, the worker experiences involuntary unemployment. It is left to the reader to formulate this in terms of the expected utility of search first when every wage found is also an offer of a job and second when that is not so. It will be obvious that involuntary unemployment is consistent with turning down jobs ($p_0 < p_0^*$). It is difficult to believe that this causes difficulty to an economic theorist.

The last point is this. Labour is in fact heterogeneous in many ways. For some, this disposes of the notion of involuntary unemployment because the worker may be comparing the expected utility of a job which he cannot do with his utility in the unemployed state. But there is no reason why in theorising we should make this mistake. It is, after all, quite obvious how to proceed. If it is then claimed that the concept is *nonoperational,* I shall point to the availability of job experience evidence of those now unemployed and to a vastness of other evidence.

Arrow and Debreu built so securely and beautifully that paradoxically to lesser mortals it appears that they have put a full stop to further enquiry. Indeed, any departure is often labeled as the sin of *ad hocery*. Arrow is not among these routinisers of thought and so I have some expectations that he might be interested in such departures from the *corpus* as the foregoing.

REFERENCES

Arrow, K. J. (1959), "Toward a theory of price adjustment," in M. Abramowitz, et al. (Ed.), *The allocation of economic resources,* Stanford: Stanford University Press.
Debreu, G. (1959), *Theory of value,* New York: Wiley.
Hildenbrandt, W. and Mertens, J. F. (1972), "Upper hemi-continuity of the equilibrium set correspondence for pure exchange economies," *Econometrica,* 40: 99–108.

CHAPTER 12

Monopolistic competition and the multiplier

Robert M. Solow

1   Motivation

The trained instinct of the modern rigorous economist is to reach first for the Walrasian model. Maybe it is – like the Army, Navy, Air Force, and Marines – a great place to start. Most of us, however, live with the ineradicable feeling that large and important areas of economic life cannot be described in that way. One of the admirable things about Kenneth Arrow's work is that even while making major contributions to the perfection of the Walrasian model, he has never blinked its deficiencies and has sought for alternatives more suited to the facts of life in modern industrial economies.

What follows is a very preliminary step in that direction. This particular story leaves very large gaps of its own. I will leave until the end my own appreciation of what they are. Some of them are patched up in a more complete and therefore more complicated version of the model that will appear as my 1985 Mitsui Lectures at the University of Birmingham.

My immediate starting point is the article by Martin Weitzman (1982). My goal is to marry it to the simplest model of effective demand. In his article, Weitzman argued that the natural habitat of any theory of persistent involuntary unemployment is an economy with nontrivial increasing returns to scale. The main reason he gives is that otherwise it is impossible to explain why bits of unemployed resources do not form tiny scale replicas of the going economy and thus employ themselves. Each such minieconomy would be at least as productive as the full economy and able to support itself on its own self-generated demand.

It is not even necessary to go so far as the minieconomy. Minifirms, once formed from previously unemployed resources, could sell their minioutput

I thank John Moore and Martin Weitzman for helpful comments.

on competitive markets. Balanced expansion takes care of the rest. If only labor is unemployed, "nonincreasing returns to scale in lending" would permit an atom of labor to borrow the purchasing power needed to hire cooperating inputs, and any infinitesimal bidding up of factor prices could be covered by the preexisting gap between the wage and the marginal disutility of labor.

To put the point slightly differently, any theory of persistent involuntary unemployment must account for the economy's inability to organize the Pareto-improving transactions that must be available. If those transactions could take place in a backyard, or on the head of a pin, it is hard to see what might prevent them. But if there is a substantial minimum scale for viable economic activity, there is at least the possibility of a plausible account of coordination failure, though of course it remains the job of theory to give that account.

This line of argument is quite general. Weitzman's formalization is of the following kind. Imagine any kind of general equilibrium model and suppose it possesses a solution, that is, an ordinary full-employment equilibrium, when the supply of labor L is inelastic. For expositional convenience, we can imagine the equilibrium solution to be unique, though that is not at all essential. Ordinarily, if there is an equilibrium with labor supply L_0, there will be an equilibrium for a range of smaller labor supplies $L \leq L_0$. Now nothing prevents us from thinking of the equilibrium with employment $L = (1-u)L_0$ as an equilibrium with unemployment rate u *provided* we have a good story explaining how the economy can be at rest with a volume of unemployment uL_0. The role of increasing returns to scale is to permit the telling of such a story.

In a model with increasing returns to scale, one of the essential characteristics of an equilibrium is the *number* of firms. In comparing two equilibria – in the sense just described – it will often be found that the equilibrium with the higher level of employment has both a larger number of firms and larger output per firm. But then, for instance, if the equilibrium concept requires zero profits, the equilibrium with higher employment will also have the higher (real) wage. The makings of an unemployment equilibrium story are clearly there. Real wage cutting in the presence of unemployment would be a step in the wrong direction. Price cutting in the hope of exploiting increasing returns by enlarging the market would be a step in the right direction; but since profits are initially zero, price cutting would involve immediate certain losses in the hope of future profits, which might not materialize anyway given that the new equilibrium will also be characterized by zero profits. That is hardly a theory, but it is certainly the promise of a theory.

I owe to James Meade the somewhat different point that nominal wage reduction might be the right reaction to unemployment provided that economic policy maintains aggregate nominal expenditure and firms respond by the even greater price reductions that are permitted by decreasing costs.

A model featuring nontrivial increasing returns to scale cannot have perfect competition as its market structure. The particular model used by Weitzman as a vehicle for his reasoning is a version of the Hotelling–Lancaster–Salop model of monopolistic competition with a circular product space, and the equilibrium concept is symmetric Chamberlinian. In the next section, I describe a modified version of Weitzman's model. The modifications are of two kinds. The first is merely technical, to correct a minor implausibility in the original formulation. The second is more substantial: I modify the demand side by introducing autonomous expenditures, in preparation for analyzing the short- and long-run response of the model to shifts in aggregate demand. The presence of an exogenous source of demand has the effect of tying down the level of employment.

2   A model

There is fundamentally only one produced good, but it can come in a continuum of "qualities," represented by points on the circumference of a circle of length H. Households are uniformly distributed around the circle with unit density. To say that a household is "located" at a particular point on the circle means that it prefers the quality represented by that point. A household consuming x units of the good at distance h from its own location achieves a utility level $u(x, h)$, where u is increasing and concave in x but decreasing and (probably) convex in h. Weitzman set $u = x - ah$, but that seems inappropriate because it makes the loss of utility with distance independent of the quantity consumed and the marginal utility of consumption independent of quality. Instead, I shall work with the utility function $xu(h)$ with $u' < 0$ and, where it matters, $u'' > 0$. Linearity in x serves a useful purpose: Each household will consume only one quality (or, at worst, be indifferent between a neighboring pair). Besides, it aggregates well. Obvious examples are xe^{-ah} and xh^{-a}; I will refer to them later.

Eventually we will come down to a symmetric equilibrium with m firms equally spaced around the circle, thus at a distance $D = H/m$ from each other, and all charging the same price. That situation must be a Nash equilibrium in prices. So imagine a typical firm looking for its best price p' when all other firms charge price p. The firm's market area will extend a distance h on each side and thus be of length $2h$, where h is determined by the condition that the consumer at that location be indifferent between the products of the two nearest firms, one at distance h and the other at distance $D-h$. Consider the consumer spending M units of "money" on the good. Indifference implies

$$\frac{M}{p'}u(h) = \frac{M}{p}u(D-h),$$

from which follows

$$\frac{p}{p'} = \frac{u(D-h)}{u(h)}.$$

Thus h is unambiguously decreasing in p' for given p. Later we will need the derivative

$$\frac{dh}{dp'} = \frac{p}{(p')^2}\frac{u(h)^2}{u(h)u'(D-h)+u(D-h)u'(h)}.$$

How much demand is generated from a market area of length $2h$ when the firm charges p' and others charge p? Let aggregate employment in the whole economy be L, uniformly distributed around the circumference with density L/H. Let the wage, in unit of account, be w. Weitzman assumes that households spend all their earnings on the good, and there is no other source of demand. Here is my main deviation from his assumptions. Households spend a fixed fraction c of their earnings on the good (or their price elasticity of demand is 1). Demand from this source is thus $(2h/H)(cwL/p')$.

In addition, there is (must be) another source of demand, government purchases, say, or perhaps, when the model can be extended that far, investment spending by firms. Suppose that nominal exogenous spending in unit of account is given; call it G. The goods bought are used in some way that does not affect private demand. I shall assume that this nominal demand is always equally allocated among firms, so each can count on G/m. Real demand from this source is thus G/mp' for the typical firm. Notice first that firms are unable to discriminate against the government but must sell to all buyers at the same price. There is a second tacit assumption. It could have been assumed that exogenous spending is equally allocated over units of circumference rather than over firms. That would have been somewhat simpler, in fact; all demand would then have the same price elasticity, larger than unity because of the responsiveness of market area to own price. When exogenous spending is divided among firms, each firm's demand is the sum of household demand, with greater than unit elasticity, and its share of the unit-elastic exogenous demand. I think the extra complication is worth bearing precisely to allow the price elasticity of demand to vary with c as well as with m, though I would not seriously defend this particular way of doing so.

The typical firm thus faces the demand function

$$d(p') = \frac{G}{mp'} + \frac{2h}{H}\frac{cwL}{p'}$$

and the revenue function

$$R(p') = p'D(p') = \frac{G}{m} + \frac{2h}{H}cwL.$$

Here, of course, L and m as well as p are parameters to the firm.

On the production side, I follow Weitzman exactly. Let y and n be output and employment of the typical firm. Then

$$y = k(n-f),$$

where the positive constant f stands for the setup labor that is the source of increasing returns. Output is zero unless n exceeds f. It follows that the total, average, and marginal costs associated with output y are

$$\text{TC} = w\left(\frac{y}{k}+f\right), \quad \text{AC} = w\left(\frac{1}{k}+\frac{f}{y}\right), \quad \text{MC} = \frac{w}{k}.$$

As in any Chamberlinian large group, the firm maximizes profits by charging a price at which

$$\text{MR} = \frac{dR}{dy} = \frac{R'(p')}{d'(p')} = \text{MC} = \frac{w}{k}.$$

The detailed calculations make use of the formula for dh/dp' set down earlier. Furthermore, for a symmetric equilibrium, we can set $p' = p$ and $2h = H/m$ after differentiation. The final result is

$$p = \frac{w}{k}\left[1+2\left(-\frac{H}{2m}\frac{u'(H/2m)}{u(H/2m)}\right)\left(1+\frac{G}{Z}\right)\right], \tag{1}$$

where, for temporary ease of notation, $Z = cwL$, which is aggregate nominal spending out of wage income. In addition, we can always write

$$mpy = G+Z, \tag{2}$$

and in symmetric equilibrium,

$$y = k\left(\frac{L}{m} - f\right). \tag{3}$$

As a final condition for long-run Chamberlinian equilibrium, suppose that free entry determines the number of firms, m, so that

$$p = \mathrm{AC} = w\left(\frac{1}{k} + \frac{f}{y}\right). \tag{4}$$

It can be checked immediately that equations (3) and (4) are equivalent to (3) and

$$mpy = wL. \tag{5}$$

Now (2) and (5) can be combined to rewrite (1) as

$$p = \frac{w}{k}\left[1 + \frac{2}{c}\left(-\frac{H}{2m}\frac{u'(H/2m)}{u(H/2m)}\right)\right]. \tag{1'}$$

Here the long-run equilibrium price is represented as a markup on marginal cost. One can easily check that the markup factor is exactly what it should be, expressible in terms of the elasticity of demand faced by each firm in a long-run equilibrium or in terms of Lerner's *degree of monopoly*. The markup factor is larger if the (absolute) elasticity of $u(\cdot)$ is larger at equlibrium and if the propensity to spend wage income is smaller. A very elastic $u(\cdot)$ means that different qualities of the good are relatively poor substitutes for one another; this gives each firm more monopoly power in the obvious way. The role of c is also simple. It will be remembered that each firm's demand curve is the sum of two components: autonomous demand with unit elasticity and household demand with greater than unit elasticity. The combined elasticity therefore exceeds 1 and is larger when c is larger so that the component with a bigger demand elasticity gets heavier weight.

3   Variations

Here I digress for a moment. It is plain that this is a Chamberlinian large-group equilibrium only by courtesy. Each firm has two neighbors whose reaction to its own decisions it cannot ignore. If one really believed in this world, it would need to be analyzed as a chain of linked oligopolies. It would be easy to hint vaguely that "quality" could be many-dimensional, so that a firm might have many immediate neighbors. Then the effects of its own price decisions would be diffused over all of them and ignored by each of them as the model requires.

In two recent papers (1985a and b), Oliver Hart has shown just how complicated it can be actually to carry out this program. Nevertheless, I think it is fair to take his results as offering a license to proceed as if we were dealing with a true large group. With enough work, it could be fixed up.

In his analysis, Hart takes it to be a desideratum that the elasticity of demand facing a typical firm should *not* go to infinity as the number of firms increases without limit. That requirement makes sense if one's goal is to prove the existence of a true Chamberlinian equilibrium of monopolistic competition. For my purpose, however, it is just as interesting to contemplate cases in which the perfectly competitive limit *is* reached as the number of firms gets large. I want to point out, therefore, that equation (1') can exhibit either kind of behavior, depending on the particular choice of the substitution function $u(h)$.

From (1'), the limiting situation is perfectly competitive if $-hu'(h)/u(h)$ goes to zero with h. The limiting situation (with large m) is monopolistically competitive if $-hu'(h)/u(h)$ goes to a nonzero limit as h goes to zero. Here are some examples:

a. Suppose $u(h) = e^{-ah}$. Then $-hu'(h)/u(h) = ah$ and (1') becomes

$$p = \frac{w}{k}\left[1 + \frac{aH}{mc}\right].$$

Here price goes to marginal cost as the number of firms gets large in equilibrium.

b. If $u(h) = h^{-a}$, of course, $-hu'(h)/u(h) = a$. Then

$$p = \frac{w}{k}\left(1 + \frac{2a}{c}\right),$$

and the markup is independent of the number of firms. This is an interesting borderline case and I shall comment on it later.

c. Suppose we would like to have

$$-hu'(h)/u(h) = s + th$$

for positive constants s and t. Then the markup will decrease to s as the number of firms become infinite (and increase to infinity as the number of firms tends to "zero"). The differential equation is easily integrated to give

$$u(h) = h^{-s}e^{-th}.$$

The fact that here and in example (b) u is unbounded as h goes to zero is unimportant, because almost no household gets to consume its very favorite quality.

d. If $-hu'(h)/u(h) = (Ah+B)/(h+C)$, then the markup goes to a non-zero value B/C as m becomes infinite and to a finite value A as m tends to zero. To make sense, we need to choose A bigger than B/C. Once again, the differential equation can be integrated to yield

$$u(h) = h^{-B/C}(h+C)^{-(A-B/C)},$$

which has all the necessary properties.

e. Finally, one might wonder if it is possible that the equilibrium markup might rise with m. (Perverse as that sounds, we have already found a case in which the markup is independent of m.) For that to happen, it must be that $(d/dh)(-hu'(h)/u(h)) < 0$. But $(d/dh)(-hu'(h)/u(h))$ has the sign of $h(u')^2 - uu' - hu''$, so this alternative pattern is possible if u'' is positive and sufficiently large. In that case, the equilibrium real wage falls as aggregate output increases. Higher output is accomplished by a more than proportional increase in the number of firms and a reduction in output per firm. Output per worker falls, and so does the real wage. In the borderline constant-elasticity case (b) above, output per firm is constant and changes in equilibrium output occur entirely through changes in the number of firms. A sharply convex $u(\cdot)$ contributes to this outcome because the marginal demand for greater variety intensifies as variety increases. Thus the degree of monopoly is greater even with a larger number of firms. This is presumably an unlikely case.

It should be remembered that the equilibrium number of firms is endogenous in this model. I have spoken of "varying" the number of firms just for clarity. But f, the level of fixed costs, is a parameter; and clearly the equilibrium value of m goes to zero as f goes to infinity and to infinity as f goes to zero. So there is no harm done.

4   The case without autonomous spending

From here on, I adopt the parameterization $u(h) = e^{-ah}$ so that I can give concrete results. It seems to be the most reasonable simple formula.

To establish the analogy to Weitzman's model, I first set $G = 0$ and $c = 1$. Then equation (2) collapses to equation (5), and there are only three independent equations, (1), (3), and (5), in the unknowns p, y, m, and L. The model economy can be in long-run Chamberlinian equilibrium with any level of employment. Then equation (1) reads

$$p = \frac{w}{k}\left(1 + \frac{aH}{m}\right),$$

and a complete solution of the model gives

$$m = \frac{aH}{2}\left[-1 + \left(1 + \frac{4L}{aHf}\right)^{1/2}\right],$$

$$p = \frac{w}{k}\left[1 + \frac{2}{-1 + [1 + (4L/aHf)]^{1/2}}\right],$$

$$y = \frac{2kL/aH}{1 + [1 + (4L/aHf)]^{1/2}}.$$

Note that m does indeed go from infinity to zero as f goes from zero to infinity. Note also that higher employment carries with it an increase in the number of firms, in output per firm, *and* in the real wage. [In the case $u(h) = h^{-a}$, the equilibrium number of firms is proportional to L, and output per firm and the real wage are independent of L.]

If this economy were to find itself in a zero-profit Chamberlinian equilibrium with unemployment, "all" it needs to set things right is for just enough new firms to appear. The added demand generated by the workers they hire will permit all firms to expand. Decreasing cost will allow the price to fall. As Weitzman pointed out, the only noncooperative way for new firms to come into existence would be to wedge themselves "between" already existing firms and force a realignment of market areas. Since the existing firms have zero profits and entering firms might have to start small, the prospect is for all-round losses, perhaps never to be made up. Of course, there may be dynamic paths starting with "nominal" wage reductions that lead to full equilibrium at higher employment. It is hard to say, if only because there is no true monetary side to the model. But it is far from obvious that a decentralized economy could find such a path quickly, even if there is one.

The fact that this model can be in neutral equilibrium at any level of employment is a consequence of the assumption, a sort of Say's law, that directs all wage income – the only income there is in equilibrium – into consumption. As soon as that assumption is dropped, the situation changes.

5   Autonomous spending: long run

When G is positive and $c < 1$, the degree of freedom disappears. Exogenous expenditure fixes the scale of the economy. The mathematical counterpart is that equations (1)–(4) now define a unique equilibrium in p, y, m, and L. Perhaps it should be mentioned explicitly that I treat the nominal wage w as given. This is not an assumption of "rigid wages" but merely a choice of *numéraire*. (I am, of course, assuming throughout that the real wage does not clear the labor market.) There is nothing in the model to determine the price level in terms of unit of account. Now it should be understood that exogenous spending is really given in wage units, not in nominal terms.

Remembering that $Z = cwL$, one sees right away that equations (2) and (5) imply that $mpy = G/(1-c)$. Across zero-profit equilibria, the simplest of all multiplier formulas holds, and for the usual reason.

In this model, however, aggregate income is the product of three endogenous variables: output per firm, the price of the good (in wage units), and the number of firms. The model can be solved for each of these, with the results

$$p = \frac{w}{k}\left[1 + \frac{2}{-1 + \left(1 + \frac{4cG/w}{(1-c)faH}\right)^{1/2}}\right]$$

$$L = \frac{G/w}{1-c},$$

$$m = \frac{aH}{2c}\left[-1 + \left(1 + \frac{4cG/w}{(1-c)faH}\right)^{1/2}\right],$$

$$y = k\left(\frac{L}{m} - f\right).$$

These bear a family resemblance to the corresponding formulas for the closed model with no autonomous demand. The ratio of price to marginal cost is higher the bigger is a. This is because large a confers more monopoly power on the firm by making alternative qualities less good substitutes. The parameter c enters in two ways. A small c weights the firm's demand in favor of the less elastic autonomous expenditure but also reduces aggregate demand. The net effect is to reduce output per firm and raise price; the effect on the number of firms is more complicated.

This particular parameterization of the model retains the convenient feature that changes in G, and thus in aggregate economic activity, work themselves out by changing employment, the number of firms, and output per firm in the same direction. The real wage moves *with* employment. I describe this as an advantage not because of any claim to descriptive realism but rather because it puts the key question of the dynamics of adjustment into sharp relief. To get further with that question, however, I define a short run for this model in the next section.

6   Autonomous spending: the short-run multiplier

The comparative-static adjustments explicit and implicit in the preceding section are strictly long run in character. The response to a change in G is a movement from one free-entry zero-profit Chamberlinian equilibrium to another; and it is achieved in this case by entry or exit of firms, if it can be achieved at all. It is more natural to think of the model's short-run response to changes in G as the profit-maximizing reactions of the existing firms, along with the associated profits, positive or negative. After all, these are the signals that are supposed to induce the appropriate long-run adjustments. Nothing much is lost and some simplicity is gained, however, if short-run responses are assumed to start from a position of long-run equilibrium.

Thus, in the short run, equation (4) is dropped and m is treated as a constant [but a constant that satisfies equations (4) and (5) initially]. The short-run comparative statics of p, y, and L come from equations (1)–(3). Actually, it is enough to work with just p and y, taking account of the fact that (3) and the definition of Z define Z as a function of y alone, with $dZ/dy = cwm/k$. The variational equations are

$$\begin{pmatrix} 1 & aHG/c(kL)^2 \\ y & p-cw/k \end{pmatrix}\begin{pmatrix} dP/dG \\ dy/dG \end{pmatrix} = \begin{pmatrix} aH/mckL \\ 1/m \end{pmatrix} \qquad (6)$$

From (6), after a lot of maneuvers making heavy use of the fact that the state variables satisfy (1), (2), and (5), one can calculate the multiplier formula

$$\frac{d(mpy)}{dG} = \frac{1}{(1-c)(1+q+q^2)^{-1}}. \qquad (7)$$

Here $q = aH/mc$. In this version of the short-run model, equation (1) reads

$$p = \frac{w}{k}\left(1 + \frac{aH}{m}\left(1 + \frac{G}{cwL}\right)\right).$$

Evaluated at the initial long-run zero-profit equilibrium, the last parenthesis is just $1/c$. Hence q is the markup. The short-run multiplier is larger when the elasticity of demand is larger, that is, the degree of monopoly is smaller. If q is near zero (the elasticity of demand is near infinite), the multiplier approaches the long-run value of $(1-c)^{-1}$. As q approaches infinity (the elasticity of demand approaches unity, its smallest permissible value), the multiplier goes to 1.

The reason for this is not mysterious. In the short run, rise in G – an upward shift in demand – permits positive profits to emerge before they are competed away by entry. In the model, these profits are not spent, and that limits the size of the multiplier. One could introduce a positive marginal propensity to spend profits with more or less obvious consequences. [If the same marginal propensity to spend applies to all income, then (2) says $mpy = G + cmpy$, and there is nothing more to be said.] But I have something ultimately more ambitious in mind. I have referred to production units as firms, but they are really just units of capacity devoted to profit maximization. Wherever I have said *entry* I could have said *investment*. One way to study the all-important dynamics of transition from short run to long run under increasing returns to scale would be to try to incorporate a serious theory of investment. According to what was said earlier, this may be the key to the notion of unemployment equilibrium. Anything so mechanical as a marginal propensity to invest profits would miss all the deeper questions about the ability of the unmanaged economy to organize the Pareto improvements that spell the difference between prosperity and recession.

In the short run, both p and y change in the same direction as G. Since the nominal wage is a parameter, the real wage falls when employment rises and vice versa. This is not what actually happens in the real world, but it is nevertheless a useful reminder that short-run forces may be perverse with respect to the achievement of long-run goals. It happens this way in the model because firms operate freely in a spot market for labor; the model concentrates on other things.

It is possible to work out the proportions in which a change in py is divided between change in y and change in p (or p/w). As it happens, the ratio of the percentage change in p to the percentage change in y, when G varies, is $q^2/(1+q)$. Alternatively, one can decompose $d(py)dG$ into $p\,dy/dG$ and $y\,dp/dG$ with the result that

$$\frac{p\,dy}{dG} = \frac{1+q}{1+q+q^2}\frac{d(py)}{dG}, \qquad \frac{y\,dp}{dG} = \frac{q^2}{1+q+q^2}\frac{d(py)}{dG}.$$

These are intuitive: A high elasticity of demand makes for a relatively small change in price and a relatively large change in output.

To fix orders of magnitude, an elasticity of demand equal to three means $q = \frac{1}{2}$. Then six-sevenths of the multiplier change in nominal output is real, and the remaining one-seventh is the change in price in wage units or, with opposite sign, the change in the real wage. The demand elasticity must get down to about 1.6–1.7 for the division between price and output change to be 50:50. The effects on the numerical value of the multiplier are more dramatic. Suppose $c = \frac{1}{2}$, so the ordinary Keynesian multiplier is 2. Then $q = \frac{1}{2}$ reduces the short-run multiplier to 1.4, and $q = 1.6$ reduces it to 1.1.

It is the essence of this formulation that short-run movements above and below long-term equilibrium are accompanied by positive or negative profits. Ultimately, it will be the investment induced by those profits that drives longer-run changes – and probably magnifies short-run fluctuations in the process. I have followed that trail for a bit in my Mitsui Lectures. For now, I just record the relevant comparative-statics derivative. If we set aggregate profit $P = mpy - wL$, then it is easily reckoned that

$$\frac{dP}{dG} = \frac{q(1+q)}{1+q+q^2} \cdot M,$$

where M is the multiplier evaluated in (7) above. Thus, if $q = \frac{1}{2}$ (the elasticity of demand is 3), profits amount to three-sevenths of the increment in income, whereas if $q = 1.6$, profits absorb 80 percent of the short-run change in income. This formula provides the weights one would use to introduce a simple marginal propensity to spend profits. But I have already argued for a different way to proceed.

7   Conclusions

It is not especially the function of simple models like this to provide prototypes for larger descriptive models. I think their purpose is rather to give "pure" illustrations of general principles. What principles emerge here?

First, further development of the model offers some confirmation of Weitzman's insight that the unassisted price mechanism may find it hard to extract an imperfectly competitive increasing returns-to-scale economy from an underemployment trap. Small-scale myopic adjustments could be self-frustrating. There are too many local Nash equilibria. Noncooperative outcomes may be inferior to what can be achieved by cooperative organization.

Second, the model suggests that the difference in orientation between investment and consumption may be fundamental, just as we used to think before Walrasian concepts and Walrasian notation infiltrated macroeconomic theory. The desirability of "pump priming" – getting a process started that will later, but only later, be self-sustaining – hinges on both the lumpiness and the durability of additions to capacity. Obviously expectations matter, including expectations about the behavior of other players, and thus another role for cooperative solutions opens up. The microeconomic foundations of macroeconomics might find room for strategic theories of investment.

Third, it may be a waste of time to try to construct macroeconomics on perfectly competitive foundations. That is already implied by increasing returns. But the model goes further in strongly suggesting that the behavior characteristics of the system, especially in the short run, may be sensitive to details of market structure.

8   Apologies

I have left to the very end my apology for the crudities of this deliberate reversion to simple 45-degree-line textbook Keynesianism. The point was to see if that old dog could produce some new tricks when placed in an unconventional framework. It seems to me that it has done so. But the crudities remain. The main ones are the treatment – or lack of treatment – of the asset market and the labor market.

With respect to the asset market, households save, but nothing is said about why they save or what they do with their savings. The most straightforward story is that households accumulate stocks of purchasing power in the form of "money." In turn, the government injects "new money" when it makes nominal expenditures. That will hardly do as anything more than a stopgap, if only because the motivation for saving is so nebulous. The key, obviously, is to introduce capital goods as a factor of production and, indirectly, a store of value. If investment is the mechanism by which the model economy gets from one long-run Nash equilibrium to another, then the financing of investment is fundamental to the outcome. The model needs some financial institutions so that household savings can finance the profit-motivated capital investments of firms. It is pretty clear how to proceed. The true difficulties with investment will come from the intrinsic uncertainty combined with economies of scale, not from the bare outlines.

With respect to the labor market, the model operates as if there is in the background an inelastically supplied labor force. Actual employment may be less than that, governed not by supply but by the price and output decisions of forms. The nominal wage is conventionally given, and the real wage is passively determined by the price of goods. If this situation is to be described as an "equilibrium," the relevant equilibrium concept must be something other than wage-mediated clearing of the labor market.

I have not tried to specify an alternative concept according to which the labor market could be at rest with involuntary unemployment, except to suggest yet another reason why the Walrasian concept has little to recommend it: because the natural disequilibrium dynamics would be misdirected. After all these years that is hardly a satisfactory treatment of the labor market. Some action should emanate from the supply side as well, and a model of endogenous wage determination should be added. But even after all these years it is not completely clear what a good model of the labor market would be.

REFERENCES

Hart, O. (1985a), "Monopolistic competition in the spirit of Chamberlin: A general model," *Review of Economic Studies,* 52(4): 529–46.

Hart, O. (1985b), "Monopolistic competition in the spirit of Chamberlin: Special results," *Economic Journal,* 95: 889–908.

Weitzman, M. (1982), "Increasing returns and the foundations of Unemployment theory," *Economic Journal,* 92: 787–804.

Author index